Aesthetics of the Natural Environment

For My Mother and Father

Aesthetics of the Natural Environment

Emily Brady

The University of Alabama Press
Tuscaloosa

Copyright © 2003 Emily Brady
All rights reserved

A copublication of the University of Alabama Press
and Edinburgh University Press

First published in the United States, 2003
University of Alabama Press
Tuscaloosa, Alabama 35487-0380

First published in Great Britain, 2003
Edinburgh University Press Ltd
22 George Square
Edinburgh

Manufactured in Great Britain
Typeface: Ehrhardt

∞
The paper on which this book is printed meets the
minimum requirements of American National Standard
for Information Science–Permanence of Paper for
Printed Library Materials, ANSI Z39.48-1984.

Library of Congress Cataloging-in-Publication Data
Brady, Emily.
Aesthetics of the natural environment / Emily Brady.
p.   cm.
Includes bibliographical references and index.
ISBN 0-8173-1374-5 (alk. paper)
ISBN 0-8173-5013-6 (pbk. : alk. paper)

1. Nature (Aesthetics) I. Title.
BH301.N3 B73 2003
111′.85-dc21   2002015643

Contents

Acknowledgements

Several chapters in the book incorporate material, in a revised form, from the following previously published papers: 'Aesthetics, Ethics and the Natural Environment' in Arnold Berleant (ed.), *Environment and the Arts: Perspectives on Environmental Aesthetics* (Aldershot and Burlington: Ashgate, 2002); 'Interpreting Environments', *Essays in Philosophy*, 3:1, 2002 (www.humboldt.edu/~essays/); 'Aesthetic Character and Aesthetic Integrity in Environmental Conservation', *Environmental Ethics*, 24:2, 2002; 'Imagination and the Aesthetic Appreciation of Nature', *Journal of Aesthetics and Art Criticism: Special Issue: Environmental Aesthetics*, 56:2, 1998; 'Don't Eat the Daisies: Disinterestedness and the Situated Aesthetic', *Environmental Values*, 7:1, 1998. I thank the journals and publishers for permission to use this material.

A Research Leave Award from the Arts and Humanities Research Board enabled me to complete a large portion of the manuscript. I thank Professor Yrjö Sepänmaa and the Finnish Academy for research funding in support of the final two chapters. Lancaster University's Committee for Research awarded a grant to carry out research for Chapter 8, with the assistance of Mary Grant.

The ideas in this book are deeply indebted to conversations with past and present colleagues in Philosophy at Lancaster University, some of whom also read and commented on draft chapters: John Benson, Isis Brook, Michael Hammond, Alan Holland, Jane Howarth, Colin Lyas, John O'Neill, Clare Palmer, Vernon Pratt, Kate Rawles and Kathleen Stock. Ronald Hepburn has been an inspiring mentor and friend, and I am grateful in particular for his comments on a substantial portion of the manuscript. My students at Lancaster, especially those in the MA programme Values and the Environment have kept me from becoming intellectually stodgy through lively and refreshing discussions.

My husband, Arto Haapala, read and commented on the entire manuscript and gave me the encouragement and support essential for bringing the project to completion. I dedicate this book to my mother, Margaret Brady, for nurturing an aesthetic sensibility in me as much through summers spent at the beach as through our frequent visits to the National Gallery of Art in Washington, DC; and to my father, Paul Brady, for encouraging an interest and respect for nature by teaching me about trees, birds and other wonders of the natural world.

Introduction

P hilosophers have only relatively recently turned their attention to studying the aesthetic dimension of our experience of the natural environment. Although a few eighteenth-century philosophers pursued this topic, Immanuel Kant, among others, it was not until the late 1960s and early 1970s that aesthetic appreciation of nature was studied seriously again. In the last decade or so this area in philosophy has become increasingly popular, however, philosophers in aesthetics are still primarily interested in the arts, and philosophers of the environment continue to be mainly concerned with our ethical attitudes towards the natural world. New work in environmental aesthetics seeks to highlight the interesting issues pointed up when we ask central questions about our experience of natural environments in contrast to artworks, and it also asserts the importance of aesthetic value to discussions of our relationships with the natural world.

One aim of this book is to explore critically central topics in the growing field of environmental aesthetics, and I hope to provide a systematic discussion that will be of use to philosophers working in both aesthetics and environmental philosophy. A second, important, aim of the book is to develop a new and distinctive theory of aesthetic appreciation of natural environments, and, therefore, to make an original contribution to contemporary debates within aesthetics. With this theory, which I call the 'integrated aesthetic', I try to find a balance between more subjective and more objective approaches to aesthetic appreciation.

The subject matter of this book is nature rather than art, but this needs clarification. Although I discuss a range of environments, the use of 'natural environment' in the title is intentional, because it captures, at least in common usage, my focus on environments that lean more towards the natural than the cultural. For example, while I shall discuss some types of modified and cultural landscapes, space does not permit me to consider gardens or built environments in any depth.

One final point about the aims and scope of this study. As a philosopher, I suspect that I am not alone in feeling pulled in two different directions. One is enticed into studying abstract, theoretical philosophical questions, while at the same time, one feels that the practice of philosophy ought to have a direct bearing on helping us to live better lives. These projects are not of course opposed, in fact they ought to go hand in hand, since philosophical methods, such as analysis and making distinctions, may be exactly what are needed for constructive critical reflection on human practice. This ideal is not always achievable, but as a philosopher studying the environment these two projects work together more easily. Here, I try to combine the careful argument and critical discussion required to unravel difficult philosophical problems with an understanding of how aesthetic valuing of the environment impacts on environmental policy and decision-making. Accordingly, parts of this study bring philosophical reflection to bear on conservation strategies and discuss concrete examples relevant to current debates. I have avoided the use of overly technical philosophical language, where possible, so that the book might also be of interest and accessible to a non-philosophical audience.

The book is organised in such a way as to provide, in the first three chapters, an understanding of the context and background of aesthetic appreciation of natural environments. The central chapters in the book, Chapters 4, 5 and 6, give close attention to theories of aesthetic appreciation of nature through a critical discussion of the current lines of debate in con-temporary environmental aesthetics, and it is here that I develop the integrated aesthetic in response to existing models of appreciation. The final two chapters bring a new understanding of aesthetic appreciation into the more practical domains of the justification of our ascriptions of aesthetic value and discussions of aesthetic value in environmental conservation.

Chapter 1 examines a set of questions which centre upon the concept of aesthetic experience What is aesthetic experience, and how is it distinct from other domains of human experience? What are aesthetic qualities? Is aesthetic value instrumental or intrinsic, and how does it relate to other environmental values? Through a critical discussion of the distinctive features of aesthetic experience, I put forward a relatively traditional account which serves as a basic foundation for my own approach as to how we aesthetically engage with natural environments. Aesthetic qualities are shown to be relational but to rest importantly upon non-aesthetic qualities. I argue for a concept of aesthetic value that is non-instrumental and captures a common but distinctive way we relate to the natural world.

In the second chapter, I ask how philosophers have understood aesthetic appreciation of nature in the past. Quite a lot has been written outside philosophy about the evolution of landscape tastes, and although I discuss some points in this history, my aim is to outline philosophical ideas that have been relevant to the contemporary debate. I give particular attention to Kant's aesthetic theories of the beautiful and the sublime, and the interesting, but problematic, category of the picturesque. My discussion of Kant also provides background on a set of ideas that have influenced my own approach to aesthetic appreciation.

The third chapter forms a bridge between the groundwork of the first two chapters and discussion of contemporary arguments in the rest of the book. My aim is to locate where aesthetic appreciation of natural environments begins. I explore differences between culture and nature, arguing that we cannot understand the distinction as a sharp one. Given differences between artworks and natural environments, what are the particular kinds of appreciative demands placed on us? Through a discussion of these differences I emphasise the need to recognise the particularity of natural environments as *environments* rather than merely as scenes or objects. In the final part of the chapter, I consider cultural landscapes and their interpretation to indicate the complexities involved in aesthetic appreciation of environments shaped by both nature and culture.

The task of Chapter 4 is to examine critically a range of contemporary theories of aesthetic appreciation of natural environments. These positions are grouped into cognitive and non-cognitive theories. Cognitive theories base aesthetic appreciation on an epistemological foundation constituted by the natural sciences. There are several problems with cognitive theories, most of which centre upon the condition of knowledge for appropriate appreciation. By contrast, non-cognitive approaches argue against the necessity of knowledge, and they embrace a plurality of both subjective-oriented and objective-oriented components of aesthetic experience to establish the appreciative framework. Overall, I argue that non-cognitive theories are more inclusive and better reflect the actual practice of environmental aesthetic appreciation, however, the more subjective-oriented components of these theories need shoring up.

In two closely linked chapters, 5 and 6, I develop a comprehensive theory, the integrated aesthetic, which builds upon the most promising features of non-cognitive theories and addresses some of their weaknesses. Through an integration of the subjective and objective components of aesthetic experience, this approach emphasises the engaged, relational and contextual character of environmental appreciation and preserves a kind of non-instrumentalism through the concept of disinterestedness.

In Chapter 5, I set out two of the basic components of the integrated aesthetic, multi-sensuous and disinterested engagement with the environment. I discuss the variety of ways that appreciation ranges beyond our visual sense, and I develop a revitalised concept of disinterestedness by showing how it is consistent with other key components of the aesthetic response to nature.

Three other components of the integrated aesthetic, imagination, emotion and knowledge, are critically examined in Chapter 6. I defend imagination against claims that it leads to trivialising or overly humanising nature, and I describe the different ways this power enhances appreciation. Similarly, I show how our emotional responses and our attributions of expressive qualities to environments are not subjective in the problematic sense of being either idiosyncratic or overly humanising. Finally, although knowledge has a relatively minor role in the integrated aesthetic, when it does have a place, I urge a broad conception of knowledge extending beyond science to include folk knowledge and other sources of meaning in relation to natural environments.

When aesthetic appreciation has a role in the practical sphere of conservation strategy and decision-making, finding the means to provide solid and convincing support for our attributions of aesthetic value becomes crucial. Using the integrated aesthetic as a foundation, Chapter 7 explains how one goes about justifying aesthetic judgements of the natural environment. I argue against the view that aesthetic judgements are private expressions of taste and formulate a type of objective approach based in the communicable, inter-subjective character of aesthetic judgements. I stress how aesthetic explanation and justification are based on a set of critical activities that are practised and developed in a public context. The concept of aesthetic communication is the starting point for an outline of environmental aesthetic education. I stress the importance of developing aesthetic sensitivity, in particular capacities such as perception and imagination, so as to better discern aesthetic value in the environment.

Chapter 8 explores the integrated aesthetic and its approach to aesthetic value in connection to more normative concerns. Through an analysis of landscape conservation designations in Britain, I show how aesthetic value has been treated as nearly equivalent to the much more narrow category of scenic value. I outline the concept of 'aesthetic character' in order to show how aesthetic value may be conceived more accurately and broadly in relation to environments. A case study is used to illustrate how aesthetic character might be applied in conservation decision-making. The second part of the chapter considers how aesthetic value conflicts and harmonises with other environmental values, especially ethical value. In a discussion of the interesting relationship between aesthetic and ethics, I point to some of the ways in which aesthetic sensitivity, and other capacities developed through this mode of experience, supports an attitude of respect for nature.

The aesthetic mode of experience has a significant role in shaping our relationship to the environment. Understanding the particular aspects of aesthetic appreciation ought to illuminate some of the reasons why, for at least some of us, contact with the natural world is such a vital and meaningful part of our lives. The continuing importance of environmental concerns and issues points to a growing need for a greater knowledge of our relationship to nature; environmental aesthetics, and philosophy more generally, can make a constructive contribution to this knowledge.

Aesthetic Appreciation

I magine walking across a rocky shoreline: the pungent salty scent of sea air; the feeling of mist across one's face as the waves crash nearby; the brilliant blue-green of the water beyond. What sort of philosophical analysis can we give of this type of experience? In this first chapter I give a critical introduction to the nature of aesthetic appreciation, aesthetic experience (or the aesthetic response) and a conception of aesthetic value that goes with it, in order to provide a conceptual framework for understanding our aesthetic relationship to the natural environment. I begin by setting out how the aesthetic domain of human experience has been identified and discussed by philosophers. In particular, I outline a relatively traditional approach, which my own view of aesthetic appreciation of nature, the 'integrated aesthetic', builds upon in later chapters.

Understanding the distinctive aspects of the aesthetic dimension of experi-ence depends in part upon an identification of the qualities that one is appreciating in the natural world. I next consider the nature and status of aesthetic qualities and to what extent they are objective or subjective. Having grasped the character of the aesthetic and its qualities, the final section considers aesthetic value within the environmental context, and how it compares and contrasts with other environmental values such as ecological value and cultural value. I argue that aesthetic value is a non-instrumental value, and that it is an important environmental value because it captures an immediate, common and distinctive way in which we appreciate our surroundings.

AESTHETIC EXPERIENCE

Consider the following: listening to music, walking barefoot on a beach, reading a novel, watching a film, beholding a rose, running through a rainstorm, stroking a cat, cooking a meal for friends, getting dressed in the morning and climbing a mountain. Philosophy studies different dimensions of our experience in the world. For example, moral philosophers theorise about human conduct and our obligations to other species, and epistemologists try to understand how knowledge is possible. Aestheticians are concerned with the 'aesthetic' dimension of our experience. All of the activities listed are potentially aesthetic experiences. They might involve what is often referred to as an aesthetic response, a response which serves as the basis of an aesthetic judgement, where one ascribes value to something: the luxurious feel of sand underfoot or the rich aroma of a fine cheese.[1]

For at least the last century, philosophers interested in the aesthetic have been predominantly concerned with the arts, painting, sculpture, music, literature and so on. But in the last thirty years or so, they have begun to recognise, albeit slowly, that the aesthetic domain is not limited to the arts, and that it reaches beyond them to include the natural environment and our more everyday environment such as the home and other parts of the built environment. The emergence of this interest goes with a more inclusive and less elitist approach to understanding aesthetic experience and its objects. Aesthetic experience happens not only in the opera house or art gallery, but also when making or appreciating a quilt, listening to rap music, or taking an evening stroll.

Philosophers have been trying to understand the nature of aesthetic experience since the eighteenth century, but (also in the last thirty years or so) interest has shifted away from this issue, and has been replaced by a study of the nature of aesthetic properties. The current state of affairs, then, is one where an interest in the environment, natural and otherwise, is gaining ground in aesthetics, while interest in aesthetic experience has largely receded from view. A problem is left in its wake. As we move away from the arts and towards more everyday objects and environments, an aesthetic vacuum opens up. With the arts, the aesthetic context is in some sense fixed by the creative activity of the artist, the meaning she or he creates through works or art, and the reception of artistic qualities by an audience. It seems that there is less concern with what constitutes aesthetic experience or the aesthetic response if we already have an object – the work of art – that presents itself for appreciation. An art work, even a political one, is something intended for attention to its perceptual, formal, expressive, symbolic, and representational properties. Even when a work of art is non-aesthetic or even anti-aesthetic, the idea of the aesthetic still 'pervades our discussion of art'.[2] When we turn to nature and more everyday environments, we are faced with objects – single objects, groups of objects, micro-environments, whole environments – that lie outside this artistic context, and may have any number of uses, functions or roles attached to them in our experience and the experience of other creatures.

When is cooking an aesthetic experience and not something just for nourishment? When does climbing a mountain involve an aesthetic response, and when is it just trying to get to the top? What makes these experiences *aesthetic* is not determined by a pre-given context, as might be the case in an art gallery or concert hall (although, of course, such contexts would not be sufficient even to show how artistic experiences are aesthetic). We don't approach these activities in every case with the appreciation of aesthetic qualities as our explicit aim.

For this reason, trying to understand the nature of aesthetic appreciation is especially important in environmental aesthetics. It is a starting point, if you like. Yet, as I hinted, the topic is rather unfashionable in philosophical aesthetics. Perhaps environmental aesthetics will give current writers a new reason to return to this central issue. The scope of this chapter allows me to put into place only the groundwork needed for a preliminary understanding of aesthetic experience.

The Traditional Account

The term 'aesthetics' was not used to describe the philosophical study of art and natural beauty until 1735, when Alexander Baumgarten defined it as the 'the science of perception' or 'science of sensitive knowing'. The term is rooted in the Greek word, *aesthesis* (*aisthanomai*), which refers to sense perception or sensory cognition and has no special application to the arts or aesthetic experience. Although some earlier philosophers, such as Aristotle, had associated our response to beauty with contemplation and perception of formal qualities such as harmony, it was not until the eighteenth century that the traditional view of aesthetic experience was formulated by a number of European philosophers, most notably, Kant, Hume, Hutcheson, Shaftesbury and Burke.

The traditional account, exemplified in Kant's aesthetic theory in his *Critique of Judgment* (1790), defines aesthetic experience as involving the disinterested contemplation of perceptual qualities. The response is perceptual rather than intellectual, and issues in pleasure in response to beauty, and displeasure in response to ugliness. (I shall have more to say about Kant's theory in later chapters but, for the moment, my aim is to sketch the traditional view more generally.) The traditional view represents a subjective turn in the history of aesthetics. Prior to the eighteenth century, interest in our experience of beauty focused on the idea of beauty as an objective quality, and philosophers such as Plato and Aquinas sought to define what sort of property it is, for example, as harmony. With Kant and others, attempts to understand beauty shifted to the subject, to the psychological state of the appreciator.

This fact has led a number of commentators to associate the traditional account with a set of theories that emerged in the mid-twentieth century. Aesthetic attitude theories claim that it is the attitude of the subject that demarcates the experience or response as aesthetic, rather than a quality or property in the object of attention. We adopt this attitude, an intentional state, to have an aesthetic experience.[3] The most well-known contemporary version, put forward by Jerome Stolnitz in 1960, defines the 'aesthetic attitude' as 'disinterested and sympathetic attention to and contemplation of any object of awareness whatever, for its own sake alone'.[4] However, it would be a mistake to define Kant's approach as an aesthetic attitude theory.[5] He argued that aesthetic judgement (and hence the aesthetic response) occurs in the immediate, spontaneous perceptual experience of the world, when something strikes us, setting our mental powers into a harmonious free play. It is not a case of putting oneself deliberately into a particular state of mind. The similarity between aesthetic attitude theories and Kant's view lies in the features picked out as characterising aesthetic experience, and it is for this reason that I shall discuss these theories together under the traditional account.

All experience of the world begins in perception, but perception lies at the centre of the aesthetic response. According to the traditional account, it is the perceptual qualities (or phenomenal qualities) of the object that we contemplate. This is sometimes put in terms of an interest in the appearance of the object rather than qualities that have to do with its function or the kind of thing it is and its place in the world. In this way, the aesthetic response is typically contrasted with perception as a means to knowing the object, or an intellectual type of attention to it. Instead, our response is grounded in an immediate perceptual response rather than one that is mediated through knowledge or factual considerations.

The response is contemplative, in so far as we contemplate, through perceptual rather than intellectual reflection, the phenomenal qualities of the object. This contemplation is not passive but rather an active engagement of our perceptual and affective capacities in relation to the object's qualities. There is a sense in which we are drawn out of ourselves as we become absorbed by the qualities of the aesthetic object. Whether or not one agrees that we put ourselves into an appropriate frame of mind, an aesthetic attitude, what is clear is that we open ourselves up to the object and allow ourselves to be thoroughly engaged by it. Not all aesthetic experiences will involve such absorption; indeed, some will be much less engaged. But perhaps the ideal responses are characterised by contemplation that is focused on perceptual and other qualities of the object.

'Sympathetic attention' describes this idea nicely, although it is open to criticisms against the aesthetic attitude, which I consider presently. As Stolnitz puts it, it is how we prepare ourselves for attending to an object, where we are in a position to 'relish its individual quality . . . we want the object to come fully alive in our experience . . . to savour fully the distinctive value of the object, we must be attentive to its frequently complex and subtle details'.[6] Part of being sympathetic is not to be distracted, to attend in the appropriate way. Compare this to having sympathy for other people, which involves attention to their feelings, trying to grasp them, and putting one's own feelings aside if there is conflict. The role of sympathetic attention has been confirmed by a recent account of aesthetic experience put forward by Noël Carroll:

> we take cognizance of the object in question and we attempt to let it guide us where it will. It may turn out that the object is a poor guide. If it is an artwork, it may be ineptly constructed. Or, it may be intended to lead us where we do not wish to go. It may alienate our sympathies. However, our experience can still be called aesthetic so long as we approach the work openly, even if the object makes our continued sympathetic attention impossible.[7]

Sympathetic attention in the aesthetic context means focusing attention on the aesthetic qualities of the object. This type of attention and the contemplation that surrounds it suggest that the traditional view is not entirely bound up with the subject. It is more precise to say that it aims to identify what is distinctive about our response, but it nevertheless gives a primary role to the object and its qualities. It is certainly not the case that the object is left behind or determined by subjective projection.

Disinterestedness has been viewed as a problematic and somewhat outdated concept, yet it has an important history in moral philosophy, and it defines another key feature of the traditional view of aesthetic experience.[8] It does not refer to indifference, but to the absence of purpose that attaches to the aesthetic response. We do not approach the object in order to use it as a means to some end, nor are we interested in discovering its function or use. Our approach is free from these concerns. For Stolnitz, it facilitates the aesthetic attitude. For Kant, it is not part of an attitude or intentional stance, but rather it is a feature of aesthetic judgement itself. In so far as the traditional view is intended as a definition, disinterestedness is not a sufficient condition because it may also characterise our moral judgements. Whether or not it is a necessary condition is a matter of debate, with traditional accounts arguing that it is.

As an approach with concern for the subject's state of mind, aesthetic experience may involve affective, cognitive and imaginative mental states. Theories of aesthetic experience vary according to how much emphasis they place on each of these different states. For example, affective approaches emphasise feelings such as pleasure and sometimes emotion, while a more cognitive approach focuses on the role knowledge plays in our appreciation of the aesthetic object. The traditional approach, as put forward by Kant and other eighteenth-century philosophers, cites the role of feeling – pleasure in response to beauty and displeasure in response to ugliness – as the basis of the aesthetic response, rather than its being based in a concept (or knowledge) of the object. (However, Kant does not extend feeling to include emotion, except in the case of the sublime, but even here its role is uncertain.)

Turning to emotion in more recent views, feeling awe, happiness or shock and so on can all be part of our aesthetic response to both artworks and nature. Proponents of an expression theory of art are known for making emotion the centre of art's meaning and appeal, but many philosophers would not want to say that emotion defines the aesthetic response. Stolnitz relates emotion to the expressiveness of the object, but he does not make it a necessary or significant component in the aesthetic attitude. This makes sense in so far as the aim is to set out what typically characterises (or even defines) aesthetic experience. Imagination also has an important place in traditional views. In Kant, for example, aesthetic pleasure is felt through the harmonious free play of the mental faculties of imagination and understanding as they connect with the qualities of the object.

Stolnitz follows Kant, but is more open to the role of knowledge. While knowledge is not central, it is relevant if it enhances our appreciation and enables us to grasp the meaning and expressiveness of the object. It is not relevant when it distracts our attention away from the object's aesthetic qualities.[9] This may be seen as an improvement on Kant's view, which has been criticised as a type of formalism by some philosophers. However, although knowledge is given no explicit role in the aesthetic response, Kant does not reject it either. His views can be interpreted as arguing that aesthetic judgements do not rest in a concept of the object, so that knowledge of the object is not necessary, nor the basis or aim of the aesthetic response.

More recent approaches to aesthetic appreciation – and ones more distant from the traditional view sketched here – argue for the significance of 'genetic studies' or information about the origins of the aesthetic object for the understanding and evaluation that is part of aesthetic appreciation. This is the case in relation to works of art, where knowledge of the artist and context of art-making (historical, social and so on) is needed for appropriate appreciation. In relation to the natural world, Allen Carlson is well known for his 'natural environmental model', which argues for the necessity of scientific knowledge for proper aesthetic appreciation.

I discuss Carlson's view at length in Chapter 4, but I should note here that aesthetic appreciation in some cases involves an attempt to understand, interpret and grasp the meaning of the aesthetic object before us. But the perspective taken on what sources are drawn upon to achieve this distinguishes one position from another. For example, one position contends that immediate perceptual experience of the sensuous surface is sufficient for such understanding so that no other source than the object itself and the individual's perspective is needed.[10] Another position claims that religious knowledge, myths and folk narratives may be the most appropriate sources. By contrast, a cognitive approach will draw upon knowledge – factual knowledge – for its main source, while not necessarily excluding the other sources as potentially relevant.

The traditional approach outlined above continues to be highly influential despite criticisms related to the concept of disinterestedness. It is probably fair to say that it is very difficult to provide a definition of aesthetic experience with necessary and sufficient conditions. A wiser move would be to argue that the features presented in the traditional approach ring true as characteristic of many experiences we would be inclined to call aesthetic. This provides flexibility, but, more importantly, should be sufficient for understanding what is meant by the aesthetic dimension of experience, at least for our purposes here.

Pragmatist-oriented Accounts

Before I move on to consider aesthetic experience in the narrower context of the natural environment, it will be useful to consider an attractive alternative to the traditional approach. John Dewey argues that the traditional concept of aesthetic experience cuts it off from everyday interaction with our world. By defining the aesthetic as disinterested and concerned with the narrow and rather elitist categories of beauty, sublimity, pleasure and fine art, the aesthetic is raised up and out of the vital stream of experience. Instead, Dewey contends that the aesthetic arises through an almost primal, active engagement between ourselves and our environment, and through ordinary activities including both practical and intellectual pursuits. The aesthetic emerges in 'an experience' when the elements of ordinary experience come together in a meaningful and vital way, creating a unified experience that is complete and whole in itself. It is not disengaged or distant, but full of meaning and expression, involving both 'doing' and 'undergoing' and engaging the 'entire live creature'.[11] As a pragmatist, although he is interested mainly in how artistic experience can enhance and invigorate human life, he is also aware of engagement with the natural world and the aesthetic dimension therein.

Dewey's view is usually sharply contrasted with the traditional approach, mainly for its pragmatist basis, its holism (and inherent critique of dualism), and its critique of disinterestedness and the elitism of theories of beauty. However, it shares with Kant and others an emphasis on perceptual absorption, active imagination and generally an active engagement of our mental powers.[12] Although it argues that aesthetic experience arises through more everyday activities, the paradigm case is our experience of art – either as maker or appreciator – and one that is infused with expression and creativity. So, although it is important to preserve the distinctiveness of Dewey's approach, it does confirm some of the traits of the aesthetic dimension of experience.

Although I can only give him brief mention, Monroe Beardsley is another philosopher who has written extensively on the idea of aesthetic experience. Writing around the same time as Stolnitz, Beardsley was influenced by both Dewey and Kant, perhaps more by Dewey in his insistence on the aesthetic as characterised by coherence and intensity. His view also reflects some the common features of the aesthetic identified by the philosophers we have looked at, but he does not present a definition as much as a set of criteria. For an experience to be aesthetic, it must meet the first criterion, plus some but not all of the others: (1) 'object directedness', similar to sympathetic attention; (2) 'felt freedom', a release from distracting or problematic concerns, perhaps not unlike the freedom identified by Kant and associated with aesthetic judgements; (3) 'detached affect', the capacity to set the object at a slight emotional distance in order to appreciate it (not disinterestedness, but perhaps a version of it); (4) 'active discovery', the constructive activity of our mental powers, where we make connections and locate meaning (similar to imaginative engagement); (5) 'wholeness', a feeling of wholeness and satisfaction or contentment (this is closer to Dewey's view of the aesthetic as life-enhancing rather than simply the pleasure or delight Kant associates with positive aesthetic judgement).[13]

Whether one chooses a strict definition that sets the aesthetic apart, or a looser set of characteristics that suggest more continuity with the rest of experience, there is some agreement on the general distinguishing marks of the aesthetic. This claim accepts that individual experiences will differ, and also that non-aesthetic experiences can share many of the features identified with the aesthetic.

Aesthetic Experience and the Environment

At the beginning of this chapter I mentioned the problem of an aesthetic vacuum – how a lack of artistic context means that an idea of what aesthetic experience is without art is especially important for any account of aesthetic appreciation of nature. That vacuum may present a philosophical problem, but it also provides an opportunity to start afresh, to consider how we can work with some important and relevant theories of aesthetic experience to understand what aesthetic appreciation of nature is all about. The openness of this perspective had been embraced by a few philosophers who have contributed to understanding the concept of aesthetic experience beyond the artworld. Since I will be discussing their views at length later on, I will only present a sketch of their views.

Paul Ziff makes one of the most interesting contributions to attempts to extend aesthetic experience beyond the artworld. In 'Anything Viewed' (1979), he compares artworks to heaps of dried dung and other atypical objects of aesthetic attention, and shows that it is false to consider an artistic context as defining the aesthetic context.

> Aesthetic value is as it were a co-operative affair. If attending aesthetically to an object is worthwhile then the object contributes its presence and possibly the conditions under which one attends to the object contribute their share while the person contributes his: what is wanted is an harmonious relation between the person and the object. It is never the case that such harmony depends solely on the contribution of the object.[14]

Objects that are fit for aesthetic attention are not distinguished solely by their context, but also by whether they are worth attending to, and Ziff is open to anything being worthy of our attention, not just great artworks.

> Consider a gator basking in the sun on a mud bank in a swamp. Is he a fit object for aesthetic attention? He is and that he is is readily confirmable.[15]

> In looking at [Leonardo's] *Ginevra* one can attend to the display of craftsmanship and the beauty of form and shape: in looking at the gator basking one can attend to the beautiful grinning display of life. Anything that can be viewed can fill the bill of an object fit for aesthetic attention and none does it better than any other.[16]

Although it is easy to agree that a sunset is a worthy object of aesthetic attention, I like Ziff's point because he is not afraid of moving away from fine art and art itself to understand the aesthetic.[17]

Ziff is not writing from the point of view of environmental aesthetics, but his views present a starting point for considering aesthetic experience in an alternative context. Ronald Hepburn's classic article, 'Contemporary Aesthetics and the Neglect of Natural Beauty' (1966), provides the first contemporary position for understanding how aesthetic experience relates to the natural environment.[18] For my discussion here, the most relevant points are, first, that in the absence of an artistic context and artistic meaning directing the appreciator, she or he is more independent, able to – but also with a greater responsibility as it were – to choreograph how the experience unfolds. We direct our attention to aesthetic qualities, and challenge ourselves by seeking those qualities that are not obviously attractive. This indicates greater freedom in aesthetic experience of nature compared to art. Carlson puts this point slightly differently, and suggests that in the absence of artistic design, we become designers of our own experience, working with the properties of the environment.[19]

Second, unlike the majority of artworks, especially traditional forms, the natural environment potentially environs us. This creates an experience of being enveloped by the aesthetic object. Although we can focus on specific objects or 'scenery', and set ourselves apart from the aesthetic object, nature is all around us. Arnold Berleant has made this fact the starting point of his 'aesthetics of engagement', arguing that our appreciation of nature begins with experiencing it as environment.[20] (I return to the problem of how aesthetic experience of nature differs from that of artefacts in Chapter 3.)

The traditional approach can meet the challenges of the natural environment (with some qualifications), which is not surprising given that Kant began with nature as the paradigm object of aesthetic experience. The freedom of perception and the mental powers unfettered by concepts or practical concern allow for a response characterised by the perceptual and contemplative absorption that the natural environment demands. Also, while some critics may find this conception of the aesthetic response empty of content, this is not the case. Nature is not devoid of meaning; unlike art, its meanings are not given mainly by an artist and presented for discovery by the appreciator. For the most part, we bring meanings to nature in aesthetic appreciation. The content of nature relevant to aesthetic appreciation can be found in its aesthetic qualities and the meanings tied to them. These aesthetic qualities are predominantly perceptual, expressive and imaginative, rather than related to art history, human culture, and the like, as is the case with art.

It would, however, be prudent to revise the traditional view in a couple of ways for the environmental context. It could be expanded to include use of all the senses, since we rely on touch, smell and taste as well in our encounters with nature.[21] Furthermore, we ought to be concerned not only with beauty, sublimity, the picturesque and ugliness but also with other categories of aesthetic value, such as the shocking. The variety of nature demands an openness to appreciation of atypical aesthetic objects – gators on dung heaps, beetles and mudflats – not just pretty flowers, sunsets and dramatic mountainscapes.

The traditional account provides one of the most widely accepted ways contemporary philosophers understand the aesthetic dimension. It has its drawbacks and needs revision in relation to the natural environment, but it serves to give a clear sense of what it means to take an aesthetic perspective on the world. Discussion of aesthetic experience is sometimes divided between those who locate the defining features of the aesthetic in the appreciator and those who locate them in the aesthetic object. As Noël Carroll puts it, an aesthetic approach may be described as 'affect-oriented' or 'content-oriented'.[22] This division is, however, too sharp. While some commentators identify the traditional approach as affect-oriented, I disagree, and contend that the traditional approach necessarily integrates the qualities of the object as equally significant in its account. This follows Kant, who although emphasising feeling in the subject, argued in his aesthetic theory and his epistemology that the possibility of experience is importantly dependent upon both the cognising subject and the perception of phenomena in the world. In the next section I consider the side of aesthetic experience that is usually associated more with the aesthetic object, aesthetic qualities or properties.

AESTHETIC QUALITIES

In our experience of a melancholy moor, the complex song of a blackbird, or the fragrance of a flower meadow, we perceive aesthetic qualities. The aim of this section is to further clarify and distinguish the aesthetic dimension of experience by considering the nature of these types of qualities (or properties) in aesthetic appreciation. This should also serve to give some insight into what grounds the value we find in the natural world from an aesthetic point of view.

Types of Aesthetic Qualities

There are a variety of aesthetic qualities, which philosophers have grouped into these categories:[23]

1. *Sensory qualities* – value added to a sensory quality such as a smell or texture, as in 'fragrant' or 'velvety soft'.
2. *Affective qualities* – these relate to some emotion or the expression of some emotion, used metaphorically, for example, 'cheerful brook'.
3. *Imaginative qualities* – these relate to imaginative associations and identification, for example, 'magical', 'mysterious', 'animated'. They often overlap with affective qualities.
4. *Behaviour qualities* – human behavioural qualities used in a metaphorical way to describe artworks or nature, such as 'lively' or 'relaxed'.

5. *Gestalt qualities* – these are to do with relations between parts, such as 'unified' or having 'integrity', and including formal qualities like 'graceful'.

6. *Reaction qualities* – these relate to the reaction or affective response of the appreciator, as in 'funny' or 'shocking'.

7. *Character qualities* – these relate to the overall character of a landscape or artwork, for example, 'majestic' or 'threatening'. Notice that there is likely to be overlap here with affective and imaginative qualities, as in the imaginative quality, 'mysterious', which might also capture the character of a place.

8. *Symbolic qualities* – this is when some aesthetic quality, for example, the fluttering, wandering flight of a butterfly, represents or symbolises something else, in this case, perhaps 'freedom'. The concept of the 'sacred' in nature and art is another possible example of a symbolic relation.

9. *Historically-related qualities* – these relate to the origins, narrative or historical feel of the aesthetic object, as in 'original', 'ancient' or even 'romantic' (in some contexts).

Not all of the types of qualities above make sense in the context of non-artefactual aesthetic objects because some of them comment on the way in which something has been crafted or to some intention embodied within it, as with 'derivative' or 'sentimental'. But like many aesthetic qualities, it could be argued that even these could be used metaphorically to describe natural phenomena.[24] Note too that the qualities listed are mainly descriptive, although they may also be used as the basis for ascribing value to a landscape or work of art. Some aesthetic qualities are evaluative in that they identify a quality but also clearly ascribe aesthetic value at the same time. They are referred to as 'pure value' qualities, such as 'vulgar', 'beautiful' or 'ugly'.

Aesthetic Supervenience

Frank Sibley has famously argued that aesthetic concepts are dependent upon non-aesthetic concepts.[25] Because aesthetic concepts identify aesthetic qualities, his claim means that aesthetic qualities are dependent upon non-aesthetic or base properties, which are often, but not in all cases, primary properties (sometimes aesthetic properties will be dependent on colour properties, so, in this type of case, the aesthetic quality is a tertiary quality). For example, the graceful sweep of a weeping willow will be dependent on the shape of the tree and its light, thin branches and leaves. In this sense, aesthetic qualities emerge from non-aesthetic ones. We simply perceive non-aesthetic qualities in things, but the discrimination of aesthetic properties, according to Sibley and others, takes keen attention and sensitivity in perception.

Although there have been criticisms of Sibley's view on aesthetic qualities, his ideas continue to be influential and have provided a sound basis for a recent defence of the realism of aesthetic qualities through the concept of supervenience. Supervenience theses argue that aesthetic properties supervene on non-aesthetic properties. Non-aesthetic properties ground aesthetic properties and therefore constitute the 'subvenient base'. Supervenience theses vary according to how narrowly or broadly one conceives of the base, and how strictly or loosely the dependency relation is expressed. In so far as Sibley's position has been viewed as supporting supervenience, it has been viewed as having a more narrow base because of his emphasis on the perceptual component of the aesthetic response.[26] Broader supervenience bases take on board base properties relating to background knowledge, acts concerning historical change and so on, and therefore support more robust versions of this type of theory.[27]

Let me say a little about Sibley's account of the nature of the dependency between aesthetic and non-aesthetic qualities. The relationship is not rule-governed, which is to say that we cannot infer from any set of non-aesthetic properties a particular aesthetic description. Fine lines and light colours will not guarantee that a painting is graceful rather than heavy. This suggests an intimate, interactive relationship between the properties there, which means that aesthetic qualities are sensitive to changes in non-aesthetic properties. Changes in non-aesthetic qualities will necessarily cause changes in aesthetic qualities. This has important implications for landscapes because any changes in the non-aesthetic properties of a landscape potentially change its aesthetic qualities.

Aesthetic Qualities and Secondary Qualities

Most aesthetic qualities, or properties, can be characterised as phenomenal properties.[28] That is, they belong to the category of things that we grasp primarily through perceptual experience, and in line with this our apprehension of them is affected by conditions of perception. These conditions include an individual person's sensory capacities, their cognitive stock, or set of beliefs and values, and the cultural and historical context of their perceptual experience. Aesthetic qualities are typically contrasted with primary or physical qualities, those qualities that are intrinsic to the object, exist independently of an observer, and which a physicist could detect and measure through physical means, such as mass, volume and shape. Instead, they are compared to secondary qualities, like colour, because they are not intrinsic to the object but rather are response-dependent. The existence and nature of aesthetic qualities are dependent to some extent upon the conditions of the observer.

The response-dependency of aesthetic qualities should not lead one to assume strong relativism or that aesthetic qualities are subjective projections. Using the analogy to colour, and other arguments, it is possible to defend a realist position on the nature of aesthetic qualities. I defend such a position here, although my position is a moderate and relational version of realism. While I recognise that aesthetic qualities are real (and defensible in aesthetic judgements), their existence is importantly dependent on the relation between the appreciator and object. My view sits between, on the one hand, objective realism, which holds that aesthetic properties exist in objects independent of observers, and on the other, subjective realism, which holds that aesthetic properties are entirely dependent on the subjective states of the appreciator.[29] I steer this course in order to show how the apprehension of aesthetic qualities draws on the conditions and situation of both the subject and object, which is consistent with a revised notion of the traditional view of aesthetic experience.

The analogy with colour establishes how aesthetic qualities may be associated with their objects, as secondary qualities, rather than as mere subjective projections.[30] When we say, for example, 'x is red', we are saying that red is a property of x, but also that it will depend upon the conditions of the perceiver, such as their perceptual capacities, the degree of light present, and so on. This fact about colour properties does not lead us to say that they are subjective properties. We do associate them with objects, and there is in most cases agreement in our colour judgements. We do not typically question that x is a particular colour, although we might quibble about the exact shade of the colour. In so far as most aesthetic judgements can be classed as perceptual judgements, of which colour judgements are also a class, we can see that there may be a similar basis for claiming that aesthetic properties have a similar status to colour properties.

That said, we must be careful to note that the analogy can only be taken so far. It is likely that there is more agreement in respect of colours than of, say, the expressive qualities of a landscape. Cultural factors and other considerations are likely to have a greater role in shaping our judgements of the landscape, so the response-dependency of aesthetic qualities will be of a different magnitude. This should not deter us from a ascribing objectivity, if limited, to them, since it is possible to identify a shared basis for judgements within many cultures, and in some cases a cross-cultural shared basis.

Many discussions of the status of aesthetic qualities go on to articulate a position in relation to their role in supporting aesthetic judgements, where we ascribe aesthetic value to things. Realists, for example, will argue that such judgements are defensible and that disagreement is not sufficient to argue for the subjectivity of aesthetic value. I shall leave that discussion until Chapter 7, where I examine how we make aesthetic judgements of the natural environment, how we go about defending them, and sources of disagreement between judgements of this kind. In this context I also draw on Sibley's views.

Some discussion of the concept of the aesthetic value of nature is required, though, to help to distinguish further the aesthetic domain. In the next section I compare and contrast aesthetic value to other types of value and locate it in relation to instrumental and non-instrumental types of value.

AESTHETIC VALUE

All the kinds of things that have aesthetic qualities can also have aesthetic value – artworks, the natural and built environments, everyday objects and so on. A discussion of aesthetic value generally would not be very helpful, since there are particular issues that arise in relation to valuing the natural environment from this perspective. How does aesthetic value stand as an environmental value? Three different issues present themselves in relation to this question. First, we need to locate aesthetic value in relation to other environmental values. Second, what are the implications for aesthetic value given that aesthetic qualities are response-dependent? Third, is aesthetic value an instrumental or non-instrumental type of value?

Aesthetic Value as an Environmental Value

'Aesthetic value' is a term commonly used in environmental aesthetics to describe the qualities ascribed to landscape, seascapes and other environments. But in other fields, such as geography, landscape architecture and environmental conservation, other terms are more commonly used for aesthetic value, such as 'landscape value', 'visual value' and 'scenic value'. Sometimes even the terms 'recreational value' or 'amenity value' are used. I find all of these terms problematic (especially 'visual value', the reasons for which I explain below). While I understand the need to use language appropriate to the aims and concerns of these other fields, each of the terms designates too narrow a perspective to appreciate fully the scope of aesthetic value in relation to the environment. The term 'aesthetic value' is certainly woolly itself, but at least it allows for a more general point of reference.

Let me begin with the term, 'visual value'. It should be obvious why this presents a problem. It rests very narrowly on visual qualities of the environment. Aesthetic qualities are not grasped through visual perception alone. Perception understood more generally, as I have used it, includes all the senses, as well as immediate thoughts and meanings attached to what we perceive. Imagination and emotion also have a role in the discovery of aesthetic qualities and value in the environment. Scenic value is similarly limited in the way it designates value related only to attractive scenery. This term suggests not only that aesthetic value is always positive, given the connotation of 'scenic', but it also narrowly circumscribes the environment as a scene to be viewed, rather like a painting is viewed at a distance, as separate from us. The environment is all around us and engages us as persons within it. Of course, we do appreciate parts of the environment from afar, and also cordon off particular objects in our perceptual field. Scenic value is used all the time in conservation literature, yet it designates an outmoded way of understanding the environment which ignores the special *environing* qualities of environments. Finally, of all the three alternative terms, 'landscape value' is the least problematic, and I may use it in specific contexts in this study. Although it is intended to refer to a variety of environments, taken literally, it does not include seascapes or marine environments, and the rich environment above our heads, the sky and space beyond it. I am also somewhat suspicious of the '-scape' suffix, which is suggestive of something stretching out before one, not unlike a scene. However, 'landscape' is a predominant term in the literature, and it has some relevant uses, so it would be foolish to abandon it. It is perhaps best simply to offer the criticism for consideration.

The next task is to clarify that 'aesthetic value' is a term I shall use to cover both negative and positive aesthetic judgements. 'Aesthetic' has acquired a connotation of positive value, as when someone says 'the interior is very aesthetic' or suchlike. It is used to describe something that has attractive qualities. Aesthetic value proper covers the wide range of judgements we make, from finding something stunningly beautiful, to finding something sublime, to finding something ugly, with a lot of variety in between. Environmental phenomena fall into all of these categories. This point is especially important in order to broaden aesthetic discussion of the environment beyond the attractive and scenic to include negative aesthetic qualities and judgements. Moreover, many phenomena viewed as unscenic or uninteresting, may be found to have positive value if we make more of an aesthetic effort and pay more attention.[31]

Finally, we need to locate aesthetic value among other environmental values. These include ecological value; rarity value; diversity value; cultural value; historical value; sacramental value; economic/resource value; and amenity value. Rather than define each one, I'd like to point out where aesthetic value overlaps with these others and show how it is a distinct value in its own right.

Interestingly, it is possible to find aesthetic qualities in the context of ecological and diversity value, but they remain distinct from aesthetic value. Ecosystems, for example, are sometimes described as having integrity or coherence. The value of biodiversity entails the quality of diversity, which alongside variety, is commonly used to identify aesthetic qualities. Variation rather than sameness or repetition is valued in works of art. In relation to more culturally oriented values, aesthetic value is still distinct. Although aesthetic value is primarily, if not exclusively, part of human culture, cultural value more specifically identifies landscapes or parts of the environment that have cultural resonance and significance for human beings. For example, the forest has special significance in many Nordic cultures as a place of solitude and engagement with nature. While aesthetic qualities may have some role in why the forest is valued, in this context it is more that the forest is seen as perhaps one thing that defines Nordic cultural identity. Aesthetic value can be clearly distinguished from historical and sacramental value, at least because we can understand the ascription of aesthetic value without explicit reference to human culture, except in the case of cultural landscapes, where reference to knowledge of human narrative of a landscape may feed into our aesthetic judgements. Below, I set out how aesthetic value can be distinguished from use values, such as recreational or amenity value.

Valuing from a Human Perspective

Aesthetic value in the environmental context is often viewed as a strongly human value. By that I mean, first, that it is seen as one of the values that is the most response-dependent. For example, it is often contrasted with scientific values, which, despite also being related to a human, cultural discourse, are viewed as less prone to human subjectivity. Second, because aesthetic judgements are strongly linked to the production of pleasure or displeasure, aesthetic valuing of nature is often viewed as an instrumental affair, and that humans value nature aesthetically for the pleasure it provides. Both of these assumptions are mistaken.

Aesthetic judgements are made from a human perspective, and from the perspective of beings with capacities like ours.[32] We bring our experience and aesthetic sensitivity to bear on base properties perceived in the environment, our experience combines with what we perceive, and aesthetic appreciation emerges. Some aesthetic judgements are described as anthropomorphic in their ascription of human qualities to nature, such as an emotion, as in a 'melancholy moor'. These facts about aesthetic judgements show that aesthetic value is anthropogenic or generated by humans. But it does not follow from this that aesthetic value is more human-centred or anthropocentric than other types of environmental values. Because aesthetic judgements are response-dependent, they are dependent on human (or other) valuers in ways that other types of judgements may be as well, such as moral judgements (although my analogy depends on taking up a moderate form of moral realism). Environmental philosophers have shown how moral judgements can be made from an ecocentric rather than anthropocentric perspective. Although there may be some grounds for suggesting that aesthetic valuing is more closely related to human perception through the sensitivity required to discern aesthetic qualities than, say, ecological valuing, this is also no more the case than with moral judgements. I do not wish to make the stronger claim that aesthetic and scientific values are both human constructions. On my more realist-oriented view, aesthetic value is response-dependent, and so more dependent on the human perspective than values based in a more objective scientific understanding of nature, but this is not to say that it is prone to either a constructivist construal of value or one that is laden with anthro-pocentrism.[33]

Aesthetic Value as a Non-instrumental Value

In discussion of values in environmental philosophy a distinction is made between instrumental and intrinsic values, or between instrumental and non-instrumental values. Much has been made of the distinction in attempts to classify natural value, ecological value and other types of environmental values as intrinsic, and to understand exactly what it means to say that something is valued intrinsically. The latter issue is important for showing why, as I shall claim, aesthetic value in the environmental context is a non-instrumental value.

Instrumental value is attributed to something in virtue of its usefulness; it is valuable as the means to some end. When nature is viewed as an instrumental value, this usually means that it is valued as a resource for human beings. Specific examples of instrumental values with respect to the environment are economic or resource value, for example, forests used to produce paper, and recreational value, where we value a forest for the recreational activities which give us pleasure, such as walking the dog or cross-country skiing.

When aesthetic value is confused with amenity or recreational value, aesthetic value is identified as an instrumental value. The confusion has a couple of sources. First, phenomenologically, it is difficult to separate our aesthetic experiences from recreational ones. Often they will be part of the same activity or situation. I take satisfaction in the fact that cross-country skiing takes me out of the stuffy confines of my office and invigorates my body, but I also simply enjoy the aesthetic qualities surrounding me, such as the soft, wispy sound of wind through the pine trees. The skiing is pursued for the satisfaction it brings, while the sounds of nature are valued for themselves rather than a means to some end. We may, of course, appreciate cross-country skiing itself for both its recreational and aesthetic value, just as we sometimes appreciate a meal for satisfying hunger and for its pleasing aromas and complex flavours. While working hard to get some proper exercise, I can also take moments to meditate on the harmonious, flowing motion of my skis on the snow.

The second source of confusion lies in the two kinds of pleasure experienced. It is not uncommon to assume that recreational activities and aesthetic experience are both instrumental because they provide us with pleasure. We have the desire to ski in the forest – and *all* that involves – because of the pleasure it brings. This view may also explain why some environmental philosophers and activists perceive aesthetic value as the 'icing on the cake', a frivolous value that has less importance and urgency in relation to conserving the environment compared to ecological or moral values.[34]

The difference between the two types of pleasure is that one is interested and the other is disinterested. We pursue recreation for the relaxation and enjoyment it gives us – and it is getting this pleasure out of the experience that motivates the activity in the first place. By contrast, in aesthetic appreciation, pleasure does not play a motivational role but rather it is merely a by-product of the experience. Jerrold Levinson provides a good working definition of aesthetic pleasure:

> Pleasure in an object is aesthetic when it derives from apprehension
> of and reflection on the object's individual character and content,
> both for itself and in relation to the structural base on which it rests.
> That is to say, to appreciate something aesthetically is to attend to
> its forms, qualities and meanings for their own sakes.[35]

Another reason to understand aesthetic pleasure in this way, as centred on the object for its own sake alone, is because aesthetic appreciation makes little sense if its purpose is the production of pleasure. If it were, then presumably any sort of experience that afforded that particular type of pleasure would do; the actual appreciation of distinctive aesthetic qualities would not matter. We could, for the sake of argument, suggest that on this view, taking a drug would be an acceptable substitute if it produced the same effect. But it would be odd to accept such a substitute for our actual experiences of aesthetic qualities. With all this said, it is also worth pointing out that the aesthetic response is not exclusively connected to pleasure. Sometimes we feel dismay, curiosity, shock and so on in our aesthetic encounters.

Understanding the nature of aesthetic pleasure brings us back to the traditional approach to aesthetic experience. Recall that sympathetic attention and disinterestedness are two important features characterising that approach. Sympathetic attention refers to the way in which we direct our attention to the qualities of the object, without distraction, to enable an open and potentially absorbed response to what we experience. Disinterestedness describes how the aesthetic response is non–utilitarian; we take no interest in how we might use the object for our ends. The upshot of this approach for appreciating the environment is that we value its aesthetic qualities for their own sake.

The idea of valuing something for its own sake is not entirely clear. In the aesthetic context, Roger Scruton has pinned down a meaning that fits with points made here:

> A desire to go on hearing, looking at, or in some way having an experience of X, where there is no reason for this desire in terms of any other desire or appetite that the experience of X may fulfil, and where the desire arises out of, and is accompanied by, the thought of X.[36]

This concedes that there is a kind of desire and interest in aesthetic experience, but it is focused on the object and terminates on it. It is, if you will, aesthetic interest.

Although construing aesthetic value as an instrumental value in relation to aesthetic pleasure is an unpopular view, some aestheticians have argued that our aesthetic experiences have value beyond themselves. Most of these views do not hold that we pursue aesthetic experiences for some further end, but that they nevertheless have benefits. For example, pragmatists such as Dewey argue that aesthetic experience is life enhancing, and others may argue that it has intellectual and social benefits. In relation to the environment, some writers have suggested that our aesthetic sensitivity and engagement with nature could lead to greater respect for the environment. In my view, there is some truth to all of these claims, but I would want to avoid any claim that aesthetic value is defined as a means to these other ends. It is more prudent to say that aesthetic experience has beneficial effects and probably supports a generally positive valuing of nature (although this may be difficult to prove empirically).

Aesthetic value, then, is a non-instrumental value. It is attributed to objects in virtue of their aesthetic qualities, rather than for some purpose, such as the production of pleasure or knowledge. Until now, I have used the term non-instrumental value to make my case. It is a clearer term in my view, and avoids the confusion often found in accounts of intrinsic value. However, a discussion of the latter cannot be avoided in the environmental context. Aesthetic value is a kind of intrinsic value, but it will be necessary to specify exactly what type it is.

John O'Neill helpfully distinguishes between three meanings of intrinsic value. (1) Intrinsic value is used as a synonym for non-instrumental value. Something has intrinsic value if it is an end in itself. The object has value in its own right, independently of its usefulness. This is the most common use among environmental philosophers; (2) Intrinsic value is used to refer to the value an object has solely in virtue of its 'intrinsic properties'. This is the view held by G. E. Moore and specifies a type of value that is internal, non-relational, and not dependent on human valuers; (3) intrinsic value is used as a synonym for 'objective value', that is having value independently of the judgements of valuers.[37] The second two meanings represent a strong realist position, making intrinsic value a real value in the world, rather than relating to valuers. A common misunderstanding is to conflate meanings (1) and (3), where it is assumed that if some entity does not have value independently of human valuers it can only have instrumental value.

I have shown that aesthetic value is response-dependent but non-instrumental. It should be clear why I subscribe to the first meaning of intrinsic value, given that it leaves room for the response-dependency of aesthetic valuing. The structural properties that ground aesthetic qualities are in the world, as intrinsic properties, but aesthetic value is dependent on grasping aesthetic qualities that relate to human or other perceivers. Aesthetic value of the environment is therefore emergent, arising out of the perception of aesthetic qualities but it is still linked to certain structural properties. My position therefore lies somewhere between a subjectivist stance where all value rests in valuers, and the objective stance where value lies in the objects independently of valuers.

This chapter began with an outline of the nature of aesthetic experience, and I put forward a revised version of a traditional approach. The nature of aesthetic qualities, as the focus of aesthetic appreciation, was considered, along with an analysis of aesthetic value as an environmental value. This background provides a basis for understanding the concept of the aesthetic that underlies the ideas in this study. In the next chapter, I continue to sketch out the setting of environmental aesthetic appreciation through a review of aesthetic perspectives on nature in the history of philosophy.

NOTES

1. Throughout the book, I shall use 'aesthetic experience', 'aesthetic response' and 'aesthetic appreciation' interchangeably.
2. Noël Carroll, *Philosophy of Art: A Contemporary Introduction* (London and New York: Routledge, 1999), p. 182.
3. David E. W. Fenner, *The Aesthetic Attitude* (Atlantic Highlands: Humanities Press, 1996), p. 4.
4. Jerome Stolnitz, *Aesthetics and Philosophy of Art Criticism* (Boston: Houghton Mifflin, 1960), p. 35.
5. This point has also been made by Gary Kemp, 'The Aesthetic Attitude', *British Journal of Aesthetics*, 39:4, 1999, p. 396n. Kemp provides a good case for reviving interest in attempts to define aesthetic experience, and he shows why George Dickie's

criticisms of such a project are unfounded (in response to George Dickie's influential article, 'The Myth of the Aesthetic Attitude', *American Philosophical Quarterly*, 1:1, 1964, pp. 55–66).

6. Stolnitz, p. 36.

7. Carroll, p. 183.

8. Disinterestedness as a feature of aesthetic experience has been attacked on a number of fronts but it has also been defended and clarified as a central concept of the aesthetic. I discuss the debate at length in Chapter 5.

9. Stolnitz, p. 58.

10. On these distinctions in the context of the natural environment, Cheryl Foster construes the debate in terms of the 'ambient' and 'narrative' accounts of aesthetic appreciation of nature. See Foster, 'The Narrative and the Ambient in Environmental Aesthetics', *Journal of Aesthetics and Art Criticism, Special Issue: Environmental Aesthetics*, 56:2, 1998, pp. 127–38. Others, including myself, distinguish between non-cognitive (or non-science-based) and cognitive (or science-based) accounts. See Chapter 4.

11. John Dewey, *Art as Experience* (New York: Perigee, [1934] 1980), pp. 48–50.

12. See Alan Goldman's comparisons between Kant and Dewey in 'The Aesthetic', in Berys Gaut and Dominic McIver Lopes, *The Routledge Companion to Aesthetics* (London and New York: Routledge, 2001), p. 186.

13. Monroe Beardsley, *The Aesthetic Point of View*, ed. Michael Wreen and Donald Callen (Ithaca: Cornell University Press, 1982), p. 290ff.

14. Paul Ziff, 'Anything Viewed' in Esa Saarinen, Risto Hilpinen, Ilkka Niiniluoto and Merrill Provence Hintikka (eds), *Essays in Honour of Jaakko Hintikka* (Dordrecht: Reidel, 1979), p. 288.

15. Ibid. p. 291.

16. Ibid. p. 293.

17. J. O. Urmson makes this sort of point, as well as claiming that it cannot be a special characteristic (against 'beauty' as a defining quality of the aesthetic), nor a special emotion (against Clive Bell's concept of aesthetic emotion), that defines the aesthetic. Instead it is the criterion of merit we use to support our aesthetic judgements, criteria which are based in the object's appearance or presentation. See J. O. Urmson, 'What Makes a Situation Aesthetic?', *Proceedings of the Aristotelian Society*, Supplementary Volume, XXXI, 1957, pp. 75–92.

18. Ronald Hepburn, 'Contemporary Aesthetics and the Neglect of Natural Beauty', in *Wonder and Other Essays* (Edinburgh: Edinburgh University Press, 1984). [First published in B. Williams and A. Montefiore (eds), *British Analytical Philosophy* (London: Routledge and Kegan Paul, 1966).]

19. Allen Carlson, 'Environmental Aesthetics', in D. Cooper (ed.), *A Companion to Aesthetics* (Oxford and Cambridge, MA: Blackwell, 1992), p. 143.

20. Arnold Berleant, 'The Aesthetics of Art and Nature', in S. Kemal and I. Gaskell (eds), *Landscape, Natural Beauty and the Arts* (Cambridge: Cambridge University Press, 1993), pp. 236–7.

21. Kant rejected the other senses besides seeing and hearing as legitimate bases of disinterested aesthetic judgement. I discuss this point further in Chapter 5.

22. Carroll, p. 168ff.

23. The list below is chiefly from lists set out by Goran Hermeren, *The Nature of Aesthetic Qualities* (Lund: Lund University Press, 1988), pp. 106–7; Alan Goldman, 'Properties, Aesthetic' in D. Cooper (ed.), *A Companion to Aesthetics* (Oxford and Cambridge, MA: Blackwell, 1992), p. 342; and Carroll, p. 190.

24. Some would add they could be used in contexts where a creator is intended to be identified, if one follows the view that nature or parts of nature are created by God or other deities. Others may contend that in the absence of a creator, there is something like teleology or purpose in nature.

25. Frank Sibley, 'Aesthetic Concepts', *Philosophical Review*, 68:4, 1959, pp. 421–50.

26. Sibley himself did not view his approach as characterised by the metaphysical suppositions of realism or supervenience because his ideas about aesthetic qualities were related more to our use of language or 'aesthetic concepts' in aesthetic appreciation. See my discussion in Chapter 7 concerning this issue.

27. See, for example, Jerrold Levinson, 'Aesthetic Supervenience', reprinted in *Music, Art, and Metaphysics* (Ithaca: Cornell University Press, 1990), pp. 134–58; and for an objection to the thesis: John Bender, 'Supervenience and the Justification of Aesthetic Judgements', *Journal of Aesthetics and Art Criticism*, 46:1, 1987, pp. 31–40.

28. I use 'quality' and 'property' interchangeably, although some writers make a distinction between the two. See Hermeren's discussion, pp. 46–8; and Jerrold Levinson, 'Properties and Related Entities', *Philosophy and Phenomenological Research*, 39, 1978, pp. 1–22, and his 'Particularisation of Attributes', *Australasian Journal of Philosophy*, 58:2, 1980, p. 106ff.

29. This formulation is used by Fenner, pp. 15–16.

30. Versions of this analogy have been suggested by other philosophers, such as Frank Sibley, in 'Colours', *Proceedings of the Aristotelian Society*, 1967–8, pp. 145–66. See also Colin Lyas, 'The Evaluation of Art', in Oswald Hanfling (ed.), *Philosophical Aesthetics* (Oxford and Milton Keynes: Blackwell and The Open University, 1992), p. 370ff.; and Carroll, p. 192ff.

31. Yuriko Saito argues forcefully for the value of unscenic nature in 'The Aesthetics of Unscenic Nature', *Journal of Aesthetics and Art Criticism: Special Issue: Environmental Aesthetics*, 56:2, 1998, pp. 101–11.

32. There is some evidence that non-humans, some birds, for instance, may have experiences of aesthetic appreciation, even if they do not consciously make aesthetic judgements. See Holmes Rolston, III, *Environmental Ethics: Duties to and Values in the Natural World* (Philadelphia: Temple University Press, 1988), p. 234.

33. Another false claim that arises as an implication of the other two is that a more response-dependent type of valuing is necessarily subjective, so that 'beauty is in the eye of the beholder'. I have provided some reasons above for why this view is mistaken, and I give more support later in Chapter 7 when I consider in detail the judgements that arise in aesthetic appreciation of nature.

34. See my discussion in Chapter 8 of aesthetic value in the practical context of environmental conservation.

35. Jerrold Levinson, 'Pleasure, Aesthetic', in Cooper, 1992, pp. 331–2.

36. Roger Scruton, *Art and Imagination* (London: Methuen, 1974), p. 148; cited in Kemp, p. 398.

37. John O'Neill, 'The Varieties of Intrinsic Value', *The Monist*, 75, 1992, pp. 119–20.

CHAPTER 2

Early Theories of Aesthetic Appreciation of Nature

T he aim of this chapter is to provide some historical and critical back-ground for understanding contemporary theories of aesthetic apprecia-tion of nature. I cannot give more than an outline here, so for that reason more attention is given to topics that have been especially influential on the recent debate, such as eighteenth-century aesthetic theory, mainly Kant's. A dis-cussion of his aesthetic theory also serves to give some foundation for my own approach to aesthetic appreciation of nature developed later in the book. Although I shall touch upon changes in landscape tastes, I concentrate on the philosophical theories which corresponded with those tastes rather than provide an empirical account of them.

AESTHETIC APPRECIATION OF NATURE BEFORE THE EIGHTEENTH CENTURY

There can be no doubt that from the beginnings of human civilisation many individuals have responded aesthetically to their natural surroundings. Before the eighteenth century aesthetic appreciation of nature would have taken place informally in pastoral environments and in the humanly modified environ-ments of gardens.[1] In the formal sense nature would have been appreciated probably only through representations in art and literature. There were no philosophical aesthetic theories specifically addressing the natural environ-ment as worthy of aesthetic appreciation in its own right. Also, 'aesthetics' as a concept and discipline was not known as such until the eighteenth century. In the overview that follows, my remarks refer to aesthetic appreciation as a topic of western philosophical study or as a formal practice.

From the classical period until the eighteenth century (apart from in-digenous people living in wilder environments), many people had little access to predominantly natural landscapes and they did not seek the environmental experience so many of us value now. Enjoying nature for its own sake or for recreation was not a common practice. While nature was studied from a pre-scientific and scientific point of view, aesthetic experience of environments took place mainly through art's Arcadian idealisations of nature. This was especially the case during both the classical period and the Renaissance. Given the predominance of the idea in western philosophical and Judaeo-Christian religious thought that humans are separate from nature, this is not surprising. Apart from the special relationships formed with natural environments by some communities, human life was conceived as sharply distinguished from natural processes, and as having dominion over the natural world.[2]

In the classical period, philosophical ideas that now belong to the field of aesthetics were mainly concerned with art. For Plato and Aristotle, nature's beauty was discussed only implicitly in the context of a representational theory of art. The aim of art was to represent the world through resemblance. Plato held an imitation theory of art, although imitations were considered inferior to the absolute and unchanging 'forms' or ideas of phenomena. The highest beauty for Plato was the form of beauty, since beauty in the physical world was impermanent. Both Plato and Aristotle discussed beauty as a quality in objects, associating it with unity, regularity and simplicity.[3] Their examples were typically of artefacts rather than nature, for example, architecture or the arts of music and literature. Artistic representations of nature sought to improve on nature's qualities through art, or to idealise nature through the mythological landscapes of Greek literature and poetry.

On the whole, nature was of little interest compared to art, however, two later classical writers made gestures towards an aesthetics of nature. Longinus' *On the Sublime* dealt mainly with the sublime in a literary context, but he also observed that mountains, great rivers, the sun and the stars were sublime.[4] Beauty was central to Plotinus' complex metaphysical philosophy, where he pays some attention to natural beauty, suggesting that it is at least as significant as beauty in art.[5] Roderick Nash points out that wild nature has been appreciated by Asian cultures since early times through art and direct experience:

> Far from avoiding wild places, the ancient Chinese sought them out in the hope of sensing more clearly something of the unity and rhythm that they believed pervaded the universe. In Japan, the first religion, Shinto, was a form of nature worship that deified mountains, forests, storms, and torrents in preference to fruitful, pastoral scenes since the wild was thought to manifest the divine being more potently than the rural. In linking God with wilderness,

instead of contrasting them as did Western Faiths, Shinto and Taoism fostered love of wilderness rather than hatred.[6]

On one level, the neglect of natural beauty continued in western thought when the early anthropocentric attitude towards nature reached a peak in the Middle Ages. Nature was viewed as a wild and frightening place, savage, irrational, disordered and evil in comparison to the safety, order and virtue of cities. Besides ideal pictures of country life, medieval art and literature reflected suspicion of nature:

> Grimm's fairy tales, Dante's Inferno, and innumerable folk tales convince us that, notably in Central Europe, forests were regarded with horror and dismay. Silent, dark, cold, airless, full of unknowns, forests are the abode of beasts and bandits, and only partially penetrable while hunting.[7]

Aesthetic appreciation of nature in terms of delight in nature's complexity, richness and beauty was virtually unknown. The pleasures of the senses, so often associated with aesthetic experience, were considered both beastly and immoral, being identified with the non-rational and non-spiritual.[8]

On a philosophical level, however, natural beauty was not overlooked. The concept of beauty was of central interest, although it was given a metaphysical and theological emphasis.[9] Aquinas built upon the classical definition of beauty, arguing that beauty is dependent upon a thing's having integrity, due proportion or harmony and clarity, with each related to divine qualities. There is some connection between his views of beauty and the natural world, since he argues that beauty has to do with the forms of living things and non-organic entities.[10] The beauties of nature were conceived as divine symbols, and nature itself as a work of divine art.[11]

During the Renaissance fear of nature subsided, and nature began to be appreciated, but still indirectly, through science and art. Renaissance thinkers were interested in the careful observation of plants and animals, and landscape painting developed more seriously to include pastoral scenes of nature as serene and civilised. During this period classical ideas of beauty as order and harmony continued to have an influence, and they underpinned the taste for elegant, idealised landscapes exemplified in neo-classical paintings. However, wild nature was not appreciated 'formally' through aesthetic categories until later, and it was still a source of fear. For example, the first European settlers in North America perceived their natural environment as an ungodly, hostile wilderness to conquer and civilise.[12]

THE BEAUTIFUL, THE SUBLIME AND THE PICTURESQUE

The eighteenth century has been described as a turning point in the history of environmental aesthetics because it was then that aesthetic appreciation of nature became important in both aesthetic thought and practice. Aesthetics as a formal discipline was founded when Alexander Baumgarten formulated the term 'aesthetics'. Most of the prominent aestheticians of this period, Archibald Alison, Joseph Addison, Francis Hutcheson, Edmund Burke and Immanuel Kant, discussed both art and nature. Landscape appreciation became an art form, a leisure activity for the educated classes. The influence of eighteenth-century English planners and theorists was so strong that its legacy can still be found in contemporary landscape tastes, in our taste for the rolling meadows of large city parks and our desire for scenic viewpoints.[13] These changes occurred for a number of reasons, including easier access to the countryside and mountains. Although many wild landscapes, such the Scottish Highlands, were still considered barren and ugly instead of sublime in the early part of the century, philosophy and art together began to encourage a more sympathetic attitude towards nature.[14] The new aesthetic tourism, the 'Grand Tour', allowed aesthetic experience of nature's landscapes 'in the raw' for the first time. From the rugged Alps of Europe to the softer green mountains in the north-eastern United States, nature was experienced directly for the aesthetic pleasure it afforded.

Changes in landscape tastes reflected new philosophical ideas which established three aesthetic categories of nature: the beautiful, the sublime and the picturesque. In the next three sections I discuss each in turn, but I shall focus on Kant's aesthetic theory in my discussion of the beautiful and the sublime.

Kant's Aesthetic Theory: The Beautiful

During the eighteenth century aesthetic theory blossomed in the formal study of taste, or aesthetic judgement, as well as the aforementioned trio of aesthetic categories. Kant was the first philosopher to offer a philosophically sophisticated theory of aesthetic appreciation of nature. His *Critique of Judgment* (1790), the third of his three Critiques, examines the nature of aesthetic judgement (and also teleological judgements, which are less relevant to aesthetic theory).[15] Kant was also interested in our aesthetic judgements of art, but he begins with examples from nature, and there is good evidence to show that nature was his main concern.

Kant sets out to solve the problem of how 'judgements of taste' are possible. He begins with an analysis of this type of judgement, and then proceeds to discover and defend the grounds for such judgements. Through his discussion, an aesthetic theory emerges which gives the distinctive features of the aesthetic response, and how it is that we make aesthetic judgements which are not merely subjective.

The 'judgement of taste' (which I shall hereafter refer to as 'aesthetic judgement') is expressed in utterances like, 'This jasmine flower is beautiful.'[16] Kant analyses this type of judgement by setting out its distinguishing qualities. First, aesthetic judgement is contrasted with cognitive judgement because it is not determined by knowledge of the object, but rather in a feeling of liking or disliking in the appreciator.[17] The jasmine is judged as beautiful not in virtue of a concept of it as a particular type of flower or because of knowing it is the source of essential oil used in many perfumes. It is called beautiful because it evokes an immediate feeling of pleasure, which is a response unmediated by the concept of what jasmine is.

The immediacy of the aesthetic response identifies a second feature of aesthetic judgement. If the judgement does not stem from knowledge of the object, then what is the basis of it? The jasmine is beautiful by virtue of an immediate response to its perceptual qualities: the soft creamy white colour, combined with its delicate petals. But although enjoyment of these qualities underlies aesthetic appreciation of it, Kant does not claim that beauty is an objective quality of the flower. Beauty does not lie in the flower's colour or forms, and these qualities do not alone cause the aesthetic response. Finding the flower beautiful is a direct consequence of an accordance or attunement between the perceptual qualities of the flower and the mental powers which Kant calls the imagination and the understanding. This attunement is characterised as a harmonious 'free play' of imagination and understanding. Freed from conceptualisation, the mental powers engage with the perceptual qualities of the object in a pleasurable activity which is directed at appreciating the object for its own sake.[18] Kant thus characterises beauty as the appreciation of something through an immediate encounter between an appreciator and a particular object. For this reason, we have no predetermined concept of beauty; it is something that arises in a relationship between subject and object.[19]

With these points in place, we are now in a position to understand more clearly why Kant thinks that aesthetic judgement is based on a feeling in the subject, and hence why he says that this type of judgement is subjective. The basis of aesthetic judgement is subjective, rather than objective, for two reasons: (1) aesthetic judgement stems from a feeling in the subject rather than an (objective) concept of the object; (2) as a judgement of beauty, aesthetic judgement cannot be other than subjective, since beauty is not an objective quality, but something which emerges through an immediate encounter between appreciator and object. These claims show the particular way in which Kant wants to identify aesthetic judgement as subjective, and they also introduce a vital point. It would be a serious mistake to associate Kant's claim that aesthetic judgement is subjective with the view that 'everyone has their own taste' or that 'beauty is in the eye of the beholder'. Kant strongly denies this, and one of the central arguments of the *Critique of Judgement* is to show that aesthetic judgement has a subjective basis in feeling, yet it nonetheless extends beyond oneself. In finding the jasmine beautiful, one is not making a singular judgement that applies only to myself, but one which implies the possibility of universal assent.[20]

Kant's defence of this claim is too complex to discuss in detail here, but it points to another important feature of aesthetic judgement, 'disinterestedness'. In this context, disinterestedness does not mean indifference or lack of interest. Kant uses the concept to describe aesthetic interest as distinct from interest in an object as a means to sensory gratification and an interest in using it as a means to some utilitarian end.[21] The disinterestedness characteristic of aesthetic judgement identifies appreciation of aesthetic qualities apart from any end. My appreciation of a seascape is aesthetically disinterested, according to Kant, when it rests on valuing its aesthetic qualities, for example, the graceful underwater movement of seals against a striking blue backdrop, rather than valuing it as a place to refresh myself after sunbathing (for sensory gratification), or as a mineral resource (where it serves a utilitarian end).

Disinterestedness operates in aesthetic judgement to distinguish this type of appreciation from the arbitrariness and subjectivity of personal desires, as well as other more practical aims which are irrelevant to the aesthetic approach. As a condition of aesthetic judgement it secures a degree of impartiality; by freeing ourselves from personal desires or preoccupations in relation to the object we are in a better position to judge the object on its terms. If this condition holds, it shows how disinterestedness provides some support for Kant's claim that aesthetic judgements do not express personal preferences. If I approach the flower or the seascape disinterestedly, and assume that others do so too, then I have grounds for expecting the agreement of others when I judge something to be beautiful.

From Kant's analysis of aesthetic judgement a significant aesthetic theory emerges. The aesthetic response is distinct from other ways in which we relate to the world because it is based in an immediate, disinterested, liking or disliking in response to the perceptual qualities of an object. Knowledge is not the basis of aesthetic appreciation, but rather the feeling that arises through perception of the object and the harmonious free play of the mental powers. The distinctiveness of aesthetic appreciation is further developed by Kant in his belief that aesthetic judgement is neither wholly subjective nor wholly objective; instead it lies somewhere in between, having a subjective basis in feeling, yet at the same time asserting the agreement of others. Aesthetic judgements are intersubjective, possessing what Kant calls 'subjective universal validity', which distinguishes them from other types of judgements we make, including cognitive and moral judgements.

Natural phenomena are the paradigmatic objects of the aesthetic response, and Kant even argues, if not entirely consistently, that only nature is the appropriate object of a 'pure' judgement of taste. But he is also interested in other categories of the aesthetic response, including our response to the sublime (which is almost exclusively a response to natural objects), and our response to art. One point from Kant's theory of art is worth mentioning here, as it relates to understanding differences between the aesthetic appreciation of art and nature. He recognises the essential distinction between art and nature, which is that the former is the product of human creation. Moreover, as artefacts, artworks are fashioned according to some idea of what the object is meant to be, so in this respect art is distinguished from nature as the product of human intentionality.[22]

KANT'S AESTHETIC THEORY: THE SUBLIME

Although the sublime had been discussed by philosophers before Burke and Kant, it is in their writings that the sublime is developed into a significant aesthetic category.[23] In her study of changes in landscape tastes, Marjorie Hope Nicolson points to the important change in aesthetic attitudes towards mountainscapes prior to the eighteenth century:

> During the first seventeen centuries of the Christian era, 'Mountain Gloom' so clouded human eyes that never for a moment did poets see mountains in the full radiance to which our eyes have become accustomed. Within a century – indeed, within fifty years – all this had changed.[24]

Before this dramatic change in aesthetic taste, a taste for the calm tranquillity of pastoral beauty dominated art and literature, as well as aesthetic taste in general. But with a new interest in wild nature, philosophers like Shaftesbury, Burke and Kant took more seriously the need for an aesthetic category which explained how wild and great things evoke an aesthetic response which was not displeasure (as associated with ugliness), but pleasure mixed with fear.

Kant's theory of the sublime reflects Burke's ideas, but it offers a more detailed and sophisticated theory. For example, while Kant is influenced by Burke's claim that the sublime is associated with large things which excite pain rather than pleasure, he refines and qualifies these claims, and he makes a distinction between two categories of the sublime. Kant's theory is of special interest to environmental philosophy because it explores a very distinctive kind of aesthetic relationship with the natural world.

After Kant makes his case for the distinctiveness of judgements connected to natural beauty, he analyses another type of aesthetic judgement, the judgement of the sublime. As with beauty, there is no determinate concept of the sublime, and Kant especially emphasises that the sublime is a feeling rather than an objective quality. The perception which serves as the starting point of the sublime is, like the beautiful, disinterested, but the object of this perception differs in important ways. In the sublime, it is the difficulty in perceiving formlessness in nature that evokes a feeling of the sublime. That formlessness can be understood either 'mathematically', that is, as the sheer magnitude or apparent infinite size of something in nature, or 'dynamically', as the power or might that we find in nature. The effect of this difficulty is to push the imagination to its very limits, so that we are unable to apprehend the object adequately using this capacity alone:

> if something arouses in us, merely in apprehension and without any reasoning on our part, a feeling of the sublime, then it may indeed appear . . . contrapurposive for our power of exhibition, and as it were violent to our imagination, and yet we judge it all the more sublime for that.[25]

> consider bold, overhanging and, as it were, threatening rocks, thunderclouds piling up in the sky and moving about accompanied by lightning and thunderclaps, volcanoes with all their destructive power, hurricanes with all the devastation they leave behind, the boundless ocean heaved up, the high waterfall of a mighty river.[26]

Experiences of nature like these demand that we make use of reason, our capacity for grasping the supersensible.[27] In a free play with imagination, reason enables us to take in the magnitude and power of nature, and in that activity we are then able to apprehend what Kant calls 'rational ideas', such as freedom and totality, which transcend phenomenal comprehension. The interaction of imagination and reason is what makes the sublime feeling what it is – one of tension between a power working at its very limits, combined with the pleasure that comes in exercising reason as it opens out the field of supersensible ideas. Indeed, as Kant remarks above, the more imagination is pushed to its limits by nature, the more we judge nature sublime.

The dialectic between imagination's ability and inability in both the mathematical and dynamical sublime is what engenders the feeling that characterises the sublime. In the mathematical sublime, Kant points to the feeling of negative and positive pleasure we feel in the aesthetic response.

We feel negative pleasure in imagination's ultimate failure to intuit an absolute whole, the infinity of nature in a representation, and we feel positive pleasure in our use of reason to apprehend the idea of infinity. Imagination and its play with reason is pivotal to the range of pleasure felt in the sublime. As Paul Guyer puts it: 'The very feeling of the inadequacy of the imagination to represent an absolute whole is the same feeling which manifests to us the existence of reason, and so this frustration turns pleasurable.'[28]

In the dynamical sublime, we find nature sublime because of its might. This judgement depends upon imagination's power to envisage the general potentiality of nature as dangerous, and the various ways in which individual sublime objects could harm us. In these situations, nature cannot actually harm us, because we are in a safe place, sheltered from the storm or walking confidently and comfortably on a mountain path. Nature's wildness evokes a mixture of anxiety and wonder, which Kant describes as fear. However, this is not actual fear, but fear incurred in imagination, so that we merely acknowledge that nature can be fearful. We are not truly overwhelmed by the fearsome quality of nature, but through imagination we are able to entertain the thought that nature could endanger us if circumstances were otherwise:

> Thus any spectator who beholds massive mountains climbing skyward, deep gorges with raging streams in them, wastelands lying in deep shadow and inviting melancholy meditation, and so on is indeed seized by *amazement* bordering on terror, by horror and a sacred thrill; but, since he knows he is safe, this is not actual fear: it is merely our attempt to incur it with our imagination.[29]

In this way imagination facilitates the kind of response that leads to a judgement of the sublime, as opposed to one in which we simply find nature frightening. Imagination's activity evokes a negative pleasure, but it has a hand too in inducing the positive pleasure of the sublime. Through imagination we entertain the thought of nature's might and feel insignificant to it, but in this imaginative activity we are also compelled to discover our capacity to resist its dangers. Imagination enables us to feel nature's might and at the same time to recognise something valuable and meaningful about ourselves, that in our freedom we feel able to cope with the challenges and dangers of nature as sublime. In that recognition we discover our strength as moral beings, not against or superior to nature, but as having a kind of independence (while also part of it). This engenders a feeling of respect for both nature, in its might, and ourselves, as moral beings.

In response to the sublimity of nature, imagination releases the mind from the limits of conceptual thought. In this freedom, rather than aiming to find order in experience, imagination enables an apprehension and appreciation of the indeterminacy and disorder confronting us. Imagination expands our experience by taking us beyond phenomenal order to discover the disjunction between ourselves and nature. Imagining nature's potential totality or its fearful aspects forces us to engage with a side of nature that creates conflict, challenging us to find a place in it and leaving us feeling as if we might never feel at home in it.

But the sublime also excites a meaningful connection to nature in the positive pleasure which comes in imagination's wake. The disorder and violence experienced in nature is exactly what enables us, in the end, to find value in nature. Sublime qualities are not objectively in nature, but they are felt qualities which we appreciate through imaginative engagement with the formlessness of nature. The discovery of value gives rise to a feeling of pleasure and respect directed simultaneously at nature and ourselves – at nature because of its great qualities, and at ourselves for discovering our capacities as non-phenomenal beings in comparison to nature. Through this type of response we explore less pleasant dimensions of our relationship with the natural world, and in doing so we find meaning and value in it. The result is a distinctive connection to nature grounded in the imaginative and affective dimensions of the sublime response.

Kant's theory of the sublime can be interpreted as defining a strongly human-centred attitude towards nature because he sometimes writes as if our freedom and capacity for reason give us 'dominion' over nature. Also, he claims that through a 'subreption' we transfer, as it were, our feeling of the sublime in nature over to ourselves. This provokes the criticism that his theory of the sublime dualises humans and nature, and moves human freedom to the centre of the experience. But this criticism overlooks some of the more interesting ways in which the Kantian sublime defines a distinctive aesthetic relation between humans and nature. It is a mistake to construe Kant's remarks as making ontological and normative claims about humanity's place in relation to nature. Through experiences of the sublime in nature, we recognise that reason gives us the ability, in our freedom, to transcend our phenomenal selves, which belong to nature, as it were. It is in that sense that we are not, in the end, overwhelmed by the phenomenal because we have resources beyond how it limits us, but we are also not above or superior to nature.[30]

By considering more carefully the role of respect in Kant's theory, sublime feeling can be shown to underpin a connection to the natural world. The respect we feel in relation to ourselves and nature arises through a direct experience of aesthetic qualities in nature. Nature itself, in all its magnitude and might, has an essential place in the feeling of the sublime; it is not used as a means to an end, if one accepts Kant's view that the sublime response is a type of disinterested aesthetic response. Sublime feeling leads to a feeling of respect for nature, the 'starry heavens above', and for ourselves, 'the moral law within'.[31] Kant's theory of the sublime does express a humanist aesthetic, but it is one that importantly anticipates the Romantic turn towards nature.

The Picturesque

A third aesthetic category of both art and landscape was developed slightly later than the categories of the beautiful and the sublime, in part because it was felt that these two categories were not exhaustive. As a quality in nature, the picturesque lies between the serene, pastoral qualities of beauty and the awesome grandeur of the sublime.

The theory of the picturesque, developed mainly by William Gilpin, Sir Uvedale Price and Richard Payne Knight in the late eighteenth century, is essentially a theory of artistic and natural landscape appreciation.[32] Its enthusiasts were keen to mark it out in its own right, identifying its qualities in paintings by Claude Lorrain and Salvator Rosa, and in literature in Gothic novels, such as Mary Shelley's *Frankenstein*. In landscape gardening, the picturesque is sometimes associated with Henry Repton, who was critical of Lancelot 'Capability' Brown's grand designs for the great manor houses of England, which involved moving earth and trees to create classical landscapes with extensive prospects across lawns, lakes and built features, such as classical temples.

The theory originates in the idea that landscapes may be appreciated according to the criteria of a picturesque painting. Price cites Gilpin's definition, which states that picturesque objects are those 'which please from some quality capable of being illustrated in painting' or 'such objects as are proper subjects of paintings'.[33] Price argued that this definition was too vague and too general, since other objects could satisfy the definition which were not actually picturesque. In response, he develops a more careful theory, one that provides a good understanding of the picturesque for us here.

In showing what the picturesque is, Price follows Burke's objective theory of beauty, where beauty is found in objects with qualities such as smoothness, uniformity of surface, regularity, smallness, delicacy, symmetry, coherence, pleasing colours, calmness, order, gradual variation, elegance, simplicity. But there is an important contrast between the two aesthetic categories. In contrast, the picturesque is associated with three main qualities: roughness, sudden variation and irregularity. Roughness was marked by rough textures, such as rough-hewn stone, but also the general feature of ruggedness in a landscape. Sudden variation refers to asymmetry of lines and contours, which cross each other or are broken in unexpected ways, and other surprising elements such as sudden 'protruberances'. Irregularity was found in intricacy and variety, but perhaps most noticeably in the effects of the passage of time, 'weather stains, partial incrustations, mosses', and also in the variety of tints on surfaces (as compared to perfectly even colour and smooth surface). Whereas the beautiful expresses peacefulness and tranquillity, the picturesque is 'splendid confusion and irregularity', tumbled masses, with everything overgrown.[34]

These qualities were exemplified in particular objects and landscapes, and they were featured in picturesque paintings. Picturesque scenery is described as broken and undulating with variety, including water, for example a lake with 'savage banks' and a surface broken rather than smooth, perhaps with a pattern in the water from the wind, or the fast-flowing water of waterfalls and whitewater. Even picturesque trees are included, trees with rugged or strongly variegated bark, especially from age. In picturesque landscapes trees are not placed evenly but irregularly and in clumps.

Picturesque landscapes often included buildings. In predominantly natural landscapes it was common to build a ruin, for this expressed the passage of time and the mystique of the past through the irregular qualities of weathered stone overgrown with ivy. Beauty was associated with classical temples, the picturesque with temples that had collapsed and decayed. Asymmetrical or intricate buildings were also favoured, including Gothic architecture with its variety of forms, and the rough-hewn character of mills, cottages and old barns.[35]

The contrast between the beautiful and the picturesque is stronger than between the sublime and the picturesque, but the distinction is still clear.[36] The picturesque shares with the sublime the move away from the calm tranquillity of the beautiful and towards an aesthetic which is more expressive and in some sense alien. Picturesque paintings are of wild and uninhabited places, and the designed landscapes which copy them present a scene which is mysterious and strange. However, the sublime is at the other extreme from the beautiful, and so it is the most wild, the most fearful, the most alien of all landscapes, at once overwhelming the senses and evoking awe. Appreciation of the picturesque is, by contrast, less anxious, less fearful and more curious and charming. It has been argued that the sublime is difficult to express through art, while depictions of nature and the art of gardening lie at the heart of picturesque theory.

The picturesque was not just an aesthetic theory but foremost a movement in aesthetic taste and design. Handbooks were available for guidance on designing landscapes, parks and gardens according to the principles of the picturesque, giving such detailed instructions as to how to group park animals in a picturesque manner and how best to develop ruins.[37] There were also recreational guides for viewing natural scenery from a picturesque perspective. The appropriate approach was defined according to the standpoint we take to landscape paintings, where we stand back and behold the design, forms and colours of the picture. Appreciators of the picturesque in the eighteenth century even used a special device, the 'Claude glass', through which they viewed natural landscapes. This instrument, a tinted convex mirror, framed the landscape like a rectangular painting, and also enabled the viewer to see the landscape through a tinted glass, giving the scene the aged appearance of a picturesque painting, such as one by Claude.

The picturesque is significant because it represents a serious step towards appreciating nature 'in the raw', nature enjoyed for qualities of its own. Prior to the picturesque, nature's imperfection was 'corrected' through neo-classicist art which sought to idealise nature's beauty. Although nature was appreciated formally through the categories of the beautiful and the sublime, for the first time landscape appreciation became a formal and recreational activity. Identifying and enjoying picturesque landscapes became the practice of upper and middle-class picturesque travellers who sought out these landscapes.

The picturesque is not unproblematic in its approach to nature, but its attention to natural qualities increased the range of positively valued aesthetic qualities in nature and added new points of interest from an aesthetic perspective. First, the picturesque recognised the temporality of nature, its dynamic, organic character.[38] Instead of attempting to freeze nature in an ideal of classical beauty, the picturesque showed nature in stages of growth and decay: in the craggy bark of an old oak, the swayed back of a worn-out carthorse, or in picturesque ruins we see the passage of time. In its temporality we also see nature's imperfection, the second point of new value revealed by the picturesque. In the stained and rough surfaces of stone or the overgrown, gnarled banks of a river, nature is not neat and tidy or symmetrically perfect. Nature is viewed as disordered, but all the more aesthetically interesting for that.[39] Third, expressiveness in nature became an important part of aesthetic appreciation. While the beautiful was found in nature's sensuous, even formal, qualities, the picturesque identified many natural features with expressive qualities, a trend that reached its height in the Romantic movement that followed. Rather than idealising nature or fictionalising it through myths or allegory, picturesque art attempted to portray a landscape's affective qualities through more natural qualities. For example, the roughness characteristic of picturesque landscapes is associated with the expressive and imaginative qualities of spirit and animation.[40] The intricacy of Gothic architecture is associated with a feeling of mystery or uncomfortable surprise. As Dabney Townsend observes:

> The formulation of the picturesque leads to a much more important and coherent way of understanding the environment as an aesthetic

object. Instead of the alternatives of neoclassical imitation and sentimental affect, the picturesque leads to the formulation of theories of aesthetic distance and natural expressiveness.[41]

All three of these new ways of aesthetically valuing nature signalled a softening of the predominant attitude which saw nature as ugly and un-controllable, and as something to be tamed and perfected by through human ideals. With the picturesque (as with the sublime) came a valuing of change, disorder and the otherness of nature. However, set against this, the pictur-esque was strongly human-centred in according value to landscapes in virtue of how well they met the standard set by picturesque paintings.

There are both aesthetic and ethical reasons for criticising the central project of the picturesque. Aesthetically, landscapes were appreciated as if they were paintings, the Claude glass representing a literal framing of nature. This is of course one way to appreciate nature, but it is an extremely narrow basis for aesthetic appreciation, for it assumes, mistakenly, that nature is appropriately appreciated in the category of pictures, as if landscapes were two-dimensional, fixed images on canvas. This impoverishes appreciation, for it focuses solely on pictorial qualities found in a landscape, such as colour and the appearance of design. This kind of approach makes some sense in so far as it provides criteria for landscapes that are in fact designed, like the grand parks and gardens of manor estates. Also, we can and do put a 'perceptual frame' around some of the natural landscapes we experience. However, to judge more natural landscapes by these criteria, as was the fashion for picturesque travellers, amounts to judging nature by artistic criteria. Natural environ-ments demand different appreciative frameworks than artworks. Nature, as environment, is a three-dimensional, dynamic space with multi-sensuous qualities. The picturesque model limits sensory attention to the visual, the main sense used in the appreciation of paintings, and fails to capture the possibility of sensory immersion in the environment, as three-dimensional space.

Townsend's remarks above indicate how the picturesque creates a kind of distance (not just physical) between humans and nature. Appreciators of the picturesque were spectators of nature's 'canvases', rather than part of it. They viewed nature through a deeply artistic lens, rather than the more situated appreciation of an individual integrated into an environment.[42] Such a position would not have been physically possible in some cases, but in more easily accessible environments a more environed appreciation could have taken place.

Finally, the view that nature has aesthetic value only when it is framed by art points up some ethical problems in the picturesque. This approach does not recognise that nature is worthy of appreciation independently of human design, and thus lacks respect for nature. Picturesque designers did not sentimentalise nature, but, arguably, their designs appropriate nature, re-creating it to look as if it were wild and uninhabited, to be viewed from the outside, usually from a privileged position, as the estate owners of eighteenth-century England would have viewed their property. Nature was appreciated for its irregularity and disorder, but only in the safe context of nature humanised, either by re-designing it, or by viewing it as if it were the work of an artist.

The picturesque expanded the boundaries of aesthetic appreciation out beyond the beautiful and the sublime, and towards an appreciation of nature for its temporal and expressive qualities. It increased human curiosity for nature's wild qualities, an appreciation for the irregular, deformed and decayed, an interest that shared some features with the sublime. At the same time, however, the picturesque continued a tradition of aestheticisation, where an aesthetic 'improvement' of nature by humans was viewed as preferable to raw nature. The picturesque is not an isolated model, for it finds its contemporary counterpart in what has been called the 'landscape' or 'scenery' model of aesthetic appreciation of nature.[43] The Claude glass has been replaced by picture postcards and the relatively superficial aesthetic experiences from scenic viewpoints which discourage multi-sensuous, envir-oned appreciation and the possibility of finding aesthetic value in less conventionally attractive environments.[44]

ROMANTICISM AND AFTER

Romanticism

The Romantic movement in Britain and Europe was to some extent a reaction against the distanced and relatively elitist aesthetic treatment of nature exemplified by the picturesque. Romantic aesthetic appreciation was grounded in a much more intimate conception of the relationship between humans and nature, and a much greater respect for natural phenomena. Although it is possible to overstate Romanticism's reverence for nature, nevertheless it represents an early peak in the appreciation of nature, at least because of its celebration of our experiences of nature in the literary and visual arts.

The philosophical ideas of Romanticism are characterised by a strong emphasis on the powers of imagination and feeling in contrast to the Enlightenment's reliance on the power of reason and its scientific outlook on the world, with its tendency to separate humans from nature. Romanti-cism's approach to aesthetics has various roots, including: the picturesque's move away from formal, ordered beauty; the sublime's exploration of human freedom in relation to nature's grandeur and mystery; Kant's theories of imagination, freedom and artistic genius; German Idealism; and Jean-Jacques Rousseau's idea of the 'noble savage', humans as primitive, wild beings living closer to nature than to civilisation. The influence from German Idealism came through the ideas of philosophers like Schelling, who gave art and aesthetic intuition the highest status in giving direct access to the 'Absolute'.[45] The Romantic aesthetic subject is exemplified by the solitary traveller exploring her or his expressive freedom through experiences of living close to the land, where that experience leads to self-understanding and self-realisation.

The leading figures of Romanticism, which began in the late eighteenth century and flourished in (about) the first few decades of the nineteenth century, were poets and writers such as Shelley, Wordsworth, Coleridge, and visual artists, primarily, Constable and Turner. Imagination was a key concept in Romantic thought, as exemplified by Coleridge's theory of creativity and Wordsworth's poetry. Through imagination we are able to close the gap between humanity and nature, and it was the essential power behind genius and originality in art. Coleridge, who had an early collaboration with Wordsworth, regarded imagination as the power which replaces reason for understanding nature. In *Biographia Literaria*, he creates a system in which imagination is given the role of 'unifying or reconciling the self and nature on three different but analogous levels. These three reconciliations are represented by perception, art, and philosophy.'[46]

The philosophical ideas of this period clearly valued nature, but they might still seem rather human-centred, in so far as nature can be understood as serving humanity for the discovery of freedom. However, some of Wordsworth's poetry is refreshing in its deeply felt attention to the variety of natural phenomena, from everyday, rustic encounters with nature to the more wild experiences of the sublime.[47] Various parts of Wordsworth's autobiographical poem, *The Prelude*, illustrate aesthetic appreciation which explores both familiar and alien environments through emotional, spiritual and imaginative modes of awareness. Also, it should not be forgotten that Wordsworth wrote a popular guide to the Lake District (with detailed landscape descriptions) that has been described as a project in the principles of landscape criticism. Eugene Hargrove points to Wordsworth's campaign to protect the Lake District from the development of a railway and describes him as a 'first-rate modern preservationist'.[48] John Clare's poetry is also worth mentioning for its sensitive observation of nature, even though he is not usually included as a central figure of Romantic poetry.[49]

Ruskin

Ruskin's thought, which came later in the nineteenth century, follows Romanticism's emphasis on artistic expressions of nature. He is especially concerned about truthful, faithful representations of nature as opposed to the idealised representations of classical landscape painters. A keen interest in science is reflected in his thought, his art criticism and in his own detailed, artistic renderings of nature, which convey an acute sensitivity to organic processes. Like Goethe and other Romantic thinkers before him, Ruskin wanted to break down the dualism between science and art, and many of his aesthetic and philosophical theories reflect this. A main tenet of his thought is the importance of encouraging both artists and appreciators to see more clearly, that is, to learn how to see the natural world through truthful, sensitive perception. In *Modern Painters*, he instructs us through rich descriptions of water, sky, earth and vegetation in relation to their artistic representation:

> Clear water takes no shadow, and that for two reasons: a perfect surface of speculum metal takes no shadow (this reader may instantly demonstrate for himself), and a perfectly transparent body, as air, takes no shadow, hence water, whether transparent or reflective, takes no shadow . . . But shadows, or the forms of them, appear on water frequently and sharply: it is necessary to explain the causes of these, as they form one of the most eminent sources of error in water-painting.[50]

Ruskin puts as much emphasis on the appreciator's experience as the artist's, while Romantic thinkers were perhaps more concerned with artistic creativity. For example, Ruskin develops a theory of imagination that applied to both artist and spectator, where he urged that, for art, 'It is not enough that it be well imagined, it must task the beholder also to imagine well.'[51]

Ruskin's concern for learning to see and his interest in truthful artistic representations suggest a more measured, other-directed attitude towards nature. The appreciator and artist are not worshipping nature through a kind of humanist dream, but rather there is a sense of respect for natural phenomena as truly distinct and independent from human beings. This perspective is probably due to Ruskin's pantheism; we ought to be true to nature, and not distort it, in order to be true to God. An approach to appreciation of nature through a thick cultural lens continues in Ruskin's thought, but his aesthetic theory succeeds in turning appreciation more outwards rather than inwards, relative to some thinkers before him.

American Transcendentalism

Some of the tenets of Romanticism found their way into American Transcendentalism in the second half of the nineteenth century, the leading figures
of which were Henry David Thoreau and Ralph Waldo Emerson. The
Transcendentalist aesthetic is best expressed as an appreciation of wilderness,
as illustrated by Thoreau's writings and the sublime wilderness paintings of
the Hudson River School. The gradual increase in aesthetic receptivity to
wilder landscapes found a kind of peak in the wilderness worship of
transcendentalism, although, like Romanticism, this worship had many
dimensions besides the aesthetic.

Thoreau's well-known essay 'Walking', expresses the value of wilderness to
civilisation, when he says that 'in Wildness is the preservation of the World',[52] and:

> My spirits infallibly rise in proportion to the outward dreariness. Give
> me the ocean, the desert, or the wilderness! . . . When I would recreate
> myself, I seek the darkest wood, the thickest and most interminable
> and, to the citizen, the most dismal, swamp. I enter a swamp as a
> sacred place, a *sanctum sanctorum*. There is the strength, the marrow,
> of Nature. The wildwood covers the virgin mould, and the same soil is
> good for men and for trees. A man's health requires as many acres of
> meadow to his prospect as his farm does loads of muck.[53]

Wild nature is not merely a place to regenerate one's spirit, rather it is
essential to one's sense of self as a source of spiritual and moral truths. Raw
encounters with nature, rather than civilisation, make this possible.

The wilderness paintings of Thomas Cole and others, such as Frederick
Church, depict mountain and river landscapes with little or no human
presence. Their canvases express the wild, sublime and divine qualities of
nature through a dramatic expression of natural forces (Church's use of light
and his *Falls of Niagara* (1857) come to mind here). But the Transcenden-
talists were also interested in local places, not just the distant and alien. Some
passages in *Walden*, which recounts Thoreau's experiment of living close to
nature at Walden pond, convey the aesthetic experience of an individual living
intimately and harmoniously with a particular natural place:

> This is a delicious evening, when the whole body is one sense, and
> imbibes delight through every pore. I go and come with a strange
> liberty in Nature, a part of herself. As I walk along the stony shore of
> the pond in my shirt-sleeves, though it is cool as well as cloudy and
> windy, and I see nothing special to attract me, all the elements are
> unusually congenial to me. The bullfrogs trump to usher in the night,

and the note of the whip-poor-will is borne on the rippling wind from over the water. Sympathy with the fluttering alder and poplar leaves almost takes away my breath; yet, like the lake, my serenity is rippled but not ruffled. These small waves raised by the evening wind are as remote from storm as the smooth reflecting surface. Though it is now dark, the wind still blows and roars in the wood, the waves still dash, and some creatures lull the rest with their notes.[54]

It is interesting to compare Wordsworth's explorations of his native Lake District with Thoreau's wilderness experiment. Both represent aesthetic situations that move between cultural and wilder aesthetic encounters with the environment.

Transcendentalism represents a less humanist aesthetic in comparison to the picturesque. The Transcendentalist aesthetic values a more direct relationship with nature, and it is much less concerned with artistic representations of nature than Romanticism. Thoreau's writings make an early contribution to a romantic conception of wilderness which has been very influential in conservation practice and environmental thought in North America. However, there has been considerable debate about the concept of wilderness and its role in valuing the environment, and a critical treatment of the transcendentalist aesthetic will be part of this discussion.[55]

TOWARDS THE CONTEMPORARY DEBATE

Philosophical attention to aesthetic appreciation of nature peaked in the eighteenth century and early nineteenth centuries but tailed off considerably afterwards. This is perhaps precipitated by Hegel's insistence on the primacy of art over nature and the subsequent influence of his views on later philosophical aesthetics. For Hegel, nature's aesthetic value is realised only when fashioned by human spirit through the production of art. His ideas signal the gradual move away from a conception of art as a representation of nature and towards art as the product of human expression and imagination. Concern for the relationship between humans and nature was displaced by a focus on artistic expression and the social value of art.

This change is also indicated by developments in the artworld after Romanticism, when art moved away from representation and towards expression and abstraction. Twentieth-century avant-garde movements gave even more persuasive reasons for philosophers to devote their attention to art rather than nature. In the face of Duchamp's *Fountain* and other works that challenged existing boundaries of art, philosophical aesthetics was presented with a formidable set of problems about the status of art.

Before concluding this chapter, I would like to note a handful of philosophers who explicitly recognised that the aesthetic response is manifested in experiences outside the arts, such as natural environments, design and everyday life. George Santayana and R. G. Collingwood, for example, devoted some of their discussion of aesthetics to appreciation of nature.[56] John Dewey was concerned mainly with art, but he insisted that aesthetic experience is not a separate domain from meaningful experiences in everyday life.[57] In Chapter 1, I mentioned Paul Ziff, who, along with other philosophers writing in the 1950s and 1960s such as Frank Sibley and J. O. Urmson, did not entirely give in to the artistic orientation of aesthetics and tried to bring attention back to other kinds of aesthetic situations. Animals, human faces, sunsets, clouds, meadows, alligators and smells and tastes, all presented aesthetic possibilities for these philosophers.[58]

Apart from these more broadly conceived aesthetic theories, the philosophical preoccupation with problems related to art has continued into contemporary aesthetics. In the late 1960s and early 1970s, however, a few philosophers reinvigorated aesthetic theories of nature and, unlike their eighteenth- and nineteenth-century predecessors, their interest emerged within a new context of environmentalism.

NOTES

1. Gardens have existed since ancient times, but they became a more formalised aesthetic and artistic practice during the Renaissance and after. Gardens vary from the more modified, artistic and formal to more informal, and 'wild'. Even though gardens can be highly artefactual, in some respects their appreciation involves an appreciation of nature, although this will vary according to the type of garden.
2. The western attitude where humans are the centre of the universe and 'man' has dominion over nature is widely discussed and debated in environmental philosophy. See, for example, Robin Attfield, *The Ethics of Environmental Concern*, 2nd edn (Athens, GA, and London: University of Georgia Press, 1991); John Passmore, *Man's Responsibility to Nature* (London: Duckworth, 1980); Val Plumwood, *Feminism and the Mastery of Nature* (London: Routledge, 1993); Keith Thomas, *Man and the Natural World* (New York: Pantheon, 1983).
3. Monroe Beardsley, *Aesthetics from Classical Greece to the Present* (Tuscaloosa and London: The University of Alabama Press, 1966), pp. 42–3, 61.
4. Longinus, *On the Sublime*, trans. W. H. Fyfe (London: Loeb Classical Library, 1953). This treatise on the sublime was probably written in the first century, but it was apparently lost and only rediscovered in the sixteenth century.
5. Beardsley, p. 85. See Plotinus, *The Enneads*, trans. Stephen MacKenna, rev. B. S. Page (London, 1956), chs II, V.
6. Roderick Nash, *Wilderness and the American Mind*, rev. edn (New Haven and London: Yale University Press, 1967), pp. 20–1.
7. J. Douglas Porteous, *Environmental Aesthetics: Ideas, Politics and Planning* (London and New York: Routledge, 1996), p. 52.

8. Ibid. An exception to this can be found in some writers, for example, in the thirteenth century, Hugh of St Victor discussed beauty in nature, claiming that there are beautiful tastes and smells. (See Beardsley, p. 99.)

9. See Umberto Eco, *Art and Beauty in the Middle Ages*, trans. Hugh Bredin (New Haven and London: Yale University Press, 1986). Notably, and in sharp contrast to the autonomy of aesthetics that emerged in the eighteenth century, classical and medieval philosophers viewed beauty, truth and goodness as closely related, if inseparable. A strong echo of this trend can be found in the more contemporary writings of the conservationist Aldo Leopold, see, for example, 'The Land Ethic', *Sand County Almanac* (New York: Oxford University Press, [1949] 1968). The strong relations between ethics and aesthetics are particularly relevant in the context of environmental aesthetics and more generally in nature conservation. I address them in Chapter 8.

10. See St Thomas Aquinas, *Summa Theologiae*, I, 5, 4 ad.1 (London: Blackfriars, 1964–76); and John Haldane, 'Admiring the High Mountains', *Environmental Values*, 3:3, 1994, pp. 97–106.

11. This view was set out in some depth by John Scottus Eriugena. See Umberto Eco, *The Aesthetics of Thomas Aquinas*, trans. Hugh Bredin (Cambridge, MA: Harvard University Press, 1988), p. 24. Note that these remarks are not inconsistent with the idea of nature as savage and evil, the difference is in how nature is understood in each case. Beautiful qualities in nature were associated with the divine, whilst that which was savage or ugly came to be associated with evil, ungodly things.

12. Nash, p. 23ff.

13. Porteous, p. 60.

14. See for example, Daniel Defoe, *A Tour Through the Whole Island of Great Britain* (Middlesex: Penguin Books, 1979); Samuel Johnson, *A Journey to the Western Islands*, ed. R. W. Chapman (London: Oxford University Press, [1773] 1944).

15. Immanuel Kant, *Critique of Judgment*, trans. Werner Pluhar (Indianapolis: Hackett, [1790] 1987).

16. For Kant, the judgement of taste is an expression of finding an object to be beautiful. He also claims that when we feel displeasure in relation to the perceptual qualities of an object, we will find the object ugly. Although Kant says little about negative aesthetic judgements (judgements of ugliness), he certainly did recognise their place in aesthetic appreciation. Ugliness is a neglected topic in aesthetics, but for some interesting recent discussions, see Frank Sibley, 'Some Notes on Ugliness', in John Benson, Betty Redfern and Jeremy Roxbee Cox (eds), *Approach to Aesthetics: Collected Papers on Philosophical Aesthetics* (Oxford: Oxford University Press, 2001); and in the context of environments that are often considered to be 'unscenic': Yuriko Saito, 'The Aesthetics of Unscenic Nature', *Journal of Aesthetics and Art Criticism*, 56:2, 1998, pp. 101–11.

17. Kant, 1987, §1.

18. Ibid. §9.

19. Ibid. §8.

20. Ibid. §6, §7.

21. Ibid. §5.

22. Ibid. §45.

23. For early accounts on the sublime, see, for example, Longinus (see above) and, later, in the eighteenth century, the Third Earl of Shaftesbury (Anthony Ashley Cooper) was influential for encouraging the study of the new aesthetic category of the sublime.

(Shaftesbury is also known for encouraging an appeal to disinterestedness as a feature of aesthetic experience. Like others of his time, he seriously considered Hobbes' challenge that human actions are selfish, and concluded that in aesthetic experience (as well as moral) we are not acting selfishly, but rather approaching the world from a disinterested perspective. Beauty is something appreciated for its own sake. The disinterested perspective was central to Kant's aesthetics, but it has also been a key feature in modern aesthetic theory. See Shaftesbury, *Characteristics of Men, Manners, Opinions, Times, etc.*, ed. J. M. Robertson (London, 1900).) The most significant contribution on the sublime before Kant is Edmund Burke's, *A Philosophical Inquiry into the Origin of our Ideas of the Sublime and Beautiful*, ed. J. T. Boulton (London: Basil Blackwell, [1757] 1958).

24. Marjorie Hope Nicolson, *Mountain Gloom and Mountain Glory: The Development of the Aesthetics of the Infinite* (New York: Norton, 1959), p. 3.

25. Kant, 1987, §23, Ak. 245, p. 99.

26. Ibid. §28, Ak. 261, p. 120.

27. Reason can be defined, in contrast to the understanding, as, 'not simply the ability to apply concepts to particular objects but our even higher-order ability to seek and find unity and completeness among concepts and principles themselves, whether of a theoretical or practical nature'. (Paul Guyer in *Kant and the Experience of Freedom* (Cambridge: Cambridge University Press, 1996), p. 207.) Kant gives different meanings to the supersensible, but, roughly, it refers to a substrate of phenomenal objects, a substrate we cannot know or experience phenomenally.

28. Guyer, p. 210.

29. Kant, 1987, Ak. 269, p. 129.

30. Kant makes an analogy that is useful for clarifying this point. Our recognition of sublime objects as fearful is compared to our fear of God. According to Kant, we fear God in the same way as nature's sublimity: we recognise God's omnipotence without fleeing from it. That omnipotence gives rise to respect, but at the same time we live in harmony with God because we recognise our own independence through our freedom. In the sublime, we appreciate nature's great and threatening qualities and respect that power, but we recognise that, as free beings, we can also live in harmony with nature.

31. Kant uses these expressions in the Conclusion to the *Critique of Practical Reason*, trans. Lewis White Beck (Indianapolis: Bobbs-Merrill, [1787] 1956).

32. William Gilpin, *Three Essays, 2nd edition* (London: R. Blamire, 1794); Uvedale Price, *On the Picturesque*, ed. T. D. Lauder (Edinburgh: Caldwell, Lloyd and Co., 1842); Richard Payne Knight, *An Analytical Inquiry into the Principles of Taste* (London, 1805). Stephanie Ross gives an excellent discussion of the complexities of picturesque theory and its different proponents in *What Gardens Mean* (Chicago and London: Chicago University Press, 1998), pp. 121–54.

33. Price, p. 78.

34. Ibid. p. 82.

35. Ibid. p. 84.

36. The distinction is clear, yet there is some overlap. For example, variety and intricacy, even irregularity, have all been associated with the beautiful and the picturesque.

37. Porteous, p. 64.

38. Dabney Townsend, 'The Picturesque', *Journal of Aesthetics and Art Criticism*, 55:4, 1997, p. 367.

39. The positive value of aesthetic imperfection is also a feature of Japanese aesthetic

sensibility. See Yuriko Saito, 'The Japanese Aesthetics of Imperfection and Insufficiency', *Journal of Aesthetics and Art Criticism*, 55:4, 1997, pp. 377–85, esp. note 38, p. 385, where Saito makes a comparison between aesthetic imperfection and the picturesque.

40. Townsend, p. 374.

41. Ibid. p. 369.

42. Ibid. p. 370. See also contemporary views on the role of distancing, detachment and disinterestedness discussed in Chapter 5.

43. Saito, 1998; Allen Carlson, *Aesthetics and the Natural Environment: The Appreciation of Nature, Art and Architecture* (London and New York: Routledge, 2000), pp. 45–7.

44. I discuss the important differences between artistic appreciation and appreciation of the natural environment in Chapter 3, and some of the practical problems of scenic-oriented interpretations of aesthetic value are addressed in Chapter 8.

45. Although Schopenhauer is not considered a central figure of German Idealism and was writing later than German Romanticism, he should not be overlooked. He is best known for his theories of aesthetic experience and music, but he wrote passionately, if sparsely, about natural beauty and the sublime. See Arthur Schopenhauer, *The World as Will and Representation*, vols I and II, trans. E. F. J. Payne (New York: Dover, [1818] 1966); and Cheryl Foster, 'Schopenhauer's Subtext on Natural Beauty', *British Journal of Aesthetics*, 32:1, 1992, pp. 21–32.

46. Samuel Taylor Coleridge, *Biographia Literaria*, vol. I [1817], in James Engell and W. Jackson Bate (eds), *The Collected Works of Samuel Taylor Coleridge*, vol. 7 (Princeton: Princeton University Press, 1983), p. lxxii.

47. T. J. Diffey, 'William Wordsworth' in Kelly, Vol. 4, 1998, p. 479.

48. Eugene C. Hargrove, *Foundations of Environmental Ethics* (Englewood Cliffs: Prentice Hall, 1989), p. 100.

49. See, for example 'The Wild-Flower Nosegay', Part 10 of *The Village Minstrel and Other Poems*.

50. See John Ruskin, *Modern Painters*, Vol. 1, Part II , edited and abridged by David Barrie (London: Pilkington Press, [1873] 1987), p. 171.

51. John Ruskin, *Stones of Venice*, edited by J. Morris (London: Faber and Faber, [1851, 1853] 1981), p. 233.

52. Henry David Thoreau, 'Walking' (1862), in *The Natural History Essays*, reprinted in Susan J. Armstrong and Richard G. Botzler (eds), *Environmental Ethics: Divergence and Convergence* (New York: McGraw-Hill, 1993), p. 111.

53. Ibid. p. 112.

54. Henry David Thoreau, 'Solitude', in 'Walden: or, Life in the Woods', in *Walden and Civil Disobedience* (New York: New American Library, [1854] 1963), pp. 90–1.

55. For critical discussion of the concept of wilderness, see J. Baird Callicott and Michael P. Nelson (eds), *The Great New Wilderness Debate* (Athens, GA: University of Georgia Press, 1998).

56. George Santayana, *The Sense of Beauty: Being the Outline of Aesthetic Theory* (New York: Dover, [1896] 1955); R. G. Collingwood, *Outlines of a Philosophy of Art* [1925], reprinted in his *Essays in the Philosophy of Art*, edited by Alan Donagan (Bloomington, IL: Indiana University Press, 1964).

57. John Dewey, *Art as Experience* (New York: Perigee, [1934] 1980).

58. See J. O. Urmson, 'What Makes a Situation Aesthetic?', *Proceedings of the Aristotelian Society*, Supplementary Volume, XXXI, 1957, pp. 75–92; Frank Sibley, *Approach to Aesthetics: Collected Papers on Philosophical Aesthetics*, ed. John Benson, Betty Redfern and Jeremy Roxbee Cox (Oxford: Oxford University Press, 2001).

CHAPTER 3

Culture, Art and Environment

The objects of aesthetic appreciation range from discrete objects in the environment to broader areas surrounding the appreciator. The genesis of these objects ranges too, from almost entirely natural to environments that are almost wholly artefactual. What exactly is meant, though, by 'natural environment', 'nature' and 'culture'? To understand aesthetic appreciation of the environment not only do we need to know what it is we experience, but we also need to know how differences between types of environments – the artefactual and cultural versus the natural – determine our appreciation. While this question could take us into the realm of ontology, the scope of my discussion here will be restricted to aiming for a basic idea of what these concepts mean, and the implications of this for appreciation. I begin by locating the distinction between the natural and cultural, and then identify the range of environments and objects that we may appreciate. This leads to an examination of the differences concerning how our appreciation unfolds across this range, and I consider in particular differences between nature appreciation and artistic appreciation. Finally, I examine the special character of cultural landscapes and the difficulties associated with appreciation and interpretation of them.

NATURE AND CULTURE

Pinning down the differences between the natural and the unnatural, nature and culture, nature and artefact is a difficult task. Perhaps the best approach is to sketch out two answers that lie at two ends of a wide spectrum. On one end is the holistic, ecological position that views nature as real and humans as part of nature rather than separate from it. Kate Soper refers to this as a 'nature-endorsing' view, and it is associated with ecocentric and green perspectives.[1]

The view that nature is not real, but rather a cultural construct, lies at the other end. Everything is cultural, and so humans are exclusively cultural beings, rather than part of nature. Soper calls this the 'nature-sceptical' view, which is rooted to a great extent in postmodern theory.

It is possible to locate a set of positions lying between these two ends. Depending on their place on the spectrum, these views range from those that identify humans as more, or less, part of nature. They make more or less of a distinction between culture and nature, and hold that there is a grey area between the natural and the unnatural so that there are degrees of naturalness and degrees of culture. I would like to locate my position as belonging to this set of views; it lies around the middle, but leans towards the ecological view without embracing it.

I am sympathetic with the belief that nature is to some extent 'other', that it involves natural processes and laws, and that it is something (largely) unmodified or untouched by human hands. The natural world exists independently of human perception and culture, so it is not entirely, at least, a cultural construct. But these claims need some qualification. Our relationship to nature is characterised by both continuity and difference. We are part of nature, but nature is also other than human, and our idea of nature is shaped by human concepts and cultural conventions. This is not to say that nature is a cultural construct. As Holmes Rolston argues:

> There is always some sort of cognitive framework within which nature makes its appearance, but that does not mean that what appears is only the framework. Maps map the world; they selectively represent some of it, and 'nature' refers to this world-making activity out there. 'Nature', if a category ('bucket') we have constructed, has real members, that is, things that got there on their own in this world-container, and remain there independently of our vocabulary. That idea of 'source' is, after all, the fundamental connotation of the word 'nature' and successfully denotes a spontaneously generated world that we encounter, producing a conviction that it precedes and surrounds us.[2]

We have to separate the relational, conceptual framework that we use to understand nature from the reality of natural processes. Nature is not subsumed by culture. By first grasping its independence we can then see how nature is affected by culture, and where humans sit in relation to it.

While nature may be thought of as that which is untouched by us, in actuality, much of it is modified in varying degrees by agriculture, humans living in the land, and the built environment of towns and cities. The concept of nature is sometimes used inconsistently when we refer to it as the opposite of unnatural, but then also employ it to describe activities or places that do not refer to untouched environments, such as a 'nature reserve' or 'natural foods'.[3] In environmental aesthetics, 'natural environment' is often used rather loosely to cover more natural rather than more cultural landscapes (and I am also prone to this usage). This use is pragmatic in so far as it recognises that pristine nature is a myth, but that more natural landscapes constitute an important area of discussion. Perhaps these various uses indicate how we have come to use the term 'nature' to mean an ideal that in actuality no longer exists.

So, nature as an untouched environment does not really exist, but this should not stop us from trying to grasp the idea of nature and trying to figure out how we are both part of it and different from it. Although many communities have become distant from nature (consider urban living and our relationship to what we eat), humans are part of nature in so far as they are biological creatures who engage in a number of activities that could be described as natural, such as child-birth, living and attempting to flourish, decaying and dying. Living and flourishing will involve a number of unnatural and more cultural activities, but some will be natural (although exactly which activities are natural and which cultural has been a matter of debate).[4] Actions that modify the environment extensively cannot be the only way to define where the unnatural, and cultural begins, since many non-human animals and natural disasters create significant change. We could add to this the idea that humans are part of the natural world, but that they are also distinct from it in their ability to control nature and transform it on a level unmatched by nature. This gives only part of the answer too, as Robert Elliot argues that we ought to focus on the type of agency involved in such activities:

> [H]uman agency is importantly different from other kinds of agency, such as the agency of non-human animals, of plants, of acids, of geophysical forces and the like. Human agency involves an array of higher-order intentional states, is mediated by a heavy intrusion of culture, social organisation and highly structured economic arrangements and is exaggerated by technological capacities. While humans are the result of, and are embedded in, natural processes, including cosmological, evolutionary and biological processes, they have transcended the natural.[5]

Human agency and intentionality are key to understanding the distinction I want to make between nature and culture and between what each produces. Although there are a number of ways to make the distinction, a common definition holds that artefacts are 'the material embodiment of human intentionality'.[6] Artefacts are the products of human making, produced with some aim or purpose, and they involve external forces imposed on nature in contrast to the internal teleology of nature itself.

Given these ways of marking out the difference between nature and culture, it is important to keep in mind that it is not a necessary separation. By taking a middle position, I do not support a sharp dichotomy between nature and culture or between the natural and artefactual. Despite being largely situated within culture, technology and social interaction, humans may be integrated in varying degrees with the natural environment. The apparent separation may be overcome, for example, by indigenous people who live closer to the land, and by individuals who adopt an ecological lifestyle. While I doubt that these ways of living will enable full integration into nature or being 'one with it', they certainly can integrate communities more fully with the natural world.

I suggest that we should be careful in how far we understand our closeness to nature. Nature is in some respects 'other', and to forget this would be to overlook the many ways in which natural creatures and their environments are wonderfully and not so wonderfully different and mysterious. At the same time, nature's otherness is not something to be devalued in relation to humans but recognised and respected as distinctive in itself. My distinction between humans and nature does not entail the set of beliefs associated with Enlightenment thought that values humans or culture over nature, mind over body, reason over emotion, and so on. I want to distance my position from hierarchical and strong anthropocentric dualism. My approach to these types of dualisms is to argue for critical integration, rather than to maintain a kind of hierarchy through reversal (for example, nature over humans) or by having one side subsume the other (for example, all nature or all culture).[7]

Many Environments

What are the implications of these conclusions about our relationship to nature for understanding the environment we appreciate aesthetically? It should be clear that I reject the notion that what humans produce is necessarily natural. Rather, in their interaction with nature, they alter and modify natural things, producing objects that are more or less cultural and artefactual, depending on the extent of modification and interaction. Cultural landscapes are one case of an environment modified by humans. Artworks present another case, but one which is artefactual through and through. They are the product of human culture, which is constituted by human creativity, beliefs, attitudes and values.[8] Degrees of naturalness, on the one hand, and culture on the other, will affect the character of the environments and objects we appreciate, and shape the aesthetic qualities experienced.

In this section of the chapter, I shall sketch out the range of environments and parts of environments that we appreciate from an aesthetic point of view. Here, too, we find that there is no sharp divide between the nearly natural and the totally artefactual. There are diverse environments, ranging from more natural to more cultural. On one end of the scale we find relatively pristine, unmodified environments and on the other, centres of human culture in urban environments. It is doubtful that there is anything untouched by human hands in nature, that is, wilderness in its true sense. There are places free from human activity – deep ocean depths and parts of the North and South Poles – but some would argue that they are at least unintentionally affected by human activity through weather and pollution. It is easier to concede that there is something we might call the entirely artefactual and cultural, which we find in the built environment of dense urban areas. But even here there are pockets of nature, some natural materials, and humans themselves, which are part of nature to some extent.

Moving along the scale from relatively unmodified environments, next there are environments that may have been modified by human beings in the past, but are now conserved and managed in ways that attempt to bring them back to their natural state. These areas are often in national parks or places that limit human activity and modification of the landscape. For example, parts of Yellowstone National Park in the USA were affected by indigenous practices of land management, but today human access is limited, and wolves have been reintroduced to the area. Within conservation areas in Britain, for example, National Parks, National Scenic Areas, Sites of Special Scientific Interest and the like, the environment will also be more or less managed, but still less modified in terms of human culture. The fact that these places are managed complicates the issue, because it could be argued that we imprint our culture on the environments we manage through planning and conservation, even when we manage them with an eye to restoring their naturalness. We cannot ignore how humans affect the landscape, and attempts to restore an environment to a more 'natural state' – however that might be determined – can be seen as having much less of an effect on nature as, say, farming does in the same environment.

Another case leads to the next type of environment, the countryside, which in Britain and much of Europe is predominantly a cultural landscape. Borrowdale, in the Lake District National Park, is an interesting case in point. In the early nineteenth century iron ore was mined in the fells, and there would have been busy activity from mining the ore and transporting it by boat on Derwent Water. Later, the fells were mostly cleared for sheep. Today, although sheep farming continues, the dale appears relatively natural to the eye. Landscape tastes in Britain, at least in much of England and Wales, are oriented towards the countryside, which is predominantly a cultural landscape. Sheep farming and other agricultural features of the landscape such as hedgerows, pollarding and coppicing are so common that it is easy to forget that they are semi-natural, with humans playing a central role in shaping the land. We may fail to realise how different many parts of the countryside would be if grazing ended and trees filled the fells. In the Scottish Highlands, where there are more wild areas, there is a greater contrast between mountains and moors, and the rural, more pastoral countryside further south, a contrast that makes it easier to recognise the cultural aspects of the countryside. Some parts of the countryside will be more or less modified by human activity. Borrowdale is relatively free from it, but there are more intensively farmed areas, from forest agriculture, wind farms, hill farms with buildings dotting the landscape, to more heavily worked environments, such as lowland farms, intensively farmed areas, mines and quarries. Besides landscapes, other cultural environments range from sparsely inhabited coastlines to the more intensively worked marine environments of fishing and mining at sea.

Within the range of environments that excludes the urban and more cultural end of the scale, there are different landscape types with topographical features that distinguish them. In Britain and much of Europe, for example, there are uplands, lowland grasslands and heaths, woodlands and hedgerows, freshwater wetlands, coastlands and islands, and so on. The variety of different features in these types of environment will give each a different aesthetic character, and different aesthetic qualities and categories of value will come into play. Uplands may be dramatic and sublime, while woodlands and hedgerows may reflect a more pastoral or tranquil beauty.

There are other environments too, more out of reach than *land*scapes, but still more or less modified by human activity. I am thinking specifically of water environments – oceans, rivers, lakes and canals – but also the atmospheric environment of the sky above and space beyond. For many people it is easy to overlook marine environments because we so often find ourselves perceiving the surface of the sea from a distance, without getting beneath it. Here, imagination comes into play in appreciation through visualising what lies under the surface – the colours and forms of the water, shells and plants, and the movement and behaviour of fish and other aquatic creatures. While the depths of the ocean may be some of the more natural areas in the world, other parts of the ocean are affected, if not modified, by humans through fishing, mining and recreational activities.

At the other extreme, the environment of the earth's atmosphere in the sky and further above, in space, provides cases of environments modified by human culture by the flight of aeroplanes, carbon dioxide's effects on the atmosphere, satellites, space stations and the exploration of the moon and other planets. Appreciation of the environment above our heads is also more difficult because it is out of our reach, but it is not impossible. A common experience is enjoying the fantastic cloud formations from the window of an aeroplane. Pilots, parachutists and paragliders engage with this environment more directly and in a very special way. William Langewiesche gives this description:

> [I]t is the richness of the genuine aerial view, something both higher and slower, that I keep returning to . . . It carries with it the possibility of genuinely free movement, and allows just the right amount of participation with the landscape – neither as distant as an old-fashioned vista nor as entrapping as a permanent involvement.[9]

One interesting feature of the aerial environment is that it offers another perspective into the landscape, another way into discovering its qualities. We experience it from the inside or from above if we are flying much higher. Viewed from below, mountains tower high above us as we crane our necks to take them in, but from an aerial viewpoint, they appear as points and crests against a smoother, dimpled background. From even further above, in space, the aerial view of a multi-coloured globe appears as a strange totality, divorced from any sense of earth as our habitual, immediate environment. From below, we experience space as filled with a great expanse of stars and planets; it is striking and sublime, even if nearly everyone is limited to appreciating it only visually, from a distance or through a telescope.

Let me return the discussion to a point much closer to home. On the urban, highly cultural and artefactual end of the scale, we find a set of environments with built or modified elements – parks, gardens and suburban environments. Parks and gardens may be more or less natural, but we should not forget that many of them are much less natural than they might appear. The designed landscapes of Capability Brown and Olmsted and Vaux's Central Park in New York, all show how moving earth and forming lakes and waterways create environments that are highly artefactual, and where a designer works with the natural landscape to create specific aesthetic qualities. All gardens are managed environments, but some gardens are more strongly designed and managed than others, such as formal gardens and topiary. Suburban landscapes present pockets of built environments that are situated within more natural cultural landscapes. In this type of human settlement, the built environment will be more or less integrated with nature, depending on the design and aims of the planner.

To the far right on the scale are the urban environments of towns and cities. These are essentially built environments that are centres of human culture, art and technology. Architecture, streets, walkways, squares, and other built structures are the human artefacts that make up this type of environment. Nature has a role here too, in a more obvious sense in the natural places we find in cities such as parks, gardens, abandoned lots and other wildlife corridors, where birds, foxes and other animals live within an urban setting. In less obvious ways, nature shows itself in some of the materials used in building – wood, stone, mud – and in weathering effects.

So far I have been discussing environments, nature and culture as they surround us, and as phenomena we interact with and experience from the inside. Within all these environments, there are discrete objects that may become particular objects of attention and appreciation. On the more natural end we find the obvious – trees, rocks, flowers, moss and other plants, birds, insects and other animals, water in the form of rivers, canals, lakes, ponds, and so on. There are also a variety of objects less obvious and less easily accessible, such as micro-organisms and crystals. Moving towards the more cultural end of the scale, we find a range of aesthetic objects. Environmental artworks, individual beds or topiary bushes in gardens, and other objects that combine the natural and the artefactual in ways that challenge appreciation. On the more clearly artefactual side, there are everyday and design objects, like furniture, fashion and graphic design; art and mass art, like paintings, sculpture, film, music, literature, TV and so on; and the more everyday technological objects we find in cars, computers and other machines.

Finally, it is important to point out that all of the environments and objects I have been discussing are more, or less, static and dynamic. Organic things live, die, thrive and decay, and evolve over time as well. Even inorganic things are affected by weather, erosion and the dynamic forces of the earth. The built environment is affected in its own way by human activity that changes it – fire destroys an area and it is rebuilt; cities expand or decline. Landscapes and ecosystems change, due to both natural and human causes. The more natural environments we appreciate are not predominantly static but dynamic, and it is possible to appreciate environments or aspects of them as events unfolding over time. Some will be events within very brief moments in time – a leaf gliding off a tree in autumn or the fragrance of a meadow; others will be over longer periods – changes in weather over a few days, the change from one season to the next, or the geological changes in a landscape over several thousand years. Although artworks are generally much more static aesthetic objects than natural environments, our appreciation of art will range from the still and static (sculpture, paintings) to that which moves or has an unfolding narrative (dance, novels, film). Our appreciation of nature will range from the relatively unchanging (inorganic things like stone and sand) to more dynamic events (the transformation of a landscape from a human settlement back to a more natural area; the life cycle of a fly). In most cases we cannot appreciate the full story of these events, but only capture some part. However, an ever-changing tableau means that aesthetic appreciation unfolds too as the environment changes around us and throws up new aesthetic qualities, while others remain constant.

APPRECIATING ART AND NATURAL ENVIRONMENTS

The differences between natural environments, cultural environments and artefacts point up a host of issues for the task at hand. Constructing an appropriate model of aesthetic appreciation requires, in particular, a consideration of how our appreciation of more natural environments compares and contrasts with that of art. My aim here is to examine how these differences affect appreciation when we turn to the environment. When presented with similarities and differences in our aesthetic encounters with nature and art, some have argued that we should view nature through the framework of our experience of art, while others have resisted this move, arguing that it reduces nature to the artistic and ignores essential differences between the art and nature. I shall also consider which approach is more appropriate to our regard for nature. The focus in this section is on predominantly natural objects, and I then address cultural landscapes in a separate, final section to the chapter.

The Object of Appreciation

There are two categories that help to organise a comparison and contrast of aesthetic appreciation of nature and artefacts: (1) the *nature* of the object, or the kind of thing it is and how its origins determine our appreciation of it; and (2) the *context* of the object, which refers to factors relating to the context of appreciation and the situation of the aesthetic object.[10]

First, the nature of the object necessarily includes its origin. This points to the most essential difference between natural environments and artworks. An artwork is first and foremost the product of intentionality. An artist brings her or his ideas and imagination to some material and through a creative and critical process makes it into an artefact. As Kant put it, '*Art* is distinguished from *nature* as doing (*facere*) is from acting or operating in general (*agere*); and the product or result of art is distinguished from that of nature, the first being a work (*opus*), the second an effect (*effectus*).'[11] As such it is an object which embodies the ideas and intentions of its maker. It is about something – it may be representational or symbolic, referring beyond itself, or it may be expressive of ideas and emotions. It follows from this that our response to artworks is shaped and guided by qualities that are created – the way a narrative unfolds in a novel, the colours and images on a canvas, or the melodies of a piece of music. Our experience is *directed* by cues in the artwork through whatever particular medium we encounter; appreciation is therefore overlaid with awareness that the object is intentional. We attribute such meanings to an artist who has created something with the expectation that appreciators should engage with its qualities and meanings.

By contrast, natural objects are caused by natural processes (but this also depends on the role of humans in altering a particular environment). Waterfalls and clouds are not planned or executed, and there is a greater degree of spontaneity involved in the generation of natural environments. Hornet's nests and ecosystems involve natural teleology of a sort, but this is different from the intentionality of artworks. Appreciation is not directed by an artist, but by perceptual attention to qualities presented by the object to us. Ziff puts it this way, in his argument that anything is fit for aesthetic appreciation, whether artwork or not:

> Imagine this: that the Henry Moore statue at Lincoln Center was in fact not an artefact by Moore but a naturally formed that is non-man-made object found in a desert and transported to Lincoln Center. Would that matter to an appreciation of the statue? Yes enormously. Knowing that one's view of the object would be restructured: one would not in looking at the work look at is as a work. One would not look for manifestations of craftsmanship. One would not look for and see signs of the sculptor's hands: there would be none. But the object would still have shape form mass and balance. The various parts of the object would still be in the spatial relations they are in. The solidity of the volumes would remain unaltered. Nor would the expressive aspects of the object be seriously impaired if impaired at all by its lacking the status of an artefact.[12]

Ziff is right to point out that the qualities remain the same, it is just that we look not for skill or creativity, but for the ways that nature has shaped the thing. We do not view nature as holding particular meanings that stem from the intentions of a creator. We make no attempt to 'read' natural objects in this way.

This point will of course not hold for individuals who regard nature as the product of divine creation. On a theistic (and western) view, beauty and ugliness in nature are the product of God's design. Our attribution of meanings will be to God as environmental artist, rather than to natural processes or to a human artist. It could be argued that design is never an appropriate category for aesthetic appreciation of nature, but I think there will be cases in which it is relevant, if only in a metaphorical sense. Kant recognised that when we find beauty in a natural object, part of this judgement stems from feeling that it is *as if* the object has been designed for our (disinterested) pleasure. He calls this 'purposiveness without purpose'. Consider the incredible forms found in orchids. They are not designed by an artist or by God, but I want to point out the sense of wonder that comes with the feeling that a natural thing is so complex that it must have been designed – even though we know it is the product of evolutionary causes (and there is a kind of natural purpose in that). A different sort of case occurs when we say, for instance, that some part or event in the countryside 'looks just like a Constable picture'. Here, our experience of artistic culture is brought to bear on our perception, so that we see an already cultural landscape *as* a painting. Taken to an extreme this type of appreciation is problematic, as Hepburn notes, 'To see nature uncritically and exclusively in the light of art can lure a person into appraising natural beauty by criteria relevant to visual art, but less relevant to nature.'[13] Hepburn cites Oscar Wilde's well-known caricature of seeing a sunset as a 'second-rate' Turner. Still, as long as this is not the only way we approach the landscape, it opens the connection between culture and nature. Besides, our experiences of art along with our other life experiences shape and influence aesthetic appreciation of the environment.

I have been focusing on predominantly natural environments, since they throw up the clearest contrasts between art and nature appreciation. However, at this juncture, it would be appropriate to consider briefly a few cases of aesthetic objects with a mixed origin, things that have both natural and human causes, such as coppicing, gardens, topiary and some environmental art. These kinds of semi-natural objects can sometimes be puzzling, because we may not know precisely how to appreciate their qualities, given that they involve both the natural and the artefactual. We are working with an aesthetic object that has both intentional and unintentional properties, and often objects where there is some conflict between the two, as in some cases of kitschy topiary, where trees are forced into shapes meant only to entertain or please humans, or even in cases of environmental art that harm the land rather than working more ecologically with it. The tension in this kind of aesthetic appreciation cannot always be resolved, which is part of what makes this appreciation so interesting and complex. One route to resolution could be by appreciating the aesthetic object in the category of art-nature, where appreciation involves the feeling that the object has emerged through a dynamic, interactive relationship between natural processes and human activity. This would seem to be the case with coppicing, the ancient and still active practice, where:

If trees are cut close to the ground several shoots will grow up from the trunk (stool); if these are cut close to the ground the stool will send up even more shoots. This natural response of the tree to intervention in its growth was used to produce long straight poles of wood which could be used for many purposes as well as easily gathered firewood . . . The tree would remain productive for centuries.[14]

In her discussion of this practice, Isis Brook argues that coppicing is ecologically sound, and has aesthetic value to boot. On the other hand, many contemporary topiary practices are so whimsical as to produce an uncomfortable feeling in some people. Faced with a bush shaped into a string of train carriages, one cannot help wondering whether organic material transformed in this way trivialises nature through human agency.[15] Even some environmental artworks, which are often aimed at disclosing the relationship between humans and nature, can create an affront, where working in harmony is overshadowed by the imposition of human goals on to natural forms.[16] Aesthetic experience of these types of objects raises moral concerns that arise directly out of potential conflict between culture and nature.

Returning now to predominantly natural environments, if we accept that they have no artist or designer, this makes them much less interpretively determinate. The positive value of the lack of a maker means freedom from the guidance of an artist in terms of her or his intention as it is embodied in the artwork. There may be more scope for various meanings to be brought to nature. We explore meaning in relation to the qualities we perceive, through what we sense, what we imagine, what we feel emotionally about nature, or by the various narratives and knowledge that may be fed into aesthetic experience (such as folklore, natural and human history, myths and religion). This is not to say that anything goes in our interpretation of nature. Although I shall argue for critical pluralism in aesthetic interpretation of nature, we must be in a position to show why a particular interpretation is a good one.

The intentionality of artworks is also reflected in their creative character. They are real objects, just like the natural environment, but in many cases their content is fictional. This is most obvious with novels, films and plays, but even the realism of portrait paintings and still life is created through the artist 'remaking the world', to use Nelson Goodman's apt phrase. As such, we approach artworks with a view to the imaginary worlds they present to us. By contrast, the natural environment is part of our real world. It does not have anything we could call fictional content, except through the cultural meanings we bring to nature through symbolic, spiritual, literary and other ways of describing the natural world. We can use imagination in our appreciation of nature, but nature is not, as such, a product of imagination.

A second important difference concerning the nature of the aesthetic object – environments and discrete objects within them – relates to the fact that artworks are bounded by both their physical borders and the conventions of artistic appreciation. For example, paintings sit within frames, films are bounded by the screen and actors are at some distance from us on the stage. We can imaginatively enter the fictional worlds of films and novels, and in that sense become part of their environments, but we can never do so literally, as we do with the land or sky. It is certainly the case that many artistic conventions have been challenged in this century, so it is becoming more common to experience art from within, as it were. Art installations, participatory theatre and environmental art are cases where it is possible to experience art as an *environment*. Music is perhaps the most obvious art form with the potential for experiencing it as an environment, especially at pop concerts, where people experience the music amidst a dancing crowd, losing themselves in sound and rhythm. It is also worth noting that there are cultural conventions that influence our appreciation of nature. There are predominant landscape tastes in different cultures and at different points in history and conservation designations that give landscapes a certain aesthetic status. Roads and paths are designed to provide vistas and panoramic views that organise our aesthetic experience of landscape.[17] But even if the differences between art and nature are more a matter of degree, art is typically experienced as a bounded object rather than environment, and under a set of conventions that are less applicable to nature.

Some natural objects stand out from their environment as single, individual objects for contemplation while others blend with it in ways that make the object of our experience a group of objects, or one vast object that reaches beyond the grasp of our senses. We can frame and select through perceptual attention, but nature comes without frames, and it may seem impossible to frame through mere perception. The case of sounds is particularly tricky, as John Andrew Fisher points out, 'Even though when we hear nature sounds we are surely guided by sounds to be heard in the environment, our acts of appreciation are far more radically undetermined than they are when we listen to music.'[18] What is interesting is not just that natural objects are unbounded, but rather that we are most often environed by natural objects. This sort of aesthetic encounter is less common with artworks since we do not typically encounter them as environments. As the focus of aesthetic attention, nature presents discrete objects – a particular birdsong; parts of environments – a streambed; and total environments – a desert.

The Context of Appreciation

This point leads to the second category for organising differences between art and nature. The *context* of appreciation is quite different given the fact that we most often experience nature as environment. Because art objects are physically bounded, our various aesthetic perspectives and engagement with them are determined by their boundaries. For example, our experience of a jazz concert is limited by our sitting in our seats and watching the musicians, and listening. We cannot go on stage and sit among them to get a more intimate feeling of the music, or to look more closely at how they work with their instruments and work together as a group. Natural objects present the possibility of appreciation while being immersed in the aesthetic object. Walking through a desert, we can turn around slowly to contemplate its colours and the shapes of the sandstorms moving through it. Furthermore, we enter into and move through environments in ways that we cannot with works of art (or at least in ways we could only do through imagination). Although the still and careful contemplation of a wildflower is a perfectly legitimate avenue to discovering aesthetic qualities, there are others open to us requiring more physical activity. We walk, climb, fly, sink, swim and even crawl through the environment.[19] An interesting effect of this is observed by Ronald Hepburn:

> We have not only a mutual involvement of spectator and object, but also a reflexive effect by which the spectator experiences *himself* in an unusual and vivid way; and this difference is not merely noted, but dwelt upon aesthetically. The effect is not unknown to art, especially architecture. But it is more intensely realized and pervasive in nature-experience – for we are in nature and a part of nature; we do not stand over against it as over against a painting on a wall.[20]

Different ways of positioning ourselves in aesthetic appreciation of environment create new perspectives on ourselves; in relation to nature we explore new ways of being. I have experienced this while swimming in lakes and the sea. There is a sense of freedom and sensuality in the water as it envelops and holds, offering a novel way to feel one's own body and its movement.

It follows from this more situated appreciation that there will be more chances for multi-sensuous engagement with the aesthetic object, as opposed to the more typical limitations of artistic appreciation to the visual and auditory. Although aesthetic appreciation tends to be ocularcentric (like experience more generally), the environment offers greater opportunity to escape this narrow approach to the world. Standing on a rock on the edge of a turbulent sea offers an active aesthetic encounter which emerges through sheer bombardment of the senses – the mist thrown up by the waves, the wet, fresh smell of the sea, the sound of the crashing waves and the taste of salt in one's mouth. This contrasts sharply with the static, yet perhaps equally exciting experience of watching a film in a dark cinema. The potential for a multi-sensuous experience also suggests the possibility of a more dynamic response in our experience of natural objects.

The dynamic character of these environmental experiences suggests another factor affecting the context of our aesthetic appreciation: *changeability*.

Unlike works of art, which are, on the whole, stable, enduring objects of perception, nature is unplanned and often spontaneous, making our encounters with it unpredictable, and full of surprises. A bird darts into view, or the faint odour of decaying flesh darkens the mood of a sunny forest walk. This points to how natural aesthetic situations are provisional, with shifts in the context of appreciation and changes in the objects themselves. We can choose to take up a variety of perspectives in light of such changes, but more often these changes force new aesthetic perspectives on us.[21]

Many natural environments and objects change on a greater scale and more rapid rate than artefacts, due to growth, decay, erosion, climate changes or the inherent movement of certain objects like the earth or the sea. Change and transience define a central feature of Japanese aesthetic appreciation of nature.[22] Art and literature are full of references to the transience of natural things – the seasons, flowers, birdsong, cherry blossoms, the moon, the wind and rain. Natural things come and go, pass with the moment or the season. This transience may partially explain their aesthetic appeal, and it may also engender an attitude of cherishing (or, perhaps negatively, an attitude of indifference for something that will soon disappear).

The unbounded, non-artefactual and changeable qualities of natural environments, as well as the potentiality of the multi-sensuousness and immersive experience they afford, suggest that they are 'aesthetically inexhaustible'.[23] That is, their indeterminacy widens the scope of our aesthetic experience in equally indeterminate ways. Their complexity provides the possibility of rich and rewarding aesthetic experience, but the aesthetic response to nature is not given. We cannot appreciate nature unless we take up the aesthetic challenges it presents to us, as argued by Hepburn:

> [W]e can contrast the stereotyped experiences of the aesthetically apathetic and unadventurous person with the rich and subtly diversified experiences of the aesthetically courageous person. His courage consists in his refusal to heed only those features of a natural object or scene that most readily come together in a familiar pattern or which yield a comfortingly generalised emotional quality.[24]

His plea for exploring the possibilities of nature aesthetically, to try out fresh perspectives rather than viewing it through the car window or a camera lens, points to a practical implication of this realm of our experience. Our aesthetic encounters with nature can range from the more distant to the more intimate. Being open in one's response would seem to be called for if we are trying to reach an understanding of appreciation in its fullest sense, in all its varieties. Through the more intimate, it is likely that one will deepen one's experience, and, through that, entertain the possibility of greater attachment to the environment. While this attachment may involve both attraction and repulsion – nature isn't always nice and pretty – there is potential for this attachment to engender an attitude of respect for the natural environment.

Which Starting Point?

The differences between art and nature appreciation cannot be ignored in understanding what is distinctive about the aesthetic response to nature, but at the same time they create some difficulties. For example, although it is the very indeterminacy of natural objects and the dynamism of our aesthetic response to them that may lead to a rich and exciting encounter, these aspects appear to make it more difficult to pin down a clear structure of appreciation.

When appreciating an artwork, such as a painting, the perceptual qualities of the work guide our visual and imaginative exploration of the canvas. But this experience may also be guided by what we know about the history of the painting and its artist, as well as by the individual experience we bring, including particular associations and any emotions that are evoked by the artwork. One might appreciate Van Gogh's *Sunflowers* through enjoyment of its colour and form, but it is more typical that interpretation and evaluation of the painting will be determined by what one perceives, supplemented by cultural and historical knowledge. When we turn to nature, aesthetic appreciation proceeds in the absence of an artistic context. Natural objects have no human maker, and no categories with respect to genre or style. What replaces artistic context in the appreciation of nature? What structures our aesthetic interpretation and evaluation of poppies and seascapes?

So far, I have put this issue in terms of a problem that needs a solution; without an artistic context we need to find some kind of framework to guide appreciation. However, I want to pause now and ask whether or not there actually is a problem. For philosophers who have spent much of their time reflecting on art, there does seem to be one in that the set of artistic categories and modes of appreciation are no longer appropriate (at least in relation to predominantly natural environments). An extreme version of this idea holds that because nature is so very different from art and is not the product of human design, it cannot be aesthetically evaluated in the first place.[25] This position argues that aesthetic judgements evaluate aesthetic objects according to criteria necessarily connected to design and are directed by questions like, is it a good painting or sculpture? Is it skilful and expressive? This view is not as odd as it first appears. Nature, as free from human design, cannot be judged according to creativity or being a good case of *x*. The upshot is that nature ought not be judged by human standards, because it is a very different kind of thing. But as Allen Carlson points out, it is an overreaction to think that nature cannot be aesthetically appreciated.[26] Surely, all that we need to do is to reorient our understanding of the aesthetic object as something very different from art and develop appropriate criteria.

There is another type of argument that claims there is no problem at all in moving from art to nature appreciation precisely *because* nature ought to be appreciated as if it were an artwork. This approach, the 'landscape' or 'scenery' model of aesthetic appreciation, has its roots in the theory of the picturesque. It defines the structure of appreciation according to the perspective we bring to landscape paintings, where we stand back and behold the design, forms and colours of the picture. Moving from the art gallery to the natural landscape, we stand in one place and enjoy what we see as a scene, a canvas laid before us, bounded not by a wooden frame but by the horizon, and the limits of the visual field. The landscape model is outdated now, mainly because of how it privileges art, as if the only way we could appreciate and value nature is through the lens of art. In the last chapter I discussed critically the theory of the picturesque. Many of the same problems are apparent in its contemporary protégé when we take on board that the natural environment, unlike a landscape painting, offers the opportunity of much more dynamic appreciation due to its changeability and the possibility of immersion in it — actually rather than merely imaginatively.

Yet another approach says that there is no problem because nature is the starting point rather than art for understanding the aesthetic response. Kant's aesthetic theory provides a clear case of this, given its original orientation towards nature as aesthetic paradigm. However, there has been some debate about whether he holds that the appreciation of art is prior to nature or whether the appreciation of nature is prior to art. The former position is adopted by philosophers who believe that art appreciation is conceptually prior, that is, that nature experience is derivative on art experience. I find this to be a strange claim indeed, and not one I wish to tackle here, except briefly. The 'art-first' view argues that the aesthetic response ought to be articulated in terms of our response to art because art cases are more central to understanding aesthetic experience than nature. This isn't much of an argument. At best, it is straightforward prejudice, but it is understandable given the priority of art in aesthetic discourse in this century. At worst, it makes the indefensible claim that we cannot appreciate nature without having first appreciated art![27] In any case, I cannot see how it applies to Kant, given his preference for nature shown by: (1) the space he devotes to nature in his discussion of the beautiful and sublime; (2) the fact that it is widely held that he struggles to make his concept of pure aesthetic judgement consistent with respect to intentional aesthetic objects (artworks); and (3) his view that aesthetic appreciation of nature better demonstrates human freedom than appreciation of art.[28]

For very different reasons, Arnold Berleant believes that there is no problem either. The environment is what it is, and we must begin there, on its terms rather than any others. Berleant argues that we misunderstand the environment if we assume that we can move easily between art and nature appreciation. If anything, the problem lies in traditional aesthetic theory based in subject–object and mind–body dualisms which creates distance between appreciator and environment through concepts like disinterestedness. As he puts it:

> Environment, in the large sense, is not a domain separate and
> distinct from ourselves as human inhabitants. We are rather
> continuous with environment, an integral part of its processes. The
> usual tradition in aesthetics has difficulty with this, for it claims that
> appreciation requires a receptive, contemplative attitude. Such an
> attitude befits an observer, but nature admits of no such observer,
> for nothing can remain apart and uninvolved.[29]

I share Berleant's concerns to some extent. He is correct to insist that the environment is essentially something that environs the appreciator. Although some artworks share this feature, the natural and built environments do it like no other thing. As outlined above, environmental appreciation is prone to a highly situated and multi-sensuous perspective. It is not an object 'out there', despite how we may feel apart from it. Aesthetic appreciation of the environment cannot be reduced to art appreciation.

But it is hard even for someone like myself who has spent some time thinking about environmental aesthetics to shake off the tendency to use some of the same appreciative structures for both art and nature. There are good reasons for not resisting this tendency. For one thing, the ideas and concepts developed in the philosophy of art can be useful for our present study, as long as they are applied critically and sensitively. Also, although environments have the quality of enclosure, they do share some features with art. Many environments are cultural, or partly artefactual, so it may be relevant to consider them in light of artistic concepts. Even if environments are not framed or bounded, we do bound them through our perceptual field, and when we zoom in on discrete objects or select for attention parts or wholes of the environment.

Unlike Berleant's holistic approach, my own favours some aspects of traditional aesthetics. I hold, for example, that there is a distinction between subjects and objects in appreciation, but that does not mean full engagement and interaction are discouraged or impossible. As I observed earlier in this chapter, human culture creates, for many of us, a distance between ourselves and nature. We do affect nature through our agency, and it affects us, but the gap is wide enough to maintain that the natural environment is distinct from ourselves. I think we ought to be realistic about the ways nature feels other and apart from us, but at the same time not to become overdistanced from it. Maintaining the subject–object dichotomy does not entail objectification of nature nor detachment from it. On the contrary, aesthetic and other modes of valuing nature can bring with them thorough-going absorption, and a sympathetic and respectful attitude towards the environment. So, although we need to embrace differences between art and nature and recognise the special features of *environmental* appreciation, we should not ignore the cultural aspects of landscape, and the human relationship to environment as defined in terms of interiority and exteriority. In line with this, I suggest an approach that takes on board some wisdom from artistic appreciation, but with selective application.

MEANING, INTERPRETATION AND CULTURAL LANDSCAPES

In the discussion so far I have highlighted differences between appreciation of art and nature, with an emphasis on natural environments as my examples. But for inhabitants of more populated regions, experience of the natural world is predominantly through cultural landscapes. On some accounts, all environments or landscapes are cultural; some constructivists contend that even pristine environments, if they exist, are experienced through cultural lenses and conventions. My view takes a much narrower conception, given that I have made a distinction between nature and culture. Cultural landscapes are those which have been intentionally modified by humans but where nature still plays some role.[30] They range from landscapes with traces of human habitation and agriculture, to the heavily modified landscapes of intensive agriculture and sparse settlements of indigenous cultures. Although urban environments would appear to be cultural landscapes, it makes more sense to keep them in a category of their own, since their urban character leaves much less room for nature compared to, say, the rural countryside. In some environmental philosophy circles, cultural landscapes are ignored in favour of wilderness, which is not surprising given that it is these environments that are often most highly cherished.[31] However, I think it important to include a discussion directed specifically at cultural environments, rather than to ignore the fact that they constitute much of our experience.

I also take the opportunity in this section to examine the problem of interpretation, not only because it is more relevant to cultural landscapes, but also because it reveals an interesting point where culture meets nature. My discussion is necessarily limited to particular aesthetic issues relating to interpretation of an environment with its origin in both human and natural causes. A wider discussion beyond philosophical aesthetics would include ideas and models from human and cultural geography and more empirical material concerning our relationship with landscape. While geographers are generally interested in understanding landscape, aesthetic interpretation of the environment will be limited to meanings that arise from and are related to aesthetic qualities, rather than solely cognitive or other meanings, such as understanding the ecological processes, the human history, or religious significance of a place.

What is Interpretation?

Interpretation is the activity of discovering meaning. It is 'making sense of' something, and involves exploration and putting together various perceptions into a coherent whole, so that we are able to grasp or take in an aesthetic object. In the artworld, one is trying to make sense of a work and the meanings it has. Because one expects for there to be something to figure out, the question directing interpretation would be, 'What do you mean?' or 'What does it mean?' The answer will be something very simple – that the painting is of a bowl of fruit, or something much more complex, such as the range of emotions expressed in a piece of music. With environments that are mostly natural, this question would be odd since there is no meaning internal to landscapes. We bring meaning to them or assign meaning through cultural frameworks. There is still an attempt to make sense of something, but not in terms of searching for meaning that already exists.

Theories of interpretation in the arts are often distinguished according to the role of biographical studies and other information in guiding and justifying interpretation. Although this is a complex debate with many different positions, basically, intentionalists argue that interpretation is tied to the artist's intention, where an actual or hypothetical intention determines a correct interpretation. Anti-intentionalists cite problems associated with understanding artistic intention and argue that the artwork is more free-floating, which allows for pluralism in interpretation and, according to more radical views, the idea that appreciators have a hand in constructing the work through interpretations of it.

The intentional distinction is not applicable to more natural environments where humans have a minor role. In cultural landscapes, such as agriculture, it may make more sense, but I would still consider it odd to apply the distinction straightforwardly in the environmental context. In the middle range of cultural landscapes, natural processes play a major role even when humans heavily manage them. When there is some obvious element of design or a kind of authorship in the landscape, as in gardens, designed landscapes and environmental art, then reference to the intention of the designer makes more sense. In any case, I would support moderate anti-intentionalism, where it would be unnecessary to refer to the artist's intention to arrive at a defensible interpretation of an artwork. Moreover, given that designed landscapes still use organic material in a strong sense and involve natural processes, an alternative to the artistic intention model is needed, one that takes into consideration the dual nature of designed landscapes as rooted in both natural and human processes.

The biographical approach could have a kind of relevance for the environment by reference to natural causes and processes (alongside human origins, where relevant) for guiding interpretation. This move is well known as the basis of Carlson's 'natural environmental model' of aesthetic appreciation, and it is relevant in his discussion of 'order appreciation' in relation to nature.[32] Carlson suggests that we replace the categories of art history with natural history for appropriate appreciation of nature. By identifying such appreciation as correct or appropriate, he assumes a standard of correctness in our interpretation and aesthetic judgement of nature. For example, in his discussion of order appreciation, Carlson says,

> First, the relevant order is that typically called the natural order. Second, since there is no artist, not even one assimilated to processes and materials, the relevant forces are the forces of nature: the geological, biological, and meteorological forces that produce the natural order by shaping not only the plant but everything that inhabits it. Although these forces differ from many that shape works of art, awareness and understanding of them is vital in nature appreciation, as is knowledge of, for example, Pollock's role in appreciating his action painting or the role of chance in appreciating a Dada experiment.[33]

This type of approach, albeit directed at appreciation more generally, entails a cognitive view of interpretation, and sets out clearly what type of knowledge is relevant for interpretation – scientific knowledge and its 'common-sense analogues'.

The cognitive approach and its focus on science as a criterion of correctness have been challenged by several environmental aestheticians, and I set out my own critique in Chapter 4. Now, though, I anticipate later criticisms by arguing here for, more specifically, an approach to interpretation that puts less emphasis on cognitive sources for discovering meaning through aesthetic appreciation. I want to show how we draw on associations, imagination and emotion, and non-scientific information in interpretation. My view aims at the middle ground between formalist and cognitive approaches to interpretation. Formalist interpretation of the environment is a perceptual rather than cognitive activity, where our making sense of something involves only those qualities available to perception, such as shapes and colours, perhaps akin to a scenery model, which rests solely on visual qualities. A cognitive model of interpretation argues for a range of *necessary* knowledge, from the knowledge of an amateur naturalist to the more sophisticated knowledge of an ecologist or geologist.

In aesthetic interpretation, meanings emerge through aesthetic qualities, as perceived by an individual who brings with her or him a set of values, preferences, and more or less background knowledge, aesthetic experience, perceptual and emotional sensitivity, and imaginative ability. Interpretation begins in exploratory perception and aesthetic description, but does not end there. Through perception, we piece together what we apprehend through the senses, grasping shapes and colours, sounds, smells and changing conditions. For example, walking through a pasture, I take in what's around me – cows grazing, green grass pockmarked with cow pats, the soft smell of grass mixed with faint sweet fragrances, perhaps from the small white flowers blooming on the tree by the stone wall, and the feeling of uneven ground underfoot, which I have to carefully walk over. My appreciation can be thin, that is, it rests on a surface rendering of what I perceive, and some of the experience will involve immediate perception rather than interpretation. Or, it may thicken, as I hear the cows munching and am reminded of the first time I walked through this pasture, when my pleasure was tinged with fear of the cows, and I stuck closer to the stone wall. This time the place has a peaceful pastoral quality, compared to the first time, when it was perhaps a little more strange. As I see some of the flower petals floating off the tree in the breeze, I imagine the leaves and fruit that will take their place. Here, the landscape becomes imbued with meaning from personal associations and my basic understanding of seasons changing. I draw on sources of meaning as the experience unfolds, determined both by how I direct my attention, and the changing conditions of the environment around me.

This is a rather ordinary, everyday example, at least in my experience. There are experiences that draw more heavily on various sources for interpretation, such as imagination, emotion and various narratives. An interesting use of imagination and perception coming together is 'seeing as'. Seeing as involves seeing objects under an aspect, and it has been described as a kind of interpretative perception. This is not mistaken perception, when one sees, for example, a black object in front of the car as a cat instead of a plastic bag, but rather when we come to see something as one thing or another thing. In his study of the neglect of natural beauty in aesthetics, Hepburn argues that 'we need not confine ourselves to the contemplating of naked uninterpreted

particulars'; we should aim to enrich the interpretive element of appreciation:[34]

> In a leaf pattern, I may 'see' also blood-vessel patterns, or the
> patterns of branching, forked lightning: or all of these. In a spiral
> nebula pattern I may see the pattern of swirling waters or whirling
> dust. I may be aware of a network of affinities, or analogous forms,
> that spans the inorganic or the organic world, or both.[35]

Notice that this is not drawing on information about the leaf itself, but rather
to bring associations or images to bear on perception. This interpretative
activity is also the source of many landscapes that are transformed into
artworks through paint, sculpture, poems, novels, films and music. For
centuries, artists have 'remade' the world, transforming their ways of interpreting their surroundings into artistic renderings. Artists are among the most
sensitive and creative interpreters of nature, and artworks provide some of the
most concrete and enduring interpretations of the environment.

Hepburn expands his more concrete imaginative interpretation to include
'metaphysical imagination':

> an element of interpretation that helps to determine the overall
> experience of a scene in nature. It will be construed as a 'seeing-
> as . . .' or 'interpreting as . . .' that has a metaphysical character, in
> the sense of relevance to the whole of experience and not only to
> what is experienced at the present moment.[36]

Through our experience of sensory qualities and an expansion of imagination
in relation to a particular landscape, we make a connection to metaphysical
ideas about 'how the world ultimately is' or, perhaps, to other fundamental
and cosmic ideas which are inexpressible in language.

Emotion is also an important source in interpretation of the environment.
The aesthetic qualities of some environment, say, the darkness and tall, heavy
trees of a pine forest, may lead to the ascription of expressive qualities of being
magical or perhaps even scary. It is these expressive qualities that often
contribute to the animation of nature, with stories of creatures – mythical or
real – lurking deep inside the forest. Expressive qualities give meaning to the
environment, and at least in this sense contribute to the interpretative
framework. Our own emotions or mood will colour how we experience a
landscape, but we have to be careful not to assume that this would be how
others see it. Disinterestedness requires that we recognise certain meanings as
personal, and separate them from more generalisable interpretations.

Last but not least, interpretation is an activity that necessarily involves understanding. By conceiving of aesthetic interpretation of nature as 'making sense of', there must be some way in which concepts enter into interpretation, but without, as I have argued, embracing a cognitive approach. One of my aims in presenting a theory of aesthetic appreciation of nature is to ensure that it is open rather than closed. I want my approach to take account of the range of aesthetic experiences that we have, and the range of abilities that appreciators have in their experience of the environment. Therefore, it makes more sense to require less of the appreciator rather than more, but at the same time to hope for the development of aesthetic sensitivity through richer experiences of the environment.[37]

In debates about interpretation in the arts, philosophers have disagreed about the proper aim of interpretation, that is, what it is that we should be doing when we interpret works of art. Some argue that the aim of interpretation is to achieve an understanding of an artwork, and this is done by reaching a correct interpretation by reference to the artist's intention. Others argue that the proper aim is to maximise enjoyable aesthetic experience, and this is achieved through a range of acceptable interpretations of the work. Still others argue that there is no single proper aim, but many.[38] This issue has relevance in the natural context too, where we need to ask what exactly the point of interpreting the environment is in the *aesthetic context*. Ecologists and some types of geographers interpret landscape for the sake of knowledge. Indigenous people living in the land want to understand and give significance to the environment that is their home through spiritual, mythological and other means. Although I find it a little on the humanistic (or even hedonistic side), the second position is more appropriate to the natural and aesthetic context. When no longer dealing with artefacts, I would argue that the proper aim of interpretation is to enrich aesthetic appreciation in ways that enhance our aesthetic encounters with the natural environment. Interpretative activity ought to be one that involves a variety of imaginative ways to discover meaning in our environment, ways that increase the value we find there. This activity ought not be directed, however, at increasing our pleasure. Rather, we should hope for, as side effects to some extent, greater sensitivity to nature's qualities and with that, greater respect for nature. This is more familiar ground to an aesthetic approach than seeking understanding through a single, correct interpretation. I am suggesting a view of interpretation that would be consistent with aesthetic education, without making such education the *aim* of appreciation.

Interpretation and Knowledge

Given these background aims to my approach to interpretation, I can now say a little more about what role knowledge will play, since this is no doubt a difficult issue to work out. Interpretation does not require more than the basic conceptual framework that we bring to our encounters with nature. Examples of this basic knowledge (and what will probably be in the background of so-called normal appreciators) range from having basic concepts, or an ability to differentiate one thing from another – this is a tree and this is a rock; to understanding the conditions or states of things – that grass is usually green, that the sun rises in the morning and sets in the evening, that flowers bloom in springtime, and so on. It is not easy to say when commonsense knowledge ends and specialist or scientific knowledge begins. As I argue later, this is one of the problems that has to be addressed before assessing the strengths and weaknesses of scientific or cognitive models of appreciation. But this basic knowledge comes into play, probably not very consciously for the most part, unless we are really puzzled by something, at which point we wonder if what we perceive is like or unlike things that are already familiar to us. Besides such concepts, whatever background knowledge the individual comes with may be fed into interpretation. This knowledge will vary, from more or less sophis-ticated, to more or less wide-ranging. Some will come with the experience of a local who walks through a pasture every day, whereas others may be visitors to the place for the first time. The local has acquired an understanding of her surroundings from repeated visits, perhaps looking more closely each time. While a visitor may compare the same place to his own familiar environments, bringing his own associations and concepts into play. In neither case is any particular knowledge necessary to find meaning in their surroundings. Both can have equally rich aesthetic experiences, although they will have different emphases. For the local, it is the familiar, and perhaps even overlooking what the visitor would notice. For the visitor, it is the new and perhaps even strange, perhaps demanding more exploration. Both interpretative frame-works may issue in reasonable interpretations.

With artworks, it is in some ways easier to differentiate between relevant and irrelevant knowledge because the aesthetic object is fixed by artistic boundaries and conventions. There are conventions that set to some extent information that is more directly relevant, and this can be shown most clearly by the fact that artworks are intentional. Artistic intention becomes the focus of debate on what is relevant, and whether additional knowledge such as influences on her or his style should be considered. Social and economic conditions are an example of information that is external to the artwork and may be viewed by some as less relevant. This suggests a movement outwards, away from the artwork as such, and towards its external relations, as opposed to the features internal to the work.

Aesthetic appreciation of the environment involves interpretation to a greater or lesser degree, depending on several factors: the type of landscape – cultural or natural; the nature of the particular aesthetic object; and the situation of the individual and context of appreciation. With nature, which has no intentional content, the boundaries of interpretation are less clear, and there is more freedom on the part of the interpreter in terms of what sources are drawn upon for interpretation. But it still holds that in terms of the interpretative framework we apply, as we move towards more cognitive sources of interpretation we also move away from the aesthetic. We move more towards attempting to understand landscape as such rather than its aesthetic qualities and the meanings connected to them.

Beyond basic knowledge, identifying the range of sources of interpretation turns on the problematic concept of knowledge. Given philosophical critiques of science, it would be slack to limit knowledge to factual categories such as the sciences, to ecology, geology and so on.[39] We ought to include so-called folk knowledge, through everyday local knowledge of an environment, including knowledge of the landscape from native sources such as mythology and other cultural meanings. We should also not forget that some appreciation draws only on perceptual experience, on knowledge acquired purely through perceptual acquaintance with an environment. Widening the scope of knowledge drawn upon does not, however, take away the problem of how we distinguish between acceptable and unacceptable interpretations of the environment. We have to pin down not which interpretations are true, but which are reasonable to make given particular cultures and types of environments. Before tackling this difficult issue, I shall first consider the range of sources of knowledge we use in making environments meaningful.

Religion and myth are perhaps one of the most common, less scientific ways people find meaning in landscape. In Hebraic-Christian thought, for example, the aesthetic qualities of landscapes are given meaning through religious symbolism. Yi-Fu Tuan describes the opposing views of the desert environment:

> From the earliest times recorded in the Bible, a harsh view of the desert existed simultaneously with its opposite . . . the prophet who recognized the repellent barrenness of the desert also saw it as the condition for spiritual uplift and exaltation, or he might see the desert itself as exhibiting an austere beauty. In the Old Testament, the Sinai wastes stood for death, disorder, and darkness, but also for God's transcendent power and redemptive love.[40]

By contrast, in the Nordic environment of Finland, the word for the Aurora Borealis is 'revontulet', which means 'fox fires'. It is said to derive from old folklore that explains the bright, pulsating, red and blue lights as the painterly effects of the arctic fox's bushy tail, which starts fires and sprays snow into the night sky.[41]

Human history, an extension of these culturally based interpretations, provides a source for making sense of an environment. The isle of Rum in Scotland is now a designated nature reserve, and it was once considered as a possible location for the reintroduction of wolves. However, much of it is a cultural landscape. Among the desolate moors and sublime mountains, one finds the overgrown ruins of blackhouses, evidence of eighteenth-century crofters who were cleared from the land to make way for sheep-farming. The ripples in the green fields that come up to the edge of the sea are not natural but rather 'lazybeds', an old agricultural practice. On the other side of the island, a more recent reminder of human history is found in a bizarre Victorian folly, an old hunting lodge built by a wealthy merchant. As we take in these parts of the environment, and feed in whatever knowledge we may gather, appreciation shifts from seeing the land as a windswept wilderness to a landscape once inhabited by humans, then sheep, and now left largely to nature, except for reserve workers and visitors.

More generally, we can talk about cultural significance, meaning that is assigned to landscapes by virtue of what they symbolise for particular cultures. Human history, but also cultural meaning, can be found in the disused quarries in Welsh mountain landscapes. One finds choppy, grey, textured expanses set against the natural contours and dramatic sweep of mountain valleys. These landscapes gain meaning through a sense of human industry set within a beautiful upland environment. More poignantly, instead of being cleared to provide prettified parks, the disused mines that were previously the mainstay of many Welsh communities have been preserved. These landscapes have significance as the cultural heritage of a community, and their qualities have significance within this context. By contrast, wilderness has significance for many North Americans for being a vast space 'untouched' by humans, at once tranquil and threatening, beautiful and sublime. It is a sacred environment, symbolising freedom and independence as well as the antithesis of modern life.

I have stressed that everyday or commonsense knowledge may also be sufficient for making sense of an environment. But what about scientific knowledge? The amateur naturalist knows something about birds or wildflowers. The hill-walker carrying a guidebook to the Yorkshire Dales is able to supplement the sensations of touch and sight with facts about the age and type of the rocks she treads upon. This may enable her to see more than first meets the eye, as she works with perceptual exploration, feeding in knowledge to take in what lies before her – 'It's soft and porous. Aha! It's limestone, and water – that's where all these fantastic shapes and holes came from.' Different meanings are brought to bear on qualities in our surroundings through the story told by science. In the case of the Aurora Borealis, the colours take on another meaning. We see them not as the fiery art of the arctic fox, but rather as caused by solar winds moving across the upper atmosphere and hitting gas molecules, which creates light. The colours are not the fox's chosen palate, but rather they correspond to the colours of gases in the ionosphere.[42]

Critical Pluralism

Which story makes the most sense for making sense of aesthetic objects? Is one interpretative story better than another, or are all stories equally legitimate? Advocates of the cognitive- or science-based models of aesthetic appreciation of nature argue that although these other stories may have some relevance, science provides the ultimate standard for interpretative activity. For example, despite the sympathy Rolston has for participatory and 'native-range' experience, he says:

> Living on the landscape keeps persons 'tuned in', and this dimension is needed, past mere science, to appreciate what is going on on landscapes. Certainly the human coping has produced mythologies that we now find incredible – Pele extruding herself as lava, Tavwoats replacing the trail to Paradise with a forbidding canyon river, the Chinese cocks on rooftops to guard off mischievous spirits, an angry God warping the Earth to punish iniquitous humans. Science is necessary to banish ('deconstruct') these myths, before we can understand in a corrected aesthetic.[43]

Although Carlson does not specifically address the question of interpretation, if we recognise interpretation as a dimension of aesthetic appreciation, science will also provide the correct framework according to his cognitive position. He accepts that mythological descriptions and other cultural information may be relevant sources for interpretation, but these stories must meet the following condition: 'cultural "outside information" contained in a landscape description must be embedded in such a way that it is accessible within that particular framework and thereby accessible independent of the particular description'.[44] According to his view, imaginative and literary descriptions do not meet this condition, so they are irrelevant sources of information. In his discussion of cultural knowledge, Carlson does not give a means for determining whether scientific or cultural knowledge takes priority in interpretation, but it is probable, given his views on the correct story within appreciation more generally, that science is the answer.[45]

Philosophers on the other side of the debate accept that multiple stories may lead to multiple acceptable interpretations, but they are sensitive to the problems, aesthetic and moral, of 'humanising nature', or of interpreting nature through only a cultural lens, rather than attempting to experience it also on natural terms.[46] For example, Yuriko Saito is particularly concerned that some cultural associations overly humanise landscapes and prevent us from appreciating their natural value. For example, she comments that tourists appreciate some landscapes 'primarily through historical/cultural/ literary associations. Plymouth Rock and the Gettysburg battlefield are the prime examples from this country'.[47] She recognises that the cultural and historical values of these places are important, but she worries that such interpretations do not approach nature on its own terms. Also, Saito allows for folk-knowledge associations because she thinks that these are not just about 'human deeds' with the landscape as a backdrop, but rather they work much more closely with nature's qualities, attempting to interpret it. While I agree with her remarks, I would add that we should avoid romanticising folk myths, and also emphasise that, where relevant in interpretation, we need to recognise rather than ignore or attempt to hide the ways in which culture shapes landscapes.

I have claimed that the aim of interpretation ought to be one that rests easily alongside the spirit of aesthetic appreciation as an enriching encounter with the natural world. Thomas Heyd argues, in a similar vein, that diverse stories can illuminate aesthetic qualities and engage us in a more concrete way than science's abstraction. Stories are determined as relevant on a case-by-case basis according to whether or not they bring out nature's qualities for appreciation in a fruitful way.[48] Given the lack of intended meaning in many natural and cultural environments, it is also the case in pre-reflective practice that aesthetic interpretation of the natural environment affords greater freedom to the appreciator. As Hepburn has suggested, environments demand 'adventurous openness' on the part of the appreciator, and there are countless new perspectives to try out.[49] These points support critical pluralism rather than critical monism. Searching for a single, correct interpretation, being guided by just one story, would be counter-productive not only to what natural environments themselves demand, but also to what we should expect from ourselves as engaged participants.

Critical pluralism sits between critical monism and 'anything goes', the subjective approach of some postmodern positions. It argues for a set of interpretations that are deemed acceptable but which are not determined according to being true or false.[50] A more pragmatic view is taken by some pluralists, where acceptable interpretations are those that work in making sense of something. An interpretation must be defensible, it cannot be outlandish, irrelevant or the whim of one person. Besides cohering with the aesthetic and non-aesthetic descriptions of the aesthetic object, the validity of interpretations must also be relativised to the background beliefs, values and cultural and historical context of interpreters. This will allow for flexibility, especially in respect of contrasting cultural meanings given to environments.

Although I am using these points to clarify what is meant by pluralism, they also reflect the fact that interpretive practice is subject to these variables. It would be harsh and overly restrictive to insist that a single interpretation is correct, given the range of appreciators' backgrounds, the dynamic conditions of many environmental aesthetic objects, and the fact that interpretations of environments span many generations. The diversity of possible interpretations does not mean that all of them make sense. A happy medium must be found between respecting environments – a normative constraint on interpretation – and allowing for the freedom and diversity of environmental appreciation. In the interpretation of the Aurora Borealis, both folklore and science provide acceptable interpretations; they give alternative ways of seeing the spectacular show in the sky. If the point were simply to understand the phenomenon before us, with knowledge as the aim, the scientist would give us the fullest factual explanation. But that is not the point of 'making sense' in the aesthetic context. Here, it is about trying out different ways of seeing aesthetic qualities, trying out different perspectives, as part of an exploration of nature and its qualities. The aim is to enhance appreciation by expanding our ways of relating to different environments, but without trivialising or appropriating them.[51]

Interpretation and Sense of Place

I want to conclude with a couple of points concerning the interpretive contexts covered here. First, as we have seen, the stories of various environments range from those told by science to those that more explicitly reflect human relations with the environment. These narratives have a greater or lesser role in appreciation, depending on the knowledge of the appreciator and the depth of interpretation in any one encounter. Second, in all of the interpretive contexts I have discussed, meaning emerges through the reciprocity of perceived aesthetic qualities and interpretive frameworks brought by appreciators to the environment. We draw on various sources, from the perceptual to the cognitive, to make sense of what we experience. This is one essential route to 'sense of place', a way of experiencing an environment that includes the aesthetic, but reaches beyond it to embrace a whole range of personal feelings and community values in relation to the distinctive qualities or 'spirit' of a place.[52] Sense of place often goes hand in hand with these different narratives, and all of them may come together with emotion to create the feeling of being at home, of attachment to a particular landscape, town, house or other part of the world. I mention these points because it is not easy to say where aesthetic appreciation ends and sense of place begins. As we move away from aesthetic appreciation and more towards an all around experience of a particular environment, we move towards sense of place. The approach taken in this book attempts to carve out a relatively distinct domain for the aesthetic, but the edges are fuzzy, and it is useful to observe where one valuing approach to the environment blends into another.

NOTES

1. Kate Soper, *What is Nature?* (Oxford: Blackwell, 1995), p. 4.
2. Holmes Rolston, III, 'Nature for Real: Is Nature a Social Construct?', in T. D. J. Chappell (ed.), *The Philosophy of Environment* (Edinburgh: Edinburgh University Press, 1997), p. 43.
3. Ibid. p. 20.
4. An interesting discussion of this in regard to hunting can be found in Paul Veatch Moriarty and Mark Woods, 'Hunting ‡ Predation', *Environmental Ethics*, 19:4, 1997, pp. 391–404.
5. Robert Elliot, *Faking Nature* (London and New York: Routledge, 1997), p. 123.
6. Keekok Lee, *The Natural and the Artefactual: The Implications of Deep Science and Deep Technology for Environmental Philosophy* (Lanham: Lexington Books, 1999), p. 2.
7. See Val Plumwood, *Feminism and the Mastery of Nature* (London: Routledge, 1993).
8. Throughout my discussion above, I do not exclude the possibility that non-human animals have something like community, culture and artefacts. Non-human animals produce homes and other kinds of shelter and modify nature in various ways as well. To keep my discussion relatively compact, I have had to limit the scope of it to applications of these concepts to the human sphere.
9. William Langewiesche, *Inside the Sky: A Meditation on Flight* (New York: Vintage Books, 1998), p. 26.
10. The differences I set out here have been recognised by various philosophers, but most notably by Hepburn, 'Contemporary Aesthetics and the Neglect of Natural Beauty' (1984a), and 'Nature in the Light of Art' (1984b), in *Wonder and Other Essays* (Edinburgh: Edinburgh University Press, 1984); Yrjö Sepänmaa, *The Beauty of Environment: A General Model for Environmental Aesthetics* (1st edn: Helsinki: Suomalainen Tiedeakatemia, 1986; 2nd edn: Denton: Environmental Ethics Books, 1992); and Allen Carlson, 'Environmental Aesthetics', in David Cooper (ed.), *A Companion to Aesthetics* (Oxford and Cambridge, MA: Blackwell, 1992), pp. 142–4. For the role of design, see esp. Allen Carlson, *Aesthetics and the Environment: The Appreciation of Nature, Art and Architecture* (London and New York: Routledge, 2000), pp. 114–17. Yuriko Saito gives a recent and interesting account of some of these differences in 'Environmental Directions for Aesthetics and the Arts', in Arnold Berleant (ed.), *Environment and the Arts: Perspectives on Environmental Aesthetics* (Aldershot: Ashgate, 2002), pp. 171–85.
11. Immanuel Kant, *Critique of Judgment*, trans. Werner Pluhar (Indianapolis: Hackett, 1987), §43, p. 170 (Ak. 303). Kant's emphasis.
12. Paul Ziff, 'Anything Viewed', in Esa Saarinen, Risto Hilpinen, Ilkka Niiniluoto and Merrill Provence Hintikka (eds), *Essays in Honour of Jaakko Hintikka* (Dordrecht: Reidel, 1979), p. 286. For shifts in appreciative perception, cf. Kant, §42, p. 169 (Ak. 302); John Dewey, *Art as Experience* (New York: Perigee, [1934] 1980), pp. 48–9; Allen Carlson, 'Environmental Ethics and the Dilemma of Aesthetic Education',

Journal of Aesthetic Education, 10, 1976, pp. 69–82; Cheryl Foster, 'Aesthetic Disillusionment: Environment, Ethics, Art', *Environmental Values*, 1, 1992, pp. 205–15.

13. Hepburn, 1984b, p. 49.
14. Isis Brook, 'Without Waste or Destruction: The Aesthetics of Coppicing', *Thingmount Working Paper Series on the Philosophy of Conservation* (Lancaster: Lancaster University Department of Philosophy, 1999).
15. Isis Brook and Emily Brady, 'Topiary: Ethics and Aesthetics', *Ethics and the Environment: Special Issue: Art, Nature, and Social Critique*, forthcoming, 2003.
16. See Donald Crawford, 'Nature and Art: Some Dialectical Relationships', *Journal of Aesthetics and Art Criticism*, 42, 1983, pp. 49–58; Allen Carlson, 'Is Environmental Art an Aesthetic Affront to Nature?', *Canadian Journal of Philosophy*, 16, 1986, and reprinted in his *Aesthetics and the Environment*.
17. See Soper, p. 242, and Alexander Wilson, *The Culture of Nature* (Blackwell: Oxford, 1992), ch. 1.
18. John Andrew Fisher, 'What the Hills Are Alive With: In Defence of the Sounds of Nature', *Journal of Aesthetics and Art Criticism*, 56:2, Spring 1998, p. 173.
19. Cf. Hepburn, 1984a, p. 3.
20. Ibid. p. 13.
21. Ibid. p. 15.
22. Yuriko Saito, 'The Japanese Appreciation of Nature', *British Journal of Aesthetics*, 25:3, 1985, pp. 245–6.
23. Hepburn, 1984b, p. 51.
24. Hepburn, 1984a, p.19.
25. For an example of this view see: Don Mannison, 'A Prolegomenon to a Human Chauvinistic Aesthetic', in D. Mannison, M. Robbie and R. Routley (eds), *Environmental Philosophy* (Canberra: Australian National University, 1980). Robert Elliot discusses this view in *Faking Nature* (London: Routledge, 1997), pp. 94–6.
26. Carlson, 2000, p. 116.
27. Proponents of the art-first view include Hegel and Richard Wollheim. For a discussion of the debate, see T. J. Diffey, 'Art or Nature?', in Emily Brady and Jerrold Levinson (eds), *Aesthetic Concepts: Essays after Sibley* (Oxford: Oxford University Press, 2001).
28. See Kant, *Critique of Judgment*, and Paul Guyer, 'Nature, art, and autonomy', ch. 7 in *Kant and the Experience of Freedom: Essays on Aesthetics and Morality* (Cambridge: Cambridge University Press, 1996).
29. Arnold Berleant, *The Aesthetics of Environment* (Philadelphia: Temple University Press, 1992), pp. 11–12.
30. Sven Arntzen has discussed cultural landscapes in relation to environmental philosophy, and I share some of his views. See his 'Cultural Landscape and Approaches to Nature – Ecophilosophical Perspectives', in Lehari, Laanemets and Sarapik (eds), *Place and Location II* (Tallinn: Estland, 2001).
31. Much more recently, some environmental philosophers have turned to addressing urban environmental problems, and this indicates a new understanding that nature exists – and is worth philosophical consideration – apart from wild nature.
32. See Carlson, 2000, esp. Part I.
33. Ibid. p. 120.
34. Hepburn, 1984a, p. 20.
35. Ibid. pp. 20–1.

36. Ronald Hepburn, 'Landscape and Metaphysical Imagination', *Environmental Values*, 5, 1996, p. 192.
37. In Chapter 7, through a discussion of aesthetic judgement, I sketch out an idea of aesthetic education in the environmental context.
38. See Robert Stecker's discussion of the debate in 'Interpretation', in Berys Gaut and Dominic McIver Lopes (eds), *The Routledge Companion to Aesthetics* (London and New York: Routledge, 2001), pp. 243–4.
39. I say more about the problem of scientific knowledge in Chapter 4.
40. Yi-Fu Tuan, 'Desert and Ice: Ambivalent Aesthetics', in Salim Kemal and Ivan Gaskell (eds), *Landscape, Natural Beauty and the Arts* (Cambridge: Cambridge University Press, 1993), pp. 143–4.
41. Recounted by Joe Brady in 'Aurora Borealis: The Northern Lights', at http://virtual.finland.fi/finfo/english/aurora_borealis.html. For a fascinating discussion of humans' relationship to the land, which involves the sensuous and the meaningful, see David Abrams, *The Spell of the Sensuous* (New York: Vintage, 1996).
42. See Joe Brady.
43. Holmes Rolston, III, 'Does Aesthetic Appreciation of Landscapes Need to Be Science-based?', *British Journal of Aesthetics*, 35:4, October 1995, pp. 381–2.
44. Carlson, 2000, p. 228.
45. Ibid. Carlson categorises science under 'factual descriptions' and myths, literary and imaginative descriptions under 'cultural knowledge'. A very recent publication indicates that Carlson may be moving away from the exclusivity of science as relevant and towards a more pluralistic position. In 'Nature Appreciation and the Question of Aesthetic Relevance', he argues that 'form, common knowledge, science, history and contemporary use [of an environment]' form the trunk of a tree of knowledge relevant to appreciation, while 'myth, symbol and art' are different branches. The trunk comprises essential knowledge while the branches are relevant depending upon the context. See Allen Carlson, 'Nature Appreciation and the Question of Aesthetic Relevance', in Berleant, 2002, p. 72.
46. Yuriko Saito is closer to Carlson in her views, but rather than emphasising correctness, she emphasises the need for appreciating nature on its own terms, which involves a moral attitude towards it. See 'Appreciating Nature on its own Terms', *Environmental Ethics*, 20, 1998, pp. 135–49. Hepburn is much farther away from Carlson, and instead, he considers respectful and serious ways of humanising nature as distinguished from disrespectful and trivial humanising. See 'Nature Humanised: Nature Respected', *Environmental Values*, 7, 1998, pp. 267–79; and 'Trivial and Serious in Aesthetic Appreciation of Nature' in Salim Kemal and Ivan Gaskell (eds), *Landscape, Natural Beauty and the Arts* (Cambridge: Cambridge University Press, 1993), pp. 65–80. I treat these views in more depth in later chapters.
47. Saito, 1998, pp. 139–40.
48. Thomas Heyd, 'Aesthetic Appreciation and the Many Stories about Nature', *British Journal of Aesthetics*, 41, 2001, p. 135.
49. Hepburn also sets out the great range of interpretations of nature through art, and is especially supportive of the multiplicity of valuable representations and 'aesthetic possibilities'. See 1984b, especially pp. 41–2 and 50–1.
50. I have found an article by Matthew Kieran helpful for thinking through these ideas, despite its focus on art. See 'In Defence of Critical Pluralism', *British Journal of Aesthetics*, 36:3, 1996, pp. 239–51.

51. In my analysis of the role of imagination in Chapter 6, I say more about the problems of serious versus trivial aesthetic appreciation of nature.

52. For a useful discussion of the variety of meanings given to sense of place or 'spirit of place', see Isis Brook, 'Can "Spirit of Place" be a Guide to Ethical Building?', in Warwick Fox (ed.), *Ethics and the Built Environment* (London and New York: Routledge, 2000), pp. 139–51.

CHAPTER 4

Contemporary Theories of Aesthetic Appreciation of Nature

I n the last three chapters I provided some background for understanding aesthetic appreciation of the natural environment. A general discussion of aesthetic experience was followed by an outline of the history of natural aesthetics theories, focusing on Kant's as the most influential. I then looked at the relationship between natural environments and cultural ones, including art. The next two chapters consider the contemporary debate on aesthetic appreciation of the environment. This chapter critically examines the two main camps, cognitive models, typified by an emphasis on the role of ecological and other knowledge, and non-cognitive approaches, which stress the importance of the sensuous surface, imagination and emotion in appreciation. After discussing criticisms of these theories, in Chapters 5 and 6 I present my own position on aesthetic appreciation of environments, an integrated model that brings together subjective and objective components of our experience.

THE CONTEMPORARY DEBATE

The contemporary debate began with Ronald Hepburn's landmark paper, 'Contemporary Aesthetics and the Neglect of Natural Beauty', published in 1966.[1] Its publication did not immediately instigate a change in orientation towards art in philosophical aesthetics. However, over the last thirty years, environmental aesthetics within philosophy has slowly developed into a growing field.

These positions can be organised into two groups: cognitive and non-cognitive theories. Their names reflect the role of knowledge in understanding what aesthetic appreciation of the environment involves. This way of construing the debate reflects more general aesthetic discussion between those who argue for the necessity of art historical or other knowledge in our interpretation and judgements of art, and those who argue that such knowledge is not necessary. It is interesting to note that although Hepburn was the first to break new ground, Carlson's theory has most clearly shaped the character of the debate. The strong objectivity of his model, coupled with the cognitive condition, has led several philosophers to present clear objections, carving out a distinctive set of theories.

Philosophers associated with the cognitive group include Carlson, Rolston and Marcia Eaton, all of whom insist that ecology, geology and other sciences constitute the guiding framework for appropriate aesthetic appreciation. They build a standard of correctness into their views for determining correct and incorrect aesthetic judgements. Without sufficient scientific knowledge, we are liable to make mistakes. Just how deep or extensive this knowledge needs to be is not always clear, and it is an important issue that I take up below. Carlson's view has been by far the most influential, but Rolston and Eaton have developed their own ideas in ways that enrich a science-based approach.

The non–cognitive camp is more diverse, but they share an inclusive stance towards the subjective side of aesthetic experience, and they are generally more pluralistic (none of them incorporates an epistemological condition for appropriate appreciation). When they do argue for appropriate appreciation, they find alternatives to knowledge for capturing this. For example, Hepburn explores a spectrum of positions lying between trivial and serious, or between overly humanising and overly distancing ways of appreciating nature. Theories on this side of the debate include Arnold Berleant's aesthetics of engagement; Noël Carroll's arousal theory; Hepburn's multi-dimensional aesthetic; Stan Godlovitch's natural (or green) aesthetics; Cheryl Foster's ambient approach; and my own view, which I describe as an integrated approach. Yuriko Saito's view belongs perhaps more on this side of the discussion than the other. She supports the role of science but challenges its centrality, and she argues for a plurality of appreciative frameworks, which begin and end in the sensuous surface of aesthetic objects and environments.

An interesting way of organising the debate is suggested by Foster, who puts the dichotomy in terms of a distinction between narrative and ambient dimensions of appreciation:

> The narrative dimension tethers perceptual features of the natural environment to diverse frameworks or conceptual information and locates aesthetic value in the capacity of the perceiver to make appreciative judgments about nature's features within the context of, or with reference to, the framework through which they are viewed . . . In the ambient dimension, the environment as an index of conceptual frameworks recedes and we encounter nature as

enveloping other, a place where the experience of one's self drifts drastically away from the factual everyday.[2]

Narratives range from mythology to natural history, and the views vary according to the stories they favour. For the cognitive camp, it is clearly scientific narratives that tow the line. By interpreting the debate in this way, Foster contests the assumption that only science counts as knowledge. The ambient dimension is characterised by sensuous immersion and extends knowledge to include that gleaned only through perception, an 'aesthetic knowledge'. However, Foster recognises that there are degrees in between and not two competing extremes.

Before looking at the variety of positions in more detail, there are a few remaining clarifications to make concerning differences between them. First, while it might be tempting to say that the cognitive side favours objectivity and the non-cognitive side favours subjectivity, this would be an overstatement. The natural environmental model is the clearest case of a strongly objective position, an object-directed approach, with little attention paid to the subjective experience of the appreciator. Rolston and Eaton at least discuss personal experience and imagination, respectively, even if they are very careful in the role they assign each in appreciation. Berleant's position is perhaps the most sympathetic to personal experience, while the others (apart from Godlovitch's approach) find different ways to incorporate the subjective dimension and at the same time to value natural environments 'on their own terms'. None of the views mentioned supports the type of postmodern approach that says 'anything goes' in deciding what constitutes an appropriate frame for appreciation. All of them recognise that aesthetic experience is coupled with a principle of respect in aesthetic appreciation and would balk at an aesthetic approach that uses nature as a device for flights of fancy or mere pleasure-seeking.

Second, some of the models argue that they represent only one way to appreciate nature, so that they may sit easily alongside other models. Carroll suggests this for his model in relation to the natural environmental model. Others, like Godlovitch's natural aesthetics, contend that theirs is the only correct one, and that Carlson, a common target, has got it wrong.

Finally, while all of the views are primarily directed at natural environments, some of them extend to cultural environments, and others require alterations in order to extend in that direction. Carlson's natural environmental model applies most consistently in the context of relatively wild nature, and he concedes that some types of cultural (non-scientific) knowledge become appropriate when we enter the realm of cultural landscapes.[3] On the other side, Berleant has given the most attention to a broad environmental aesthetic that stretches from the natural landscapes of Maine wilderness to the human, built environments of cities and Disney World.[4]

COGNITIVE THEORIES

The Natural Environmental Model

I begin a closer examination by focusing on the most established of the cognitive approaches, the 'natural environmental model', which Carlson developed in a series of papers beginning in the 1970s and culminating in his collected essays published in 2000. Carlson's model responds to the problem of how to guide aesthetic appreciation in the natural context and in the absence of the more familiar artistic framework. He also wants to show that aesthetic judgements of nature are not arbitrary or subjective, and that they can be justified by reference to a knowledge base.

Carlson's strategy for establishing this knowledge base is to consider what would provide the most suitable epistemological framework in the non-artistic context. He is searching for relevant and appropriate appreciative categories for nature, categories that he believes will provide the most factual and truthful knowledge we can have of nature. By analogy, Carlson draws on a well-established cognitivist position put forward in the context of art by Kendall Walton in his article, 'Categories of Art'.[5]

Walton argues that categories of art history, origin, artistic medium and, in some cases, artistic intention provide the relevant information needed for appropriate appreciation. Appropriate appreciation must be guided by knowledge that enables us to perceive it in the correct category, so for example, we appropriately appreciate Picasso's *Guernica* if we perceive it in the category of cubist rather than impressionist paintings. What counts as the correct category for individual works is determined according to a set of criteria: (1) the work has a large number of properties that are standard to the category; (2) the work is more aesthetically pleasing when perceived in that category as opposed to others; (3) the work was intended by the artist to be perceived in that category; and (4) the category is established and has societal recognition. Without such categories, we are liable to get appreciation wrong by incorrectly perceiving aesthetic properties. Walton wants to challenge the narrowness of formalism, which argues that the perception of form, design and colour, to the exclusion of content and external information, is all that is needed for appropriate appreciation.

Although Walton's ideas are mainly in relation to art, he claims that there is no correct appreciation with respect to natural environments. Because nature as aesthetic object is something quite different from art, appreciative categories cannot be determined as correct according to the third and fourth criteria. He concludes that natural aesthetic categories are therefore relative to what we perceive. Aesthetic judgements of nature are relative rather than true.

Carlson objects to this conclusion and associates Walton's approach with views that hold that aesthetic judgements of nature are impossible. He argues against Walton by showing how categories of nature can be discovered which provide a standard for appropriate appreciation. Art historical categories are replaced with knowledge of the natural sciences and their 'commonsense predecessors and analogues':

> The analogous account holds that there are different ways to
> perceive natural objects and landscapes. This is to claim that they,
> like works of art, can be perceived in different categories – not, of
> course, in different categories of art, but rather in different
> 'categories of nature.' Analogous to the way *The Starry Night* might
> be perceived either as a post-impressionist or as an expressionist
> painting, a whale might be perceived either as a fish or as a
> mammal . . . Further, for natural objects or landscapes some
> categories are correct and others not.[6]

It follows from this that appropriate and significant aesthetic appreciation of natural environments and their objects 'requires knowing what they are and knowing something about them . . . In general, it requires the knowledge given by the natural sciences'.[7] Science not only serves to deepen aesthetic appreciation, but without it we are unlikely to make aesthetic judgements that are *true*. We may overlook or misapprehend some aesthetic quality in nature unless aesthetic appreciation is supported by scientific categories, as Carlson's own example illustrates, 'The rorqual whale is a graceful and majestic mammal. However, were it perceived as a fish, it would appear more lumbering, somewhat oafish, perhaps even a bit clumsy (maybe somewhat like a basking shark).'[8]

The use of science to ground aesthetic appreciation of nature also establishes how aesthetic judgements of nature are objective. By combining perceptual qualities with the objectivist epistemology of science, Carlson pins down something close to general criteria for the aesthetic evaluation of nature. What we know about nature informs our perception of it by providing categories through which to correctly perceive it. I would be wrong in my judgement that the whale is clumsy if I perceive it in the incorrect category, just as I would be mistaken if I judged one of Picasso's cubist works to be a poor attempt at impressionism.

In addition to the knowledge requirement, Carlson's model has two other features. First, his model incorporates an object-oriented or object-focused approach. He argues that we ought to turn away from a subject-oriented approach, and that the individual object's qualities should determine what knowledge or other information becomes relevant from our cognitive stock.

Different objects make different demands, and for this reason each particular aesthetic situation determines what becomes relevant:

> Appreciating objectively in this sense is appreciating the object as and for what it is and as and for having the properties it has. It is in opposition to appreciating subjectively in which the subject – the appreciator – and its properties are in some way imposed on the object, or, more generally, something other than the object is imposed on it.[9]

Relevant information ranges from scientific facts to much deeper scientific knowledge, and it excludes that which cannot be deemed as factual or objective.

Second, Carlson points to how the perceptual dimension of appreciation connects to the cognitive dimension through his concept of 'order appreciation'. Nature is not designed (unless one adopts a theistic perspective), so it is more appropriate to explain its appreciation through the natural order. In 'order appreciation' the appreciator's perception selects aspects of the natural object, and 'focuses on the order imposed on these objects by the various forces, random or otherwise, which produce them'.[10] The exercise of selecting and focusing is guided by a non–aesthetic and non–artistic story, provided by science, and it is this story that enables the perception of order.

These three features of Carlson's approach, its science/cognitive base, its object-directedness and order appreciation, come together to establish a strongly objectivist model of aesthetic appreciation. This cannot be understated. The knowledge provided by ecology and other sciences is a necessary condition of appropriate appreciation. Appreciation without such knowledge occurs all the time in practice, but, on Carlson's account, such appreciation is superficial, badly informed or incorrect, and thus cannot count as aesthetic appreciation in any important sense. Alternative bases of knowledge would not give alternative, acceptable judgements.

It ought to be emphasised that the natural environmental model is intended to apply only to predominantly natural environments; Carlson himself suggests this limited application to so–called virgin nature.[11] When discussing agricultural and urban environments scientific knowledge is replaced with knowledge about the function of the landscape or building. How he would approach other types of cultural landscapes is less clear, although he does acknowledge the use of alternative stories to science in some cases, where the information is sufficiently culturally embedded so as to count as objective. I address this point below when I discuss some of the problems in his model.

Other Cognitive Theories

Cognitive positions held by Rolston and Eaton contend that ecology and other sciences are necessary to shore up aesthetic appreciation. Both of them appear to be more open and less reductionist or essentialist in their thinking compared to the natural environmental model.

Rolston embraces the immediate, engaged and participatory dimension of our encounters with nature, and he recognises the range of values that enter into aesthetic appreciation, such as the symbolic, cultural, historic and sacred or reverential meanings that arise in the relationship between humans and the natural world. It could be said that he combines a phenomenological approach with a scientific one, especially when he discusses the significance of bodily engagement and kinaesthetic sensation.[12] Immediate perceptual experience alone is 'impressionistic', and it must be supported by scientific knowledge. Even though mythology may play a role in our encounters, it is only entertained and never taken as a serious way of knowing. If such alternative stories were taken on board, they would amount to 'mistaken interpretative frameworks' and possibly lead to illusion rather than truth:[13]

> Forests have to be, in a certain measure, disenchanted to be properly
> enjoyed, although, as we shall insist, forest science need not
> eliminate the element of the sublime, or even of the sacred.
> Indigenous and premodern peoples typically enchanted their forests.
> After science, we no longer see forests as haunted by fairies,
> nymphs, or gnomes Forests are biotic communities; we have
> naturalized them.[14]

Rolston's view is reminiscent of Aldo Leopold's interplay of immediate perceptual experience of nature – the mark of the aesthetic and the observations of an ecologist.

Leopold also falls into the cognitive camp because of his emphasis on ecology and having solid knowledge as the basis of our enjoyment of nature. Not surprisingly his aesthetic ideas have been described as an 'ecological aesthetic' by some commentators. This is underlined in his well-known claim that the beauty, integrity and stability of environments are interdependent. If beauty exists only in ecologically sound or healthy environments, grasping the ecology of an environment must be central to aesthetic appreciation. But Leopold also celebrates the sheer immediacy of aesthetic experience, without mediation by knowledge. I quote from Leopold's observations in the chapter 'October' in *Sand County Almanac* to show this movement between the two dimensions:

It's hard on such a day to keep one's mind on grouse, for there are many distractions. I cross a buck track in the sand, and follow it in idle curiosity. The track leads straight from one Jersey tea bush to another, with nipped twigs showing why.

This reminds me of my own lunch, but before I get it pulled out of my game pocket, I see a circling hawk, high skyward, needing identification. I wait till he banks and shows his red tail . . .

Lunch over, I regard a phalanx of young tamaracks, their golden lances thrusting skyward. Under each the needles of yesterday fall to earth building a blanket of smoky gold; at the tip of each the bud of tomorrow, preformed, poised, awaits another spring.[15]

Rolston himself cites Leopold's remarks on Daniel Boone's ignorance of ecology, and therefore the limitations of his appreciation of the wild environment he explored. It is not difficult to align the aims of Rolston and Leopold in this particular context.[16]

Eaton is influenced by Carlson's approach and stipulates a cognitive cognition of ecology for appropriate appreciation. Her concern is to combine aesthetic theory with ecological awareness, so that natural beauty is intimately related to ecological health and sustainability.[17] Ecological knowledge enables us to discover aesthetic qualities and to know what to look for. Appreciation of landscapes in the absence of this knowledge risks misunderstanding, which may lead to harmful environmental practices. Without knowledge to support the aesthetic value of landscapes, it is unlikely that a rational basis for the evaluation of their ecological sustainability is possible.[18] Like Carlson, Eaton has done extensive work in applied aesthetics, having examined various case studies to support her views.

While Eaton recognises some role for imagination and emotion in aesthetic appreciation, she does not allow for much flexibility. In the case of imagination, she fears that imagination fictionalises nature and makes it into something it is not, thereby trivialising or sentimentalising it. Where imagination is present, it ought to be grounded in a solid knowledge base. I return to a discussion of her views on imagination in Chapter 6.

Objections to Cognitive Theories

Cognitive theories, especially Carlson's natural environmental model, face several persistent criticisms. The main problem centres on the knowledge condition and the way this condition restricts what counts as appropriate appreciation. Some of the objections I raise are aimed at the cognitive approach in general, and others are aimed more specifically at the natural environmental model, since it has had the greatest impact on the debate.

There are three types of objections, with specific problems related to each one: (1) the objection to Carlson's argument by analogy; (2) the knowledge objection; and (3) the essentialism objection.

In developing his natural environmental model, Carlson wants to locate the correct information for fixing appropriate appreciation in the absence of artistic categories, given that they would be inappropriate to nature. Using an argument by analogy, he claims that the appropriate categories are fixed by science, which is the source for understanding nature as nature. But there are a couple of weaknesses in his argument. Carlson does not make a strong enough case to show why science is more appropriate than other categories. Science is assumed to be objective and less susceptible to personal views, and therefore the most likely source for valuing nature on its own terms rather than imposing cultural or personal frameworks on to it. But this view of science has been challenged on a number of fronts, so in order to show why its categories are better than others, Carlson has to provide some kind of argument. As Carroll points out, why does he so quickly settle on science without considering relevant alternatives?[20]

Carlson rejects other frameworks, namely, those provided by art, the 'object of art model' and the 'landscape or scenery model'. The contrast to art models is made on the basis that nature is environmental, not a single object such as a sculpture or a two-dimensional painting, and it demands engagement in a different manner and through a different epistemological framework. These claims are sound. What is odd is the leap he takes in his move away from art. It makes sense, of course, to argue that knowledge about artistic intention and art history have no relevance to the natural world, but rather than consider other possible aesthetic frameworks he moves into an entirely different body of knowledge, and one that has traditionally been contrasted with the arts. Art, imagination and creativity have been typically contrasted with the realm of science, truth and knowledge. Such a contrast is strained because science is infused with creativity and imagination, and aesthetics is not divorced from knowledge. Furthermore, naturalists and ecologists aesthetically engage with the things they study, just as artists and poets bring real world experience and truth into their works, and in some cases aim to teach through art.

I want to emphasise, however, the counter-intuitive way that Carlson chooses an alternative framework. Given that the context is an aesthetic one, why turn to the experience and knowledge of scientists, rather than the aesthetic experience of poets, painters, photographers, environmental artists and others, such as indigenous people living in the land, or even visitors to their local natural areas? These groups have arguably developed a greater aesthetic sensitivity to particular environments than other groups, such as naturalists or ecologists. Someone with the knowledge of a naturalist will have more scientific knowledge, but why is this more appropriate in aesthetic appreciation than, say, Wordsworth's intimate experience of the Lake District or a dog-walker's daily experience of a forest? Poets and painters actively reflect on nature's qualities, and in our experience of art we recognise that they provide interpretations of their experiences. As Donald Crawford points out:

> What the picturesque painter shows, and what we experience when we adopt the painter's eye in viewing natural scenery, are *the effects of nature* on us as perceivers. The impressionist painters, for example, self-consciously represented nature's effects in the realm of reflected and refracted light in natural settings. The effects of visible nature not only include light, but also texture (as in the face of a cliff), color gradations (as in a canyon), shape, pattern and movement, as well as powerful forces (waterfalls, ocean waves crashing against the shore). Perceiving these effects in nature need not exclude but does not always require scientific knowledge as guiding appreciation in order for that appreciation to be both aesthetic and directed toward nature as it truly is.[21]

My point concerning artists should not be taken to mean that we ought to appreciate environments exclusively through art or that art 'improves' on nature, as held by the picturesque theory. The tools for aesthetic discovery gained through the experience of artists provide one way to appreciate nature.[22] This claim also does not represent a failure to understand nature as an environment rather than an object, but rather seeks to show the relevance of artistic vision in relation to nature. Moreover, I have suggested that there are several frameworks, based on a range of experiences, which may serve as the background knowledge that is potentially fed into appreciation.

   The second main objection to the natural environmental model involves the precise nature of the knowledge that is supposed to guide appreciation. This problem has several different layers. First, we should ask, what is the proper aim of aesthetic appreciation of nature? On cognitive views, one is led to believe that the aim is to understand nature. Although Rolston claims that environments cannot be aesthetically experienced at second hand – we must encounter them for ourselves – the aim of aesthetic appreciation is clearly knowledge of nature. Enjoyment of aesthetic qualities alone is too superficial an aim in his view.[23] In his attempt to underpin the aesthetic with the ecological, Rolston almost confuses the two and comes close to reducing the aesthetic to gathering scientific knowledge. It appears that he has in mind the scientist who appreciates aesthetic qualities and connects them to a set of scientific concepts. There is no reason that ecologists cannot appreciate aesthetic qualities with their knowledge in tow, as long as it does not detract from the immediacy of aesthetic experience. But the priority is misplaced here. The aesthetic domain is distinct from other domains in so far as it is characterised by the sensuous, expressive/emotional and imaginative. Although we feed background beliefs into appreciation, the experience is predominantly characterised by non-intellectual engagement with the world.

Saito illuminates the problem in Rolston's approach through her discussion of unscenic nature. Rolston argues that if appreciated within the wider context of natural processes in an ecosystem, maggots feasting on an elk's carcass will not appear ugly, but rather beautiful. But Saito points out that it becomes unclear where the aesthetic appreciation lies, since the experience becomes mainly conceptual. In her view, 'the *aesthetic* value of the elk with maggots is not simply our conceptual understanding of its role in the ecosystem, but *the way in which* its various sensory qualities illustrate or express their important role'.[24] In other words, the sensuous surface cannot be left behind.

Carlson wants correct aesthetic judgements, and these are based in knowledge, so the aim is to make aesthetic judgements of nature that fully know it. In a debate with Godlovitch on the concept of appreciation, Carlson confirms this cognitive aim: 'Appreciation has an essential cognitive component' in the sense that we 'size up' the object at hand.[25] But as Godlovitch deftly points out, appreciation has several meanings, and the proper emphasis for the aesthetic context is a sympathetic, positive valuing, rather than a logistical reference to knowledge.[26]

Other philosophers have suggested different aims to aesthetic appreciation, and these are more in keeping with the character of the aesthetic. Dewey argues for a pragmatic aim – aesthetic experience is instrumental for vivifying and vitalising life experience more generally.[27] His view sits within the context of art and is therefore more humanistic. Breaking away from this, Saito claims that the aim of appropriate aesthetic appreciation is to engender an attitude of respect for nature, which is why she argues that we ought to appreciate nature on its own terms through its sensuous surface, science and folk knowledge.[28] Following Kant, my own view is that aesthetic appreciation of nature is directed at aesthetic qualities themselves, where they are valued for their own sake alone. Aesthetic appreciation is a disinterested activity, so appreciation itself is not a means to some further end. There will be outcomes of appreciation, but they are not outcomes tied to intended aims. On this more traditional and non-cognitive view, knowledge of environments and even a moral attitude towards them are welcome effects of aesthetic appreciation, but they are not its aims.

A second layer of the knowledge objection concerns the very nature of the knowledge stipulated by the cognitivists. There are two related questions that are not clearly answered by Carlson, in particular: what type of knowledge meets the necessary condition; and what depth of this knowledge is required? In earlier work, he holds that 'something like the knowledge and experience of the naturalist is essential'[29] for appropriate appreciation, but he also says that knowledge of the sciences *and* their 'common-sense predecessors and analogues' is required.[30] Most recently, he states that the natural environment must be appreciated, 'in light of knowledge provided by the natural sciences, especially the environmental sciences such as geology, biology, and ecology'.[31] But also, scientific knowledge is to be thought of 'as only a finergrained and theoretically richer version of our common, everyday knowledge of it, and not as something essentially different in kind'.[32]

Robert Stecker points out that Carlson 'appeals to three different, though not sharply different, kinds of knowledge: common sense, scientific, and the naturalist's'.[33] Given other remarks by Carlson, it is probable he favours a necessary condition constituted by deeper knowledge, but this raises problems, for it is not easy to pin down where everyday knowledge ends and scientific knowledge begins. If Carlson is going to set up a necessary condition, he needs to say exactly what level of knowledge is required, and how we are to understand the difference between a naturalist's knowledge and its commonsense analogues.

Because he does not provide a set of cases or examples to clarify matters, we are left in the dark. We could assume the stronger requirement, but Carlson seems to want things both ways, which makes matters worse. In a reply to criticisms of his model put forward by Carroll, Carlson says:

> The primary case Carroll presents of something that is not meant to be commonsense knowledge of nature in the relevant sense is, in the waterfall example, 'that the stuff that is falling down is water.' However, it is not completely clear why such knowledge is not commonsense knowledge in the relevant sense. Is it not the product of the commonsense predecessors and analogues of natural science?[34]

Here, Carlson minimises his knowledge requirement in such a way as to make it ineffective for determining the categories of appreciation he wants. If all that is needed to fix appropriate appreciation is having a concept of the object, then this knowledge cannot do the work that Carlson requires of it. By his own argument, it would appear that to appreciate a waterfall we need to know not just that it is water, but that it is a waterfall, that is, lots of water pouring with great force, having been channelled through a relatively narrow area. Only this depth of knowledge would equip us to appreciate the waterfall's grandeur. This point fits with the whale example above, where he claims that appropriate appreciation requires not merely that we know it is a whale, but also that we perceive it as a mammal because we could not appreciate its grace if it were perceived as a fish.[35]

Furthermore, Carlson bases the depth of knowledge required by reference to Walton's categories of art, which involve knowledge of art history and criticism, but the analogy breaks down in the waterfall example. Carlson weakens his requirement to identifying an object under a very general category – the stuff that is falling down is water, not soil – yet this is not analogous to Walton's categories, where correct appreciation involves more specific knowledge than the capacity to identify a work of art as a painting as opposed to a sculpture. Recall that to judge correctly Picasso's *Guernica*, we must perceive it in the more specific category of a cubist rather than an impressionist painting.

The consequence of the disanalogy is that the natural environmental model cannot provide a clear answer to the problem of what grounds aesthetic appreciation of nature. This weakness is internal to Carlson's own strategy of replacing artistic categories with scientific ones: the aim of his categories is lost when he generalises them so much as to include everyday knowledge of objects. To avoid this, he could more clearly specify the depth of knowledge necessary for appropriate appreciation, but if this path is chosen we are back to problems concerning why we should choose scientific knowledge over other frameworks in the first place.

In his criticism of two non-cognitive models, Carlson raises an excellent question, what makes these models of nature appreciation types of aesthetic appreciation?[36] Above, I challenged Carlson's choice of scientific categories over others, but now we should ask whether these categories work in the way he claims they do. It is odd to claim that scientific knowledge is essential for appreciating nature from an aesthetic point of view. Scientific knowledge may be a good starting point for appreciation characterised by curiosity, wonder and awe, but is it really necessary for locating aesthetic qualities? Counter-examples are not difficult to find. One can appreciate the perfect curve of a wave combined with the rushing white foam of the wave crashing on to sand without knowing how waves are caused. The judgement of the wave as spectacular and exhilarating can be dependent solely on an appreciation of perceptual qualities and any associations or feelings that give meaning to these qualities. The appreciation is not ill-founded or inappropriate.

It might be argued that this response also involves the very basic knowledge that what one perceives is a wave, but this cannot count as an appreciative category for Carlson (as shown by the waterfall example above). I am not at all suggesting a formalist approach, which makes knowledge irrelevant to aesthetic appreciation, for that would 'purify away' the richness of aesthetic experience of nature. Rather, as I explained in relation to interpretation, I urge that we embrace pluralism, that there may be a number of other frameworks that do not distort nature. Scientific knowledge may be drawn on in appreciation, and in some cases it can even thicken aesthetic appreciation in desirable ways, but the cognitive models run into problems when they make science a necessary framework and the only correct one.[37]

Carlson's emphasis on science rather than more aesthetically inclined categories raises some practical problems, and these represent a third layer of the knowledge objection. One motive for fixing the appreciative context of aesthetic judgements with scientific categories is to achieve objectivity, so that conservationists and other environmental decision-makers might more easily use it to determine the aesthetic value of some part of the natural environment. However, alongside this possible advantage is the disadvantage that scientific and aesthetic value might become indistinguishable in the deliberative process. Ecological value in particular plays a dominant role in the process which leads to a decision about how to conserve or manage the natural environment, yet aesthetic value is often dismissed as too subjective and too difficult to measure, and thus loses an important place alongside other types of value. To ensure that aesthetic value is treated seriously in practice requires a model that carves out a distinctive place for *aesthetic* appreciation and provides an understanding of aesthetic value as not merely personal or arbitrary. Carlson's model meets the second criterion, but it does it at the expense of the first. By attempting to tie aesthetic judgements too closely to science, his model risks obscuring what is distinctive about aesthetic valuing. In emphasising some of the more traditional features of aesthetic experience, non-cognitive approaches have an advantage over cognitive ones.

The other practical consequence of emphasis on knowledge is that it threatens to leave out non-expert judgements. If knowledge equivalent to a naturalist's is required for appropriate appreciation, or for aesthetic judgements to be taken seriously, this limits the role of pluralism in environmental policy-making. The intellectual demands that cognitive models place on appreciators potentially disqualify their accounts of aesthetic experience in the deliberative process because they are not grounded in sufficient knowledge. By ignoring the significance of perceptual knowledge or aesthetic knowledge – the knowledge that comes through aesthetic experience and sensitivity to place – cognitive models close off the possibility of these other voices counting in planning and decision-making. It is possible to conceive of a model that welcomes these voices without sacrificing their reliability or effectiveness due to accusations of subjectivity. I am not suggesting that only these voices be heard, but rather that local non-experts as well as experts ought to be given a legitimate place. Expert knowledge of environments is obviously needed to understand harmful practices and to outline conservation measures, but it rarely provides the full story.

These points reveal a third main criticism of cognitive theories. By making science a necessary condition, all the cognitive theories, but especially the natural environmental model, are too restrictive on the range of aesthetic appreciations that are considered reasonable. The problem stems from the essentialism inherent in Carlson's model. This is characterised by the choice of a single epistemological framework as correct, and by the assumption that any frameworks other than science inappropriately impose human ways of valuing on to nature. Although his position does not rule out a set of appropriate appreciations that are all grounded in the necessary condition of science, his view, as well as the other cognitive theories, does not allow for 'serious' appreciations that lie outside science.

Carroll, for example, criticises this approach for excluding a category of very common responses as appropriate, those that involve being emotionally moved by nature.[38] Others have also argued that there may be alternative frameworks, including cultural ones, which do not give misinformation. Why, one feels compelled to ask, is there not some ground in between a single framework and anything goes? Saito wonders why Carlson entirely rejects Walton's relativism in relation to nature, and she counters that there may be a variety of appreciations that are not improper, and in fact serve to increase interest in aesthetic qualities of nature.[39] Full-blown relativism is not the answer, but some relativism makes appreciation broader and more flexible.

It is a little puzzling why Carlson's model is so narrow in its conception of appropriate appreciation. Why not explore other ways to discover aesthetic qualities, if they do not threaten to impose overly human-cultural projections on to nature? There is no question that a normative aim is bound up with the cognitivists' arguments. Science, as they see it, reveals nature's real properties, rather than other narratives that may falsify it. But it has not been shown that all non-scientific stories lead to partial or misleading appreciation. Some of them do – appreciating nature only as if it were a work of art, or valuing a landscape only for its symbolic qualities are cases of partial appreciation.

Science can also be seen as a cultural framework that imposes anthropocentric views on to nature. Carlson recognises that science is a human framework, but nowhere does he consider whether or not it fails to reveal nature's properties as they are. On the contrary, science is clearly accepted as objective and factual, and he puts it in a separate category rather than in the category of 'cultural information'.[40] Godlovitch, Saito and Heyd have all pointed to this problem, and Saito in particular raises the issue that science has been credited as one of the causes for the hierarchical dualism of humans over nature.[41] None of these philosophers argues that nature is a human construct, but they raise the issue that science cannot be taken at face value. Rather than arguing that science enables us to grasp nature as it is, Carlson simply assumes it; as Godlovitch complains, 'If cognitivist aesthetics banks on the presumption of hard truth in science, it must face the challenge of Antirealists, Internal Realists, and Relativists.'[42]

Interestingly, Carlson makes a small concession to cultural information in the context of natural environments. In a discussion of the landscape descriptions in Tony Hillerman's mystery novels (set in the American South-west), Carlson distinguishes three categories of potentially relevant information for aesthetic appreciation of landscapes: the formal, the factual and the cultural. Science belongs to the second category. The cultural includes nominal, imaginative, mythological and literary descriptions, and their relevance depends upon whether or not they are sufficiently 'culturally embedded' as to be objective and 'generally available'.[43] Out of the four categories, nominal descriptions (for example, a local name for a geological feature) and mythological descriptions meet this condition. For example, Navajo descriptions of local geological features, such as 'Evening Twilight Mountain is the mountain built by First Man for Abalone Shell Boy', can enhance appreciation.[44] The problem is that Carlson doesn't say enough about their claim to truth, which seems odd, given that he so consistently aims for truth through science. What exactly is the role of this information in relation to scientific information? Which is more appropriate or are they both equally legitimate bases for proper appreciation? These questions are left unanswered. Carlson's attempt to incorporate mythological descriptions, while welcome, is simply not developed enough to make it significant, or to counter criticisms against his view.

Finally, in relation to the problem of essentialism, we should not forget that another distinctive aspect of aesthetic appreciation is its *free* yet disinterested character; in particular we are freed up from instrumental or intellectual concerns. Too much knowledge brought to the fore of appreciation potentially impedes attention to aesthetic qualities by detracting from them. Again, the problem stems from making scientific knowledge a condition of appropriate aesthetic appreciation, with another undesirable implication – the necessary condition potentially constrains the aesthetic response. Although Carlson's theory includes an excellent account of the differences between artworks and natural environments and how this shapes our aesthetic response, it does not adequately address the demands of aesthetic appreciation when we move from art to nature. In this context, we need an approach that allows for the freedom and creativity demanded by nature *qua* aesthetic object. Hepburn makes some room for scientific knowledge in his view of appreciation, but he insists also on the subjective side of experience. I quote him at length, as he nicely sums up some of the problems discussed here:

Science, rightly and necessarily, gives precedence to *objectivising* movements of mind; probes behind the human perspective with its phenomenal properties; abstracts from our emotion- and value-suffused, perceptually selective, view of the world, and works ultimately towards a mathematically quantifiable and imperceptible reality. In the course of that abstraction, most or all of the features of the world that are of human concern are eliminated. Yet the very pursuit of that scientific enterprise has dynamics that belong only within the human life-world, the world of perception and feeling, curiosity and striving to know, and vanish in the objective view. The *aesthetic* mode of experience, the development of which is a very different enterprise indeed from that of science, far from admitting a *nisus* to leave the subjective, human perceptual, evaluative and emotional experience, seeks to explore it and intensify it. And, crucially, the aesthetic experience of nature – notably of landscape – is a prime means of enriching, enhancing, increasing our powers of discrimination, as members of that life-world; a world which has as great a claim to reality as the objective world of the physicist. Some thought-elements concerning the geological past of the region we contemplate, some thought of the ecological unity of its plants and animals, may well enter and enhance our experience. But we are under no rational imperative to allow the scientific to displace the human perspective or to play down the centrality of that perspective to any experience that can be called aesthetic.[45]

The natural environmental model is problematic with either a weak or strong foundation of science: minimising the requirement to everyday knowledge of objects makes the foundation of the natural environmental model ineffective for directing appreciation, while strengthening the requirement makes it both difficult to distinguish aesthetic from scientific value and excessively restrictive on the aesthetic response. The best course would be to abandon essentialism in favour of more flexibility, so bringing our attention to non-cognitive theories.

NON-COGNITIVE THEORIES

Non-cognitive approaches to aesthetic appreciation range from the traditional, disinterested theory offered by Kant, to the phenomenological, personally engaged theory put forward by Berleant. The integrated aesthetic that I defend in the next chapter is a non-cognitive position, so although I present objections to non-cognitive theories, my overall aim is to defend them. Before considering the variety of these theories, a discussion of Saito's position will serve as a useful transition.

Saito's Pluralistic Approach

Saito stresses that aesthetic experience 'begins and ends' with the sensuous surface, but perceptual qualities express natural qualities which can be known through science. She is especially concerned that our aesthetic encounters are grounded in a moral attitude towards the natural world.[46] To this end, she argues that appreciation of nature must be on its own terms rather than human terms; nature tells its own story through its sensuous qualities, but also through science, myths, folklore and indigenous tales. As she puts it, 'Both scientific explanation and folk narratives are our attempts at helping nature tell its story to us concerning its own history and function through its sensuous surface.'[47]

Saito does not think that science is desirable on the grounds that it gives true or correct appreciation. Scientific knowledge informs appreciation that may be more respectful of nature, but she is not uncritical of this type of knowledge. It prevents overly humanising appreciation, but it is not the only route to treating nature on its own terms. Saito recognises that science is not free itself from cultural influences, and gives a very balanced approach to its role. While science 'attempts to humanise nature by relying on *our* observations and by making them comprehensible to *us*', scientific stories 'are stories of natural objects' own lives, suggested by their specific perceptible features, even if they must be told by means of *our* images and vocabulary'.[48] Also, Saito narrows the scope of relevant scientific categories, specifically to those categories that are based on observation and perception of secondary qualities in time and space. This is related to her view that while science can certainly enhance appreciation, in some cases scientific information can distract us away from aesthetic qualities: 'For example, the molecular structure of a rock or the medicinal value of a spring seems too removed from our immediate perceptual arena to be realizable on the sensuous surface.'[49]

For these reasons, science does not have exclusive domain; some folk narratives – local and bioregional narratives – enable valuing nature on its own terms.[50] Saito emphasises frameworks that connect to perceptible qualities and lived experience, but those which do not humanise nature needlessly, as it were. While her approach clearly underscores the importance of science, it gives a more reasonable picture of the nature of science as a source of knowledge, and it is more pluralistic than cognitive approaches.

Hepburn's Multi-dimensional Aesthetic

Most non-cognitive theories urge a multi-dimensional aesthetic encounter with environments, and this is one way to characterise Hepburn's views. Carlson has recently described his views in terms of the 'metaphysical imagination' model, and although this is an accurate portrayal of Hepburn's most recent thinking, it does not entirely capture the themes in his work that have been developed and explored since he published 'Contemporary Aesthetics and the Neglect of Natural Beauty'.

In that article, Hepburn shows why environmental appreciation is distinctive, and some of these points were raised in my discussion of the appreciation of art versus nature. In particular, he highlights the many dimensions of environmental appreciation, through perception, emotion, imagination and thought. Perception enables us to focus on particular details, or to choose a wider sensory field for aesthetic attention, while expressive qualities in nature are grasped through both perceptual and imaginative exploration. The suggestive sensuousness of a red poppy is only grasped when it is experienced up close, and our response to a field of poppies may be different altogether if viewed from the distance.

Through his analysis of these activities, Hepburn also provides an answer to the role of knowledge in our aesthetic response to nature. Scientific knowledge has no fundamental role in aesthetic experience of nature, although it may be part of the beliefs fed into appreciation. Like other non-cognitivists, Hepburn foregrounds immediate, perceptual experience and backgrounds knowledge, and this also shows the influence of both Kant and phenomenology on his thinking. He describes the role of beliefs in two distinctive ways, which avoid an overly intellectual or factual perspective.

First, beliefs and reflections in relation to the aesthetic object come through the component of 'thought-content' in our response, where we 'think-in' beliefs about the object in relation to perceived qualities or thought-content not available to our present perception. Thoughts are not necessarily conscious or verbalised, but intimately interact with feeling and perception.[51] Here, Hepburn tackles the difficult issue of finding a balance between the sensuous surface and thought:

> We are working here, implicitly, with a scale. Near one end of it aesthetic experience attenuates towards the perception-transcending substructure of its objects. We do not have an obligation to place ourselves there; with the aesthetic, it is on the phenomenal, the *Lebenswelt*, concrete and abstract both, that we must focus attention. At the other end of the scale, as we have just noted, we exclude all thought, and leave sensuous immediacy only. At both extremes we lose what John Findlay singled out as aesthetic essentials, the poignant and the perspicuous in combination.[52]

Hepburn sees a role for this thought component, but little depends upon it, and there is no condition 'to think-in *perception-transcending* ideas or explanations'.[53]

Second, there is a kind of discovery or aesthetic understanding which comes through perceptual and imaginative activity in relation to the aesthetic object. Hepburn calls this 'realizing' where, as an episode of experience, it

> involves making, or becoming, vivid to perception or to the imagination . . . it is a coming-to-be-aware, a 'clock-able' experience. In the aesthetic setting that interests us, it is an experience accompanying and arising out of perception . . . Realizing, in our sense, is not estimating or calculating.[54]

This is best understood through his own example:

> If suddenly I realize the height of a cumulo-nimbus cloud I am not simply *taking note* of the height, but imagining myself climbing into the cloud in an aeroplane or falling through it, or I am superimposing upon it an image of a mountain of known vastness . . .[55]

As a feature in the aesthetic response, imagination enables us to become aware of various aspects of a natural object, and to make connections between objects through analogy and metaphor. This approach is not objective in the sense that we come armed with facts or information that we use as categories through which to perceive nature. Instead, our understanding of the cloud arises from gazing at it and contemplating its forms through projection – through a sort of bodily 'feeling-as'. Hepburn, like Carlson, is aware of the difficulties involved in strong subjectivity; fantasy, pleasure-seeking and trivialising responses have no role in his theory. The pitfalls of subjectivity are best avoided, he argues, by keeping our imaginings relevant according to the perceptual qualities of the object and the individual qualities that make the object distinctive.

Hepburn addresses the problem of anthropocentrism and subjectivity by articulating a scale of serious versus trivial aesthetic appreciation of nature. He argues that we should avoid an aesthetic response that 'distorts, ignores, suppresses truth about its objects, feels and thinks about them in ways that falsify how nature really is'.[56] The boundary between true and false approaches is not determined by a standard of correctness prescribed by the objectivity of science, but on a case-by-case basis, taking into consideration the variability of nature and the individual experience of the appreciator. He sets a mean whereby we do not overly humanise nature or overly distance ourselves from it, and this is also the search for an aesthetic response that is consistent with respect for nature, although he does not ground the aesthetic in the ethical.

Hepburn's most recent phase of thought has emphasised the metaphysical dimension of aesthetic engagement with the natural world. The influence of Kant is most apparent here, for recognition of nature's otherness is bound up with respect for nature and the more metaphysical category of aesthetic experience, the sublime. Through a meditative, 'metaphysical imagination', we seek to engage with nature as other, and through this experience certain metaphysical ideas concerning our relationship to nature and the cosmos are brought to life or made more vivid.

Hepburn's philosophy continues to influence aestheticians, and I count myself among them. The richness and diversity characteristic of his approach, as well as his dislike of extremes or necessary conditions, make it very attractive. Besides his philosophical insights, it would be interesting to see how he might bring his theory to bear on practice by tackling a particular environmental case study.

Berleant's Aesthetics of Engagement

Many of the philosophers on this side of the debate favour a more *phenomenological* aesthetic approach, and this is most explicit in Berleant's engagement model.[57] Phenomenology functions as both a critical and descriptive framework in his account. It is critical of the subject–object and mind–body dichotomy implicit in Kant's aesthetic theory, the landscape/scenery model and the natural environmental model. One of the fundamental drawbacks of these models is the assumption that environments are appreciated as objects from the perspective of disembodied, contemplative appreciators. For Berleant, there is no sharp separation of subject and object, but rather appreciator and environment are interactive. Aesthetic appreciation demands fullness of participation. A critique of disinterestedness is therefore integral to his theory; all the traditional notions of detachment, distancing and passivity are rejected:[58]

> Perceiving environment from within, as it were, looking not *at* it,
> but *in* it, nature becomes something quite different; it is transformed
> into a realm in which we live as participants, not observers . . . The
> aesthetic mark of all such times is not disinterested contemplation
> but total engagement, a sensory immersion in the natural world that
> reaches the still uncommon experience of unity.[59]

Berleant's aesthetics of engagement values activity rather than passivity, involvement rather than distancing.

In the move away from a traditional or modernist aesthetic, engagement is accompanied by attention to the context or situation of the appreciator. In this way the experience of the individual appreciator, and his or her emotions, values, beliefs, associations, memories, becomes as important as the aesthetic environment. Thus, the aesthetic response, including any judgements we make, is determined as much by what the appreciator brings to the experience as by the environment. It is important, though, not to assume that emotions, values, and so on constitute merely a mental engagement; Berleant's emphasis on sensory perception in aesthetic experience centres on the body-subject, our bodily engagement with the world.[60]

Despite the critique of science by phenomenologists, Berleant does not exclude it as one of the possible cultural frameworks brought into environmental experience (he would not want to exclude any component). However, he is critical of Carlson's position for its rationalistic and objectifying perspective. The aesthetics of engagement endorses personal experience and personal meaning in relation to nature, so in comparison to some other non-cognitive positions, the subjectivity in the aesthetic response is more broadly conceived.

The engagement model, unlike others, applies to the broadest range of environments – from our appreciation of artworks and built environments to the least modified natural environments. Rather than drawing up a special framework for nature as opposed to art, Berleant argues consistently for engagement in all aesthetic situations. This, as well as his view that humans are not separate from their environments, explains why Berleant's approach is more culturally oriented than any other discussed here. Body and environment alike are cultural 'products', and cultural influences permeate our aesthetic encounters.

> The aesthetic dimension . . . is bound up with the physical,
> historical, and experiential aspects of an environment, and an
> actively participating human presence lies at the center of
> environmental meaning and value. In living in the landscape, then,
> we not only shape the environment but also establish its values . . .
> The critique of an environment is at the same time a critique of a
> civilization.[61]

A strength of this account is surely the way it captures the variety of environments and shows that humans are integrated with them rather than separate from them. On the other hand, his emphasis on culture suggests an overly human-oriented view towards the natural world. Berleant stresses a holistic understanding of humans and aesthetic valuing of nature, but the result is pan-culturalism.

Carroll's Arousal Model

Besides stressing somatic experience, Berleant does not emphasise one component of aesthetic appreciation over others, but the richness of all of them coming together. Carroll, however, wants to show that feeling and emotion are common in our aesthetic responses to nature. Kant's theory emphasises a feeling of delight or enjoyment, but this is simple pleasure, something different from the ways in which we might be moved emotionally by viewing a waterfall or standing under its cascade of water. While Berleant believes that his approach should supplant others, and although Carroll is critical of the natural environmental model, he wants his 'arousal model' to sit alongside other models.

Because philosophers typically view emotion as felt by the subject and unpredictable compared to reason, it is placed within the subjective realm of aesthetic experience. The arousal model, however, adopts a cognitive theory of emotions, and sets out to show how emotion can be part of an appropriate response to nature. One of Carroll's aims is to include the subjective side of experience in ways that meet some common objections, such as the problem of sentimentalising nature and the claim that our emotional responses are not communicable. The role of emotion meets a standard of objectivity in so far as it can be shown to be shareable and not wayward or arbitrary.

Emotional responses are deemed appropriate or inappropriate according to their objects and aspects of the emoter underlying them, including beliefs and thoughts. Whether or not it is appropriate to feel melancholy when standing in the middle of a desolate moor depends upon the nature of the particular moor, but, also, the beliefs and thoughts that underlie the response. Furthermore, we must ask whether the thoughts and beliefs that underlie that response can be reasonably shared by others.[62] Emotional responses are not subjective projections on to the landscape (which would be Carlson's criticism of such responses). They are not one-sided (from the subject), but are in part due to something about the object we perceive.

If we want to give explanations of emotions generally, then we have to explain them in terms of having objects, and in terms of those objects. I must be afraid *of* something or angry *with* someone. Carroll contends that if one finds a waterfall grand, and feels excited before it, being moved in this way can be explained through particular non-aesthetic features of the waterfall that cause that response, for example, its large scale. These non-aesthetic features serve to justify the response; it is grand and exciting because of its sheer size.

Another aspect of explaining emotions has to do with the *beliefs* of the subject, that is, the beliefs that person has concerning the object of her or his emotion. So how we explain emotions – why they occur, and so on – depends upon both people's beliefs and the way they relate to the object of their emotion. Carroll uses the example of someone's fear of an oncoming tank. To explain this fear, we have to understand something about tanks (they are powerful and heavy), and one's beliefs about tanks (one is afraid of them because one knows that they can harm people).

We assess emotions according to the nature of the object, and according to whether an individual's beliefs about some object accord with other people's beliefs. Carroll argues that the beliefs are reasonable if they *cohere* with other people's beliefs: one's fear of an oncoming tank would appear to be an appropriate response given that tanks are in fact powerful and heavy, and that it is reasonable (at least in relation to other people's beliefs) to believe that they are harmful. So we can assess this emotional response as appropriate to that object.

Applying this argument to aesthetic appreciation of nature, Carroll claims that his theory of emotions and their explanation and assessment is relevant and useful:

> All things being equal, being excited by the grandeur of something that one believes to be of a large scale is an appropriate emotional response. Moreover, if the belief in the large scale of the cascade is one that is true for others as well, then the emotional response of being excited by the grandeur of a waterfall is an objective one. It is not subjective, distorted or wayward.[63]

Carroll argues persuasively that our emotional responses are explained in terms of the object's properties and the beliefs of the person having the emotional response, and this determines the inappropriateness and appropriateness of our responses.

Godlovitch's Natural Aesthetics

Apart from Saito, none of the non-cognitive theories is concerned with bringing together aesthetic and ethical valuing in their models of aesthetic appreciation of nature. Godlovitch is one writer who seeks to integrate environmental aesthetics more deeply into environmental philosophy. He achieves this by arguing for an aesthetic perspective that fully takes on board nature's mystery and otherness. As such, his position is anti-cultural and strongly natural; it rejects any humanising subjectivity and is at the same time non-cognitive.

The first stage in Godlovitch's natural aesthetics is the development of what he calls an 'acentric aesthetic'.[64] Here, he argues that a concept of nature as other in aesthetic perception ought to replace humanistic or Romantic conceptions of it. Even ecologically sensitive conceptions such as Gaia are rejected as imposing culture on to nature.

Although he believes that Carlson's model provides more human distance from nature than other approaches, he doubts science's capacity to give us a true picture of reality, remarks on how many scientific categories have been falsified and laments science's rationalisation of nature:

> Science de-mystifies Nature by categorising, quantifying, and patterning it. Under those frameworks, science makes intelligible the Nature it divides, conquers, and creates in theory. So, the object is still ours in a way; a complex artefact hewn out of the cryptic morass . . . Science ultimately disappoints the acentrist because it offers a gallery of our own articulated images.[65]

Rather than pick apart nature and attempt to understand its processes, we approach it appropriately only when we recognise its ineffability. Aesthetic appreciation with any other guiding framework – science, emotion, sensuous engagement – risks human appropriation of nature and an unethical attitude towards it.

What is left is a position where we see ourselves as insignificant in relation to nature and appreciate nature as independent from humans, as autonomous. The aesthetic attitude we take up towards nature is characterised by 'aesthetic aloofness' and a sense of mystery, but one where we do not attempt to get to know nature (as if to solve a puzzle), rather, we simply regard it at a distance and as unknowable. Godlovitch is careful to distinguish this approach from respect, sublimity and wonder, which in their own ways are still tied to human views.[66]

What Godlovitch asks for, he admits, may be an impossible perspective. Can we successfully distance ourselves from cultural concepts of the natural world? Can we, as aesthetic valuers, give up our human perspective? The second stage of his natural aesthetics is to forward the vision of a green aesthetic, where natural aesthetics is intimately linked to environmentalism. Through a fusion of aesthetic and moral value, he hopes for a more caring attitude towards nature. These aims are laudable, and the radical break he wants is refreshing in a way. But, as yet, it is difficult to understand how one can value nature aesthetically on his terms in any recognisable way. No one framework except aloofness secures the requirement of nature's auton-omy, yet aloofness appears to be empty. Not only is it a radical departure from the aesthetic domain, but it is unclear what if anything is left of an aesthetic response as we know it.[67] Godlovitch wants to achieve a kind of anti-aesthetic – not aesthetics as we know it – but this is at odds with common ways of appreciating the natural world. How can we truly care for nature if we do not in some sense attempt to get closer to it? A much more realistic option would be to couple intimacy through aesthetic engagement with distance through disinterestedness, and the respect that may follow from both.

Strengths and Weaknesses of Non-cognitive Theories

I have pointed to a few of the problems with non-cognitive approaches, but there are other criticisms that have been raised, mainly by cognitivists. The main criticism centres on the problem of subjectivity: non-cognitive positions, it is argued, humanise nature unacceptably and therefore fail to take nature on its own terms. Some positions can, I believe, be defended against this charge, while others cannot.

The first criticism, raised by Carlson, claims that appreciation which lacks cognitive content is empty. He points in particular to the sensory immersion that is the basis of Berleant's engagement model.[68] Mere sensory immersion is tantamount to emptiness, that is, to the 'blank cow-like stare' of disinterestedness that Berleant himself wants to avoid with his idea of engagement. Rolston's insistence that sensuous appreciation alone is super-ficial is another way of arguing for a lack of content in non-cognitive views. Neither Carlson nor Rolston suggests that non-cognitive views share the faults of formalism, so their arguments are aimed more at the need for cognitive content.

Carlson's argument goes on to claim that without the cognitive content supplied by science, perception, emotion and imagination in varying degrees lead to subjectivity of the 'beauty is in the eye of the beholder' sort.[69] The danger is that we project on to nature a whole set of properties that it does not actually have. This leads to trivial rather than serious appreciation, to appreciation prone to whatever the subject wants. Here, too, Berleant is the main target. The worst offender, however, is a postmodern approach that says any cultural framework is appropriate, and none is misleading:

> Such a view would compare nature to a text, contending that in reading a text we appropriately appreciate not just the meaning its author intended, but any of various meanings that it may have acquired or that we may find in it. And, moreover, none of these possible meanings has priority; no reading of a text is privileged.[70]

But to my knowledge, there is no model in the current philosophical debate that takes such a view. All of the non-cognitivists, except Berleant to some extent, would reject outright this position.

Carlson is critical of aesthetic subjectivism for good reasons, and this is surely a strength of his account, for the ethical implications of subjectivism are potentially quite dangerous to the natural environment. If beauty is in the eye of the beholder, then it could be argued that there is no way to arbitrate between personal opinions. One person's view will be as sound as the next person's, so that, for example, nature conservationists who wish to prevent a road being built through a forest will have no defensible aesthetic grounds for arguing their case. Carlson's broad aim is to show that we can make aesthetic judgements of nature that have some claim to truth, and if aesthetic value is to play any role in environmental decision-making, then it cannot be reduced to the arbitrariness of extreme subjectivity. I agree to the extent that these are the possible undesirable implications of a position like Berleant's. The subjectivity in his view could make it difficult to fix any general criteria in practice. For example, the range of individual experience that would have to be taken into account from a variety of individuals presents the practical problem of incorporating this diversity into the deliberative process. However, Carlson is wrong to assume that all accounts not grounded in science are necessarily prone to trivialising nature.

Insight into the rigidity of Carlson's position can also be gleaned from his portrayal of the contemporary debate. He takes up Hepburn's scale of serious to trivial by placing the natural environmental model on the serious end, sharply contrasted with postmodern and subjectivist views, including all non-cognitive views (except Hepburn's) at the trivialising end, as if there were no in between. Also, positions put forward by Berleant, Carroll and Foster's ambient approach are lumped together and criticised for focusing 'primarily on sensory and formal qualities', but none of these views rule out the role of narratives, and even Carroll argues that the arousal model ought to sit next to the natural environmental model rather than replace it.[71] Even Hepburn's ideas are interpreted in such a way as to support Carlson's cognitivism, despite the fact that Hepburn is clearly not on this side of the debate. For example, Carlson uses an example from Hepburn, and interprets it through a cognitive lens, which is not Hepburn's original intention. Also, while applauding Hepburn's metaphysical imagination model as setting a future agenda for environmental aesthetics, he then claims that it will be science that provides an understanding of our fundamental relationship between nature and humanity, which is not at all what Hepburn has in mind.[72] Carlson's criticisms of non-cognitivist models are weak because they attack a straw person. More careful attention to the specific problems in each view would serve his argument better.

One particular version of the subjectivity criticism is aimed at the role of imagination in aesthetic appreciation of nature. While Eaton and another critic, Robert Fudge, accept that imagination can play a positive role, it must operate within a cognitive context. Without proper ecological knowledge, Eaton is worried that imagination's flights – seeing all deer as Bambi – fictionalise and sentimentalise nature.[73] Fudge argues along the same lines, and sees a positive role for imagination when it is grounded in scientific knowledge.[74] Carlson, on the other hand, gives no place to imagination – recall that both imaginative descriptions and those issuing from literary imagination are not sufficiently culturally embedded to be warranted. The first two criticisms are directly aimed at my own discussion of imagination in aesthetic appreciation of nature, so in my discussion of the integrated approach in Chapters 5 and 6, I take up this issue and defend imagination's role.

All of these criticisms concerning trivialising nature raise an important question, What exactly does it mean to take nature on its own terms? Rolston, Eaton and Carlson take for granted that it means grasping nature through its true qualities, those known through science. Saito argues that taking nature on its own terms is achieved through a moral attitude towards it and building the aesthetic upon that. Godlovitch maintains that taking nature on its own terms means not knowing it at all. Except Saito, these philosophers maintain that any other conceptual framework, including minimal commonsense knowledge, amounts to not taking nature on its own terms. What it is to take nature on its own terms is not at all easy to answer. Can we ever know what terms nature would have us appreciate it on, or that we could even specify such terms, assuming they exist? The cognitivists too easily assume the answer is science, without providing adequate support.

In a way, this problem harks back to the issue of appropriate appreciation. Is there a single correct framework – just one way to take nature on its own terms, or are there several different ways that fit the bill? A promising suggestion is offered by Hepburn in his analysis of the spectrum between the serious and trivial. Science is not the answer, as overreliance on it threatens to 'dissolve' or 'overwhelm' the perceptual aspect of appreciation. Straightforward respect also runs into problems, because it is liable to overmoralise a natural world that has its own disturbing events. Aesthetic respect involves finding the right degree of various aesthetic components in appreciation and not overdoing one at the expense of another. Perception, imagination, emotion and thought-content all balance to appreciate nature on terms that are part-human, part-natural, without distorting nature.[75] Such appreciation would be likely to be characterised by sympathetic attention to aesthetic qualities. In this sense, then, there is no criterion of truth for establishing the appreciative terms of aesthetic engagement, but rather a proper balance executed on a case-by-case basis.

One final worry expressed by Carlson and others is that a non–cognitive approach leads to incorrect aesthetic appreciation. There are two strands to this objection. The first is simply that appreciation without any knowledge, let alone sufficient knowledge, may result in partial or incomplete appreciations.

An example that originates in Hepburn is used by Carlson to make this point (and in a critique of Carlson, Stecker presents the most compact summary of it for our purposes here):

> The shore of a tidal basin is sometimes above water and is then (part of) a beach, and is sometimes below water and is then (part of) a sea-bed. Here are (initially) three ways one can appreciate this bit of land: as beach, as sea-bed, as sometimes beach – sometimes sea-bed.[76]

Without perceiving the tidal basin in the relevant categories, we are liable to incomplete appreciation. Only the third option gives us full appreciation. But as Stecker points out, there are no good reasons to accept this conclusion or to believe that any partial appreciation is ill-founded. What constitutes complete appreciation in this case is not evident, since one could say that each appreciation is complete under each interpretation. In any case, we might ask why complete appreciation is the goal in the first place. For one thing, it may be difficult to specify what complete appreciation would be in each case, given that the object of aesthetic appreciation of nature is often a changing, dynamic environment. We also have to consider the aim of appreciation. If one accepts the cognitive position, then correct appreciation – according to science – is the aim. But I have already questioned whether this is an appropriate aim for appreciation. If one wants to enhance appreciation, if that is the aim, this is not persuasive either, for it is not clear how partial appreciation in this case (and others no doubt) represents diminished appreciation.

The second strand has an ethical tinge: without appropriate knowledge we are liable to be mistaken in our aesthetic judgements. Saito, for example, cites Leopold, who worries that damaged landscapes will be 'invisible' to the untutored eye.[77] In other words, uninformed judgements of beauty may be mistaken and suspect if they fail to grasp an unhealthy ecosystem or other harm to the environment. An interesting variation on this sort of case is a charred landscape. Imagine coming upon a burned-out section of moorland. You judge it to be ugly, without knowing whether it is caused by a controlled burning, a natural fire, an accident, or vandalism. Upon discovering it is the result of vandalism, you still find it ugly. You no doubt feel dismayed to learn that someone has harmed the landscape deliberately, and perhaps you morally condemn the vandal, but whether the fire is due to natural or human causes, you still find the black earth ugly. The new knowledge does not change your judgement. Perhaps you come upon it a few days later and you see young, green shoots coming up through the black earth. Now, you find it poignant, expressive of renewal. The aesthetic judgement changes, but this is due to observable changes in non-aesthetic qualities.

My point is that aesthetics is not in the business of uncovering actual damage. This ought to be left to ecologists, whose enterprise focuses on understanding nature through science. It is, of course, possible that aesthetic value may be found in an ecological system; an ecosystem can be harmonious or beautiful, which is an aesthetic judgement, just as when I judge a chess move to be elegant. This does not show that the ecological and the aesthetic are bound up with one another, but rather it indicates how we bring aesthetic sensitivity to environments perceived under their different aspects, whether approached as an ecological system or an environing place for aesthetic engagement. Preserving the autonomy of the aesthetic does not lead to the conclusion that the edges between aesthetic and other environmental values are clear and sharp. Wonder, for example, combines intellectual curiosity with rapture, which suggests aesthetic sensibility. The autonomy of the aesthetic also does not privilege aesthetic over other values, and it does not suggest that aesthetic valuers would be unaware of harm done to nature. Rather, it seeks to preserve the distinctiveness of aesthetic value so that this special part of human experience can be recognised, with a view to carving out a place for it in environmental debate. By keeping their focus on aesthetics, non-cognitive views have the advantage of enabling this.

Various aspects of the aesthetic response – perception, imagination, emotion – are given both stronger and weaker emphasis in the different theories that fall into the non-cognitive group. A notable strength of these theories is the way they open up aesthetic appreciation by including rather than excluding various modes of aesthetic attention. This makes them more flexible than cognitive models and even creative, so they are more able to cope with the complex demands of natural environments, in their ever-changing variety. Furthermore, they make room for, and in fact encourage, some subjective elements of the aesthetic response, including the situation of the appreciator. This last point is of particular importance in the practical context, where attention to detail and localised knowledge is imperative for good judgement. Attention to the aesthetic experience of local residents and their sense of place, coupled with the perspectives of the ecologist and the developer are all voices that have a role in the deliberative process. The thoughts of the local residents stem from their individual experiences, thoughts that are both included and valued in the non-cognitive approach. Some of these experiences will be shareable, others not, but those that are found to be reasonable, through an intersubjective exchange, are valuable in the deliberative process.

Another strength of non-cognitive views (apart from Godlovitch's) is their awareness that aesthetically valuing nature involves bringing ourselves to the natural world as *cultural* beings. We can never get around this state of affairs, and we ought not pretend that science will achieve a perspectiveless aesthetic valuing. What we can do is embrace the richness of human life in its engagement with nature and at the same time heed nature's otherness. As I argue in later chapters, to follow Kant's lead of disinterested aesthetic appreciation will be a fruitful way of achieving this.

NOTES

1. Ronald Hepburn, 'Contemporary Aesthetics and the Neglect of Natural Beauty', first appeared in Bernard Williams and Alan Montefiore (eds), *British Analytical Philosophy* (London: Routledge and Kegan Paul, 1966); and later in Hepburn's *Wonder and Other Essays* (Edinburgh: Edinburgh University Press, 1984). (I refer hereafter to this article as 1984a.)
2. Cheryl Foster, 'The Narrative and the Ambient in Environmental Aesthetics', *Journal of Aesthetics and Art Criticism Special Issue: Environmental Aesthetics*, 56:2, 1998, pp. 128, 133.
3. Allen Carlson, *Aesthetics and the Environment: The Appreciation of Nature, Art and Architecture* (London and New York: Routledge, 2000), ch. 14.
4. Pauline von Bonsdorff also develops an engaged, multi-dimensional model of environmental aesthetics which she applies to a wide range of environments, especially cultural and built environments. See von Bonsdorff, *The Human Habitat: Aesthetic and Axiological Perspectives* (Jyväskylä: Gummerus, 1998).
5. Kendall Walton, 'Categories of Art', *Philosophical Review*, 79, 1970, pp. 334–67.
6. Carlson, p. 89.
7. Ibid. p. 90.
8. Ibid. p. 89.
9. Ibid. p. 106.
10. Ibid. p. 118.
11. See Allen Carlson, 'Saito on the Correct Aesthetic Appreciation of Nature', *Journal of Aesthetic Education*, 20:2, 1986, p. 91.
12. Holmes Rolston, III, 'Aesthetic Experience in Forests', *Journal of Aesthetics and Art Criticism*, 56:2, 1998, p. 162.
13. Holmes Rolston, III, 'Does Aesthetic Appreciation of Landscapes Need to Be Science-Based?', *British Journal of Aesthetics*, 35:4, 1995, p. 383.
14. Rolston, 1998, p. 161.
15. Aldo Leopold, *Sand County Almanac* (New York: Oxford University Press, [1949] 1966), pp. 61–2.
16. See Rolston, 1995, p. 377.
17. Marcia Muelder Eaton: 'The Role of Aesthetics in Designing Sustainable Landscapes', in Yrjö Sepänmaa (ed.), *Real World Design: The Foundations and Practice of Environmental Aesthetics, Proceedings of the XIIIth International Congress of Aesthetics*, vol. II (Lahti: University of Helsinki – Lahti Research and Training Centre, 1997), pp. 51–63; and 'The Beauty that Requires Health', in Joan Nassauer (ed.), *Placing Nature: Culture and Landscape Ecology* (Washington: Island Press, 1997).

18. Marcia Muelder Eaton, *Merit, Aesthetic and Ethical* (Oxford and New York: Oxford University Press, 2001), p. 184.
19. Marcia Muelder Eaton, 'Fact and Fiction in the Aesthetic Appreciation of Nature', *Journal of Aesthetics and Art Criticism*, 56:2, 1998, pp. 149–56.
20. Noël Carroll, 'Being Moved By Nature: Between Religion and Natural History', in Salim Kemal and Ivan Gaskell (eds), *Landscape, Natural Beauty and the Arts* (Cambridge: Cambridge University Press, 1993), p. 250.
21. Donald Crawford, 'Allen Carlson's Aesthetics of Nature', paper read to American Society of Aesthetics Annual Meeting, Reno, October, 2000.
22. Robert Stecker has also argued that art can provide one appropriate avenue of appreciation. See Robert Stecker, 'The Correct and the Appropriate in the Aesthetic Appreciation of Nature', *British Journal of Aesthetics*, 37:4, 1997, pp. 394–6. See also Hepburn's discussion of interpretations of nature through art in 'Nature in the Light of Art', in *Wonder and Other Essays* (Edinburgh: Edinburgh University Press, 1984). (I refer hereafter to this article as 1984b.)
23. Rolston, 1998, pp. 160–1.
24. Yuriko Saito, 'The Aesthetics of Unscenic Nature', *Journal of Aesthetics and Art Criticism: Special Issue: Environmental Aesthetics*, 56:2, 1998, p. 104. (Saito's emphasis. This article is hereafter referred to as 1998a.)
25. Allen Carlson, 'Nature, Aesthetic Appreciation, and Knowledge', *Journal of Aesthetics and Art Criticism*, 53:4, 1995, p. 396.
26. Stan Godlovitch, 'Carlson on Appreciation', *Journal of Aesthetics and Art Criticism*, 55, 1997, pp. 53–4.
27. Richard Shusterman, 'Pragmatism', in Berys Gaut and Dominic McIver Lopes (eds), *The Routledge Companion to Aesthetics* (London and New York: Routledge, 2001), p. 98ff.
28. Yuriko Saito, 'Appreciating Nature on its Own Terms', *Environmental Ethics*, 20, Summer 1998, p. 142 (hereafter referred to as 1998b).
29. Carlson, 2000, p. 68.
30. Carlson, 1995, p. 399.
31. Carlson, 2000, p. 6.
32. Ibid. p. 7. Later in the book, in Chapter 14, he distinguishes within factual knowledge, 'the ordinary, the scientific, the historical, and the functional', where the ordinary covers 'commonplace descriptive terms like "mountain" and "sunset"'. See p. 220.
33. Stecker, p. 397.
34. Carlson, 1995, p. 399. For Carroll's quote, see Carroll, 1993, p. 253.
35. Carlson, 2000, p. 89.
36. Carlson, 1995, pp. 394–5.
37. Patricia Matthews has recently presented a cognitive position similar to Carlson's. Her own position expands and refines Carlson's views, especially in relation to the categories of art analogy. She defends the cognitivist approach against several common objections, but like Carlson she does not question the status of scientific knowledge. For example, she supports the view that it is science that gets at 'the nature of nature' (p. 47), but why this is so, and why science does this better than other narratives is left unanswered. ('Scientific Knowledge and the Aesthetic Appreciation of Nature', *Journal of Aesthetics and Art Criticism*, 60:1, 2002, pp. 38–48.)
38. Carroll, p. 245. Other writers also make the point that common responses are left out, according to Carlson's model. See Saito, 1998b, pp. 147–8; Stecker, p. 399.

39. Yuriko Saito, 'Is There a Correct Aesthetic Appreciation of Nature?', *Journal of Aesthetic Education*, 18:4, 1984, pp. 35–46. See also Saito, 1998b.
40. Carlson, 2000, p. 220.
41. Stan Godlovitch, 'Icebreakers: Environmentalism and Natural Aesthetics', *Journal of Applied Philosophy*, 11:1, 1994, p. 23; Saito, 1998b, pp. 142–3; Heyd, pp. 135–6.
42. Godlovitch, 1994, p. 22.
43. Carlson, 2000, p. 228.
44. Ibid. p. 231.
45. Ronald W. Hepburn, 'Landscape and Metaphysical Imagination', *Environmental Values*, 5, 1996, pp. 194–5.
46. Saito, 1998b; and see Saito, 1998a.
47. Saito, 1998b, p. 147.
48. Ibid. pp. 143–4. Saito's emphasis.
49. Ibid. p. 144.
50. Saito, 1998b.
51. Hepburn, 1993, p. 67.
52. Ibid. p. 73.
53. Ibid. p. 71.
54. Hepburn, 1984a, pp. 27–8.
55. Ibid. p. 27.
56. Hepburn, 1993, p. 69. See also his 'Nature Humanised: Nature Respected', *Environmental Values*, 7, 1998, pp. 267–79.
57. Arnold Berleant, *Aesthetics of Environment* (Philadelphia: Temple University Press, 1992).
58. See Berleant, 1992; and Arnold Berleant, 'Beyond Disinterestedness', *British Journal of Aesthetics*, 34:3, 1994, pp. 242–54.
59. Berleant, 1992, p. 170.
60. See Berleant 1992; and Arnold Berleant, *Living in the Landscape: Toward an Aesthetics of Environment* (Lawrence: University Press of Kansas, 1997), Ch. 6.
61. Berleant, 1997, p. 24
62. Carroll, 1993, pp. 257–8.
63. Carroll, 1993, p. 258.
64. See Godlovitch, 1994, pp. 15–30.
65. Ibid. p. 23.
66. Ibid. pp. 27–8.
67. Cf. Carlson, 2000, p. 8; and Ronald Hepburn, *The Reach of the Aesthetic: Collected Essays on Art and Nature* (Aldershot and Burlington, VT: Ashgate, 2001), p. 145. Carlson refers to Godlovitch's approach as the 'mystery model'.
68. Allen Carlson, 'Appreciating Art and Appreciating Nature', in Salim Kemal and Ivan Gaskell (eds), *Landscape, Natural Beauty and the Arts* (Cambridge: Cambridge University Press, 1993), p. 226n.
69. Carlson, 2000, pp. 9–10.
70. Carlson, 2000, p. 9.
71. Ibid., p. 429. Elsewhere, Carlson claims that rather than being a subjective view, the arousal model collapses into the natural environmental model because appropriate emotional responses depend upon reasonable beliefs (i.e., knowledge). Besides the fact that Carroll's model stands in strong contrast to Carlson's, one is left wondering which of Carlson's criticisms holds. See Carlson, 1995, p. 398.
72. Carlson, 2000, p. 11; Hepburn, 1993, p. 71.

73. Marcia Muelder Eaton, 'Fact and Fiction in the Aesthetic Appreciation of Nature', *Journal of Aesthetics and Art Criticism*, 56:2, 1998, pp. 149–56.
74. Robert Fudge, 'Imagination and the Science-Based Aesthetic Appreciation of Unscenic Nature', *Journal of Aesthetics and Art Criticism*, 59:3, 2001, pp. 275–86.
75. Hepburn, 1993, pp. 71–3.
76. Stecker, p. 398. Carlson's discussion can be found in Carlson, 2000, pp. 60–1. For Hepburn's original example, see Hepburn, 1984a, p. 19.
77. Saito, 1998a, p. 103.

CHAPTER 5

The Integrated Aesthetic I: Multi-sensuous Engagement and Disinterestedness

I n the last chapter, I worked through a set of contemporary approaches to aesthetic appreciation of nature. Several problems were found in cognitive theories of aesthetic appreciation of nature, as put forward, mainly, by Carlson. Alternative approaches, without the necessary condition of science, presented a more open and richer account of appreciation. While I identify with the non-cognitivists, my aim now is to develop a comprehensive theory of aesthetic appreciation which builds upon the strengths of this group of theories but also addresses some of their weaknesses. I call my aesthetic approach the 'integrated aesthetic' After setting the context, I discuss two components of the integrated aesthetic: multi-sensuous engagement and disinterestedness. The next chapter continues with an analysis of three other components: imagination, emotion/ expression and the role of thought and knowledge.

THE INTEGRATED AESTHETIC

The integrated aesthetic is 'integrated' in the sense that I want to draw upon both the situation of the subject and the situation of the object for guiding appreciation. As I argued in Chapter 1, along the lines of a more traditional view, appreciation comes about through the subject's appreciative capacities – perception, imagination and so on, coupled with open, sympathetic attention to qualities of the aesthetic object. Approaching the problem in this way prevents leaning too heavily towards a subject-oriented or object-oriented account and captures the potential richness of as many relevant features as may be present in any particular encounter with an environment. My intention is not to provide a definition stipulating necessary and sufficient conditions, but rather to analyse some of the main features of aesthetic appreciation of nature.

My preference for 'integration' underscores how aesthetic appreciation of nature involves a relationship between appreciator and environment. First, it captures the environing experience of nature, as it surrounds the appreciator, as opposed to an experience of perceiving landscape from a distance, as a spectator would observe a painting. Second, given that environments change from day to day, season to season, year to year, and so on, my approach intends to capture the fact that each aesthetic appreciation of the same landscape is potentially different. Some features of the landscape may stay the same, but others change, and things may happen during the time we are appreciating it. There is movement, new things to smell or see, and changes in light, wind and temperature. The aesthetic situation reflects the complexity of environmental appreciation, where appreciation is more like a *happening*, and where that happening creates the conditions of the situation we are in.

The integrated aesthetic stresses the idea of situatedness but I am not putting forward a full-blown engagement or holistic account such as Berleant's. Aesthetic experience is characterised by a relationship between appreciator and environment, rather than becoming one with nature, where every aspect of one's being would be part of appreciation. The appreciator is placed in a certain way – aesthetically – in relation to an environment. This is not merely a spatial relation, as when we say that 'the glasshouse is situated at the back of the main house'. It is meant to capture all the possible types of aesthetic relations that can arise through participating with, or even interacting with, what one is situated in – the environment. In these relations, some distance is maintained, rather than our being fully integrated with the environment. Recognition of nature's otherness is implicit in appreciation. More specifically, this is expressed through the concept of disinterestedness, which I put forward as one component of appreciation. I shall argue for a renewed understanding of disinterestedness, where its negative connotations are stripped away to reveal it as a concept that supports engagement and sympathetic attention, without the problems associated with overly detached responses.

Besides expressing a degree of distance between nature and us, disinterestedness will also help to filter out idiosyncratic features of the appreciator. In this respect, the integrated aesthetic falls short of embracing all aspects of the subject. Some aspects will not be given prominence mainly because they may be idiosyncratic or not easily shared by others making aesthetic judgements of the same object. In this way, I distinguish aesthetic appreciation as a shared activity from the more private or personal activity of expressing preferences.

The sources or inspiration for the integrated aesthetic are Hepburn and Kant. I have already drawn substantially on Hepburn to explain and argue for differences between nature and art appreciation. Here, I follow the spirit of his ideas by integrating the various components of appreciation and finding a balance between more objective and more subjective approaches to appreciation. Also, although he takes imagination in a more metaphysical direction than do I, I credit his discussion of imaginative possibilities in appreciation of nature for motivating my emphasis on imagination in the integrated aesthetic.

Kantian aesthetics provides several core ideas for the integrated aesthetic, but the limitations of his theory must be carefully drawn. His views continue to be influential in contemporary aesthetics, but many philosophers find that various problems in his theory make it impossible to take it on board without important qualifications. Given that in Chapter 1, I already sketched a relatively traditional theory of appreciation which draws on Kant, it should be clear at this stage that I draw on the following Kantian ideas for understanding aesthetic appreciation: the nature-first (rather than art-first) emphasis in his view of appreciation; the immediate and first-hand experience of the aesthetic; the non-cognitive nature of aesthetic appreciation; the dependence on both subject and object for the aesthetic response; the role of the free play of imagination; and disinterestedness. (Later, in Chapter 7, I draw on his theory of aesthetic judgements, aesthetic communication and ideas on connections between aesthetics and other aspects of human life to support my approach to aesthetic judgement and aesthetic education.)

There are several significant points where my account departs from Kant's.[1] One divergence is the need to broaden and update the aesthetic domain. Although Kant recognises a range of aesthetic objects, from wilder nature and gardens to design objects, fine art and architecture (and to this extent he covers objects of the everyday), his treatment of aesthetic value is narrower. Like other philosophers of his time, he works exclusively with the categories of beauty, sublimity and ugliness. He says little about ugliness, and excludes the variety of categories of aesthetic value that we are more familiar with today. I want to include his categories, but embrace others too, such as the magical, humorous, unappealing, marvellous and so on.

I also set aside formalist interpretations of his aesthetic theory and pursue the richest possible interpretation. As we shall see, a Kant-influenced, integrated view of aesthetic appreciation will be rich in content rather than empty. I elaborate on this below in my discussions of disinterestedness and imagination. One dimension of this issue involves the non-cognitive nature of Kant's aesthetic theory. It can be shown that while non-cognitive, there is room in his theory for indeterminate concepts and the very basic organising concepts needed for experience of the world. While still maintaining the predominantly non-cognitive nature of appreciation in the integrated aesthetic, I shall go beyond Kant to some extent by suggesting that it is sometimes appropriate to feed in background knowledge.

On one point, the role of emotion, I break entirely from Kant. Kant is well known for his suspicion that the unpredictable and idiosyncratic nature of emotion undermines moral judgements. In the aesthetic domain, he worried that 'charm' and 'emotion' would undermine the impartiality of disinterested judgements. Even in his discussion of the sublime, it is not real fear, but a sort of quasi-fear that is involved in the aesthetic response.[2] There is some textual evidence for Kant's recognition of expressive aesthetic qualities, but this is limited to the expression of aesthetic ideas rather than emotion.[3] Many writers would agree that emotion has a role to play in aesthetic appreciation of both nature and art, so this factor cannot be ignored. As Carroll shows, we can identify emotional responses and expressive qualities that are justifiable rather than mere subjective projections. In this way, I seek to incorporate Kant's views in ways that are consistent with the aims of disinterestedness and shareability of aesthetic judgements.

Given these clarifications, it would be an overstatement to call the integrated aesthetic a neo-Kantian view. The best way to characterise the relationship is to describe my strategy as an attempt to draw on a useful set of ideas from Kant's aesthetic theory, but to reinterpret them in a contemporary context. Kant was right to begin his analysis of aesthetic judgement with natural objects, and this is a distinct advantage, but without renewal and expansion, his ideas are less applicable in current environmental aesthetics.

Regarding the context of environments, the integrated aesthetic is intended to apply across the scale, from relatively wild nature to cultural landscapes to gardens and parks. It is possible that it also applies to more artefactual environments such as the built environment and artworks, but that discussion reaches beyond the scope of this study.

MULTI-SENSUOUS ENGAGEMENT

Aesthetic appreciation begins in perception. The immediate, first-hand experience of environments and their objects constitutes the basis of all aesthetic valuing of nature. Perception, though, has many dimensions. It includes all of the different types of our sensory contact with the world – seeing, hearing, smelling, tasting and touching, combined with thoughts, imagining and beliefs. All of our senses, alone and in conjunction with other capacities, enable the perception of aesthetic qualities.

Perceptual exploration of environments involves a range of potential perspectives as well as a range of different senses to draw upon. A landscape can be perceived from far away, as a view, or close up, within it. We can select particular objects for close scrutiny, such as a moss-covered rock, or allow our senses to wander from one object to the next, shifting attention and focus, perceiving more or less carefully depending on how our aesthetic interest is activated by our surroundings. As discussed in Chapter 3, we also choose different perspectives or find ourselves placed in different ways in relation to the environments we perceive. We can walk slowly through them, or experience them from a car window, or swim, climb or fly through them.

The sensuous perspectives active in aesthetic appreciation are mutually determined by subject and object. We may consciously choose to experience a lake by swimming in it rather than rowing through it. We can choose careful attention or a more cursory glance, but environments and their objects significantly shape our perceptual perspectives. Nature's careful appreciation demands slow ambulation, rather than a fast cycle ride, although both perspectives offer legitimate appreciation. Environmental qualities stop us in our tracks and demand our attention: the vivid colour of the sea; the melodious song of a thrush; the spectacular drama of thunder and lightning; the inviting fragrance of jasmine; or the luxurious feel of cool sand underfoot. In many cases, some of which constitute our most highly valued experiences, there is little conscious choice and just spontaneity. These situations occur by natural processes and spontaneity – rain falling on our faces; leaves falling from the trees; or clouds moving across the sun. Also, the dynamic character of natural environments is perhaps most evident in the way that perceptual qualities change. Our visual, aural, tactile, olfactory and gustatory experiences of nature are all subject to change caused by atmospheric conditions, and so on.

Depending on how many senses we draw upon, sensuous engagement can be thick or thin. The most common senses used are seeing and hearing, and like the rest of experience, aesthetic experience is dominated by them. Ocularcentrism results in experiencing nature only, consciously at least, through one perspective. It is also responsible for some of the problems in the landscape/scenery model, and its predecessor, the picturesque. However, seeing should not be devalued as our main tool for perceptual exploration; perception begins with vision, and vision can direct the other senses to a broader sensuous engagement. Seeing, sometimes in conjunction with other senses such as touch, is responsible for the perception of formal qualities in nature, and there are some truly fantastic forms, such as the intricate form of a snowflake and the alluring forms found in orchids.

The sounds of nature are all around us, and they significantly contribute to the environing quality of natural aesthetic appreciation. Birdsong, rippling water, wind through the trees, creaking tree limbs, distant sounds of human culture, such as aeroplanes, voices, farm machinery, cars and so on, all may create a soundscape. We are often unaware of these sounds until they actually capture our attention, when for example, a sound enters our experience in a vivid way – a curlew's mournful cry is heard as it passes into range, or we come upon a crashing waterfall. There is great pleasure in nature's tranquillity, which is not silence but natural sounds, and we may balk at the intrusion of human noise upon it.[4]

Aural aesthetic qualities are picked out through attention to sound events. We can listen to all sounds together – an ensemble – or focus on a group of sounds or one individual sound. An individual bird's song is perhaps the most accessible or everyday natural sound, and it occurs in all sorts of environments, from the deep forest to the city. The sound event of a starling's song evokes wonder at the range of sounds produced, and the almost humorous imitations of other sounds, usually other birdsongs. Other birdsongs may have more melodious qualities and invite comparison to the intentionally arranged melodies of human music. Still, it is important to recognise that much of our delight is due to the unpredictability and otherness we hear in this and other types of natural sounds.[5]

John Andrew Fisher points to how very changeable nature's soundscapes are:

> Whereas a landscape's visual appearance may be merely enhanced at dawn and dusk, natural soundscapes change dramatically as various species of birds, insects, and other animals (as well as weather events) either make sounds or cease to make them. Birds, although beautiful in themselves close up, do not significantly affect the visual appearance of a landscape, whereas the daily cycle of their sounds have a powerful affect on the soundscape. (This is even more true of insects, such as crickets and cicadas, that we seldom see. Their stridulations create a rich blanket keynote for many soundscapes.) Both landscape and natural soundscape change significantly by season as well.[6]

Fisher's point, as well as his excellent examples, show how important a broader sensuous approach to environments is for enabling appreciation which does justice to nature's dynamic qualities.

In the natural environment, there is great potential for using the other three senses. Without them, appreciation fails to meet its full potential, and may only be one or two dimensional. Touch is one of the most intimate ways we explore nature; it is the least distanced and most interactive of all the senses. When we reach out to touch nature, it touches us back, if not intentionally. Touch gives us the feel and texture of our world, and invites bodily engagement through our face, hands and feet, and in some cases, our whole body.

Consider the various textures or feel of these objects: wet moss; different textures of tree bark; a layer of pine needles underfoot; sand; fur; fish skin and scales; cold water; a rose petal; pebbles, rocks and shells and so on. Diane Ackerman describes with relish these kinds of experiences:

> Consider all the varieties of pain, irritation, abrasion, all the textures
> of lick, pat, wipe, fondle, knead; all the prickling, bruising, tingling,
> brushing, scratching, banging, fumbling, kissing, nudging . . . The
> feel of a sweat bee delicately licking moist beads from your ankle . . .
> Pulling your foot out of the mud. The squish of wet sand between
> the toes.[7]

We can also experience tactile qualities from a distance, visually, when we
perceive waves in the sea, waves in fields of grain and the different textures
and patterns created by rocks, trees and other vegetation on mountains.
Textural aesthetic qualities range from the soft, blue haziness covering a
mountain range to the stiff, unpleasant feel of heather that has been burned,
leaving only short, coarse vegetation behind.

Nature's smellscape also has distinctive environing qualities and contributes just as much to the aesthetic character of an environment as hearing
and touching. Despite this, smells (and tastes) have been neglected in
philosophy and aesthetics due to a prejudice which has its roots in mind/
body dualism and the belief that qualities associated with the body have less
value than those associated with the mind. In aesthetics, smells are viewed
as lacking features of other aesthetic objects that would make them
candidates for appreciation. It is claimed they lack stability (they are
short-lived and supposedly difficult to identify as objects); and that our
experience of them is limited to mere sensation rather than having the
mental component – reflection or contemplation – considered essential to
aesthetic appreciation.[8]

But smells are much more aesthetically interesting than these claims
suggest. I have argued elsewhere that smells (and tastes) have duration,
complexity and structure, and that smell events can serve as objects of
aesthetic appreciation.[9] They have expressive properties and evoke associations from imagination and memory. The most obvious evidence for smells as
aesthetic objects are the established, critical appreciative activities of wine-
tasting, the culinary arts, perfumery and so on. But olfactory aesthetic
judgements also take place in our everyday encounters with smells in the
immediate environment, when walking through a park to work, choosing
ingredients for a meal, or showering, dressing and scenting our bodies each
day.

In the natural environment, we are often unaware of smells around us; like
sounds, they constitute a sensuous backdrop and are appreciated only when
we attend to them or when they impose themselves upon us. The fragrance of
a pine forest, for example, operates at a general level, while more specific
smells might then enter our experience, such as the peaty, moist smell of a
rotting log, or the putrid odour of an animal carcass. Like sounds, smells come

and go, as we move past them or come upon them, and when the wind shifts direction.

Tastes too have a role, but gustatory experiences are less common than the olfactory in the environmental context. The Nordic custom of wandering through the forests to collect blueberries and mushrooms may involve gustatory appreciation that is not merely instrumental. When I was growing up, part of the appreciation of the forest for my father involved chewing on Black Birch (or Sweet Birch) twigs to savour their wintergreen taste. Other examples are drinking spring water on the way up a mountain, or tasting salt from sea-air and mist. Disinterestedness applies in these cases in so far as we appreciate gustatory qualities for themselves and not merely for consumption.[10]

Appreciation of aesthetic qualities through sensory engagement is directed to a great degree by qualities perceived, but what is picked out for appreciation depends to some extent on the effort made with respect to engaging perceptual capacities. With art, a lot depends on the ability of the artist to create an engaging and imaginative work of art. With nature, the character of the natural object significantly determines how much perceptual effort is required. It may take less effort to see the beauty of a particularly grand landscape compared to a 'wasteland'. However, unscenic nature also has aesthetic value, and perceiving that is dependent upon the effort of the individual.

An example from my own experience helps to illustrate this point. The local government where I live has been working with the local community to decide how to manage a landscape that was formerly the site of an oil refinery. Besides some remnants of building foundations and an old road around the site, it has become a habitat for various plants, insects and birds, and pondlife in two ponds that have formed from shallow holes in the ground where storage tanks had once stood. Initially, some argued for digging up the landscape to replace it with a neat and trim park. Others argued for it to be left as it is, with the exception of building a boardwalk or path and a few information boards to facilitate exploration of the area and its history, for visitors, and it is this course that the planners have chosen for the site. After spending some time exploring the place, I discovered that what appeared to be a dull landscape was in fact aesthetically interesting. Through careful attention to various aspects of that environment, I discovered the graceful flight of birds, the soft fragrance of various wildflowers, and an elegant pair of swans in one of the ponds. My delight in these aspects of the place was heightened by my background knowledge of the debate and the history of the place (and that knowledge led me to explore it in the first place), but the aesthetic value I found there did not depend upon such knowledge, rather it depended on perceptual interest and immersion in the landscape.

The senses enable aesthetic engagement with environments and provide a primary route to the discovery of aesthetic qualities. But using all the senses takes an effort. Nature calls for active perception and sensuous participation, rather than passivity or laziness. Practising multi-sensuous perception may lead to greater aesthetic sensitivity and a closer relationship with our natural surroundings. I want to underline that sensuous aesthetic appreciation is not hedonistic. While feelings of enjoyment or, alternatively, displeasure accompany many of our aesthetic experiences, these feelings are other-directed, that is, they closely relate to the qualities of the object. As a characteristic of the integrated aesthetic, disinterestedness provides an explanation of this feature of aesthetic appreciation.

DISINTERESTEDNESS

The concept of disinterestedness has had a long tradition in aesthetics going back to eighteenth-century British moral philosophy and aesthetics, but it gets its most important treatment as a defining feature of aesthetic judgement in Kant's philosophy. It continues to have contemporary relevance, and several philosophers recognise its value for characterising aesthetic appreciation. At the same time, disinterestedness has been the target of a number of criticisms. In Chapter 1, I introduced it as part of a traditional view of aesthetic appreciation. Here, I discuss objections to it and refresh the concept by clarifying and defending its place in the aesthetic response to nature.

One might ask, why bother reviving this concept? Why not drop it altogether and find other ways to describe this feature of aesthetic experience? There are a few good reasons for avoiding this tactic. One fruitful effect of thinking about philosophical problems in relation to the environment is the way it forces us to re-evaluate particular concepts. Discussion of the natural environment raises new questions and throws new light upon concepts like diversity, rarity and, perhaps most of all, morality. I believe that disinterestedness is an instance of this particular critical enterprise.

Disinterestedness moves more easily in the space of natural aesthetics, where the concerns of politics and society are of less relevance than in the context of art. Many artworks do have social aims, and, in this context, to insist on disinterestedness might limit the scope of our appreciation of them. Although natural processes have their own functions, these are less the concern of aesthetics than ecology. In the case of artworks, a social aim is expressed through a creative artistic medium, so we attend to the artwork to discover its message. With nature it makes less sense to appreciate it in this way. Nature operates spontaneously, without such intentions, so that aesthetic appreciation is freed from such 'responsibility'. In other words, our encounters with nature lend themselves more easily to the concept of disin-terestedness. (I shall say something later in this chapter about modified landscapes in relation to this point.)

Moreover, if the environment is something we ought to protect, then we are required to adopt a moral attitude towards it. If this is accepted, then it follows that we should seek a conception of aesthetic value that is consistent with this stance. This means finding an alternative to hedonistic 'aesthetic' appreciation, where aesthetic value is reduced to amenity value, where nature becomes ours for our pleasure and where scenic views are for our consumption rather than having value in themselves in virtue of their aesthetic qualities. Disinterested aesthetic appreciation provides such an alternative. It achieves this by showing how aesthetic valuing can be conceived in a way that backgrounds personal preferences and utilitarian concerns in our approach to nature, and foregrounds an appreciation of its qualities.

Kant distinguishes judgements of aesthetic appreciation, judgements of taste, from other types of judgement in two ways. First, judgements of taste are grounded in a feeling of pleasure or 'liking' in the subject in response to the form or appearance of some object, rather than being grounded in a determinate concept of the object. This marks off aesthetic judgements from cognitive judgements. Second, and more importantly for my argument, the feeling of pleasure or liking which grounds aesthetic judgements is *disin-terested*. Disinterestedness does not mean indifference, but rather it identifies appreciation of an object apart from any 'interest'. It operates as the logical condition which distinguishes judgements of taste from both judgements of the agreeable and the good, both of which involve appreciating objects in relation to an 'interest'.[11]

For Kant, to have an 'interest' in an object is to have a concept of it in terms of its capacity to satisfy some desire.[12] In particular, he identifies two kinds of interest that are not involved in the aesthetic appreciation of the judgement of taste: (1) interest in or desire for an object for sensory gratification (which he classifies as a liking for the agreeable); and (2) interest in or desire for an object as a means to some practical or utilitarian end (which he classifies as a liking for the good). Both types of interest involve valuing objects for some purpose that they serve, which may also be understood in terms of satisfying some desire we have. In the first case, we like or value an object, maybe a cold drink, because it serves the purpose of quenching our thirst. The second case involves liking or valuing an object because it serves another type of purpose, either utilitarian or moral. To use Kant's example, we like health and say that it is good because it enables us to perform the tasks of life. Valuing something as morally (or intrinsically) good is connected to purpose and desire because we find something morally good when it satisfies an end according to duty (Kant's 'moral law'). Aesthetic appreciation involves no interest in this sense because the judgement of taste is a judgement that is free from any (determinate) concept of the object, and thus any desire connected to this.[13]

Aesthetic appreciation through the judgement of taste is therefore distinguished from valuing an object in virtue of its capacity to fulfil some desire. The judgement of taste is a 'free liking' arising from the mere contemplation of an object for its aesthetic qualities, rather than a liking arising from the ways in which that object might satisfy our needs, whether as a means to our own (self-interested) ends, or other ends. Kant articulates this when he says, 'only the liking involved in taste for the beautiful is disinterested and free, since we are not compelled to give our approval by any interest, whether of sense or of reason.'[14]

In Chapter 1, I pointed out that Stolnitz brings the concept into his own contemporary interpretation of a traditional view to argue that aesthetic appreciation involves 'disinterested and sympathetic attention to and contemplation of any object of awareness whatever, for its own sake alone'.[15] In environmental aesthetics, although Hepburn does not give disinterestedness a major role in his theory, it is certainly there, since Hepburn characterises the aesthetic response as involving *some* degree of detachment and a non-utilitarian relationship to nature. At the same time he wants to ensure that this sits within an engaged response.[16] Although reasonably critical of some uses of the concept, Carlson recognises the value of disinterestedness, and he has defended it against the claim that it is incompatible with active, participatory aesthetic appreciation.[17] On the other hand, disinterestedness is the main target of Berleant's critique of traditional aesthetics, and his rejection of it is essential to clearing the way for his aesthetics of engagement.[18]

Criticisms of Disinterestedness

Criticisms of disinterestedness come from a variety of perspectives and from several different philosophers. There are three perspectives in particular: criticisms from philosophical aesthetics; criticisms from sociological aesthetics; and criticisms from feminist philosophy and aesthetics.[19] Because there is overlap between them, and for convenience, I shall proceed by grouping them together, whilst recognising that their objections are bound up with the different projects for each of them. The common criticisms are:

1. disinterestedness wrongly characterises aesthetic appreciation as a 'blank cow-like stare'; and
2. disinterestedness necessarily underpins a formalist aesthetics, which is indefensible because it claims that the aesthetic is identified exclusively with the perception of form.

The first objection rests on the association of disinterestedness with distancing, detachment and passive contemplation.[20] This association stems from the idea that through disinterestedness we detach or distance ourselves from concerns about ourselves in order to be in a better position to appreciate an object for its individual qualities. Unfortunately, distancing and detachment have given rise to the belief that aesthetic experience involves passive contemplation of an object.

From this there arise a number of problems for the concept of disinterestedness. For the aesthetician, detachment, distancing and passive contemplation are often taken to mean that aesthetic experience is typified by 'the blank cow-like stare', that is, inactive perceptual contemplation. The blank cow-like stare is challenged by the claim that many experiences that we might want to call aesthetic are active and exciting instead of still and restful. The feminist and sociological aesthetician concur, arguing that the detachment of disinterestedness yields a passive and abstracted standpoint rather than an active and embedded one. Their objection rests on the belief that disinterestedness requires that almost everything about the individual subject is set aside (values, beliefs, desires, life experience), so that one is disconnected from both situation and context. Disinterestedness is thus accused of insensitivity to the individual circumstances and details of a situation (in this case the natural object or landscape of our aesthetic attention).

The associations at the foundation of the first criticism give rise to the second, that disinterestedness is responsible for the worst kind of aesthetic formalism. In aesthetic formalism, detachment from personal concerns associated with the disinterested standpoint becomes detachment from concern for everything but form. Exclusive attention to form has two consequences for the aesthetic response. First, formalism sets up a dichotomy between form and content and claims that only the perception of form is relevant to aesthetic appreciation. Form is usually associated with combinations of lines, colours, and shapes, while content pertains to what the painting, poem, or music is about. Second, it is argued that in aesthetic appreciation 'we need bring with us nothing from life', as Clive Bell puts it.[21] The aesthetic response is cut off from knowledge of the artist's intention, the genetic history of the artwork, and more, generally, life experiences, except the response of aesthetic emotion, an emotion exclusive to the perception of 'significant form'.[22]

Many aestheticians object to both tenets of formalism. The first is rejected on the grounds that the form/content dichotomy is difficult to uphold.[23] In response to the second point, critics argue that the exclusion of both life experience and knowledge of the aesthetic object devalues our input into the aesthetic experience by making irrelevant knowledge, beliefs, imaginative associations, memories and so on. The feminist and sociologist agree, but put a slightly different slant on their objections. Formalism represents a 'closure' of the aesthetic response because it sharply defines it in terms of disinterested perception of form. This closure seals off the aesthetic from the rest of our experience, which has the additional consequence of making aesthetic appreciation available only to a select elite, namely those who possess the aesthetic sensitivity to perceive significant form.[24]

Defending Disinterestedness

To the extent that these criticisms have been seen as effective, they have prompted a view of disinterestedness as a distanced, even elitist approach, which is connected to a dispassionate, abstracted perspective. I shall argue that these criticisms about the idea and value of disinterestedness can be traced back to misconceptions of the concept as it was originally understood. By returning to the historically accurate roots of the concept, I aim to clarify it and thus expose the misguided nature of these objections.

The original meaning of disinterestedness lies in eighteenth-century moral philosophy, where Shaftesbury identifies the disinterested standpoint with morality. Moral action is motivated by affection for something for its own sake, and it is therefore contrasted with desiring an object as a means to an end, for one's own pleasure or for any other use. Arguing against Hobbes, Shaftesbury opposes 'interestedness' or self-love to disinterestedness or actions that are not motivated by self-concern or thought of any other outcome.[25] Disinterestedness thus begins in this ethical context and is then brought smoothly into aesthetic theory to characterise the standpoint that we find in Kant.

The significance of Shaftesbury's remarks, together with Kant's, is to show that disinterestedness does not entail the passivity, abstraction and formalism assumed by its critics. Aesthetic appreciation does not require that we set aside who we are, it requires only that we set aside *what we want*. Disinterested aesthetic appreciation does not have to be impersonal or detached from the self; we approach the object from a concrete standpoint and, if we choose, relate the object to ourselves but apart from wants and desires. With this clarification in mind, we can now consider more carefully how this type of standpoint can meet the two objections above.

The first criticism began with the claim from within aesthetics that disinterestedness turns aesthetic appreciation into a blank cow-like stare, an approach marked by passive contemplation. Here, the objection also rests on a mistaken assumption, the assumption that there is some conflict between disinterestedness and engagement with the aesthetic object. But if disinterestedness is merely freedom from certain kinds of interest, then it certainly does not follow from this that aesthetic attention can be likened to the blank cow-like stare. Aesthetic attention involves the active use of the capacities of perception, thought and imagination.

To support this point I return to Kant, since his aesthetic theory sets disinterestedness side by side with the aesthetic contemplation of the object. Although he says that the judgement of taste is characterised by *passive* delight or contemplative pleasure, a closer look provides an important clarification. Kant attributes a special meaning to 'passive' by connecting it to an 'interest', which was shown above to mean having a desire connected to an object, whether for sensory gratification or to use as a means to some end.[26] Only judgements of taste are characterised in this way because the activity of the perception is complete in itself. So, the passivity of the aesthetic response means only inactivity in respect of interest, and it does not preclude active contemplation. But just what does this active contemplation consist in? I would like to discuss the role of imagination as one aspect of this engagement to show that aesthetic attention is rarely passive and that there is no conflict between disinterestedness and participation with the aesthetic object.

Recall that for Kant, the contemplation of the aesthetic response is characterised by the 'harmonious free play of imagination and understanding'. The freedom of the mental powers here refers to freedom from cognising the object, that is, seeking determinate knowledge about it, but it also refers to the very nature of imagination's activity as free. Its activity is not constrained or directed by determinate concepts of the object. Thus Kant sets up an active role for the mind in aesthetic experience, one which involves playing with the perceptual features of both artworks and natural objects. Although he uses the term 'contemplation' to describe this mode of attention, this is no still, passive state of mind, as illustrated in these remarks:

> This pleasure is also not practical in any way . . . yet it does have a causality in it, namely to *keep* [us in] the state of [having] the presentation itself, and [to keep] the cognitive powers engaged [in their occupation] without any further aim. We *linger* in our contemplation of the beautiful, because this contemplation reinforces and reproduces itself.[27]

It is in fact this activity that gives rise to the feeling of pleasure that coincides with the judgement of taste, so the activity is characteristic of every act of aesthetic appreciation. He also gives an active role to the imagination in a particular kind of aesthetic experience, the sublime. Here imagination is active in trying to grasp the magnificent size or power of awesome natural objects, although in the end it fails to apprehend the object because it is stretched to its capacity, pushed beyond its limits. It is important to note, however, that in both cases imagination's freedom is tied to the object; there is no room for self-indulgent fantasy in Kant's account.

Kant's view of aesthetic contemplation is characterised by engaged attention rather than a blank cow-like stare, but where does this leave the subject as participant? Recall that further problems related to the first criticism were raised by feminists and sociological aestheticians, namely, the claim that the disinterested subject is abstracted from the situation and context. This problem stems from mistaken associations which are in part due to the unfortunate connotation of the terms, 'disinterestedness', 'distancing' and 'detachment'.

'Disinterestedness' is too often taken to mean indifference rather than interest or attention to aesthetic qualities alone. 'Distancing' is mistakenly coupled with the idea of creating distance (physical or otherwise) between subject and object rather than distancing oneself from desires and needs which might get in the way of appreciating the object itself. This mistake is not surprising given the conventions that hold in viewing artworks, and the physical barriers that we sometimes put between ourselves and the natural environment. 'Detachment' is understood not as setting aside utilitarian interests in relation to an object, but rather, mistakenly, as cutting oneself off from one's own experience.

Referring back to the logic of disinterestedness outlined above, these associations look misplaced. There is nothing in the concept of disinterestedness which excludes an approach that is sensitive to context, narrative and the situation of both subject and object. To show how disinterestedness can support a more embedded aesthetic, I focus first on the role of the subject and defer consideration of the aesthetic object to my response to the formalism objection. What is required here is a better understanding of exactly what aspects of the subject are precluded by disinterestedness, and I begin by considering this problem within ethics.

In the domain of human conduct, some philosophers have argued that the impartiality of Kantian disinterestedness does not entail that moral judgements are made from an abstracted standpoint.[28] To see how this might be possible, consider two different cases: the impartial juror deliberating on the innocence or guilt of the accused; and the counsellor who provides guidance as both listener and adviser. First, a juror in an armed-robbery trial acts as an impartial observer of the proceedings because she is expected not to act on personal biases towards the defendant. If the defendant is a particularly arrogant person, a juror who has a particular dislike for arrogance, and in fact mistrusts it, has a duty to background this preference, to make it irrelevant to her judgement. Nonetheless, the juror deliberates from a situated perspective rather than a view from nowhere. For example, let's say that she is a young woman with a keen eye for detail, which she will use to examine carefully the facts of the case and to make a reasonable judgement as to innocence or guilt. She herself has been robbed once and is thus able to relate to the situation of the victims, but she adds to this the fact that it must have been even more frightening for them because her assailants were not armed. She uses her own past experience to relate to the victims, yet she tells herself not to assume the guilt of the defendant out of her own fear. My example illustrates a disinterested approach to judging the situation, in which the juror judges from a position embedded in her particular experience, knowledge and ability. The concrete features of the juror are not left out of deliberation, but rather they play an essential role in her assessment of the case.

My second example shows how a disinterested perspective can be essential in the more intimate context of a counsellor–client relationship. In order to help clients with their problems, counsellors require a detailed understanding of each case which they achieve by discovering the background and needs of the client. This essential sensitivity and familiarity with the client's situation is coupled with the counsellor's own situated perspective. The counsellor is also an individual with particular experience, beliefs and needs, some of which may be absolutely essential to his expertise in this context. His experience as a supportive member to the rest of his own family may be what has enabled him to develop the particular stance he takes with all his clients, and it may also enable him to address the problems of a particular client. But alongside this we expect the counsellor to be disinterested, so that his own needs and desires do not impede his ability to help his client. His needs and desires remain a part of him, but they are not acted upon in this context. For example, a session may evoke thoughts and feelings about his relationship with his partner, yet he must set these concerns aside and work them out in his own time, unless they can be redirected away from his own concerns and used to work through the client's problem. An advantage of backgrounding needs and desires is that the counsellor is open and receptive, more able to focus on the client's needs.

The two examples show how some very individual or personal features of the subject are compatible with a disinterested standpoint, while others are deemed to interfere, and hence are set aside. Although the aesthetic stand-point does not involve the practical reasoning and deliberation of a moral agent, we can begin to see how a disinterested, embedded standpoint works in the appreciation of aesthetic qualities. When appreciating a butterfly, I am not detached from who I am in my response. I take delight in the graceful weightlessness of its flight, which may be because I delight merely in the gaiety I see expressed in the creature, or it may turn on personal associations I relate to the experience – perhaps I identify with the freedom of its flight. My own experience shapes and deepens my appreciation of the aesthetic object; it is shaped by who I am and deepened by the meanings that I attach to the object. My response, is still disinterested because although my own associations shape my response I am not preoccupied by them; I value the butterfly for its grace and beauty rather than for any end it might serve.

The potential fruitfulness of disinterestedness for the integrated aesthetic has so far been described in terms of how the subject's experience contributes to the aesthetic response, but I have yet to show how disinterestedness helps to sustain attention to the aesthetic object. This also provides the opportunity to reply to the formalism objection, which claimed that disinterestedness underpins aesthetic formalism. One source of the formalist position is Kant's claim that aesthetic judgement is unlike cognitive judgement because in aesthetic judgement we do not apply a determinate concept to an object. Rather, the aesthetic response is characterised by a feeling of pleasure in the perception of the form or appearance of an object.

However, although formalists trace their roots back to Kant, most commentators argue that he is not a formalist.[29] For example, Salim Kemal points out that one of the reasons Kant has been viewed as a formalist is that, for a long time, only that aspect of his theory had been emphasised. Advances in recent Kant scholarship show that his theory is much less narrow. A richer and less dry or empty interpretation of disinterested perception works against formalism.[30] This interpretation stresses active perception and imaginative engagement. Perception of form is accompanied by imaginative associations, and what Kant calls 'aesthetic ideas', the poetic and metaphorical ideas (described as indeterminate concepts) that arise in the free play of imagination and understanding.[31]

Paul Crowther also interprets Kant to show that it does not follow from Kant's claim that *only* form is relevant to aesthetic appreciation:

> The key *logical* significance of the pure aesthetic judgement lies in what it does *not* presuppose in order to be enjoyed. To take pleasure in the way things appear to the senses is just that. We may find that our being in a position to experience such pleasure has required a certain path through life; it may also be that a lot of factual knowledge and practical considerations impinge upon our pleasure. However, such factors are not *logical* preconditions of our enjoying beauty: they are contingent elements. We do not *have* to take account of them in appreciating formal qualities for their own sake.[32]

This points to the negative logic within Kant's aesthetic theory. Knowledge of the background of the aesthetic object, for example knowledge of the function of a whale's blowhole, is not *necessary* for appreciating the shimmering grey skin across its back. Crowther's point is useful for clarifying the logic of Kant's judgement of taste, and it suggests that contingencies such as knowledge of whale biology *could* be fed into aesthetic appreciation.

Disinterestedness and Knowledge

Disinterestedness does not go hand in hand with formalism, but how do concepts figure in this kind of appreciation? To explain this, once again, I discuss Kant's own ideas to show how robust his account in fact is, but I will also build freely upon his ideas in order to clarify a renewed understanding of disinterestedness.

I want to reiterate Kant's aim in introducing disinterestedness. It is first and foremost to distinguish different types of judgements that we make. Aesthetic judgements are not preferences, and they are not concerned with the function or purpose of an object. This means that concepts may be part of the background of appreciation, but we do not base our judgements on these determinate concepts. Aesthetic appreciation of the beauty of a rose does not arise from facts about its biological functions but simply from perceptual-imaginative reflection on its colour and form (and, in my view, its fragrance as well). That appreciation is different from scientific appreciation, for it has no aim.

Although Kant is quite clear in saying that determinate concepts do not form the basis of aesthetic experience, it does not follow that concepts such as 'rose' or 'nightingale' are absent from appreciation. This is the sense in which they may form a backdrop in the aesthetic response. Kant's point is that what it is to be a rose or a nightingale in terms of their function or purpose – facts about their existence – does not determine appreciation of beauty. Malcolm Budd supports this when he remarks that

> Although Kant often writes as though his conception of a pure
> judgment of taste requires the subject to experience an object
> without conceptualising it as being an instance of some kind – a
> requirement that would render his conception nugatory – he is aware
> that it does not: 'A judgement of taste about an object with a
> definite intrinsic purpose would be pure only if the person judging
> either had no concept of this purpose, or abstracted from it in
> making his judgement' (CJ, §16, 231).[33]

So, Kant's account does not exclude (determinate and purposive) concepts in the background.

Departing a little from Kant now, if we actually pick out knowledge, or come upon knowledge (such as reading an information board on a nature trail), we may consciously feed it in in order to supplement perception. But this is not to suggest that our appreciation is grounded in or determined in any direct way by that knowledge. Rather, the knowledge may enable an expansion of perception of aesthetic qualities.

Returning to the butterfly example, my appreciation may be shaped not only by associations I make, but also by my background knowledge of butterflies. Knowing that a butterfly emerged from a caterpillar in a cocoon may increase my appreciation of the vibrant colours if it enables me to recognise the contrast of colours before and after the metamorphosis. This knowledge is part of the story of the butterfly, yet it becomes a legitimate part of aesthetic appreciation because it adds meaning to the perceptual qualities I enjoy. But some knowledge clearly conflicts with the condition of disinterestedness. When I identify with the butterfly's free flight, thoughts may distract me from disinterested attention to the butterfly *qua* aesthetic object. For example, if I bring to the experience the knowledge that one of my siblings is not so free, but rather trapped in a painful relationship, I have used the butterfly to articulate my thoughts and feelings around something oriented towards my own needs or desires. In this way I have become preoccupied not with the beauty of the butterfly, but with concern for my sibling.

Other uses of knowledge are inconsistent with disinterestedness in cases where they shift our focus away from aesthetic appreciation. Scientific knowledge can supplement the aesthetic response, as my point about metamorphosis shows, but it can also dominate appreciation in ways that divert attention from aesthetic qualities. If I value the butterfly because it has particular qualities that make it a good specimen of its species, then I value it in virtue of biological rather than aesthetic qualities. Furthermore, even if the scientific approach is disinterested, as some have argued, it lacks what makes the disinterestedness of aesthetic appreciation valuable to nature conservation. Scientific value is grounded in wonder and curiosity and aims at acquiring knowledge, while aesthetic appreciation is grounded in the experience of aesthetic qualities, but it has no explicit aim; it is not *for* knowledge, nor *for* sensory gratification.

So far I have discussed only natural environments and objects, but what happens to disinterestedness in the context of modified landscapes, where human intentionality (and function) plays a role? In the case of agricultural landscapes, a type of cultural landscape, no inconsistency arises in claiming that the disinterested response applies in this context too. On the account I have given, knowledge or concepts may be part of the backdrop of the response. There is likely to be an implicit understanding that the land is farmed or used for grazing (something we can most likely see, and which would be commonsense knowledge in most cultures). Upon observing non-aesthetic qualities of furrows in a field (and therefore assuming it is agricultural land), we may perceive it as fertile and bountiful. But in this case and others, we do not require a concept of the purpose of the object for our aesthetic judgement. Also, when we appreciate objects with both natural and artefactual origins (those standing outside the artworld), it does not appear to involve making a direct connection between an aesthetic quality and its creator.

My discussion here in some ways reflects Kant's discussion of 'free' and 'dependent' beauty. Without digressing into the debate concerning problems with his distinction, let me consider a few relevant points. Kant recognises that aesthetic appreciation of natural things is not governed by a concept of what the object is meant to be. One would assume that free beauties are natural things and dependent beauties are not, but this is not so. Free beauties include birds, but also some types of design, and music without words. Dependent beauties include architecture, but also horses and human beings.[34] Aesthetic judgements of dependent beauties may be conditioned by a concept of what the object is intended to be.[35] As Henry Allison puts it, 'this concept functions as an external, that is, extra-aesthetic, constraint or condition on what may properly be deemed beautiful'.[36] However, according to Allison's interpretation, the judgement remains aesthetic and therefore disinterested, if less 'pure', because although a dependent beauty is constrained by its function, 'this function does not become the determining ground of the aesthetic liking itself'.[37]

Kant's ideas help in understanding how differences between nature and artefact affect aesthetic appreciation, and how our judgements continue to be disinterested. As we move along the spectrum towards urban environments (including some environmental artworks and gardens), a concept of what the object is meant to be does not determine appreciation, but it pushes itself more into the foreground of appreciation. In more formal gardens, where design is apparent, such as in the sculpted bushes of topiary, we cannot help but see nature under an artefactual aspect. In cases of highly artefactual environmental artworks (many are not), here too our appreciation is more conditioned by experiencing environment as artistically modified. Christo's pink-cellophane wrapped islands (*Surrounded Islands*, 1983) comes to mind here.

With art and architecture, although not always necessary, we may find that knowing the artist's or architect's aims or the function of a particular building helps us to locate expressive qualities, for example, or meanings connected to perceptual qualities. Appreciation can still be characterised as disinterested, if the much richer, non-formalist interpretation I have developed is upheld. As Kemal argues:

> the aesthetic judgement can bring in all the factors of social and
> political background, the place of the work in the history of arts, the
> intentions of the artist, and so on, without deriving conclusions
> about the validity of his judgement from any of these factors . . .
> Thus, this work continues to be the focus of his attention, and his

judgement on the work will be about the meaning, order and significance of the parts of the work, and so will consider the work itself, clarifying it by reference to the background.[38]

I have argued that disinterestedness is a central feature of the integrated aesthetic, and that it applies to more natural environments, including some types of cultural landscapes. My claims may also apply to art, but it is not my intention to make a case for that here.

DISINTERESTEDNESS AND VALUING NATURE

My discussion of disinterestedness shows that it can support a more open and less rigid type of aesthetic appreciation, where the situation of appreciation is embedded rather than superficial or formal. I have provided a picture of what disinterestedness *includes*, rather than what it excludes. It is not merely a concept that works negatively to set the logical parameters of aesthetic judgement, but it also works positively to encourage open receptivity to aesthetic qualities because it frees up the mind from personal preoccupations.

Disinterestedness characterises attention directed outwards rather than inwards. Iris Murdoch eloquently expresses this selfless way of seeing things:

> I am looking out of my window in an anxious and resentful state of mind, oblivious of my surroundings, brooding perhaps on some damage done to my prestige. Then suddenly, I observe a hovering kestrel. In a moment everything is altered. The brooding self with its hurt vanity has disappeared. There is nothing left but kestrel. And when I return to thinking of the other matter it seems less important.[39]

She illustrates how we can be drawn in by natural objects and become engaged so thoroughly in perception that their qualities pull us out of ourselves.

The positive value of disinterestedness is echoed in aesthetic theories after Kant. Schopenhauer is perhaps best known for characterising how aesthetic experience releases us from the ceaseless striving of the will. Disinterested aesthetic appreciation is a state of will-lessness in which we are cut off from desire and fully absorbed by the object:

> [we] sink ourselves completely therein, and let our whole consciousness be filled by the calm contemplation of the natural object actually present, whether it be a landscape, a tree, a rock, a crag, a building, or anything else. We *lose* ourselves entirely in this

object, to use a pregnant expression; in other words, we forget our individuality, our will, and continue to exist only as pure subject, as clear mirror of the object, so it is as though the object alone existed without anyone to perceive it, and thus we are no longer able to separate the perceiver from the perception, but the two have become one, since the entire consciousness is filled and occupied by a single image of perception.[40]

Schopenhauer presents perhaps the extreme of disinterested perception, where we nearly become one with the object. In any case, this passage suggests how disinterestedness enables object-directed appreciation.

In the early 1930s, Dewey explicitly argued against Kantian theories of beauty and disinterestedness; nevertheless his account of aesthetic perception is interestingly similar to the focused perception facilitated by disinterestedness:

Not absence of desire and thought but their thorough incorporation into perceptual experience characterizes esthetic experience, in its distinction from experiences that are especially 'intellectual' or 'practical' . . . The esthetic percipient is free from desire in the presence of a sunset, a cathedral, or a bouquet of flowers in the sense that his desires are fulfilled in the perception itself. He does not want the object for the sake of something else.[41]

Later, he says, 'Perception is so thorough-going that the work of art is detached or cut off from the kind of specialized desire that operates when we are moved to consume a thing physically.'[42] Dewey does not deny that desire is related to aesthetic experience, but he reframes its role. All of these views show how disinterestedness allows us to become absorbed with the qualities of the object before us. This underlines how aesthetic experience of nature involves immersion rather than spectatorship, and a grasp of the object's situation through attention to its qualities.

Disinterestedness as the basis of aesthetic appreciation defines a standpoint that backgrounds the concerns of self-interest and utility in relation to nature and foregrounds its aesthetic qualities as valuable in their own right. Against the claims of the blank cow-like stare and formalism objections, I have shown that this standpoint does not entail abstraction from every aspect of individual experience, nor from the context in which the aesthetic object is situated. Instead, it supports appreciation that is sensitive to the particularities of the experience and works positively to shift focus away from the self and towards aesthetic qualities for their own sake, rather than as a means to fulfilling some personal or practical goal.

In this way, disinterestedness supports a less human-centred approach to aesthetic appreciation of nature. We have seen that aesthetic valuing, like other types of valuing, depends upon the human subject. But in particular, aesthetic appreciation is relational, since aesthetic qualities depend upon the subject's perceptual capacities as well as qualities of the object. For this reason, aesthetic valuing has been viewed as either anthropocentric or hedonistic, but as a central feature of the integrated aesthetic, disinterestedness precludes hedonistic valuing.

Also, it becomes clearer how disinterestedness characterises valuing of nature that achieves a degree of distance, but does not detach us from features of ourselves and nature that enable us to become aesthetically intimate with it. Aesthetic appreciation in this sense may be akin to friendship that evolves into a close relationship with some degree of intimacy while at the same time maintaining enough distance to allow others to be themselves.

Finally, it should not be surprising that a disinterested, integrated aesthetic potentially supports an environmental ethics characterised by respect and care (disinterestedness, after all, originated in moral philosophy). Respect is a moral concept that depends upon allowing the other to be who they are, without using them as a means to one's ends. Aesthetic and moral values are distinct, but each type of valuing may complement the other for developing an appropriate attitude towards the natural environment.[43]

NOTES

1. On a general level, as much as possible I set aside his metaphysical and epistemological architectonic. I am sympathetic to his philosophical system, but it would be inappropriate to launch into a critical discussion of it here, so it is best to leave it.
2. Kant calls sublime feeling an emotion, but he never elaborates on this point in the *Critique of Judgment*, so it is very difficult to know where he actually stands. Henry Allison provides some explanation in a note in, *Kant's Theory of Taste: A Reading of the Critique of Aesthetic Judgment* (Cambridge: Cambridge University Press, 2001), p. 399n.
3. One exception is the expression of 'joyfulness and contentment' of a bird's song, but Kant mentions this only in passing, and it could be read more as symbolic than emotional expression. See my further discussion of aesthetic ideas in the section on imagination in Chapter 6. See Immanuel Kant, *Critique of Judgment*, trans. Werner Pluhar (Indianapolis: Hackett, 1987), §42, Ak. 300, p. 168.
4. Tranquillity has been cited by visitors to natural areas as the second most important aesthetic feature they enjoy (the first is scenic beauty). John Andrew Fisher provides an interesting explanation and argument for why we appear to have a preference for natural over artefactual sounds. See John Andrew Fisher, 'The Value of Natural Sounds', *Journal of Aesthetic Education: Symposium on Natural Aesthetics*, 33:3, 1999, pp. 26–42; John Andrew Fisher, 'What the Hills Are Alive With: In Defense of the Sounds of Nature', *Journal of Aesthetics and Art Criticism*, 56:2, 1998, pp. 167–80.

5. Fisher, 1999, pp. 34–6.
6. Fisher, 1998, p. 168.
7. Diane Ackerman, *A Natural History of the Senses* (New York: Vintage, 1990), pp. 80–1. Cheryl Foster has also written about the rich aesthetic experience of texture in 'Texture: Old Material, Fresh Novelty', in Pauline von Bonsdorff and Arto Haapala (eds), *Aesthetics in the Human Environment*, International Institute of Applied Aesthetics Series, vol. 6 (Jyväskylä: Gummerus, 1999), pp. 48–68.
8. This view has been held by Aquinas, Kant, Hegel and some recent philosophers such as Roger Scruton. See Aquinas, *Summa Theologiae* (Oxford and London: Blackfriars with Eyre and Spottiswoode, 1963–75); Kant, *Critique of Judgment*; G. F. W. Hegel, *Aesthetics: Lectures on Fine Art*, trans. T. M. Knox (Oxford: Clarendon Press, 1975), vol. 1, p. 35; Roger Scruton, *The Aesthetics of Architecture* (London: Methuen, 1979), pp. 113–15. For Kant, tastes and smells belong to the realm of the 'agreeable'. In his distinction between the beautiful and the agreeable, the beautiful involves disinterested contemplation of an object's form or appearance, while the agreeable involves interest and merely what 'the senses like in sensation', and so it is not disinterested and not contemplative. The agreeable also lacks the imaginative engagement of the contemplation of the beautiful (*Critique of Judgment*, §3, Ak 205–7, pp. 47–8). Kant's view assumes that there must be something more than mere sensation; there must be some form or structure in an object in order for it to give rise to an aesthetic judgement (§14, Ak. 224–5, pp. 70–1). This assumption becomes more explicit when Kant dismisses colour alone as a proper object of aesthetic contemplation, as well as single tones of music. If smells and tastes lack structure, like colours, they can never be included in the category of aesthetic objects. But these claims rest on a limited concept of aesthetic objects, and it can be shown that smells and tastes exhibit structure, and go beyond mere sensation in their appreciation, to include associations and imagination.
9. Emily Brady, 'Sniffing and Savoring: The Aesthetics of Smells and Tastes', in Andrew Light and Jonathan M. Smith (eds), *The Aesthetics of Everyday Life* (New York: Seven Bridges Press, 2002). For other discussion of smells and tastes in aesthetics, see Frank Sibley, 'Tastes, Smells, and Aesthetics', in John Benson, Betty Redfern and Jeremy Roxbee Cox (eds), *Approach to Aesthetics: Collected Papers on Philosophical Aesthetics* (Oxford: Oxford University Press, 2001), pp. 207–55; Carolyn Korsmeyer, *Making Sense of Taste: Food and Philosophy* (Ithaca: Cornell University Press, 1999).
10. Brady, 2002.
11. Kant, §2.
12. I follow Paul Guyer's interpretation here when he defines Kant's notion of 'interest' as 'a conception of an object which furnishes an incentive for the will, or as a conception of an object and its relation to the subject whereby the faculty of desire is determined to seek its realization'. Paul Guyer, *Kant and the Claims of Taste* (Cambridge, MA, and London: Harvard University Press, 1979), p. 187.
13. Kant also connects 'interest' to being concerned about the 'real existence' of the object. This is an odd way of putting it, but interpretations show that it means having an interest in the object that is determined by concepts of its utility or its goodness (or more generally, its 'empirical existence'). See Guyer, 1979, p. 183ff.; Henry Allison, *Kant's Theory of Taste* (Cambridge: Cambridge University Press, 2001), ch. 4; Paul Crowther, 'The Significance of Kant's Pure Aesthetic Judgement', *British Journal of Aesthetics*, 36:2, 1996, p. 111; Salim Kemal, *Kant's Aesthetic Theory*, 2nd

edn (New York: St Martin's Press, 1997, p. 38ff.). This interpretation is supported further when Kant says that the judgement of taste is a free liking, in which what matters is 'not the [respect] in which I depend upon the object's existence' (Kant, §2, Ak. 205, p. 46).

14. Kant, §5, Ak. 210, p. 52.

15. Disinterestedness also plays a role in other aesthetic attitude theories, such as Edward Bullough's theory of 'psychical distance', and Roger Scruton's neo-Kantian aesthetics. See David Fenner, *The Aesthetic Attitude* (Atlantic Highlands: Humanities Press, 1996); and Roger Scruton *Art and Imagination* (London: Methuen, 1974). Gary Kemp and Oswald Hanfling have also reconsidered, in favourable terms, the notions of disinterestedness and distancing, respectively. See Kemp, 'The Aesthetic Attitude', *British Journal of Aesthetics*, 39:4, 1999, pp. 392–9; and Hanfling, 'Five Kinds of Distance', *British Journal of Aesthetics*, 40:1, 2000, pp. 89–102. Since I am not putting forward an aesthetic attitude theory, criticisms of disinterestedness as defining a special kind of attitude are not relevant to my discussion.

16. Ronald Hepburn, 'Contemporary Aesthetics and the Neglect of Natural Beauty', *Wonder and Other Essays* (Edinburgh: Edinburgh University Press, 1984) pp. 13; 21, and *The Reach of the Aesthetic: Collected Essays on Art and Nature* (Aldershot and Burlington, VT: Ashgate, 2001), pp. 133–4.

17. Allen Carlson, 'Aesthetics and Engagement', *British Journal of Aesthetics*, 33:3, 1993, pp. 220–7, and Allen Carlson, *Aesthetics and the Environment: The Appreciation of Nature, Art and Architecture* (London and New York: Routledge, 2000). He makes some of the same points as I do in defence of disinterestedness.

18. Berleant has raised criticisms of disinterestedness and traditional aesthetic theory in many of his writings, but see especially, 'Beyond Disinterestedness', *British Journal of Aesthetics*, 34:3, 1994, pp. 242–54.

19. Examples from aesthetics include: Friedrich Nietzsche, *On the Genealogy of Morals*, trans. Walter Kaufmann (New York: Vintage Books, 1969); John Dewey, *Art as Experience* (New York: Perigee, [1934] 1980), p. 252ff.; Richard Shusterman, *Pragmatist Aesthetics: Living Beauty, Rethinking Art* (Oxford: Blackwell, 1992), pp. 8–10; Berleant, 1994; David Novitz, *The Boundaries of Art* (Philadelphia: Temple University Press, 1992), p. 64ff.; Noël Carroll, *Philosophy of Art* (London and New York: Routledge, 1999), pp. 182–9. From sociological aesthetics, for example, see Pierre Bourdieu, *Distinction: A Social Critique of the Judgement of Taste* (London and New York: Routledge and Kegan Paul, 1984). From feminist philosophy and aesthetics, for example, see Christine Battersby, 'Situating the Aesthetic: A Feminist Defence', in Andrew Benjamin and Peter Osborne (eds), *Thinking Art: Beyond Traditional Aesthetics* (London: ICA, 1991), p. 35ff.; and *Gender and Genius: Towards a Feminist Aesthetics* (London: Women's Press, 1989). George Dickie criticises aesthetic attitude theories, in which disinterestedness plays a role, in 'The Myth of the Aesthetic Attitude', *American Philosophical Quarterly*, 1:3, 1964; pp. 56–66. There are also critiques of the abstraction associated with disinterestedness in ethics. These are too numerous to list here, but one worth noting because it combines both a feminist and environmental point of view is Val Plumwood's *Feminism and the Mastery of Nature* (London and New York: Routledge, 1993), p. 169ff.

20. Bullough's concept of 'psychical distance' may be partly responsible for the association of disinterestedness with distancing, but Bullough also never intended to suggest a passive, detached experience. One meaning of Bullough's concept is quite useful, where distancing simply means turning our attention away from the practical aspects

of a thing, and instead attending to aesthetic qualities. This is certainly very similar to what Kant had in mind with his use of 'disinterestedness'. See Edward Bullough, ' "Psychical Distance", as a Factor in Art and an Aesthetic Principle', *British Journal of Psychology*, V, 1912, pp. 87–117; and Hanfling, pp. 89–91.

21. Clive Bell, *Art* (London: Chatto and Windus, 1931), p. 72.

22. 'Significant form' is exclusive to Bell's formalism. His formalism applies only to art and not to nature.

23. Noël Carroll, 'Clive Bell's Aesthetic Hypothesis', in George Dickie, Richard Sclafani and Ronald Roblin (eds), *Aesthetics: A Critical Anthology*, 2nd edn (New York: St Martin's Press, 1989), p. 87.

24. Paul Crowther, *Critical Aesthetics and Postmodernism* (Oxford: Clarendon Press, 1993), p. x.

25. Jerome Stolnitz, 'On the Origins of "Aesthetic Disinterestedness"', *Journal of Aesthetics and Art Criticism*, 20, 1961, pp. 132–3.

26. Immanuel Kant, *Metaphysics of Morals*, in *Ethical Philosophy*, trans. James Ellington (Indianapolis: Hackett, 1983), p. 10.

27. Kant, 1987, §12, Ak. 222, p. 68. Translator's brackets.

28. See, for example, Barbara Herman, *The Practice of Moral Judgment* (Cambridge, MA, and London: Harvard University Press, 1993), pp. 184–207; Onora O'Neill, *Constructions of Reason* (Cambridge: Cambridge University Press, 1989), pp. 145–62.

29. See Kemal, pp. 145–51; Eva Schaper, *Studies in Kant's Aesthetics* (Edinburgh: Edinburgh University Press, 1979), p.78ff.; Crowther, 1993, p. 56ff.; Anthony Savile, *Kantian Aesthetics Pursued* (Edinburgh: Edinburgh University Press, 1993), ch. 5. Henry Allison interprets the formalist strand in Kant's thought quite broadly, and argues not only for its compatibility with the content that comes through aesthetic ideas, but he also claims that form and the expression of aesthetic ideas are mutually dependent upon each other. See Allison, pp. 286–90.

30. Kemal, p. 111.

31. Ibid. pp. 44–5. Kemal and others have pointed out that aesthetic ideas arise in both appreciation of art and nature for Kant.

32. Crowther, 1996, p. 112.

33. Malcolm Budd, 'Delight in the Natural World: Kant on the Aesthetic Appreciation of Nature. Part I: Natural Beauty', *British Journal of Aesthetics*, 38:1, 1998, p. 4n.

34. Kant, 1987, §16.

35. They are not necessarily so conditioned, since Kant thinks it's possible to abstract from the concept in one's judgement. See Kant, 1987, §16, Ak. 231, p. 78.

36. Allison, p. 139.

37. Ibid. p. 141. Kemal makes a similar interpretation in Kemal, pp. 145–51.

38. Kemal, p. 50.

39. Iris Murdoch, *The Sovereignty of the Good* (London: Routledge, [1970] 1991), p. 84.

40. Arthur Schopenhauer, *The World as Will and Representation, Volume 1*, trans. E. F. J. Payne (New York: Dover, 1969), pp. 178–9.

41. Dewey, p. 254.

42. Ibid. p. 258.

43. See Chapter 8.

CHAPTER 6

The Integrated Aesthetic II: Imagination, Emotion and Knowledge

In the last chapter two fundamental elements of the integrated aesthetic were examined: perception of sensuous qualities and disinterestedness. In this chapter, I examine those elements that are more oriented towards content in our aesthetic responses to the natural world: imagination, emotion and knowledge. The imaginative and affective components build upon the sensuous to broaden and deepen aesthetic engagement. The integrated aesthetic also makes room for knowledge, although as I have emphasised, it is not given a major role, but is fed into appreciation where appropriate, as I shall explain.

IMAGINATION

Why Imagination?

One might assume that imagination has more to do with the creation and experience of art than with the appreciation of nature. Imagination is a humanistic concept – the hallmark of human creativity and genius in both the arts and sciences. When we deal with works of art we approach them as products of a human imagination, and when we enjoy works of art, one of the things we are trying to do is to unlock their imaginative content. However, imagination has a place in many other human endeavours and experiences. It is present in all sorts of contexts, for example, when we envisage possibilities, bring to mind a person or thing that is absent from perception, and when we attempt to identify with another person's feelings. In other words, imagination is not a capacity defined by our engagement with the arts, rather, it is a capacity we bring from the everyday into the aesthetic domain. While imagination may be most fully exercised within the aesthetic domain, it does not originate there.

Indeed, several philosophers have argued that our very experience of the world presupposes imagination. Although I think this may be true, I am not prepared to make a case for it here. What I do claim is that imagination is present in a range of human experiences, and art is only one of them.

If this point is accepted, then one can begin to grasp how imagination may be present in our encounters with the natural environment – and most explicitly in our aesthetic encounters. Both Kant and Hepburn argue that imagination has a significant role in aesthetic appreciation of nature. For Kant, imagination is central in aesthetic judgements of nature. It frees the mind from the constraints of intellectual and practical interests and enables a play of associations and creative reflection in relation to nature's qualities. Hepburn's ideas resound Kant's, but Hepburn also wants to highlight imagination's power to 'shift attention flexibly from aspect to aspect of the natural objects before one, to shift focus from close-up to long shot, from textural detail to overall atmospheric haze or radiance; to overcome stereotyped grouping and clichéd ways of seeing'.[1] Imagination enables us to adopt several different perspectives, as well as entirely new ones. It gives us ways to reach beyond stereotyped modes of appreciating environments: to come afresh to familiar or everyday environments and to locate previously undiscovered qualities. Heyd makes a similar point when he argues that we can overcome aesthetic boredom or fatigue 'by increasing the contrast in our perceptual experience, and, generally, by enhancing the possibilities for the play of imagination', which is partly achieved by integrating various non-scientific stories of the land into appreciation.[2] Essentially, imagination facilitates free play, a creative approach to appreciation that leads to the discovery of aesthetic qualities.

By bringing a range of experience and ideas to bear on perception, imagination contributes to the meaning and context of aesthetic objects, and to situating ourselves in relation to them. It opens up new relations and connections and adds to the context of appreciation. Contrary to Kant's position, I do not believe that imagination is a necessary condition of aesthetic experience. In some cases aesthetic objects will not evoke imagination, and sometimes we may simply rely on perceptual capacities and just engage the senses. Some imaginations are less developed than others, which is also a factor in limiting its role. But when imagination is active, it opens up the aesthetic horizon and deepens the aesthetic response. As an important component of the integrated aesthetic, it has the potential to encourage a more intimate engagement with our natural surroundings.

What is Imagination?

Imagination is a notoriously difficult concept for philosophical analysis. Peter Strawson draws on remarks by Hume and Kant when he says that it is the 'concealed art of the soul, a magical faculty, something we shall never fully understand'.[3] Many philosophers have tried to uncover its workings, but in the history of philosophy it is typically cast aside as an unruly, irrational power that creates fictions and misleading representations of reality rather than truth. Because imagination is commonly associated with fancy, fantasy, daydreams and the like, it is treated as a capacity that must be kept in check by reason. Apparently, Descartes gave up reading fables because they 'make one imagine many events possible which in reality are not so'.[4] That view now seems rather old-fashioned, but there is nevertheless some remaining suspicion in recent philosophy. Although the existentialists lauded imagination for its capacity to construct creatively the self (as if a work of art), and to live 'poetically', at the same time they were wary that a life of imagination could become a life of illusion, where we no longer face our responsibilities as free human beings. The work of some contemporary philosophers has contributed to restoring imagination's reputation, but much work has yet to be done.[5] A careful, better understanding is needed of the various activities of imagination.

I cannot tackle such a project here, but I want to make a few clarifications about this distinctive mental power before turning to a discussion of its role in aesthetic appreciation of the environment. My aim is to show that imagination is in fact a very broad concept, fantasy being only one of its many modes of activity. Imagination is not opposed to truth; a proper understanding of its relationship to truth will enable a better grasp of the real value of this mental power.

Theories of imagination typically divide its modes into two categories: sensory imagination and creative imagination.[6] Sensory imagination is the mental power that makes our experience of objects coherent by 'bridging the gap' between concepts and sense perceptions. This category includes imagination's power to bring together past and present perceptions of the same object, and its imaging role in connection to memory and recollection. These modes of imagination have been referred to as 'reproductive imagination' because imagination 'reproduces' past perceptions as images that facilitate the identification of an object of a present perception.[7] This category also includes mental images that do not involve creativity or invention.

The second category, creative imagination, describes the creative power responsible for reaching beyond the ordinary. The most obvious modes which display creativity are those in which we use imagination to entertain possibilities, to be inventive, to solve difficult problems – scientific, moral, artistic or to create fantastic scenarios such as those of make-believe and daydreams. These various activities have been referred to as the 'productive imagination' because imagination's activity is not mimetic, but poetic. Imagination enables us to reach beyond the given by bringing together the elements of experience in novel ways so that we can, for example, imaginatively transform ourselves into a trees swaying in the wind; imagine a better alternative to a harmful practice; or envisage life on a planet without an atmosphere such as earth's.

Dewey recognised that creative imagination spans all experience, aesthetic and non-aesthetic alike. It brings meaning into experience, which emerges from the interaction of live creature with environment. Within experience itself, it presents new possibilities, a departure from the ordinary or habitual. Although imaginative activity is heightened in art and crucial to it, it is a capacity exercised in everyday encounters and in technical invention.[8] In the context of art, Dewey is careful to distinguish between the 'imaginative' and the 'imaginary', where the imaginary is equated with mere fancy, and 'mind and material do not squarely meet and interpenetrate. Mind stays aloof for the most part and toys with material rather than boldly grasping it.'[9]

There is no doubt that imagination's many activities range from the serious to the trivial. Artistic creativity and technical invention lean towards the serious. The imaginative leaps underlying scientific discovery are also serious. Moral philosophers, at least as far back as Hume, have extolled our capacity to imagine what it is like to be in another person's situation in order to determine better one's own course of action. What should not be overlooked, however, is that the creative, inventive and transformative power of creative imagination is behind more trivial activities as well as these more serious ones. The power to reach beyond the given, to bring the not-present together with the present, is also what marks the freedom of mind to imagine oneself on a desert island instead of in the office marking essays. Disclosing the value of creative imagination in aesthetic experience requires not that we condemn its very powers, but that we distinguish between the imaginative and the imaginary, relevant and irrelevant imaginings, and find the right balance between the serious and trivial. I shall say more about this below, when I defend imagination against some of its critics within environmental aesthetics.

Although imagination's greatest power is its capacity to reach beyond the beliefs and knowledge that we rely upon for day-to-day living, it does not follow that imagination is unrelated to these. Imagination depends upon our beliefs about the world. Putting yourself in someone else's shoes begins with a set of beliefs about that person's situation and proceeds by entertaining beliefs about her or his possible behaviour or state of mind. Imagining a pink polka-dotted elephant begins from the belief that elephants are normally uniformly grey, and the imagining has no meaning unless it is contrasted with what is actually the case. When we imagine p, the pink polka-dotted elephant, we entertain the belief that p, while also having the belief that not-p (that is, the belief that elephants are not actually pink polka-dotted). Having a false belief and accepting it as true are distinct from entertaining a false belief through imagination.

Roger Scruton conceives of imagination as a rational activity that is not reducible to fantasy or whim:

Imagination is not simply producing descriptions of an object which one is unprepared to assert. It involves thinking of these descriptions as appropriate in some way to the primary object. Imagination is a rational activity. The man who imagines is trying to produce an account of something, and is, therefore, trying to relate his thoughts to their subject-matter: he is constructing a narrative, and to do this it is not sufficient merely to go beyond what is already 'given'. It is necessary that he should attempt to bring what he says or thinks into relation with the subject: his thoughts must be entertained because of their 'appropriateness'.[10]

Scruton's point also emphasises how imagination works along lines of relevance rather than complete arbitrariness.

In cases where imagination operates at an extreme, we lose contact with our beliefs: obsessive fans believe that a rock star is singing about them, rather than just about anyone in love. Sometimes imagination leads to delusion, but such cases are generally exceptional, and rare in our aesthetic encounters. Even when engrossed in a novel or a film we maintain aesthetic distance; imagination enables us to engage with fictional events and characters but we do not believe they are real. This is due to both the conventions of aesthetic appreciation, and the way the qualities of the artwork direct our imaginings.

Although, as a creative power, imagination is distinct from knowledge, some philosophers have argued that it supports our intellectual endeavours. We are already familiar with its role in science, where it allows for the freedom of mind that leads to new insights and discoveries. The constructive and narrative capacities of imagination are highlighted by Collingwood, who makes a fascinating case for the essential role of imaginative re-enactment in the service of historical knowledge. Imagination, distinct from knowledge on the one hand and fancy on the other, 'does the entire work of historical construction'.[11] In the context of aesthetics, David Novitz argues for 'romantic realism', in which imagination is required for the acquisition and growth of knowledge in the most basic sense. It is also essential to the creation of literature and metaphor, which themselves contribute to the acquisition of knowledge.[12]

IMAGINATION AND NATURAL ENVIRONMENTS

I now turn to a consideration of imagination's particular role in aesthetic appreciation of environments. In comparison to other components of the integrated aesthetic, my discussion of imagination is in more depth, but this is not to suggest that it necessarily has a more dominant role. Imaginative activity in aesthetic appreciation admits of degrees. While in most cases imagination (working along relevant lines) enhances appreciation, aesthetic qualities may be appreciated in many cases without using imagination. The degree to which imagination is active depends upon individual appreciator, the nature of the aesthetic object and the aesthetic situation itself. More space is devoted to the topic here because I would like to redress misunderstandings of this important capacity in environmental aesthetics discussion and reply to some criticisms of my position as it was originally set out in my article, 'Imagination and the Aesthetic Appreciation of Nature'.[13] Also, although some writers have given it attention, imagination remains a largely unexplored problem in this area of aesthetics. That we use imagination when viewing paintings, listening to music, or reading poetry is undisputed, but even here some aestheticians have disputed the proper role of imagination.[14]

Kant's View of Imagination

Kant's view of imagination in the aesthetic response, although somewhat vague, provides a starting point for understanding how imagination is active. Although also present in cognitive judgements, 'productive imagination' is exercised to its fullest in the judgements of taste that characterise the aesthetic response. In judgements of taste, imagination is engaged in a free, harmonious play with the understanding. In contrast to its activity in cognitive judgements where it submits to the laws of the understanding, in aesthetic judgements imagination is free from these laws. More specifically, imagination does not function to support the understanding in the application of a concept to the object. This description of the relationship between the two powers is one way that Kant shows that there is no cognitive aim in aesthetic judgement.

In its free play, imagination makes connections and associations in relation to the object's qualities for their own sake. However, imagination does not have an entirely free rein; Kant is not putting forward imagination as 'fancy', the power behind fantasy. Although free from the laws of the understanding, imagination operates within a relationship with the understanding and the very basic concepts of cognition. Imagination's trajectory is constrained by the manifold of the object but not by any determinate concept of it.[15] We could say that imagination's activity is choreographed to some extent via the perception of qualities in objects.

While the free play of imagination is necessary for aesthetic judgements, imagination is given a less murky role by Kant in the production of 'aesthetic ideas':

by an aesthetic idea I mean a presentation of the imagination which
prompts much thought, but to which no determinate thought
whatsoever, i.e., no [determinate] concept, can be adequate, so that
no language can express it completely and allow us to grasp it.[16]

In the imaginative expression of aesthetic ideas, it is poetic, metaphorical and
symbolic images or associations that give content to our aesthetic reflection.
Here, imagination is explicitly creative, as it presents a host of 'kindred
presentations', and reaches beyond the limits of rational language.[17] Here too,
although at the height of its productive powers, imagination is not free to do
whatever it pleases. In Kemal's words:

> [T]he indeterminate use of concepts sustains a free play of the
> faculties. These concepts proceed by associations of ideas, metaphor,
> metonymy, and catachresis, and do not follow causal determinations,
> ordered into a system of scientific knowledge, as a standard. Rather,
> we use reason to guide the associations into a theme – an aesthetic
> idea – which we explore through association of ideas. No exactness
> according to causal factors or 'particular rule of cognition' is at issue
> here, though we may refine and direct associations of ideas to their
> theme.[18]

Kant's discussion of aesthetic ideas is primarily in the realm of fine art and
genius, specifically poetry, but aesthetic ideas are also expressed in relation to
natural beauty.[19] In the same discussion where he claims that natural beauty
has superiority over art, he says that we may find in 'the beautiful in nature
. . . a voluptuousness for the mind in a train of thought that we can never fully
unravel'.[20] Natural beauty is a symbol of morality (through nature's moral
purposiveness), but although he gives several examples, he does not elaborate
on the ways that nature expresses aesthetic ideas.[21]

> Thus a lily's white color seems to attune the mind to ideas of
> innocence, and the seven colors [of the spectrum], from red to violet,
> [similarly seem to attune it, respectively, to the ideas of] (1)
> sublimity, (2) courage, (3) candor, (4) friendliness, (5) modesty, (6)
> constancy, and (7) tenderness.[22]

> . . . beautiful objects of nature or of art are often called names that
> seem to presuppose that we are judging [these objects] morally. We
> call buildings or trees majestic and magnificent, or landscapes
> cheerful and gay; even colors are called innocent, humble, or tender
> because they arouse sensations in us that are somehow analogous to

the consciousness we have in the mental state produced by moral judgments.[23]

These examples have been interpreted as moral-aesthetic images but aside from this they are clearly products of imagination. They are the sorts of imaginative associations we might be inclined to make when perceiving expressive qualities in natural objects or landscapes.

Metaphorical Imagination

Kant's discussion of aesthetic ideas is suggestive not only of associative imagination, but also metaphorical imagination. The metaphorical imagining underlying metaphors involves bringing together two different things in novel ways – an aesthetic object or aspect of it is fused with some image that is not an image of that object nor an image of another instance of that object.[24] Working with language (and not necessarily with mental images), imagination creates a novel connection between the different semantic relations that constitute a metaphor. To borrow Carlson's example of a geological feature in the American South-west (mentioned in Tony Hillerman's mystery novels), if we say, 'Ship Rock is a free form gothic cathedral,' we speak metaphorically.[25] We are not, of course, saying that a cathedral actually exists there, just as in our nominal description we are not saying that a ship actually exists in the desert. In using imagination to make a novel connection, we work from our experience of the qualities of one thing and work towards a creative comparison to another thing. 'Ship Rock is a free form gothic cathedral' is a metaphorical expression used to capture the character of a massive protuberance of complex forms which rises towards the sky out of the flat desert. The jagged forms are reminiscent of the pointy parts of towers and detail in Gothic cathedrals.

The metaphorical connection made here is not arbitrary. The two objects' forms resemble one another, and the sheer scale of Ship Rock is reminiscent of the scale of a great cathedral which dwarfs buildings around it. More importantly, the imaginative description, when we read it in a novel or when someone says it while in the landscape itself, accentuates and draws attention to the perceptual qualities of the object. We pick out the pointiness more clearly, or begin to notice the contrast between the rounded end section and the taller, pointier sections of the shape. Metaphorical descriptions are used readily in our aesthetic responses; they help us to make sense of what we see. Not only do they direct appreciation, but they also succeed in offering images of other things for comparison, and work both to refine and enrich our apprehension of aesthetic qualities.

Exploratory Imagination

Besides the novel connections and relations made through associative and metaphorical imagination, I identify four additional modes of imaginative activity in relation to nature: *exploratory*, *projective*, *ampliative* and *revelatory* imagination.[26] There is some overlap between Kant's ideas on imagination, the activity of metaphorical imagining and the variety of modes I set out below. Also, I should point out that we use none, some, or all of these modes in appreciation, as our responses range from imaginatively thin to imaginatively thick, depending on the aesthetic object and the imagination of the appreciator.

Exploratory imagination is the most deeply tied to perception of the various modes we use. Here, imagination follows the lead of perception and explores the various perceptual qualities and relationships between qualities as we attend to the aesthetic object. While perception does much of the work in simply taking in the various features of the object and cordoning it off in our perceptual field, imagination reaches beyond this in a free contemplation of the object. As imagination brings meanings to bear on perceptual qualities, we identify aesthetic qualities and broaden our grasp of the object. In this way exploratory imagination helps the appreciator to make an initial discovery of aesthetic qualities. For example, in contemplating the bark of a locust tree, visually, I see the deep clefts between the thick ridges of the bark. Images of mountains and valleys come to mind, and I think of the age of the tree, given the thickness of the ridges and how they are spaced apart. I walk around the tree, feeling the wide circumference of the bark. The image of a seasoned old man comes to mind, with deep wrinkles from age. These imaginings lead to an aesthetic judgement of the tree as stalwart, and I respect it as I might a wise old sage. My interpretation of the locust tree is tied to its non-aesthetic qualities, such as the texture of the bark, and the associations spawned by perceptual qualities.

Another feature of the exploratory mode is that imagination sometimes undeliberately searches for unity in a scene where perception is unequal to the task. Imagination may struggle to bring together the various aspects of a moor which stretch beyond sight by supplying missing detail or filling in what is not seen, such as images of the landscape beyond the horizon. (Although I am specifying an environmental context, this activity is also common in the appreciation of naturalistic paintings, when we imaginatively 'fill in' the space beyond the edges of the canvas.)

Projective Imagination

Projective imagination draws on imagination's projective powers. Projection involves imagining 'on to' what is perceived, such that what is actually there is somehow replaced with or overlaid by a projected image. In this way projective imagination is associated with deliberate 'seeing as', where we intentionally, not mistakenly, see something as another thing. We put 'seeing as' to work in order to try out new perspectives on objects by projecting images on to them.

In visually exploring the stars at night, imaginative activity overlays perception in attempting to unify the various forms traced by individual stars, perhaps by naturally projecting geometrical shapes on to them. Sometimes we take the further imaginative leap of projecting ourselves *into* natural objects and 'scenes'. For example, to appreciate the aesthetic qualities of an alpine flower, I might somatically imagine what it is like to live and grow under harsh conditions. Without imagining such conditions I might be unable to appreciate the remarkable strength hidden so beautifully in the delicate quality of the flower. Both of these examples show how imagination provides a more intimate aesthetic experience, allowing the exploration of aesthetic qualities more deeply than through perception alone.

Stephanie Ross has identified an interesting use of imagination in gardens which seems to involve projective (and perhaps also exploratory) imagination, where we project ourselves into an environment:

> In some cases imagination is a natural prelude to action, for
> instance, when we deliberate and then choose to walk along a
> particular path. In other cases, we are for practical reasons restricted
> to imagination alone. Thus, while viewing an extensive prospect . . .
> I can imagine ascending a craggy peak or following a road to the
> horizon when either task is clearly beyond my physical abilities. In
> sum, a central feature of our enjoyment of gardens, and of other
> natural landscapes as well, is imagining ourselves performing some
> sort of action in that landscape, or in response to it, coupled with
> the possibility of actually going on and doing one or all of these
> things. Let me call this feature of gardens *invitation*.[27]

Many other features of gardens are designed to capture imagination. Grottos and winding paths create the quality of mystery and invite us to explore them. The romantic, fake ruins built into grand gardens are rich in suggestion, encouraging us to 'imaginatively live for a moment in the irretrievable past while simultaneously aware of the power of time to negate the present'.[28] Although gardeners intentionally create opportunities for imagination, in more natural landscapes, natural qualities invite us to explore them in similar ways. Openings in forests and rocky scrambles are common examples of natural invitation.

Projective imagination is especially interesting due to its participatory character. Through imagination, we attempt to gain access to nature's ways, to explore its otherness. This type of imaginative activity also facilitates a sympathetic or empathetic identification with nature. As R. K. Elliott puts it:

> Empathy, which is attributed to imagination, is the capacity for entering imaginally into the situation of another person or animal, and assuming its expression; or into the situation and expression of some quasi-person, such as a literary character; or of entering into and assuming the anthropomorphized expression of some plant or inanimate object.[29]

Such explorations are related more to moral concern and care rather than an aesthetic perspective but imaginative identification often begins in the imaginative exploration of aesthetic qualities, drawing the appreciator more deeply into the situation.

Ampliative Imagination

The third mode of imaginative activity, ampliative imagination, involves the *inventive* powers of imagination, and need not make use of images. It is marked by heightened creative powers and a special curiosity in its response to natural objects. Here, imagination amplifies what is given in perception, thereby reaching beyond the mere projection of images on to objects. This activity is therefore more penetrative, resulting in a deeper imaginative treatment of the object. It is imagination in its most active mode in aesthetic experience.

This use of imagination involves both visualising and the leaps of imagination that enable us to approach natural objects from entirely new standpoints. In contemplating the smoothness of a sea pebble, I visualise the relentless surging of the ocean as it has shaped the pebble into its worn form. I might also imagine how it looked before it became so smooth, this image contributing to my wonder and delight in the object. Merely thinking about the pebble does not vivify the silky smoothness that is emphasised by contrasting its feel with an image of its pre-worn state. Ampliative imagination enables us to expand upon what we perceive by placing or contextualising the aesthetic object with narrative images. Andrew Wyeth illustrates this with another example from the sea, 'A white mussel shell on a gravel bank in Maine is thrilling to me because it's all the sea – the gull that brought it there, the rain, the sun that bleached it there by a stand of spruce woods.'[30]

Ampliative imagination also accounts for a non-visualising activity in which we try out novel ways to appreciate aesthetically some object. Calling on imagination in this way facilitates the perspective of experiencing a valley as lush and green, imbued with tranquillity, or, by contrast, perceiving the valley's shape as carved out by icy glacial forms.

This narrative imagination has a special use in relation to the transitory quality of natural objects. Many natural phenomena come and go, changing from moment to moment. Saito discusses how this plays out in Japanese aesthetics, in the writings of Yoshida Kenkō:

> As in a love affair between a man and a woman, 'in all things, it is the beginnings and the ends that are interesting' because such stages of the phenomena are more stimulating to one's imagination. In particular, we appreciate the exquisite contrast between the present condition and the imagined condition of the previous or following stage. Even when an object is at the peak of its beauty, the appreciation is deepened by pathos based upon the apparent contrast between its present appearance and what it will become later on.[31]

This shows how imagination may be sensitive to the temporal qualities of natural objects and environments.

Revelatory Imagination

Where ampliative imagination leads to disclosure, I call this imaginative activity *revelatory*. In this mode, invention stretches the power of imagination to its limits, and this often gives way to new ideas and meanings; revelation in the non-religious sense. When my alternative contemplation of the valley, glaciers and all, reveals the tremendous power of the earth to me, a new understanding emerges through a distinctively aesthetic experience.

This new understanding is not gained through intellectual endeavour. It is not sought out. Revelatory imagination is part of an aesthetic experience, and in this respect the revelation that occurs is not an extra-aesthetic truth that is disclosed. Rather, an idea, belief or value is crystallised through heightened aesthetic experience, where perceptual and imaginative engagement with nature facilitates the kind of close attention that leads to revelation. A quick glance at a lamb reveals little except an acknowledgement of its sweetness. But the fuller participation of perception and imagination brings about a stronger grasp of the nature of innocence. Contemplating the fresh whiteness of a lamb and its small, fragile stature evokes images of purity and naivety. It is through dwelling aesthetically and imaginatively on natural phenomena that we may achieve new ways of seeing.

Revelatory imagination is reminiscent of the poetic apprehension conveyed through Kant's aesthetic ideas, where imaginative devices – symbolic images, metaphor – open out new meanings beyond the limitations of literal language.

It is also suggestive of Hepburn's metaphysical imagination, where heightened imaginative experience through deep encounters with nature vivify and open out certain metaphysical ideas.

Not all imaginative revelations are pleasant and positive. Imaginative engagement also reveals the horror and suffering of humanity and the natural world. Witnessing human evil, natural disasters, or even the everyday encounter of a cat stalking and killing a bird, all strike imagination in ways that spread meaning more deeply, and in ways that also make these experiences more demanding and difficult to undergo.

Imagining Well

The metaphorical, exploratory, projective, ampliative and revelatory modes of imagination distinguish the varieties of imaginative activity in aesthetic appreciation of nature. However, objections have been raised against imagination, the charge being that it sometimes leads to inappropriate responses. When functioning in its most fanciful mode, imagination may produce personal fantasies that distract attention from the aesthetic object, and possibly lead to trivialising and sentimentalising nature. Nature is transformed into something it is not, and we fail to respect it. But imagination is a much more sophisticated power than these claims suggest. It operates in a variety of modes distinct from fantasy, and additionally, it is possible to identify ways of keeping imagination on track so as to prevent trivialising responses. Our appreciation of nature draws valuably on imagination's powers without distorting or disrespecting nature.

In my original discussion of imagination, I set out three ways that our imaginings are guided (these also help to locate the distinction between relevant and irrelevant imaginings): (1) the way the object's qualities evoke and direct our imaginings; plus two explicit guidelines: (2) disinterestedness; (3) imagining well, which is characterised by comparing imagination to a virtue, so that we 'imagine well' when we use imagination skilfully and appropriately according to the context of aesthetic appreciation. These guidelines are intended to be flexible, since inflexibility will conflict with the range of responses demanded by the diversity of natural objects and appreciators.

The perceptual attentiveness discussed in the previous chapter indicates where imagination begins, and it also helps to guide imaginative activity. There is a close relationship between the two capacities in appreciation: the perceptual qualities of the aesthetic object guide imagination by giving it direction, and through suggestion by sensory cues. The deep ridges in the locust tree's bark, alongside the belief that the tree is old, suggest to imagination the image of an old man with wrinkles in his face. Wyeth's reflection on the seashell is guided by attention to perceptual qualities of the aesthetic object and its immediate environment of the seashore.

In some cases our imaginings will be only tentatively tied to perceptual qualities of the object, so we cannot rely solely on the connection between imagination and perception to pinpoint relevant imaginings. For example, when coming upon Beachy Head, a high cliff on the south coast of England, one is awestruck by the dramatic, sheer drop to the sea, and this feeling is heightened by the knowledge that this is a favourite suicide spot. Imagining the feeling of jumping off the cliff, and the fear of someone standing at the top of it, accentuates the sublimity of the place. But this train of images would become irrelevant to aesthetic appreciation of the cliff if one then imagined, vividly and rather gruesomely, the fallen body at the bottom of the cliff and the specific kinds of wounds that the cliff face might have inflicted on the body. As we focus our attention on thoughts about the body and its particular set of wounds, our imaginings become distanced from qualities of the cliff.

Furthermore, although many images evoked by an object are obviously connected to its perceptual properties, some imaginings do not emerge through attention to perceptual properties alone. Aldo Leopold's appreciation of a mountain as wild and majestic is achieved through 'thinking like a mountain', or an empathetic, imaginative identification with the mountain.[32] Leopold may have tried to project himself into the mountain, and sensory images would help, but it might also just involve an attempt to identify with the feeling of height and mass and the sublime feeling that might accompany it.

Perception directs imaginings in many cases but other forms of guidance may be needed. Disinterestedness characterises aesthetic appreciation as non-practical and non-instrumental. Adherence to this guideline eliminates the danger of self-indulgence by the imaginative subject. As I have argued, there is no tension between the active engagement of the subject's imagination and the detachment typically associated with disinterestedness. Properly understood, it is the active detachment of disinterestedness that clears the ground for the free activity of imagination, but it is also what helps to keep it in check, preventing self-indulgent responses. In freeing the mind from self-interested and instrumental concerns, imagination can underpin appropriate appreciation of the aesthetic object. Disinterestedness functions to check thoughts or imaginings that stray from an aesthetic focus in my appreciation of a seascape, such as fantasising about the abundance of shells I might collect if the waves weren't so big.

Disinterestedness specifically addresses the concern that the use of imagination leads to self-indulgence, while the second guideline has more to do with training imagination, as a skill, where we try to keep imagination in line with relevant features of the object. It requires a more active role by the appreciator in that she or he is expected to 'imagine well'. Just as keen rather than slack perception enables the discovery of aesthetic value in a dull landscape, imagination can be used effectively or ineffectively in the context of aesthetic appreciation.

An analogy to virtue is helpful for explaining how to imagine well. For Aristotle, virtue is not a natural capacity, but rather it is learned and acquired through practice. We reach a comfortable point where we exercise a virtue as a matter of habit. Imagination, too, is developed through practice, and it gains a habitual footing just like virtue. We can begin to see how an effective use of imagination might develop, but how exactly would such a use sort relevant from irrelevant imaginings? An important aspect of virtue provides an answer to this question. The proper assessment of the context or situation of a moral problem (using practical reason), as well as practice, provides the foundation of the appropriate virtue. In the aesthetic context, imagination is mobilised and exercised according to the demands of the aesthetic object, so that we become able to determine the irrelevance of, for example, some of the Beachy Head imaginings. Imagining well means spotting aesthetic potential, having a sense of what to look for, and knowing when to clip the wings of imagination. This last skill involves preventing the irrelevance of shallow, naive and sentimental imaginative responses which impoverish rather than enrich appreciation.[33] Imagining a lamb dressed up in baby clothes might underline the aesthetic truth of innocence, but it is sentimental and shallow, and it fails to direct an appreciation appropriately. Such discriminations are not always easy to make nor by any means clear-cut, but through practice it is possible to develop the skill of keeping imaginings on track.

Despite the fact that I intend only to draw an analogy between imagination and Aristotelian virtue, the comparison suggests that the exercise of imagination involves choices that could be described as normative. As Scruton remarks:

> we often distinguish among the activities of the imagination between those which are really imagination and those which are merely fantasy and whim. This is not a genuine distinction between imagination and something else, but it is an instance of a derivative use of 'imagine': it marks a distinction based on our own sense of what is appropriate in describing an absent thing.[34]

Elliott agrees with this observation when he argues against the aesthetic objectivist's belief that imaginative activity could leave the aesthetic object behind altogether or lead to chaos. If we are attending to the aesthetic object, then we should expect imaginative activity to be related to the work:

[Imagination] seems to have a double movement: an expansive moving out from the work along lines of relevance, and a turning back upon the work which concentrates the additional ideas or images around it like a nimbus. One might add that Imagination obeys not only a rule of relevance but a rule of decorum, for the rapt state would be at an end if a thought or image which was felt to belittle the work obtruded into it.[35]

Although Scruton's and Elliott's claims are directed at art, they are relevant to nature too. Neither philosopher's argument depends upon a relationship between the artist's intention and imagination. Their views share with mine an insistence on the kind of capacity imagination really is: imaginative activity is tied to qualities of the aesthetic object broadly conceived; and our ability to make choices to direct our imaginings in appropriate ways. Imagination sometimes functions in the mode of fantasy, but it is more accurate to say that in our aesthetic encounters, it operates rationally and appropriately according to the demands of the object.

Directing imagination in appropriate ways is not only in the interest of valuing the object for its own sake. Developing effective imaginative ability is desirable outside of aesthetic contexts too. Fantasy may be entertaining, but it does not serve us well in life, except very occasionally as a psychological release. Instead, by drawing on imagination's most effective modes, and giving them some practice, we achieve the focus required to use it in positive ways. Developing imaginative skill in order to relate better to others, make moral choices, decide how to live one's life, be creative, make discoveries and so on, is unquestionably a good thing.[36]

Criticisms of Imagination

Above, I remarked on imagination's bad reputation in the history of philosophy. A few environmental aestheticians are also suspicious, and their scepticism also rests on problems concerning imagination's relationship to truth. Imagination, it is argued, is not concerned with truth but rather with entertaining possibilities (and, worse, falsity), and when it comes to aesthetic appreciation of nature, truth is the bottom line. But this is where they make a crucial mistake: the failure to grasp that imagination is not reducible to 'fantasy'. It is a much broader concept, involving several valuable modes of engagement with the natural environment. Imagination's opponents come mainly from the cognitivist camp, so their criticisms arise out of a common theoretical basis, the objective epistemology of science. Aesthetic objectivism relies on an objective framework for appreciating, interpreting and evaluating aesthetic objects. In the context of art, for example, the aesthetic objectivist fears that imaginative activity in appreciation is prone to subjective flights of fantasy that leave the artwork and its qualities behind, replacing them with an individual, arbitrary fantasy. In environmental aesthetics, the same objection is raised, and it is argued that appreciation must be guided by knowledge provided by the sciences.

Apart from Carlson, the cognitive camp recognises that imagination may have some positive role but they insist that it should be constrained by the necessary condition of scientific knowledge.[37] Eaton, who supports imagination informed by scientific knowledge, is nonetheless critical of many of its uses. These objections are raised in her response to my original article on this subject.[38] In particular, she objects to my examples of having the mental image of the wrinkled face of an old man when perceiving the deeply textured tree bark, and the truth of innocence revealed through the aesthetic experience of the lamb, on the grounds that knowledge is required to ensure that imaginings are appropriately directed:

> Knowledge does not simply deepen the experiences that imagination provides, it directs them, or should direct them if we hope to preserve and design sustainable landscapes. Concepts such as imagining well make no sense unless one knows what the object is that one is talking about, something (in fact, as much as possible) about the object, and something (in fact, as much as possible) about the context in which the object is found.[39]

As I have indicated, knowledge plays some role in the form of basic concepts and everyday knowledge, and so is likely to be present in many of our aesthetic experiences (and to this extent some basic concepts and beliefs will be presupposed in our imaginings). But the more specialised demands of scientific knowledge, and in-depth knowledge of this kind, present problems if made a necessary condition. The way Eaton puts the matter here puts unrealistic and unacceptable intellectual demands on appreciators in order to have 'correct' appreciation. What does she mean by 'as much as possible'? Are we required to read up in the nature centre before we head out? Many people will possess basic concepts of what they appreciate, but is it fair to expect each of us to try to find out as much as possible about the ecology, geology and so on of the environments we aesthetically appreciate? I do not want to deny that aesthetic appreciation can be accompanied by the pursuit of knowledge if so desired, but it is unreasonable to expect every appreciator to find out as much as possible in the context of aesthetic valuing.

As I have indicated, there are other ways to ensure that imagination is put to the best use possible, rather than stipulating a necessary condition. Eaton does not engage very deeply with my discussion of constraints on imagination.

When describing my agreement with Kant's views of aesthetic imagination, she writes, 'Aesthetic experience is marked, he [Kant] argued, by disinterestedness. We put aside ordinary scientific, ethical, or personal interests and respond to objects *as we please*. We allow imagination full rein.'[40] But disinterestedness operates both negatively and positively, and in the former sense, we do not respond as we please; disinterestedness constrains self-interested appreciation. Furthermore, Kant's free play of imagination is not unbridled. Without assuming some direction to imagination in line with qualities of the aesthetic object, he would have had to contend with the subjective flights of fancy of which an entirely free imagination is, in some modes, susceptible.

Ronald Moore is also critical of the role given to imagination, but, unlike Eaton, he is equally critical of the role given to scientific knowledge.[41] Moore urges a 'syncretic aesthetics' that combines knowledge and imagination. Like Eaton, however, he misconceives my position by assuming that a free imagination is an imagination without limits. He is generally critical of non-cognitivist approaches put forward by Berleant, Carroll and me because he believes that:

> [T]he fundamental problem with these views and all other non-conceptualist approaches is the inherent limitlessness of the non-conceptual. If, as between understanding and imagination, nature is committed to the unrestricted province of the latter, there can be no bounds on what we make of it.[42]

This is a difficult claim to support. First, although non-cognitive views do not give knowledge a central place or make it a necessary condition, they do give it some role. They do not emphasise knowledge but they are also not subjectivist in the extreme sense supposed by Moore. If the non-conceptual were limitless, then we would have only facts on the one hand and nonsense or complete arbitrariness on the other. Moore's portrayal is strikingly similar to Carlson's, where the debate is put in terms of two stark alternatives with no subtle or careful distinctions concerning positions lying in between.

Second, Moore overlooks possible ways, other than knowledge, to guide and warrant imaginative activity, and, interestingly, he makes a similar mistake in relation to his criticisms of Carroll's arousal theory. Carroll makes a strong case for grounding emotional responses to nature through a cognitive theory of emotions. Recall my discussion in Chapter 4 concerning the way in which emotional responses are anchored in the object and beliefs surrounding it. Moore ignores the thrust of Carroll's argument and portrays him as a subjectivist. When addressing my position, Moore does not engage with or even acknowledge my case for guiding imagination. If he thinks that attempts to warrant emotional and imaginative activity fail, then he needs to present an argument for why this is so.

Robert Fudge has also argued that scientific knowledge provides the appropriate backing for giving a limited role to imagination in aesthetic appreciation of the natural environment. In particular, he argues that science is a necessary condition for appreciation of unscenic nature, which we often find difficult to appreciate compared to scenic landscapes (he concedes that scenic nature may be appropriately appreciated without scientific knowledge). Fudge makes some persuasive points in relation to how knowledge can enable appreciation of the unscenic, as opposed to unreflective revulsion, but he does not succeed in his attempt to bring together science and imagination in appreciation, and his claims against some imaginative responses are unconvincing.

His strategy is to show that, ultimately, science is needed to back up our imaginative (aesthetic) responses to nature; imaginings not backed by science threaten to downgrade appreciation. However, in the end he succeeds only in making a weak case for the role of science. Despite arguing that science and imagination working together reveal the unscenic as aesthetically delightful, his account of how the two come together is underdeveloped, and his case is largely based on an interpretation of my examples. Without a positive account of how imagination – as an inventive capacity that amplifies or reveals – works with scientific facts, imagination gets buried under the weight of knowledge. The effect is to reduce imaginative engagement to a type of cognitive engagement.

Fudge presents a case specifically against exploratory and projective imagination, but his objections are unconvincing. In respect of exploratory imagination, he questions whether seeing the tree bark as the wrinkled face of an old man is an appropriate imagining and concludes that, 'Though seeing the bark as the skin of an old man may lead to our noting previously ignored aesthetic properties of the bark, it may also mislead our appreciation, as wrinkled skin and tree bark are only incidentally related.'[43] Science provides the standard of appropriateness by giving us knowledge of trees that we then transform into appropriate images through imagination.

In his discussion of this example, Fudge appears to rely on my own point concerning the way perceptual qualities guide our imaginings. The deep clefts of the bark are like the wrinkles of an old man. This could be the only way that the relevant relationship is formed which leads to 'noting' new aesthetic qualities. Yet, Fudge then expresses concern that the tree and the man are only 'incidentally related'. He never explains why or how this imagining misleads appreciation. In any case, more than an incidental relationship exists in my original example. The connection is established through the resemblance between the perceptual qualities in the bark and the face, coupled with recognition of the tree as old. This contributes to evoking the image of an old man (rather than a young one with a smooth face). The example was used to illustrate exploratory imagination, which is the most closely tied to perception of the various modes.

Fudge cites a second example, his own, which he assumes would be acceptable on my account. He does not think that 'aesthetic appreciation of a mountain is enhanced when we project onto it an image of an upside down ice cream cone' because 'seeing the mountain as an ice cream cone brings in a way of thinking about the mountain entirely unrelated to it'.[44] In this example, there is clearly a problem surrounding the relationship between the mountain and the projection of the ice-cream-cone image. I agree with Fudge, although I'm not sure if I understand correctly what he has in mind. If his example intends to bring together an upside-down ice-cream cone and a mountain covered in snow two-thirds of the way up, with a brown or grey rocky, pointed top, then the connection is too tenuous to be relevant. Snow is cold, so is ice cream, but our associations with the shapes might be too strained to arrive at such an imagining. There is not sufficient resemblance, in my view, to evoke this imagining, and if there were, I doubt it would be shareable. Given these points, we could conclude that not only is it irrelevant, but it is rather trivial. Its triviality is partly due to its not being easily shareable, and as just the result of whim.

My account of imagination clearly recognises that a relevant connection must exist between the aesthetic object and our imaginative activity, so there is agreement on this point. But there is a problem with Fudge's description of imagination's capacities. In his view, imagination's primary activity is 'thinking in' *facts*, but surely this move reduces imagination to intellectual thought. 'Thinking in' describes what we do when we feed knowledge into aesthetic experience. Imagination, like knowledge in some cases, functions to open up new aesthetic qualities or deepen engagement with qualities already perceived. Its activity, although related to thought, makes a creative break from facts and knowledge given in experience, and makes novel connections. In this respect imagination is a transformative power in relation to given experience.

Fudge's next move is to argue that ampliative and revelatory imagination depend upon scientific knowledge.[45] My examples of the worn sea pebble and the glacial valley are interpreted to show how imagination works together with scientific knowledge to give the pebble's narrative and to reveal truth about the valley's geological history. The problem for all cognitive theories arises again in relation to Fudge's argument. How exactly are common sense and scientific knowledge distinguished, especially given the diversity of appreciative communities? In the sea-pebble case, the narrative is an imagined one, but it is plainly connected to common sense beliefs about the sorts of things one finds on beaches: it is common sense that most objects found on beaches have spent time in the sea! The glacial valley is a more promising example for

Fudge's case, but even here the example as set out illustrates how imagination tries out different perspectives on the valley – as lush and green or then as icy. When the latter imagining leads to revelation, the basis of the information is speculative. Our imaginative activity is not directed at perceiving the valley according to actual geological facts about the place, but rather to entertain a narrative related to the forms of the valley, where the narrative gives meaning to the place. The activity involves imaginative interpretation (along lines of relevance) rather than a straightforward application of scientific knowledge. Imaginative attention opens out relevant, new meanings and enhances our present perception through an image of the valley's long-past glacial state, but without the scientific-epistemological condition of verification.

It is possible that there is little disagreement between our accounts, but to determine that, Fudge, like Carlson, needs to specify exactly what degree of scientific knowledge is required, how this knowledge differs from common sense, and what our expectations should be with regard to knowledge possessed by appreciators. Fudge gives an example of a rotting elk carcass (drawing on Rolston's discussion of this type of case), which suggests that knowledge of ecological processes is required to perceive aesthetic qualities in this example of the unscenic. In any case, I have presented arguments to show how imagination is tied to the aesthetic object, and how it is not necessarily divorced from basic concepts. Later in this chapter, I discuss the difference between commonsense beliefs and scientific knowledge.

By limiting his discussion to an interpretation of my examples to show how imagination and science work together, another problem arises for Fudge's account. His ultimate aim is to show that science and imagination reveal aesthetic value in the unscenic, but my examples are not directed at this category of environments, and, as he acknowledges, my overall position is not specifically aimed at the unscenic. Earlier in his article he discusses interesting examples of the unscenic and the role of science in aesthetic appreciation (including the elk carcass). But Fudge does not return to the unscenic after his discussion of imagination and science, and therefore he gives no explicit treatment of how imagination enables aesthetic valuing of the unscenic. Generally, Fudge's preoccupation with defending the role of science is at the expense of adding anything substantial to accounts of imagination's role in aesthetic appreciation. We are told that imagination opens up new ways of seeing that which we otherwise avoid, but Fudge does not provide any content or any specific discussion of how imagination is *imaginative*.[46]

Defending Imagination

Many of the criticisms against my position on imagination do not specifically tackle the actual examples I give to support my position but, instead, rely on extreme examples to make a case. For example, Eaton never says why the old man and innocent lamb examples, as they stand, represent irrelevant imaginings. Instead, she turns to Felix Salten's *Bambi* to show that fiction and imagination may have such a strong cultural influence that we become unable to appreciate deer on their own terms, seeing them *only* through Bambi/ cultural spectacles. This type of strategy makes two logical errors. First, it sets up a straw person by presenting more extreme cases than my own. Second, it relies on a slippery slope in the sort of claim made against imagination: if imagination has freedom in cases like the tree and the lamb, isn't it also in danger of leading to the problems apparent in seeing all deer as Bambi, or projecting whatever we please on to nature's forms?

I point to the use of cases/examples because of the general difficulty in distinguishing relevant from irrelevant imaginings. Defending imagination must be done largely on a case-by-case basis. Arguing against it, that is, that it has a role but also that it can lead to harmful fantasy, must also rely on distinguishing between sound and unsound uses of imagination. Both arguments are not easy. It is also worrying that many of the objections to imagination do not recognise our ability to check flights of fancy.

I have already discussed a few examples to indicate irrelevant or otherwise problematic imaginings, but further discussion is needed to clarify my position. In her critique, Eaton says I do not clearly show cases where imaginative activity falsifies nature. Above, I presented the case of a lamb dressed up in baby clothes, a clear sentimentalisation of nature (or more accurately, a domesticated animal), which describes a falsification of it. However, I am concerned about relying on an explicit standard of truth or falsity. Imagination engages in entertaining beliefs and propositions, not in ascertaining facts. But as I pointed out above, imagination is also not opposed to belief or reducible to fancy. Apart from delusions, imagining is accompanied by an awareness of the relationship between an imagining and the beliefs that surround it. Consider a boy who sees a hill as a giant's head: he sees a huge, looming hill, shaped somewhat like a head, with a bumpy bit that suggests a nose, so he imagines a giant's head. Compare this to the experience of a geologist and imagine the two sharing each other's experiences. The child's response can be characterised as more playful, and it brings attention to the great scale of the hill and its distinctive shape and form through the identification of imaginative qualities. The boy does not run away frightened, because he doesn't really think that the hill is a giant's head, he only imagines it to be like that and he is aware of his imagining. The geologist tells the child about the rock that constitutes this great natural phenomenon, and the geologist sees the aesthetic qualities of solid bulk and sublimity too, but as grounded in her knowledge of geology. Is one response more legitimate than the other as an aesthetic response?

In distinguishing between relevant and irrelevant imaginings or more and less reasonable ones, the standard ought not be fixed by truth and falsity in the strict sense but rather by determining relevance based on the guidelines I have set out. Although I referred earlier to the serious and trivial scale in other contexts concerning appreciation of nature, I shall not use it here. Trivial imaginings there are, and they have no role in my account, but I am not inclined to describe imaginings as 'serious' either. Some perfectly reasonable and acceptable imaginings will be playful, and this does not fit very well with describing them as 'serious'. The serious/trivial scale fits better with Hepburn's original use, where serious represents science-based appreciation and trivial represents arbitrary or falsifying appreciation. As an alternative, I suggest that we work with a scale of relevant versus irrelevant, with irrelevant imaginings thrown out.

Irrelevant imaginings are those that do not meet the condition of disinterestedness and those that can be shown to have no relationship (or only a very tentative one) to the qualities of the aesthetic object. In this respect, imaginings are object-directed while also shaped to some degree by the particularity of the appreciator. Imaginings must relate to the aesthetic object in specifiable ways that enhance appreciation and are consistent with the practical guideline of imagining well. In relation to practice, imagination in many cases operates naturally along lines of relevance, so my guidelines are intended to operate as an encouragement for appreciators to develop a skilful imagination.

There is more to be said about the relevance of specific examples of imaginings. Moore's argument against my account of imagination presents a set of more outlandish cases, which I assume he believes are acceptable on my account. Three fanciful examples[47] are given, but in fact each one would be excluded by my guidelines: (1) Seeing a river as a bookmark. This is strange, as there is no apparent relationship between perceptual qualities in this case, or any way in which one image illuminates the other. Rivers are never straight like the sides of a bookmark (canals might be), and they're usually rippled from the wind and current. (2) Taking a star to be a good luck charm. It's not clear how this activity relates to perceiving aesthetic qualities, unless one related the brightness and shine to the positive qualities of good luck. In any case, this does not meet the condition of disinterestedness either, since one wants to use the star to bring about one's own good fortune. (3) Seeing a raven as a writing desk is offered as an example of unbridled imagination.[48] This is a clear case of fancy and just bizarre. There is no connection through cultural associations nor any remote similarities in perceptual qualities that would be shareable (ravens don't have flat surfaces, which writing desks have when folded down, and black desks are uncommon). One association might be a black quill pen made from feathers, but this is rather remote, at least because it refers to a pen and not the desk. If upon seeing a raven, lines from Edgar Allen Poe's poem, 'The Raven' come to mind, this literary association would be relevant, even if shareable only by the appreciative community familiar with this famous poem.

The Poe example raises the problem of imaginings that could be argued to bring human culture too strongly into our responses to nature, and therefore threaten to negate nature's qualities through anthropomorphism of the worst kind, or just by hindering our ability to recognise that some part of an environment has both cultural *and* natural value.

Saito objects to one way in which we invoke associations in relation to nature, although it is not always clear whether these are aesthetic uses of imagination. Recall her concern that some cultural associations overly humanise landscapes, preventing appreciation of their natural value (see Chapter 3). She worries that tourists appreciate some landscapes in human rather than natural terms, and imaginative associations are part of the problem. The reduction of a landscape to a cultural association is, in the absence of recognition of natural qualities, problematic but there are a couple of points that help to defend some associations.

Many landscapes are cultural in the sense that humans have shaped the land or events that have taken place there. This is especially the case with Saito's example of the Gettysburg battlefield. Such landscapes are not entirely natural, but lie somewhere along the natural/cultural scale. It should therefore be possible to value a landscape as both a cultural symbol and a natural place, indeed, many cultural landscapes have this character. Although she seems to recognise this, she claims that 'for associationist appreciation, the specific sensuous features of the object remain irrelevant'.[49] But this is not the case for all cultural, associationist appreciation, because quite often it is the play between natural and cultural qualities that creates aesthetic and other types of values. The landscape in and around Gettysburg, where the battle took place, features rolling hills, forests, farmlands and the town itself. In experiencing this pleasant, semi-rural place today, a visitor imagines the same landscape covered with thousands upon thousands of dead and wounded soldiers. The contrast of the present with the past brings home the poignant feeling of the place. Similarly, imagining the terrible battle at Culloden in the Scottish Highlands is connected to perceiving the qualities of the heather-covered, windswept moor, and the heavy weather that can affect such a place. It is possible to distinguish between overly humanising imaginative responses and imaginative responses that work legitimately with both cultural and natural aspects of a place.

Godlovitch raises stronger objections to imagination on the grounds that it does not value nature on its own terms. Like emotion, science and indeed any human framework, imaginative activity necessarily distorts nature, and prevents us from conceiving of 'nature *qua* nature', that is, without human categories and frameworks.[50] I argued in Chapter 4 that such a stance is either impossible or makes aesthetic appreciation empty. I have established sufficient grounds for understanding how imagination can deepen our engagement and how it can be checked so as not to distort nature. We come to nature with human ways of seeing and human ways of aesthetically encountering the world, but rather than attempt to throw these off entirely, we ought to harness imagination's powers in ways that bring out nature's value.

THE COMMUNICABILITY OF IMAGINATION

Let me conclude my discussion of imagination by explaining how to warrant imaginative activity through a cluster of ideas that relate to the communicability of aesthetic judgements. (I make a general case for the communicability and justification of aesthetic judgements in Chapter 7.)

I pointed out above that Kant was not deeply worried about a wayward imagination, and this is shown also by his argument for the intersubjectivity of aesthetic judgements. The basis for his argument is the *sensus communis* or 'common sense'. This designates the basis of communicability of aesthetic judgements as grounded in the similar capacities of individual appreciators. With it (and his deduction of pure judgements of taste), Kant wants to show how individual judgements based in feeling nonetheless claim subjective universality. We demand agreement with our judgement because we assume that the conditions for making such judgements (including the free play of imagination and disinterestedness) are met, even if they are not met in actuality. Kant's idea has been influential on other accounts that show how aesthetic judgements, although unlike cognitive judgements, lay some claim to communicability.

Hepburn echoes Kant when he says:

> if we share a common environment, the annexed forms [of imagination] can range from the universally intersubjective, through the shareable though not universal, to the highly individual and personal. Basic natural forms are interiorized for the articulating of a common structure of the mind. Through these, the elusively nonspatial is made more readily graspable and communicable.[51]

Although our imaginings are marked by particularity rather than generality, it does not follow that they are idiosyncratic. They are potentially shareable, just as the other elements of the aesthetic response, perception, emotion, cognition, are potentially shareable.

As we have seen, it is a common mistake to assume that imagination is characterised by waywardness. Like emotion, imagination is an individual power shaped by the events and values in any individual life. It is this particularity that gives our imaginings their richness. At the same time, our imaginings are not unrelated to the objective world, indeed, they centre upon it; imaginings are connected to qualities in objects and surrounding beliefs.

So, we can suppose that imagination, too, may be warranted through the communicability of the aesthetic situation. The critical discourse that is part of aesthetic appreciation of art and the natural environment can be part of the actual activity of revising and redressing our aesthetic responses. Just as we are able to discover more aesthetic value by sharing aesthetic experiences, in so far as we believe our judgements ought to be communicable, we discard imaginative descriptions that cannot be reasonably shared by others experiencing the same object, or by a culture or community.

I shall revisit Carlson's discussion to demonstrate my claim here. His criterion for cultural information (nominal descriptions, mythological descriptions, imaginative descriptions and literary descriptions) is that they are required to be culturally embedded, and in this sense they are more 'generally available'.[52] While 'Ship Rock', the proper name of a particular geological feature, is culturally embedded, descriptions of that landscape feature as a 'blue thumb' or as a 'free form gothic cathedral' are not. Carlson thinks that both imaginative and literary descriptions are not relevant because they cannot meet his conditions.

This exclusion of imaginative descriptions is both odd and unnecessary. It is odd because the metaphors we use in our imaginative descriptions depend upon concepts which are part of language in common use. It is unnecessary because such descriptions are actually descriptive and direct our attention to aesthetic qualities. In other words, some imaginative descriptions, not all of them, meet Carlson's criteria of relevance.

I've never seen Ship Rock at first hand, but judging by pictures, it appears to be majestic in character. Two images give us a strong sense of the majesty of Ship Rock: a ship moving with a great wake through the calm sea, or a great cathedral impressive in its proportions. These sorts of comparisons are part of common understanding for many of us. They do not represent highly individualistic associations. The Ship Rock example, as well as others, shows that some imaginative descriptions meet the criterion of cultural embeddedness.

However, although the concepts used in metaphor are commonly known, this is not sufficient to make metaphors work, since the connection made could be bizarre or arbitrary. Imaginative descriptions can be misleading, just as metaphors can be misinterpreted. But this is no reason to exclude them as irrelevant. Determining which imaginative descriptions or metaphorical descriptions are appropriate or which ones make sense, given the non-aesthetic qualities of a particular landscape, forms a key part of critical discourse. For example, Ship Rock was also described by Hillerman as sticking up 'like a blue thumb on the western horizon seventy miles away'.[53] Although this description might make sense under very specific light and weather conditions, it is likely that it is so specific as to be of little interest or importance. I agree with Carlson that highly individualistic descriptions like this one will have little if any role in *appropriate* aesthetic appreciation, because they are unlikely to be easily shared or accessible to others.

Another example cited by Carlson is 'Table Mesa'. Descriptions of flat-shaped geological features are quite common across the world. These names are based in local language use, and they emerge from figurative descriptions that have become used as proper names. This is how they have become culturally embedded, and Carlson accepts this. However, he rejects Hiller-man's imaginative description of Table Mesa as 'the ultimate aircraft carrier' because it is not sufficiently culturally embedded. It is clear that it is not embedded in the sense of being a proper name, and it is unlikely to become a proper name, unless of course it makes its way into common use among locals and Hillerman fans who visit the place.

However, the description, also a metaphor, draws on ordinary or com-monsense concepts. Tables are a part of our daily lives, aircraft carriers are not. But this is why the metaphor works so well. It makes a creative link to a concept which suggests not only flatness, but massive bulk beneath it as well. It is a description that may be less ordinary but is certainly more suggestive of the aesthetic qualities that exist. Cultural embeddedness is a reasonable condition of relevance, but it ought to be broad enough to include imaginative descriptions which get their impact and novelty by starting from the ordinary and reaching beyond it in ways that are still comprehensible. Not to accept this would be to limit unacceptably the scope of poetic language in landscape descriptions.

The inventiveness characteristic of imagination does not always lead to positive value, but to put imagination aside altogether or to be too wary of its powers is not the answer. This strategy suppresses an aesthetic tool that has great potential for enabling both the discovery of aesthetic qualities and a creative engagement with nature.

EMOTION, EXPRESSIVE QUALITIES AND NATURE

I looked up dizzily, and beheld a wide expanse of ocean, whose waters wore so inky a hue as to bring at once to my mind the Nubian geographer's account of the *Mare Tenebrarum*. A panorama more deplorably desolate no human imagination can conceive. To the right and left, as far as the eye could reach, there lay outstretched, like ramparts of the world, lines of horridly black and beetling cliff, whose character of gloom was but the more forcibly illustrated by the surf which reared high up against it its white and ghastly crest, howling and shrieking for ever.[54]

The affective dimension of environmental appreciation, as illustrated by these lines from Edgar Allen Poe's 'A Descent into the Maelström', is common to our aesthetic experiences of nature. In some responses there is felt emotion, as when we feel exhilarated when taking a morning walk through a forest. In other responses we may not feel any particular emotion, but rather we just find expressive qualities in what we experience, such as a landscape that is bleak and forbidding.

In this section my primary concern is how to make sense of and justify attributions of expressive qualities to the natural environment. In relation to the question of our emotional responses, where we actually feel moved in some way by nature, I rely mainly on the argument already provided by Carroll's arousal theory (discussed in Chapter 4). Of course, appreciation is often characterised by experiencing expressive qualities and emotions at the same time, but for the purposes of my explanation, I treat them separately. Both types of experiences have a place in the integrated aesthetic, and together they define the affective component therein.

Emotions and the Environment

Like imagination, emotion is a valuable resource in aesthetic appreciation but it too suffers from caricature: it is commonly viewed as too subjective and arbitrary to pin down as a legitimate part of appreciation. Any discussion of it needs to show not only how nature can evoke emotion and be expressive, but also give some assurance that emotion will not lead to wayward or distorting responses.

Carroll addresses the specific problem of justifying emotional responses to nature, that is, the particular emotions we feel when we experience great waterfalls, richly textured mosses, or tiny spiders. He adopts a cognitive theory of emotions and sets out to show how emotion can be an appropriate response to nature. An emotional response is appropriate or inappropriate according to its object and aspects of the subject having the emotion, including particular beliefs surrounding the object. In Carroll's view, justifying the feeling of excitement from the grandeur of a waterfall depends upon the qualities of the waterfall and the beliefs and thoughts that underlie the response. The thoughts and beliefs cannot be subjective, but rather must be reasonably shared by other people.[55] Using this strategy, he shows how emotional responses are not subjective projections on to the landscape and how they relate to the whole aesthetic situation – subject, object and context.

Carroll makes a strong case for warranting our emotional responses, and I am inclined simply to support it as the best account available. I would just add two points of clarification. First, Carroll is quite clear that the beliefs that support our emotive responses are not based on scientific knowledge. They are not specialist beliefs, but rather serve as background, commonsense beliefs that cohere with other people's beliefs. Although Carroll relies on a cognitive theory of emotions, his arousal theory is intended as an alternative to Carlson's natural environmental model, with its necessary condition of scientific knowledge. That model does not capture the common experience of being moved by nature.

Second, while beliefs are relevant to warranting emotion, they do not provide the fullest account of the grounds for our emotions. Some recent theories of emotion in philosophy argue that emotions may also rest on imaginings or thoughts that are merely entertained. Carroll has picked up on this discussion, and in his more recent work he revises his cognitive theory of emotions by adding that our emotional responses may also be legitimately grounded in thoughts, or propositions that are merely entertained:

> I may view a cloud formation – entertaining the metaphor that it is a mountain range – and that belief-like state (that imagining) may engender emotions of awe in me, calling my attention to the massive, powerful shapes in the sky. Nor need this imagining on my part be idiosyncratically subjective. Everyone else can see why I see it as a mountain range and can agree that my metaphor is apposite . . . But I do not believe that the cloud is a mountain. I merely entertain the thought in a way that raises an emotional response in me, which, in turn, enables me to organize my perception of . . . some of its features.[56]

I welcome these new ideas because they enrich his theory by recognising that our affective responses reach beyond beliefs for their grounding and context. They also suggest a way that imagination and emotion are linked in aesthetic appreciation. Overall, Carroll provides a useful explanation and justification of our emotional responses to the natural world.

Nature's Moods

I give special attention to the problem of expressive qualities in nature because there has not been much discussion of it in environmental aesthetics. Various writers have considered expressive qualities, such as Hepburn, but there has been only one detailed philosophical treatment of them, by Jane Howarth, and her discussion has a particular focus. Before I set out my own position, and in order to provide some background, I shall give an outline of her discussion of the problem.

In 'Nature's Moods', Howarth considers one dimension of the problem of expressive qualities, the role of moods in environmental experience.[57] She turns her attention not to the emotions we feel, but to the expressive qualities we perceive. Although her account is limited to moods, it gives a useful survey of some of the problems that arise when we use emotion terms to describe nature and points in the right direction for developing an account of expressive qualities.

There are various ways we might attempt to explain how environments and their objects are expressive. A first attempt can be dismissed easily. We might say, literally, that a natural environment, perhaps a loch and dark images of the hills surrounding it, actually is sombre. But this strategy fails if we are ascribing an emotional state to the loch. Inanimate objects, objects without minds, do not have emotional states.[58]

Other possible arguments stem from attempts to say how art is expressive of emotions. Howarth considers whether or not a 'Croce-Collingwood expression theory' might be relevant, which claims that we call works of art sad, happy and so on because the artist is expressing her or his feeling of sadness through the medium of art. However, according to this view, we necessarily make reference to the artist, and this is nonsensical in the context of natural (as opposed to heavily modified) environments. We might bypass the artist and argue that the artist's emotion is embodied in the artwork's form, but this still makes an implicit reference to a creator with an intention.

Yet another approach focuses on the response of the appreciator. This is more hopeful and much more appropriate to nature, since it sets aside intentionality. A causal theory of emotions holds that when we ascribe an expressive quality to something, it is because the thing causes one to feel a particular emotion. However, consider this example. The loch environment may make someone feel content and calm, relaxed and satisfied, rather than sombre, and so in this case it would be odd to call the loch sombre. The fact that one says it makes one feel sombre isn't sufficient to show why it is sombre, since it could affect others in a different way. Besides this problem, it may also be the case that we judge the loch to be sombre without actually feeling anything at all, so the causal account cannot explain this type of response either.

Howarth then asks us to consider the projection of emotions. For example, it is common for children to project emotions on to dolls and teddy bears. We have already seen that there is no mind in inanimate natural objects, and we know that when we call a loch scene sombre, we are certainly not saying the loch feels sombre. There may be some room here for saying that in some cases our emotional states colour our particular aesthetic experiences, but unpacking this must be very carefully done.

Given the problems with these strategies, Howarth suggests an alternative explanation using the concept of moods. We could perhaps talk about experiencing objects under different emotional aspects. Moods are not tied to a more narrow account of what emotions consist in such as the object of emotion, response and behaviour. Moods are typically objectless, with no clear characteristic behaviour, and it is sometimes difficult to pin down reasons for them. Feeling gloomy or cheerful are moods that seem to 'descend upon us without reason'.[59]

But how is this account not just another subjective projection of emotions on to nature? Rather than adopting a cognitive theory of emotion that would not fit easily with moods (since moods do not have explicit objects), Howarth argues that moods have appropriate backdrops and are specified by atmospheres, and these atmospheres resemble our moods:

> The cheerful brook moves much as a cheerful person might: it
> babbles and plays, pauses awhile, rushes on, darts, has a quick, light
> movement . . . The wind's moaning 'echoes' the human moaning.
> There is a sense in which the moaning wind can actually sound like
> a person moaning or sighing.[60]

Furthermore, she claims that we can understand our own moods better through aesthetic experience of nature, and we can understand nature better by discovering resemblances between ourselves and nature's moods. In addition to this strategy for avoiding subjectivism, Howarth adopts a phenomenological description of moods and our interaction with nature through the philosophy of Heidegger and Merleau-Ponty.

Howarth's account is informative, for she explains the drawbacks of several different explanations of nature's expression. The main problem lies in nature's not having intentional states, and thus being mute in terms of actual expression – whether it is emotion or the communication of ideas. In art, this particular issue does not arise, although the existence of an artist capable of expressing emotion through an artwork produces its own set of problems for philosophers. Howarth is also correct to point out the resemblance between emotion qualities in nature and our own behaviour when we are feeling the same emotion. Although her discussion is more concerned with moods than expressive qualities more broadly understood, her general conclusion is very promising for finding a solution to the problem of expressive qualities in nature.

Expressive Qualities in Nature

Interestingly, elsewhere, in a discussion about expressive qualities in art, Carroll raises some examples of expressive qualities in nature. He does not develop a position specifically in relation to the natural environment but he brings to the surface some useful ideas that follow Howarth's strategy (without relying on phenomenology). Their views are similar in the way they invoke a relation of resemblance between expressive qualities in nature and the characteristic behaviour expressed when people are in various emotional states.

Carroll argues that we can attribute expressive qualities to nature in somewhere near a literal sense regardless of the fact that sinister forests and cheerful brooks do not possess mental states. Carroll's argument, which I think is a good one, is based on the idea that we attribute expressive properties to things – namely artworks and natural objects – because of their 'configuration', or the way they 'look or sound'. (Presumably, he would be willing to accept that something's configuration could also be based in other sensory properties, such as texture or smell.) For example:

> We see the gnarled branches of barren trees and call them anguished because they call to mind the twisted appearance of human suffering. But that does not entail that we are not speaking literally. For we are not saying that the tree is suffering (that it possesses a psychological state), but rather that it is anguished-looking – that it exhibits characteristic aspects of the physiognomy of anguish.[61]

There are other examples too – a weeping willow is sad or sad-looking because we recognise in it the posture of someone feeling down. The activity of a furious storm 'reminds us of how the behaviour of a furious person appears'.[62] Poe's howling and shrieking storm sounds like the cries of humans. On Carroll's view the reference point is human behaviour because that is what we know so well, but it is possible that the resemblance works both ways. When my friend is furious, she 'storms' around the house. Nature, too, may be a reference point for recognising characteristic emotional behaviour in humans, who are, after all, part of nature themselves.

One advantage of this approach is its externalist emphasis. It relies on the perception of non-aesthetic qualities, the configuration of something, and characteristic behaviour, so that our identification of expressive qualities is easily explained to others, whom we would expect to make similar ascriptions. That particular expressive qualities exist is therefore not dependent on the subjective experience of the appreciator.

This strategy is very similar to philosophical theories of musical expression which have been called '*appearance-of-expression*-based views' or more simply, 'similarity theories'.[63] For example, Stephen Davies' argues that the emotion terms which are used to describe what Carroll has called 'configurations' are deeply rooted in the way we use these terms to describe emotional states. In relation to musical expression, he says that 'emotions are heard in music as belonging to it, just as appearances of emotion are present in the bearing, gait, or deportment of our fellow humans and other creatures'.[64] We can identify emotion characteristics in appearances – in human faces, music, weeping willows, cars and St Bernard dogs. The claim is not that these objects feel emotions. There is no reference to a feeling of emotion but only to the *look* of an emotion.[65] In the context of natural environments, we might say that we can identify emotion characteristics in appearances – the sensuous surface, or dynamic context of some landscape, natural object or phenomenon.

Peter Kivy also puts forward a type of similarity theory of musical expression. The idea of 'contour' is used to describe the type of resemblance that exists between expression in an object and the expression of human emotion. The similarity exists structurally, and he describes a piece of music as a 'sound map' of particular emotional expression. To hear music as having expressive qualities is to recognise in music a resemblance to human emotional behaviour through speech, gestures and bodily movement.[66]

In these theories of musical expression, the role of the composer and performers is considered less relevant because the relation is based on qualities in the music alone. This move makes sense in the context of nature too, for it leaves out reference to intentional states. However, we still have to ask what place the experience of the listener has in relation to the music they hear, for little has been said about this. Critics have argued that similarity theories need to take account of the role played in hearing the music and the interpretive process that leads to the ascription of expressive qualities. The existence of resemblance alone does not provide a sufficient explanation for the existence of expressive qualities. This type of criticism of similarity theories in musical expression enables us to locate what is missing from the same type of view as applied to natural environments. The approaches of Carroll, Davies, Kivy and Howarth give some explanation of expressive qualities in nature, but some questions are left unanswered.

The shortcomings surface when we consider the fact that some attributions of expressive qualities to landscapes will not be traceable or indeed reducible to similar emotional expression behaviours. There are two ways we can identify this problem. The first dimension is set out clearly by Hepburn, so I quote him at length:

A person who contemplates natural objects aesthetically may
sometimes find that their emotional quality is describable in the
vocabulary of ordinary human moods and feelings – melancholy,
exuberance, placidity. In many cases, however, he will find that they
are not at all accurately describable in such terms. A particular
emotional quality can be roughly analogous to some nameable
human emotion, desolation for instance; but the precise quality of
desolation revealed in some waste or desert in nature may be quite
distinctive in timbre and intensity. To put this another way: one
may go to nature to find shapes and sounds that can be taken as the
embodiment of human emotion, and in so far as this occurs, nature
is felt to be humanized. But instead of nature being humanized, the
reverse may happen. Aesthetic experience of nature may be
experience of a range of emotion that the human scene, by itself,
untutored and unsupplemented, could not evoke.[67]

We should not assume that there will always be a correlation between human
and natural qualities. Sometimes the correlation will be inexact or not exist at
all. Hepburn is also saying that too narrow a correlation between expression in
nature and expression in humans threatens to overly humanise nature and to
overlook nature's own distinctive otherness. While humans themselves are of
course natural creatures, there are great differences between us and other
animals, and between us and other natural things. This fact is perhaps most
dramatically shown in cases where we experience the wonder and the
sublimity of nature.

One way to overcome the problem (at worst a sort of projection of emotion
on to an environment) is to emphasise a point made earlier by Howarth. She
recognised the reciprocal relationship between human emotion and expression
in nature. It is often the case that natural expression will influence our moods
or determine them altogether, so that we reflect nature's qualities rather than
the other way around. In the context of music, Davies describes this as a
'mirroring response' where the listener's emotions mirror the music's emotional expression.[68] An interesting variation of this is *mono no aware*, a concept
of Japanese aesthetics that describes our emotional identification with natural
objects or environments. The concept was developed by the eighteenth-
century Japanese scholar, Motoori Norinaga, and as Saito describes it, the
term can be translated as ' "pathos of things" or "sensitivity of things" . . .
sometimes compared to the Latin notion of "*lacrimae rerum*" ("tears of
things")'.[69] Knowing *mono no aware* enables an emotive affinity to develop
between aesthetic object and appreciator, where it seems to be the object that
determines the type of identification that takes place.

Another problem in similarity theories relates back to humans and their cultural relationship with environments. We might, for example, describe a landscape as an expression of poignant pride. Although I cannot speak for Welsh communities, it may be the case that for some people, the disused quarries found, for example, in North Wales – choppy, grey, textured expanses set against the natural contours and dramatic sweep of mountain valleys – express such feelings. Instead of being tidied up or cleared away, some disused quarries that were previously the mainstay of many communities have been left as they are. The landscapes may appear to some as ugly or scarred, but they are deeply associated with and in some sense express the hard work and hard lives of the community. These landscapes have significance as cultural heritage, and their qualities have significance within this context.

In this case, there are no non-aesthetic qualities of the landscape that bring to mind emotional behaviour linked to feeling proud. That pride is also not reducible to the simple projection of feeling on to the landscape, for the quarried mountainside, and all of its distinctive qualities, are deeply associated with the lives of people who worked there. Their associations cannot be separated from the objective, non-aesthetic qualities of the landscape: 'the slate stairways, the hewn caverns, and the exposed slate face'.[70] This example shows that in many cases the connections between a landscape and its expressive qualities are more complex than the similarity theory can account for. Those connections will reach beyond resemblance to include 'complex chains of association and belief',[71] including cultural and historical associations, and aspects of our experience of environments that are better described through the concept of a 'sense of place'.

Sometimes associations will be based on cultural conventions, and this phenomenon may not be dissimilar to what is happening in the quarry case. Kivy recognises this, for he adds to his contour thesis another concerning how conventions dictate some correlations of expression through the 'customary association' of expressive qualities in music and emotion.[72]

In the context of the natural environment, Saito has pointed out that Japanese literature has so often associated natural phenomena with certain emotions that these associations have become conventions: 'cherry blossoms (especially when they are falling) are often associated with sorrow in classical Japanese literature because they epitomize the transience of beauty'.[73]

Where resemblance is missing as the basis of the attribution of expressive qualities, another explanation is needed. An account of expressive qualities that has been suggested but not fully developed by Saito and Carlson may help here. They draw on George Santayana's 'two-term' account of expression to show how natural and cultural landscapes are expressive. Santayana argues that aesthetic expression occurs when two terms are fused together, or 'lie together in the mind': 'The first is the object actually presented, the word, the image, the expressive thing: the second is the object suggested, the further thought, emotion, or image evoked, the thing expressed.'[74] He offers an example of how the association brings about expression when appreciator and aesthetic object interact: 'moonlight and castle moats, minarets and cypresses, camels filing through the desert – such images get their character from the strong but misty atmosphere of sentiment and adventure which clings about them'.[75] Saito applies Santayana's ideas specifically to landscapes:

> Many instances of our aesthetic appreciation of nature are based upon this 'fusion' between the object's sensuous surface and various associated facts such as scientific facts, historical or literary associations, or practical values. For example, we may appreciate the way in which the fierceness of a battle is *reflected* in a disfigured landscape with poor vegetation.[76]

Santayana and Saito together show how a broad range of expressive qualities may be attributed to landscapes. We might call this approach the 'embodiment' account, because it suggests how environments embody history, emotions, memories and so on, and we can use it to supplement the explanations given by similarity theories.

Another strength of the embodiment account is that it addresses the relational character of expressive qualities. This is brought out in Carlson's discussion of Santayana:

> for an object to express a quality or life value, the latter must not simply be suggested by it. Rather the quality must be associated with the object itself; that is, what Santayana meant by saying that the object must seem to embody that which it expresses. Clarified in this way, expression is not typically due to the unique associations resulting from an individual's own personal history.[77]

Carlson does not work out in detail how such expressions are held by a community as opposed to certain individuals, and this needs some careful working out. Acknowledgement of the role of the appreciator's feelings, associations and perceptions is important, but less relevant if the aim is to find a shareable, practical understanding of the expressive character of environments. In any case, through the embodiment account it is now possible to understand how the Welsh quarry may be expressive of pride: for a community of individuals, the landscape is fused with memories and associations of their working lives in that landscape.

The embodiment account helps with the unanswered questions left by similarity theories, but one might argue that the concepts of fusion and embodiment are vague. What exactly does it mean to say that environments or objects are 'drenched' with emotions or images? I am reminded of Wittgenstein's explanation of 'seeing-as' as an image coming into contact with the thing perceived. Perhaps aspect perception could provide a more concrete understanding of the embodiment account, but I do not think it ought to replace it, since concepts like 'embodiment', 'fusion' and 'drenched', although metaphorical, capture the mood and atmospheric qualities that characterise some of our experiences of expressive qualities in environments.

I have not explored theories of metaphorical exemplification, which have been used to explain expressive properties in artworks. It is certainly the case that we can explain expressive qualities in nature through the use of metaphor. Poe's 'howling, shrieking surf' is metaphorical; we grasp the expressive quality of the surf by comparing it to a wild, screaming being, sputtering and flailing about. Metaphorical imagination may have a role here too in making the connections that expressive qualities rest upon. Metaphorical exemplification is not unlike the explanation given by the embodiment account but the latter is broader because it accounts for types of expression that do not involve the application of a metaphor, and this makes it more attractive as a general theory.

I have argued that the similarity account provides part of the answer to the problem of expressive qualities in nature but that it needs to be supplemented by the embodiment account. Even though the embodiment account is a little vague, bringing the two accounts together is probably the best way to explain expressive qualities in nature, and we must be content with the fact that an entirely clear explanation may be difficult to attain (as is also the case with musical expression).

Let me finish by saying that finding a balance between the more descriptive, similarity approach and one that is perhaps more sensitive to the experience of the appreciator or appreciative community is something we also ought to aim for in the practical context of environmental planning. When we explain how expressive qualities contribute to descriptions of landscapes, we should not simply rely on discerning resemblances, which could in fact be arrived at by gathering together data on the non-aesthetic qualities of a landscape, and drawing conclusions from that. What is needed is attention to the situated context, cultural and otherwise, of the aesthetic appreciator, and the affinities we can locate between their feelings and the expressive qualities of landscapes.

When we can identify expressive qualities, we have a better idea of the predominant aesthetic characters of various landscapes. Expressive qualities, along with other aesthetic qualities, such as perceptual or imaginative qualities, provide more detail and depth to the aesthetic descriptions that issue from aesthetic responses than more general and scenically-oriented descriptions. A solid philosophical account of expressive qualities provides a clearer, non-idiosyncratic understanding for discussions in the practical context of conservation.

KNOWLEDGE IN THE INTEGRATED AESTHETIC

At this stage, it ought to be clear that like other non-cognitivists I do not view knowledge as a necessary condition of aesthetic appreciation of nature. The intellectual component of the integrated aesthetic is not significant, but it can have a place. So far, I have argued that commonsense beliefs may be in the background in aesthetic appreciation (this would be true of any experience of the world), but on some occasions it is helpful to appreciation to feed in knowledge. In my discussion of interpretation in Chapter 3, for example, I showed how folk knowledge as well as scientific knowledge underpin equally reasonable interpretations of nature.

The type of knowledge that is fed in and the occasions on which it is fed in depend very much on the demands of the object and the appreciator's cognitive stock. In Chapter 4, supporting other non-cognitivists, I argued that scientific knowledge can impede appreciation of *aesthetic* qualities, and that it does not provide more appropriate knowledge than other alternatives, such as religious or mythological narratives. I questioned the implicit claim in cognitive theories that science provides the truest foundation for appreciating nature on its own terms, and showed why science too relies on a cultural framework.

One of the main problems in cognitive theories is their lack of explanation for what actually counts as scientific knowledge in appreciation. I have said a little about how this problem might be addressed, but it would be useful to return to it here, because a better understanding helps to show why commonsense beliefs are more likely to have a role in the actual practice of aesthetic appreciation, and why it is unreasonable to demand that scientific knowledge be taken as a necessary condition or as a main component in appreciation.

That there is really no treatment of this problem by, for example, Carlson, is not altogether surprising, since distinguishing the two types of knowledge is no easy task. However, Ernst Nagel provides one of the best attempts to sort out the difference:

It is the desire for explanations which are at once systematic and
controllable by factual evidence that generates science; and it is the
organization and classification of knowledge on the basis of
explanatory principles that is the distinctive goal of the sciences.

More specifically, the sciences seek to discover and to formulate in general terms the conditions under which events of various sorts occur, the statements of such determining conditions being the explanations of the corresponding happening.

A marked feature of much information acquired in the course of ordinary experience is that, although this information may be accurate enough within certain limits, it is seldom accompanied by any explanation of why the facts are as alleged . . . Much that passes as common sense knowledge certainly is about the effects familiar things have upon matters that men happen to value; the relations of events to one another, independent of their incidence upon specific human concerns, are not systematically noticed and explored.[78]

Scientific knowledge involves explanations and clear methodology, while common sense does not set out to search for facts, explanations and verification. Commonsense knowledge is more indeterminate while science aims at certainty. This is not to say that common sense is unreliable or always inaccurate; some scientific explanations grow out of common sense beliefs. I do not mean to devalue common sense, but rather to show that it is characterised by a more practical, everyday form of knowing. This kind of knowing comes through experience (what some philosophers have called 'knowledge by acquaintance'), and this fits more easily with the strongly perceptual character of aesthetic appreciation. This type of knowledge is more in line with a more pluralistic approach to appreciation.

Local knowledge can be described as a type of commonsense knowledge which is based in the experience of a place and local practices in relation to the land. Although I am speculating, it may be the case that common (and even more local vernacular) names for flora and fauna originate in conversations about the aesthetic or other qualities of individual plants and animals. For example, in *Flora Britannica*, Richard Mabey writes that 'Queen Anne's Lace', 'Fairy Lace' and Spanish Lace' are given as vernacular names for the plant, *Anthriscus sylvestris*, because of its lacy appearance.[79] It is more humbly known as 'cow parsley', probably because it grows in or near pastures. Mabey's project covers vernacular names, folklore and literary references, art references and so on, and depends significantly on contributions of local knowledge supplied by residents of Britain. The 'Biodiversity Stories' website, sponsored by Scottish Natural Heritage and the Royal Botanic Gardens Edinburgh, brings together in one place a range of knowledges about species and habitats and our cultural relationship to them.[80] The public is invited to contribute audio- and text-based stories about the wildlife, ecology and landscapes of Scotland, with folktales, old legends, poems, ecological accounts and stories about practical uses of nature.

Hepburn provides probably the most balanced account of the role of thought and knowledge in aesthetic appreciation, and I have already said something about this in earlier chapters. The thought-content in aesthetic appreciation is distinguished from the cognitive component and is like a reflective backdrop that fuses with other elements of appreciation: 'thought is present, as we implicitly compare and contrast *here* with *elsewhere*, *actual* with *possible*, *present* with *past*. I say 'implicitly'; there may be no verbalizing or self-conscious complexity in the experience'.[81] The explicit, and 'serious' side of knowledge – science – has some role to play for Hepburn, as the appreciator may sometimes feel obliged to take into account facts described by science (or, for example, data of history). In his view, aesthetic appreciation is not hostile to science, but it has different aims and modes of approach to nature from the sciences.

It might be most accurate, then, to describe the thought and knowledge elements of the integrated aesthetic in terms of a reflective component that ranges from thoughts and beliefs in the background, to actively fed-in thoughts and beliefs, which are constituted by a range of knowledges, including common sense, folk and other cultural knowledges, including scientific knowledge. This kind of account makes room for the range of experience brought to appreciation by different appreciators, and it also allows for a flexible approach to truth, where a fixed or universal truth is replaced with the idea of local truth and bioregional truth.[82]

In all cases, the content and degree of knowledge fed in is dependent on the situation of the appreciator and the demands of the object. Relevance is determined according to the qualities of the object and the appreciative situation, which includes the context of the object, the appreciator and the relationship between them. In Chapter 5, through the butterfly example I showed how disinterestedness is consistent with relevant knowledge fed into appreciation.

The aim in formulating the integrated aesthetic has been to provide a non-cognitive model that incorporates the various dimensions of aesthetic appreciation of nature. It emphasises the relationship between subject and object by recognising the way human capacities such as perception, imagination, emotion and thought, respond to features of the aesthetic object or environment. My model is intended to be inclusive of a range of individual experience without the problems associated with a strongly subjectivist stance. Disinterestedness functions to characterise my approach accordingly.

The integrated aesthetic does not require specific knowledge from the appreciator. This is especially important in the practical context where environmental decision-making involves a wide variety of individuals who enter into the deliberative process with more or with less expertise. My model is potentially more inclusive, more open to the aesthetic experiences of inhabitants, visitors, developers, local government and so on, in working out the best solution to environmental problems.

NOTES

1. R.W. Hepburn, 'Nature in the Light of Art', in *Wonder and Other Essays* (Edinburgh: Edinburgh University Press, 1984), p. 47.
2. Thomas Heyd, 'Aesthetic Appreciation and the Many Stories About Nature', *British Journal of Aesthetics*, 41, 2001, p. 130.
3. Peter Strawson, 'Imagination and Perception', in *Freedom and Resentment* (London: Methuen and Co., 1974), p. 47.
4. Alan White, *The Language of Imagination* (Oxford: Blackwell, 1990), p. 24.
5. Recent studies on imagination include: White; Mary Warnock, *Imagination* (London: Faber and Faber, 1976); Richard Kearney, *The Wake of Imagination* (London: Hutchinson, 1988) and *The Poetics of Imagining* (Edinburgh: Edinburgh University Press, 1998); various pieces by Roger Scruton: *Modern Philosophy* (London: Sinclair Stevenson, 1994); 'Imagination', in David Cooper (ed.), *A Companion to Aesthetics* (Oxford: Blackwell, 1992), p. 212; and *Art and Imagination* (London: Methuen, 1974).
6. See Scruton, 1994, 1992. Gregory Currie also follows this distinction, but he gives it a special twist, by describing sensory or reproductive imagination as 'recreative imagination', which simulates but does not copy actual objects and events. Creative imagination, on his view, is truly creative, and does not involve simulation. See Gregory Currie, 'Imagination and Make-believe', in Berys Gaut and Dominic McIver Lopes (eds), *The Routledge Companion to Aesthetics* (London and New York: Routledge, 2001), pp. 253–62.
7. Adherents to this view are numerous in the history of philosophy, including Aristotle, Aquinas, Hobbes and Hume. Kant makes a distinction between reproductive and productive imagination, and claims that imagination is the power that 'makes the absent present' (*Anthropology*, AK,VII, 167), but he makes the further distinction between productive or transcendental imagination and reproductive or empirical imagination. The productive imagination is a transcendental condition that synthesises intuitions into conceptual experiences. Kant contrasts it with the reproductive imagination which is empirical, that is, it is given the role of image-maker for calling up images of things we have already experienced, and thus of making associations between past experiences. See Kant, *Critique of Pure Reason*, trans. Norman Kemp Smith (London: Macmillan, 1929), B151–152, p. 165. In the *Critique of Judgment*, the productive imagination is the free imagination which is the subjective ground of judgements of taste. See Immanuel Kant, *Critique of Judgment*, trans. Werner Pluhar (Indianapolis: Hackett, [1790] 1987), Ak. 241, p. 91.
8. John Dewey, *Art as Experience* (New York: Perigee, [1934] 1980), pp. 272–4.
9. Ibid. pp. 267–8.
10. Scruton, 1974, p. 98. Richard Moran also argues against the assumption that imagination is always associated with make-believe, and he points to the different ways our imaginings are deeply related to real-life situations and commitments. See Richard Moran, 'The Expression of Feeling in Imagination', *The Philosophical Review*, 103:1, 1994, pp. 75–106. Kathleen Stock makes a persuasive case for the rationality of

imagination and how imagining is a means to belief: 'Imagining is an active, rational, structured process which essentially involves the possibility of conceptually constrained inferential transitions from imaginary state of affairs to imaginary state of affairs. In imagining I do not passively contemplate a picture in my head: I explore possibilities by considering conjunctions of states of affairs and what would follow from them; I *think.' The Nature and Value of Imaginative Responses to the Fiction Film*, Ph.D. dissertation, 2002, p. 49.

11. R.G. Collingwood, *The Idea of History* (Oxford: Clarendon Press, 1946), p. 241.

12. David Novitz, *Knowledge, Fiction and Imagination* (Philadelphia: Temple University Press, 1987).

13. *Journal of Aesthetics and Art Criticism: Special Issue: Environmental Aesthetics*, 56:2, 1998, pp. 139–47.

14. Work on imagination in aesthetics has more recently focused on fiction, make-believe and simulation theory. See, for example, Kendall Walton, *Mimesis as Make-Believe* (Cambridge: Harvard University Press, 1990); Gregory Currie, *Image and Mind: Film, Philosophy and Cognitive Science* (Cambridge: Cambridge University Press, 1995). A first of its kind, the University of Leeds held a conference on 'Imagination and the Arts' in 2001.

15. See Paul Guyer, *Kant and the Claims of Taste* (Cambridge, MA, and London: Harvard University Press, 1979), pp. 250–1; Henry Allison, *Kant's Theory of Taste: A Reading of the Critique of Aesthetic Judgment* (Cambridge: Cambridge University Press, 2001), pp. 46–51, especially, p. 50. Malcolm Budd also conveys this interpretation when he says that even in free play, imagination is 'monitored' by the understanding, and that imagination must still provide an image that is 'a representation of the way the object actually is, and, accordingly, the imagination is not free to manufacture whatever form it pleases'. See Malcolm Budd, 'Delight in the Natural World: Kant on Aesthetic Appreciation. Part I: Natural Beauty, *British Journal of Aesthetics*, 38:1, 1998, pp. 6–7. Imagination's free play indicates the fact that judgements of taste are reflective judgements, having to do with indeterminate rather than determinate concepts. Also, the harmonious free play of the two faculties is what underlies the 'subjective purposiveness' of judgements of taste, and the pleasure that issues from judgements of the beautiful.

16. Kant, *Critique of Judgment*, §49, Ak. 314, p. 182.

17. See Guyer, 1979, pp. 233–4; Salim Kemal, *Kant's Aesthetic Theory*, 2nd edn (New York: St Martin's Press, 1997), pp. 45–7.

18. Kemal, p. 47. For textual evidence, see Kant, 1987, §49, Ak. 314–15, pp. 182–3.

19. See Kant, 1987, §51, Ak. 320, p. 189.

20. Ibid. §42, Ak. 300, pp. 166–7.

21. Allison, pp. 258–9; 262–3.

22. Kant, 1987, §42, Ak. 302, p. 169. Translator's brackets.

23. Ibid. §59, Ak. 354, p. 230. Translator's brackets. Kant does not argue that we do in fact judge them morally, but he wants to make an analogy.

24. Further discussion of metaphorical imagination and its connection to constructing metaphors can be found in Emily Brady, 'The City in Aesthetic Imagination', in Arto Haapala (ed.), *The City as Cultural Metaphor: Studies in Urban Aesthetics* (Lahti: International Institute of Applied Aesthetics, 1998). See also Ronald Hepburn, 'Trivial and Serious in Aesthetic Appreciation of Nature', in Salim Kemal and Ivan Gaskell (eds), *Landscape, Natural Beauty and the Arts* (Cambridge: Cambridge University Press, 1993), pp. 74–5.

25. Allen Carlson, *Aesthetics and the Environment: The Appreciation of Nature, Art and Architecture* (New York and London: Routledge, 2000), pp. 227–8.
26. The exploratory, projective and ampliative modes of imagination are loosely borrowed from Anthony Savile who discusses them in relation to narrative paintings. See Anthony Savile, *Aesthetic Reconstructions* (Oxford: Basil Blackwell, 1988). The fourth, revelatory imagination, is my own, although it resembles some other views on the revealing power of imagination. For example, see John Ruskin's discussion of 'penetrative imagination' in Volume Two, Section II of *Modern Painters*, edited and abridged by David Barrie (London: Pilkington Press, [1873] 1987). Dewey also refers to the revelatory (but non-theistic) power of imagination through art: 'revelation in art is the quickened expansion of experience'. See Dewey, p. 270. Hepburn's metaphysical imagination and the role of imagination in Kant's 'aesthetic ideas' also refer to its revelatory power.
27. Stephanie Ross, *What Gardens Mean* (Chicago and London: University of Chicago Press, 1998), p. 166. Invitation is a device also used by some artists. An interesting example of this is Caspar David Friedrich's *Rückenfigur* paintings, which usually depict a single figure with her or his back turned to the (external) viewer so that the figure in the picture is a spectator of the landscape or other scene. This positioning of the figure invites the external spectator to identify with her or him, and enter the painted scene. See Joseph Koerner, *Caspar David Friedrich and the Subject of Landscape* (London: Reaktion Books, 1990), p. 211.
28. Donald Crawford, 'Nature and Art: Some Dialectical Relationships', *Journal of Aesthetics and Art Criticism*, 42, 1983, p. 54.
29. R. K. Elliott, 'Imagination: A Kind of Magical Faculty', in Paul Crowther (ed.), *Collected Essays of R. K. Elliott* (Aldershot: Ashgate, forthcoming).
30. These remarks are from an interview with Andrew Wyeth. (Wanda Corn, *The Art of Andrew Wyeth* (Greenwich: New York Graphic Society, 1973), p. 55.) I thank Fran Speed for drawing my attention to this quote.
31. Yuriko Saito, 'The Japanese Appreciation of Nature', *British Journal of Aesthetics*, 25:3, 1985, p. 247. She refers to Kenkō's passage from *Essays in Idleness*.
32. Aldo Leopold, *A Sand County Almanac* (New York: Oxford University Press, [1949] 1968), p. 129.
33. See also Hepburn, 1993, for issues related to this point.
34. Scruton, 1974, p. 98.
35. R. K. Elliott, 'Imagination in the Experience of Art', *Royal Institute of Philosophy Lectures, vol. six, 1971–1972: Philosophy and the Arts* (New York: St Martin's Press, 1974), p. 101. Anthony Savile has also tackled this problem in the context of art. He defends the view that imagination has a proper role in aesthetic experience, but, unlike Elliott, he emphasises the importance of checking the activity of imagination though at the same time allowing it the freedom required for the richest possible experience of the work. The artwork itself controls the imaginative activity through the 'signs that the artist lays down'. Furthermore, Savile argues that the careful use of imagination by the spectator ensures that the picture is always at the centre of the aesthetic experience, such that it never becomes a mere stimulus for some private fantasy (Savile, 1988, esp. p. 72). Unlike Savile, however, Elliott does not rely on an explicit reference to artistic attention, so his position is more easily brought into the context of natural objects. Some discussion of ways to sort relevant from irrelevant imaginings are suggested by Hepburn in Hepburn, 1993; and in 'Landscape and the Metaphysical Imagination,' *Environmental Values*, 5:3, 1996, pp. 191–204. In the

context of fiction, see Peter Lamarque, 'In and Out of Imaginary Worlds', in John Skorupski and Dudley Knowles (eds), *Virtue and Taste, Philosophical Quarterly Supplementary Series, Vol. 2* (Oxford: Blackwell, 1993).

36. Susan Feagin presents a persuasive argument for the general benefits of developing imagination's 'affective flexibility' through the aesthetic experience of reading fiction. See *Reading with Feeling* (Ithaca: Cornell University Press, 1996), ch. 11.

37. Rolston is one cognitivist I do not discuss in this chapter, and who does not appear to give any role to imagination. He does not make any explicit objections to my position, but he does worry that what he calls an 'expressionist' view of nature treats it as a 'smorgasbord of opportunities that humans can do with as they please. No one aesthetic response is more or less correct than any other; what counts is the imaginative play, and what is remarkable is nature's richness in launching this play.' See Holmes Rolston, III, 'Does Aesthetic Appreciation of Landscapes Need to Be Science-Based?', *British Journal of Aesthetics*, 35:4, 1995, p. 376.

38. Marcia Muelder Eaton, 'Fact and Fiction in the Aesthetic Appreciation of Nature', *Journal of Aesthetics and Art Criticism: Special Issue on Environmental Aesthetics*, 56:2, 1998, pp. 149–56.

39. Ibid. p. 152.

40. Ibid. p. 150. My emphasis.

41. Ronald Moore, 'Appreciating Natural Beauty', *Journal of Aesthetic Education: Symposium on Natural Aesthetics*, 33:3, 1999, pp. 42–58.

42. Ibid. p. 53.

43. Robert Fudge, 'Imagination and the Science-based Aesthetic Appreciation of Nature', *Journal of Aesthetics and Art Criticism*, 59:3, 2001, p. 282.

44. Ibid. p. 281.

45. Ibid. pp. 281–2.

46. Fudge is also concerned with defending the role of science against some of the criticisms I raised in the original article. To respond to these I refer the reader back to my arguments against cognitive theories in Chapter 4, where I deal with many of the same issues. There, I discussed some of the problems related to science as a dominant component in appreciation, and I also cited arguments by others, such as Stecker and Hepburn, to support my case.

47. Moore, pp. 53, 55.

48. I assume that the example refers to a riddle in Lewis Carroll's *Alice in Wonderland*, where the Mad Hatter asks, 'Why is a raven like a writing desk?' As a riddle, the question just challenges and puzzles us and does not lead imagination smoothly or easily to make connections.

49. Yuriko Saito, 'Appreciating Nature on its Own Terms', *Environmental Ethics*, 20, 1998, p. 140.

50. Stan Godlovitch, 'Valuing Nature and the Autonomy of Natural Aesthetics', *British Journal of Aesthetics*, 38:2, 1998, p. 181 and p. 181n.

51. Hepburn, 1993, p. 73.

52. Carlson, 2000, p. 228.

53. Tony Hillerman, *A Thief of Time* (New York: Harper, 1988), p. 148, quoted by Carlson, 2000, p. 227.

54. Edgar Allen Poe, 'A Descent into the Maelström' in *The Complete Tales and Poems of Edgar Allen Poe* (New York: Modern Library, 1938), p. 128.

55. Noël Carroll, 'Being Moved by Nature: Between Religion and Natural History', in Kemal and Gaskell, 1993, pp. 257–8.

56. Noël Carroll, *Beyond Aesthetics: Philosophical Essays* (Cambridge: Cambridge University Press, 2001), p. 391.

57. Jane Howarth, 'Nature's Moods', *British Journal of Aesthetics*, 35:2, 1995, pp. 108–20.

58. Non-human animals raise another set of issues that cannot be addressed here. A sad-looking dog may resemble the human appearance of sadness, but we cannot be sure what emotional states dogs are experiencing or how those states compare to human emotional states. See Stephen Davies, *Musical Meaning and Expression* (Ithaca and London: Cornell University Press, 1994), p. 227.

59. Howarth, p. 113.

60. Ibid. p. 115.

61. Noël Carroll, *Philosophy of Art: A Contemporary Introduction* (London and New York: Routledge, 1999), p. 101.

62. Ibid.

63. Jerrold Levinson, *The Pleasures of Aesthetics: Philosophical Essays* (Ithaca: Cornell University Press, 1996), p. 93; John Spackman, 'Expression Theory of Art', in Michael Kelly (ed.), *Encyclopedia of Aesthetics*, vol. 2 (New York and Oxford: Oxford University Press, 1998), p. 142. Exponents of this view include Peter Kivy and Stephen Davies.

64. Davies, p. 103.

65. Ibid. p. 223.

66. From Peter Kivy, *Sound Sentiment* (Philadelphia: Temple University Press, 1989), discussed by Mark DeBellis, 'Music', in Berys Gaut and Dominic McIver Lopes (eds), *The Routledge Companion to Aesthetics* (London and New York, 2000), pp. 531–44.

67. Ronald Hepburn, 'Contemporary Aesthetics and the Neglect of Natural Beauty', in *Wonder and Other Essays* (Edinburgh: Edinburgh University Press, 1984), p. 20.

68. Davies, ch. 6.

69. Saito, 1985, p. 243.

70. As described by Alan Holland and John O'Neill in 'The Integrity of Nature Over Time: Some Problems', TWP 96-08, *The Thingmount Working Paper Series on the Philosophy of Conservation* (Centre for Philosophy, Lancaster University, 1996), p. 2.

71. Spackman, p. 143.

72. DeBellis, p. 534.

73. Saito, 1985, p. 245.

74. George Santayana, *The Sense of Beauty: Being the Outline of Aesthetic Theory* (New York: Dover, [1896] 1955), p. 121.

75. Ibid. p. 130.

76. Saito, 1985, p. 244.

77. Carlson, 2000, p. 143.

78. Ernst Nagel, *The Structure of Science: Problems in the Logic of Scientific Explanation* (Indianapolis and Cambridge: Hackett, 1979), pp. 3–6.

79. Richard Mabey, *Flora Britannica* (London: Sinclair Stevenson, 1996), pp. 283–5. Mabey's current project is compiling a *Birds Britannica*.

80. www.biodiversitystories.co.uk

81. Hepburn, 1993, pp. 66–7.

82. These types of truth are suggested by Jim Cheney, as cited by Saito in 'Appreciating Nature on its Own Terms', *Environmental Ethics*, 20, 1998, p. 148.

CHAPTER 7

Aesthetic Judgements of the Natural Environment and Aesthetic Communication

I n this chapter I set out to establish the objectivity of aesthetic judgements of nature. My case is not only a theoretical one in relation to theories in philosophical aesthetics. If aesthetic value is to be taken seriously in the practical context of environmental planning and policy-making, objectivity, of some degree at least, is essential. Aesthetic value is often viewed as reflecting mere personal preferences rather than rational aesthetic judgements. We do argue about our aesthetic judgements, and this presents a promising starting point. Why would we bother if such matters were merely expressions of personal taste? Our own experiences do, however, matter, so the case I make here is for objectivity in terms of the intersubjective validity of aesthetic judgements, rather than a rigid objectivity that would leave out the subjective dimension of aesthetic experience altogether.

I begin with a critical discussion of a few models of objectivity, and I defend the very distinctive foundation of our judgements through the practice, explanation, and support we give in aesthetic justification. The position I put forward, which is based on the ideas of Kant and Sibley, provides a strong foundation for the idea of aesthetic communication. I argue that this type of communication gives further support to the idea that aesthetic judgements are not private expressions of taste. I conclude the chapter by showing how my model of aesthetic justification and communication encourages an environmental aesthetic education that enables the education of capacities for the discovery of aesthetic value in the environment.

AESTHETIC JUDGEMENTS AND OBJECTIVITY

The problem of establishing the objectivity of aesthetic judgement continues to be a vexing problem in philosophical aesthetics. It is possible to identify a few different strategies for locating the objectivity of aesthetic value. In what follows, I sketch out the territory of the debate to give some background to later discussion on this problem within environmental aesthetics.

Aesthetic Realism

A popular contemporary strategy adopts a metaphysical approach through realism of aesthetic properties. If one can show that aesthetic properties are real and not subjective projections on to the world, then it is more likely that we can provide an objective basis for evaluations. Within this approach there are stronger and weaker varieties. Strong aesthetic realism argues that aesthetic properties are objective but also intrinsic, so they are non-relational. Their existence is independent of our aesthetic judgements about them and the values and beliefs we hold.[1] Moderate varieties of aesthetic realism argue that aesthetic properties are relational to some degree and supervene on non-aesthetic objective properties.[2] Supervenience theses are primarily aimed at explaining aesthetic descriptions, but they also have force in establishing an objective basis for our aesthetic judgements (as involving evaluations).[3] While aesthetic descriptions ground evaluations, more support may be required to justify the objectivity of the evaluative component of attributions of aesthetic value.

Anti-realists object to the independent and real status of aesthetic properties and they play up the relational character of aesthetic judgements. They also point out that there may be disagreements among even fairly skilled judges. Moderate varieties of anti-realism try to locate some agreement among judgements, while stronger ones argue for the deeply relative and subjective nature of aesthetic evaluation.[4]

In my discussion of the nature of aesthetic qualities in Chapter 1, I set out why I hold a moderate realist position on aesthetic qualities. This position, a robust, relativised, and pragmatic version of aesthetic supervenience, is assumed as a starting point in my discussion of the justification of aesthetic judgements below.

Ideal Judges

Another common strategy gives empirical grounds for aesthetic justification by appeal to competent judges, that is, individuals with developed aesthetic sensibilities and experience. The most well-known proponent of this position is David Hume, from his essay 'Of the Standard of Taste.'[5] Hume recognises that there is divergence in our aesthetic responses and, ultimately, he argues that a standard of taste is needed to settle disputes and fix objectivity of value. This standard is set by an ideal judge or 'true critic', who is free from 'defects' in taste. These defects include a lack of 'delicacy' and 'good sense' (the ability to perceive and reason through all the relevant aesthetic features or qualities of an artwork); failure to have practised and failure to have made comparisons, that is, not to have practised aesthetic discernments and to make comparative judgements between cases of excellent works, and finally to be prejudiced or to allow biases and other irrelevant factors to affect one's judgement.[6] Hume has in mind literary and art critics but this type of position could be extended to include other appreciators with relevant sensibility and experience. The development of taste occurs (in one way) through the social process of communication by which people initiate one another into, and progress in mutual refinement of, the perception of aesthetic qualities and the making of aesthetic judgements.

While variations of this approach have been popular, it is strongly art-oriented and less useful for environmental appreciation.[7] With artworks, a large part of our judgement will relate to whether or not the artist has succeeded in producing a work of skill, originality and creativity. Knowledge of what skill, originality and creativity mean within the artworld may be needed in some cases, or at least it may be the case that we would rely on the best art critics if we have no idea where to begin our criticism of a piece. With nature we are not judging the aesthetic object within such a context, so we would not apply concepts such as skill, creativity and originality, nor would the art critic have any role. A cognitive model of aesthetic appreciation of nature would argue here that we ought to turn to ecologists, geologists and so on to tell us how to appreciate the environment, a claim that I dispute given my criticisms of cognitive theories of appreciation (although it is both perceptual discernment and knowledge that Hume requires of the true critic).[8] These experts might be able to tell us whether or not an ecosystem is healthy or how old a mountain is, but why would we put faith in these facts rather than in someone who brings keen aesthetic interest and sensitivity to her or his appreciation of the environment? We would be more likely to rely on a nature poet, an avid hill-walker, or just a friend whose judgement we trust to help us to grasp aesthetic value.

A further objection arises from Hume's claim that there are principles of taste established by the standards set by true critics. Hume argues that there are 'rules of art' which can be established, like other rules or principles (for example, in science), through empirical observation.[9] Establishing such principles seems far-fetched, even though there may be agreement over time on exemplars of beauty in art and in nature. My main worry is the attempt to establish such rules through generalisation and induction. Aesthetic judgements are not susceptible to this kind of proof. Arguments by Kant and Sibley, below, show why this is true.

Kant on Aesthetic Justification

In contrast to Hume, Kant argues that judgements of taste claim (subjective) universal validity *a priori*, that is, not by reference to the empirical evidence of critics. The apparent paradox that Kant is faced with in giving justification for the subjective universal validity (or intersubjectivity) of judgements of taste is that such judgements are 'singular' (particular) judgements grounded in feeling in the subject. Yet at the same time we have the right to 'demand' agreement from others. To show why this is not inconsistent, Kant argues against both rationalist and empiricist explanations. He does not posit rules or principles of taste; beauty is not a concept or an objective quality in the world. Rather, beauty is connected to the first-hand perception of the structural qualities of the object as they attune with and set the mental powers of imagination and understanding into free play.

Judgements of taste do have necessity, but a special kind: 'a necessity that does not depend on any a priori bases of proof by the presentation of which we could compel [people to give] the assent that a judgment of taste requires of everyone'.[10] That is, they are not making general claims about some object that would apply to all objects of that kind. My judgement, 'This rose is beautiful', applies only to this particular rose, not to all roses. Aesthetic judgements are open to argument but are, according to Kant, *unprincipled*.[11] They do not rest on inductive or deductive proof. So, in so far as reasons have to be generalisable to have any force, we do not give reasons for our judgements of taste:

> There can be no rule by which someone could be compelled to acknowledge that something is beautiful. No one can use reasons or principles to talk us into a judgment on whether some garment, house, or flower is beautiful. We want to submit the object to our own eyes, just as if our liking of it depended on that sensation.[12]

Kant recognises that empirical arguments have also been made for aesthetic judgements, including arguments based on ideal critics and the 'test of time', and he explicitly refers to Hume in this context.[13] In this respect, Kant is equally insistent that such arguments do not establish the validity of the judgement of taste:

> universal validity is not to be established by gathering votes and asking people what kind of sensation they are having; but it must rest, as it were, on an autonomy of the subject who is making a judgement about the feeling of pleasure . . . , i.e. it must rest on his own taste; and yet it is also not to be derived from concepts.[14]

we demand that he judge for himself: he should not have to grope about among other people's judgments by means of experience, to gain instruction in advance from whether they like or dislike that object; so we demand that he pronounce his judgment a priori, that he not make it [by way of] imitation.[15]

Kant's justification for these claims about the judgement of taste is given in different stages in the *Critique of Aesthetic Judgment*, although his formal argument appears in §38. The judgement of taste, while subjective, is still a type of judgement we make, and by virtue of that it involves the essential faculties of cognition, imagination and understanding. Both reflective and determinate judgements rest on a mental state in the subject. This mental state involves the faculties necessary for 'cognition in general', imagination and understanding, and it makes our judgements 'universally communicable'. We can assume in others the basic capacity for cognition in general, in terms of the two mental powers and their activity as necessary for cognition. Hence we can presuppose that the 'subjective conditions' hold in the judgement of taste for ourselves as well as others.[16] Kant puts this in terms of the *sensus communis*, the 'common sense' or universally possessed sensibility.[17] Therefore, we demand agreement and intersubjective import for our aesthetic judgements. The communicability of aesthetic judgements (and indeed of all judgements) is extremely important to Kant, and I return to a discussion of this below.

An extra point of support for his argument is the concept of disinterestedness. If this condition holds, which is a condition of the possibility of the judgement of taste, Kant claims that 'private conditions' – personal biases and idiosyncrasies related to interest or desire in relation to the aesthetic object – will not be present to create disagreement.

Kant's attempt to prove the right to demand agreement, the evaluative force of aesthetic judgements, is successful but limited in that it does not show that such agreement actually exists or that we will succeed in making unbiased aesthetic judgements.[18] In his overall analysis of the normativity of judgements of taste, he is able to show their essentially public nature; communicability is inherent to them. This is not insignificant, and we at least have the promise of agreement. He only asserts that in making the judgement of taste we postulate the *possibility* of agreement and does not attempt to establish agreement in fact but only to show what conditions would make it possible. Kant is well aware that there will be disagreement and that there are likely to be 'private conditions' or biases and prejudices that will create disputes about taste. Indeed, we are just as susceptible to making impure aesthetic judgements as we are to making impure moral judgements.

Although Kant's aesthetics is not explicitly sensitive to differences in taste between cultures, he is not ignorant of possible differences either. It could be argued that his quest for universality is unrealistic, but not if one takes on board his more modest attempt to establish that we have the right to demand agreement, even if there is no guarantee of disinterested judgements. The warrant for such a demand is based on similar capacities, detachment from biases and awareness of how personal interests affect our judgements. Even though 'demand' is a strong term, there are certainly cases where we feel indignant when others disagree. In cases of being deeply moved or struck by something, it would not be odd to say that we would be surprised if others disagreed. In my discussion of Sibley, I show how some of Kant's ideas can be given contemporary import in the context of aesthetic appreciation of environments.

AESTHETIC JUDGEMENTS OF NATURE

In the context of aesthetic appreciation of nature, there have been some attempts to show how our judgements are grounded in some kind of objectivity, rather than being merely preferences. I shall take a critical look at objectivist positions on aesthetic judgement of nature by Allen Carlson and Janna Thompson. I construct a third approach that offers an objectivity that stresses the activities involved in explanation and justification, rather than reference to a standard of truth. As we shall see, Sibley's idea of 'perceptual proof' leaves room for the kind of aesthetic engagement that fits well with the integrated approach to aesthetic appreciation for which I have been arguing.

Carlson's Categories of Knowledge

A theory of aesthetic justification in relation to the arts usually grounds objectivity either in some kind of realism about aesthetic properties or epistemologically in a solid knowledge base. Kendall Walton's 'categories of art' is an example of the latter, and Carlson uses it to produce an analogous account in relation to appreciation of nature. It is worth mentioning that Carlson's natural environmental model provides a complete theory of aesthetic appreciation, that is, it includes a theory of justification. Carlson not only argues for the grounds of appreciation of nature as opposed to art, but also that aesthetic judgements can be shown to be true or correct. The standard of correctness for our judgements is found in the categories of natural science.

Carlson's position is valuable as a serious, recent attempt to show why our aesthetic judgements of nature are not hopelessly relative. His argument is set against Walton's claim that aesthetic judgements of nature are relative while judgements of art are not, and the 'Human Chauvinistic Aesthetic', which argues that aesthetic judgements necessarily involve 'artistry', being essentially tied to human production (to artworks).[19] The latter view holds that aesthetic evaluation cannot take place in the context of natural objects. Carlson argues forcefully against these views, and I agree with him that they are highly problematic and difficult to defend.

I have already set out criticisms of Carlson's position on appreciation in Chapter 4, and many of these also apply to his views on aesthetic justification. Therefore, here, I shall just emphasise a couple of points made earlier. Carlson puts forward strong objectivity by determining correctness according to a scientific conception of nature. However, we have seen that he relies on an uncritical conception of science as a standard of objectivity, without considering the view that science might not give us a 'transparent mode of access to the world'.[20]

Carlson might reply by arguing that science nonetheless provides the best framework for securing objectivity in our judgements. But I would reiterate that aesthetic appreciation is a very different kind of activity than science, and that it would be odd to rely on the content of this type of knowledge as our guide to objectivity. This is not only true of the experience of appreciation and the aesthetic descriptions we give, but also in the activity of aesthetic justification, which forms an important part of appreciation. The activity of justification is quite distinctive in aesthetic appreciation as I show, below, in my discussion of Sibley's idea of perceptual proof.

I have argued that science is too narrow a basis for appreciation for a number of reasons that are relevant to the problem of justification. Cognitive theories' central reliance on scientific knowledge excludes other legitimate stories of the environment. Science may also be exclusive in narrowing the range of appreciations that are considered appropriate, such as those that are not informed by science. The use of a range of sources for grounding appreciation – perception, non-scientific knowledge, emotion, imagination – avoids strong objectivism but does not necessarily lead to subjectivism. Rather than following Carlson's essentialism, I have argued that our appreciation of the natural world ought to be understood more flexibly and openly.

In the context of interpretation (Chapter 3), I argued for a critical pluralism that sorts out a range of acceptable interpretations according to their reasonableness and relevance rather than truth or falsity. Instead of a single correct interpretation, there may be a set of interpretations that make sense in respect of the aesthetic object. This strategy avoids rigid objectivity, but it also does not accept eccentric or idiosyncratic interpretations. A deep assumption of this pluralistic stance is that our aesthetic responses are not private. While aesthetic responses will have their individuality, they are shareable and communicable.

In this spirit, our evaluations of nature and the justifications we give of them are also deemed acceptable not on the basis of being true or false but rather as being reasonable and understandable. It is possible to have objectivity without truth. Determining the reasonableness of our judgements will not be a matter of an appeal to a standard of correctness found in science or 'professional/expert nature critics'. Instead, it will be through the activity of giving both explanations and justifications for our judgements, where the appeal is to a range of sources, as opposed to a single one.

Apart from my concerns about the strictness in Carlson's approach, it also gives little explanation about how to make comparative judgements of natural objects. Although in his writings Carlson has discussed modified environments, his model of aesthetic appreciation of nature is framed around natural environments, or at least this is what his view of 'positive aesthetics' indicates. Positive aesthetics is the view that, 'All virgin nature, in short, is essentially aesthetically good.'[21] In the case of wild nature – or, I take it, nature that is predominantly untouched by humans – nothing can ever be ugly. There are no grounds for attributions of negative aesthetic value. I discuss this type of criticism below through objections raised by Thompson.

The Analogy with Art Criticism

A more promising theory of objectivity in aesthetic judgements of nature is put forward by Janna Thompson.[22] She argues for objectivity, but not in the strong sense supposed by a scientific model. Her approach emphasises the practice of justification rather than a standard of correctness as such.

Thompson begins by pointing to the problem of how aesthetic value has been neglected in environmental philosophy in comparison to ethical value. To rectify this she argues that our aesthetic judgements of nature are objective and that aesthetic value is a kind of intrinsic value. Thompson wants a minimal objectivity, where we are able to give reasons and justification for our judgements, even when there is disagreement.[23] Aesthetic value should not be confused with instrumental values such as amenity or recreational value; we do not value nature aesthetically for the pleasure or satisfaction it gives us, rather it has value in itself. The intrinsic value she argues for is not that nature has value independently of human perceivers, but rather that a thing is valued for its own sake, or respected as having value in its own right.

Although Thompson finds Carlson's view attractive in some ways, she believes that his strategy for establishing objectivity is unsuccessful. She questions his positive aesthetics because it automatically privileges the aesthetic value of wilderness over cultivated nature. Cultivated nature will always be aesthetically inferior to wild nature, and while the former can be ugly, the latter can only ever be beautiful. Moreover, this makes it very difficult to make meaningful comparative aesthetic judgements between different wild environments. How do we judge the value of a wild swamp compared to a wild mountain in Carlson's view?[24] Thompson asks why natural history should be privileged over another history as that which grounds the objectivity of aesthetic judgements of nature, and in so doing she also sheds light on the fact that Carlson's position on aesthetic judgements is less applicable to modified nature: 'A rural neighborhood, a city, a trash dump, or a garden all have a history, a complex relationship between parts, that we can come to appreciate. It is not clear why a history of human interference should require us to value an environment less.'[25]

Together, these problems lead to an unsatisfactory objectivity for the aesthetic value of nature; Carlson cannot provide an adequate basis for making aesthetic discriminations in this context. Thompson suggests an interesting alternative strategy for fixing that objectivity. Her argument is straightforward: aesthetic appreciation of nature involves many of the same practices as the aesthetic appreciation of art, and the practices we find in the latter have an objective basis:

> The ability to make good judgments about art is demonstrated in the practice of making and justifying judgments about particular works of art. So too our ability to make aesthetic judgments about nature is demonstrated by the way we make and justify judgments about particular environments or objects.[26]

Support for these claims comes through examples of how we justify our judgements about art, with analogous cases for nature. She notes differences between art and nature, for example pointing to the role of the artist's intention as lacking in the latter. However, she avoids falling foul of the view that such differences undermine her position and instead she draws usefully on aspects of the aesthetic response that are common to our experiences of art and nature. She notes aspects such as the appeal of colour and light, challenges to imagination and perception, and the role of culture and history in our appreciation of nature.

Thompson is on the right track, and I agree with her criticisms of positive aesthetics. Her discussion provides a good starting point for showing how to ground our aesthetic judgements, but as it stands there is a central weakness. The argument underestimates the complexities in establishing the objectivity of aesthetic judgements. She is right to claim that, as with art, we can in fact provide explanations and justification for our aesthetic judgements of nature, so this meets a minimal standard of objectivity. But she does not offer sufficient support for her case. We are left wondering about the nature of that justification – how exactly do we back up our judgements? Thompson gives examples to show the ways we go about making defensible judgements, but her explanation of the structure of that justification and the nature of our explanation is sketchy. We are not shown how critics are discriminating in their judgements. Without a better idea of what grounds objectivity, we have no solid account to underpin our aesthetic judgements.

I do think that Thompson's general approach is sound, and it provides the seeds of an alternative approach. In the next section, I shall build on the strengths of her ideas to make my own case for objectivity.

Sibley on Aesthetic Explanation and Justification

My alternative approach to showing how aesthetic judgements of nature are objective relies heavily on Sibley's theory of aesthetic evaluation. There are several strengths in his account. First, like Kant, he is able to pin down the very distinctive nature of aesthetic judgements and their objectivity. Sibley shows why we do not rely on logical proofs for our judgements, but rather on the first-hand, perceptual experience of the aesthetic object. As I see it, his approach aims for practical objectivity. This objectivity does not make a case for the universality of aesthetic judgements, and it rejects the view that aesthetic justification involves applying rules categorically. Rather, it rests on the concrete experience of appreciators who use aesthetic language to communicate their judgements to others. Being more concrete, Sibley's approach has a clearer, more direct bearing on the practice of making aesthetic judgements and determining their force in the context of environmental conservation.

Second, of the different views discussed here, Sibley's view has the advantage of being an open and egalitarian approach to understanding the status of aesthetic judgements. It does not rely on expert knowledge, but rather only on sensitive perception for noticing and discerning aesthetic qualities. Although he uses the term 'taste' to describe this sensitivity, his use is opposed to elitism and special expertise. Rather, it is connected to capacities for perception shared by almost everyone, including children.[27] We can make better judgements if we develop our abilities to discern aesthetic qualities; his idea of aesthetic education is not one of being taught by experts, but rather seeing for oneself and showing others.[28] In Sibleyan terms, the activity of aesthetic justification relies on shared experience that is accessible to all. Also, as I hope to show, the 'aesthetic conversation' which takes place in the Sibleyan model has great potential for fostering an environmental aesthetic education.

Third, Sibley's views are not art-oriented but instead are neutral in terms of the aesthetic object. Although he does not give a theory of aesthetic judgements tailored for the environment, his aesthetic–non-aesthetic distinction and his theory of aesthetic evaluation are aimed at a range of aesthetic objects, including artefacts (artworks and design objects) and natural objects and environments (for example, animals, human faces, sunsets, clouds and meadows).[29]

Sibley's account of aesthetic evaluation involves three different types of remarks.[30] The first type is a straightforward non-aesthetic description, where no aesthetic sensitivity is required, and where agreement is expected. For example, I might say that a particular tree has a full, rounded shape, or that a piece of moss is green and wet. The second type of remark is an aesthetic description, such as, 'the horse moves gracefully', or 'the desert sand ripples like a vast ocean'. Aesthetic sensitivity and discrimination are needed to make this kind of remark, and the possibility of disagreement is increased. Third, there are 'overall verdicts', when we make aesthetic judgments that express a general verdict or evaluation of the aesthetic object, for example, 'What a magnificent horse!' These different remarks may be linked in aesthetic criticism. Our aesthetic descriptions are supported through non-aesthetic descriptions, and we give substance to our overall verdicts through our aesthetic descriptions. I might say, for example, that one of the things that makes the horse magnificent is the way it moves so gracefully.

In Chapter 1, I explained Sibley's aesthetic–non-aesthetic distinction and how it shows a particular kind of dependency relation between aesthetic and non-aesthetic qualities.[31] Non-aesthetic qualities determine aesthetic qualities, so that any change in the former causes changes in the latter. Sibley never describes his theory as a supervenience thesis, and he was not in favour of conceiving of aesthetic properties as real in a metaphysical sense.[32] Instead he was primarily interested in the use of aesthetic language, or 'aesthetic concepts'. In any case, the force of that dependency relation holds. Given agreement in non-aesthetic qualities and by tying aesthetic to non-aesthetic qualities, this dependency provides grounds for explaining our aesthetic descriptions. The explanations we give, however, are not arrived at through inductive or deductive methods.

Aesthetic qualities are not positively condition-governed, which is to say that we could never infer from the existence of a set of non-aesthetic qualities that particular aesthetic qualities exist. Aesthetic judgements are particular rather than general judgements, so our aesthetic descriptions and evaluations are not a matter of inference from general criteria.[33] We do not apply rules or standards in order to justify our judgements. Against Hume, and with Kant, Sibley argues that aesthetics is not a science.[34] In this respect we do not give inferential reasons for our aesthetic judgements, but rather explanatory reasons only.[35]

For Sibley, aesthetic judgements begin in first-hand, perceptual experience of some aesthetic object. In Chapter 1, I discussed the comparison that has been made between aesthetic and colour judgements in order to show why philosophers think that aesthetic qualities are similar to secondary qualities. Aesthetic qualities, like colour (a secondary quality), are relational, that is, they involve a perceiver in relation to some sense data. Aesthetic qualities are not independent of human perceivers. Colour judgements are also dependent on first-hand perception of something, and clearly depend upon human visual apparatus in addition to sense data. With colours, notice also that we generally expect that others will recognise the same colours that we do (assuming normal colour vision). There is variation and disagreement in colour judgements, as in aesthetic judgements, but less so. As a type of perceptual judgement, aesthetic judgements involve perceptual discernments that are not unlike colour discriminations. And in so far as colour judgements involve objectivity and rest in 'a certain kind of appeal to agreement in reaction and discrimination', we may say that aesthetic judgements share something important with colour judgements.[36]

Perception is therefore where attributions of aesthetic value begin. The objectivity in our aesthetic justifications is explained through this context, which is essentially the context of aesthetic criticism where aesthetic descriptions and attributions of value are carried out and discussed. Sibley identifies two critical methods that comprise two stages in the process of justification, 'explanation' and 'perceptual proof'.[37]

Explanation 'consists largely in showing how aesthetic effects are achieved . . . by isolating and pointing out what is (notably, mainly, in part) responsible'.[38] The appreciator, or critic, if sensitive enough, is able to point out where aesthetic and non-aesthetic qualities lie and why the object has the aesthetic character that it does. This activity not only enables us to recognise the basis of our judgement and to have greater confidence in it, but as

> we come to realize how boldly or subtly, with what skill, economy, and exactness, the effect is achieved, how each detail is judged to a nicety and all work together with a fine precision, our appreciation is deepened and enriched and becomes more intelligent in being articulate.[39]

Justification of aesthetic judgements primarily involves giving 'perceptual proof', the second stage in the justificatory process. In this critical activity, which Sibley sees as more important than explanation, we are trying to help others 'to see and judge for themselves' aesthetic qualities.[40] We are successful if we are in fact able to get others to see the qualities we have seen. This activity and the discussion that ensues from it enables one to grasp a quality that was overlooked or a relationship that has been missed between a non-aesthetic and aesthetic quality. It is still possible of course that one may be unsuccessful in getting someone to see an aesthetic quality.

Although Sibley refers to this proof as perceptual, as we shall see, it is only the context and justificatory method, as first hand, that he describes as perceptual. Not only do some of the critical activities draw on sources beyond perception (such as imagination), it is also significant that the aesthetic qualities that are identified are not merely perceptual ones, but may include a range of aesthetic qualities, for example expressive and imaginative qualities.

Perceptual proof is a method whereby appreciators use a set of critical devices to demonstrate and support the explanation they have given of their aesthetic judgement. Appreciators are trying to show others that the aesthetic qualities are there by getting people to see those qualities for themselves. This kind of public, persuasive method is a type of proof, laying claim to objectivity, yet of course very unlike other kinds of proofs:

> an activity the successful outcome of which is seeing or hearing cannot, I think, be called reasoning. I may have reasons for thinking something is graceful, but not reasons for seeing it is. Yet aesthetic perception, as I have said, is essential to aesthetic judgement; one could not therefore be brought to make an aesthetic judgement simply as the outcome of considering reasons, however good. It is a confusion of disparate activities to suppose that in this sense one could have a 'rational justification' for making an aesthetic judgement. Thus the aesthetic judgment I am concerned with can neither *have* nor *lack* a rational basis in this sense, namely, that they can either be or fail to be the outcome of good or bad reasoning. Perception is 'supported' in the manner described or not at all.[41]

To explain how this alternative type of proof works, Sibley lists seven critical activities that describe the various ways we demonstrate our aesthetic judgements.[42] To illustrate these activities, I shall use the example of the Lancaster Canal. If I wanted to defend my judgement that the canal has an aesthetic character of pastoral, yet sometimes eclectic, beauty, I could justify this through these methods of support.

The first activity is just directly pointing to non-aesthetic qualities. Sibley says: 'We may simply mention or point out non-aesthetic features . . . we are singling out what may serve as a kind of key to grasping or seeing something else.'[43] This has the effect of getting someone to notice an aesthetic aspect that might otherwise go unnoticed. I could point to the mixture of human and natural features (characterful canal boats as well as elegant swans) of the canal to show that the place isn't pristine or attractive in a conventional way and use this to support my claim that the canal has a sort of eclectic beauty. Or, I might point to the mixture of built and natural features of the canal – the towpath verge itself – to support my judgement of the canal as having a comfortable, familiar and unthreatening feeling about it because it is on a human scale.

The second critical activity is directly mentioning aesthetic qualities. In this instance, I note all the aesthetic qualities I want my companion to find there: 'The use of the aesthetic term itself might do the trick; we say what the quality or character is, and people who had not seen it before see it.'[44] I might say things like: 'notice the elegance of the swans' or 'listen to the soft sound of the canal boat passing quietly through the water' or smell the complex and wonderfully intermingled scent in the air – it brings together town and country in one whiff'.

The third activity involves at once directly 'linking remarks about aesthetic and non-aesthetic features'. I might say things like: 'The common occurrence of swans contributes to the elegant and pastoral aspect of the canal as a whole', or 'The almost comic activity of the moorhens and ducks adds to the light and relaxed feeling I experience when I'm here.'

In the fourth activity we use the figurative language of similes and metaphors to bring out aesthetic qualities. Here, there is a place for both imagination and emotion. If I say that the canal is a green life-line between nature and culture, through an image I am trying to capture the distinctive integrated character of the canal. We might use this technique especially in reference to expressive qualities when we ask our companion to recognise particular expressive qualities that contribute to the place's character. Maybe the ducks are real comedians – not of course suggesting this in a literal sense, but in order to find expression in their movement.

The fifth activity makes use of contrasts, comparisons and reminiscences in reference to aesthetic qualities. 'We use what keys we have to the known sensitivity, susceptibilities, and experience of our audience.'[45] Here, too, imagination has an important role because it helps us to envisage possible objects of comparison and contrast. For example, consider a canal in large contrast to Lancaster's. Although the Telemark Canal in Norway is also situated within cultural landscapes and inhabited areas, some parts of it (especially where it passes through lakes) are on a much larger scale, with steep mountains on each side of it. Parts of this canal will feel much more dramatic and grand, perhaps even sublime, as compared to the more ordinary setting of the Lancaster Canal, which is on a smaller scale, surrounded by fields, villages and towns. Reminiscences are especially interesting because they suggest how more personal experience joins with the experience of other people to justify the ascription of aesthetic value. I might recount my experience of walking or jogging along the canal and describe various things that happened on those occasions – the mood of the place at a particular time, the sighting of a tern or other birds, or the practices of fishermen along the canal. I could also introduce and convey stories told by others – from canal boat traditions to local folktales. Here the use of narratives helps to explain why I have found particular qualities in the place.

The sixth activity involves 'repeating with some variation and development points and observations already made'.[46] This is an essential persuasive part of the critical process. Through 'repetition and reiteration' I underline points already made in order to convince my companion, 'as if time and familiarity, looking harder, listening more carefully, paying closer attention may help . . . When one epithet or one metaphor does not work, we throw in related ones.'[47] This is also an opportunity to bring together an overall aesthetic description of the place in an attempt to sum up the aesthetic value found there and to sum up the critical explanation I have given. I might take my companion back to the place several times or try different activities in the place – boating, walking – all the time supporting my aesthetic claims.

Alongside all these verbal activities, Sibley wants to emphasise the role of appropriate *gestures* to make one's case. In a sense one gives a performance, but not just a verbal one. Sibley says: 'We accompany our talk with appropriate tones of voice, expression, nods, looks gestures.'[48] We point to things, encouraging others to look more closely, we make sweeping motions with hands and arms, we speak loudly to emphasise a point, or more softly to put across a quiet mood. This creates an opening for new and different perspectives of appreciation, provides emphasis where needed for persuasion and encourages the discovery of aesthetic qualities.

Practical Objectivity and the Environment

In discussing Sibley's critical activities, I have tried to show that subjectivity has some place in a critical process that is, at heart, an exercise in a particular sort of objectivity. The activity of justification sketched out does not exclude imagination, emotion and individual background experience, as these may reasonably enter into the kinds of explanations and support that one gives. These subjective components of appreciation are not problematic in the sense that they could not be part of an intersubjective explanation of Lancaster Canal's aesthetic qualities and value. The imaginative and expressive qualities that I grasp are connected closely enough to aesthetic and non-aesthetic qualities to be a justifiable part of my aesthetic judgement.

Of course, there will be cases of personal experience and imaginative or emotional linkages that are irrelevant or eccentric, but these can be identified and excluded through the critical process. Critical explanation and discussion enables the recognition of judgements that are largely out of sync with other appreciators. It should also be possible to sort self-interested aesthetic judgements from those that allow the environment itself to reveal its aesthetic value to us. This suggests a further dimension of objectivity; a focus on the object, such that its qualities are shown to us, as it were.

The practical, perceptual type of justification not only indicates the type of 'proof' most appropriate to aesthetic judgements, but this type of justification is also well suited to environmental appreciation. Because Sibley anchors his theory in perception, we do not have the burden of knowledge or the potential elitism of an 'expert critic' to challenge the appreciator. As I have argued, aesthetic appreciation does not require the cognitive framework set out by the natural environmental model. When we turn to explaining and defending our judgements, here too we find that knowledge is not required to make sound aesthetic appraisals. Our judgements make a claim to objectivity without reference to scientific categories.

A central feature of aesthetic judgements, as shown by both Kant and Sibley, is their particularity, that is, they entail the particularity of the aesthetic object, the appreciator and the aesthetic situation. In the aesthetic domain, then, we move from the particular to the communicable. This is not particularity as private experience. The practical approach to objectivity is an active, perceptually engaged method that encourages aesthetic communication between individuals. Through argument and conversation about our aesthetic judgements we learn from others and may develop a critical aesthetic vocabulary that is designed and developed with the special demands of the environment in mind.

AGREEMENT, DISAGREEMENT AND THE PROBLEM OF TASTE

Reasons for Divergence in Aesthetic Judgements

Arguments against objectivity of aesthetic judgements usually overstate the extent of disagreement. There is more consensus in aesthetic judgements than the common saying, 'beauty is in the eye of the beholder', suggests, especially in respect to great works of art and architecture and great landscapes. We would seriously question the judgement of someone who found Chartres Cathedral or the Grand Canyon ugly. While it would be an overstatement to say that there are aesthetic universals across cultures or even within them, there are some exemplars of excellence in art and beauty in the natural world.[49]

Every theory of aesthetic justification, though, faces the problem of divergence in judgements. On the one hand, the very fact that we dispute aesthetic judgements shows that they express more than just personal tastes.

On the other hand, such disputes reveal deep disagreements, many of which are never settled. I shall argue that although disagreements there are, it does not follow that our aesthetic judgements of nature are strongly relative or subjective; they maintain their objectivity.

Our first task is to identify the different reasons behind disagreement (which includes reasons for being able or unable to discern aesthetic qualities). Their identification makes it possible to explain away a good deal of disagreement, although some will no doubt remain. These reasons can be organised under four headings: (1) inappropriate attention; (2) differences in experience; (3) prejudice or bias; and (4) multiple legitimate experiences of aesthetic objects.[50]

(1) Inappropriate attention covers a range of problems related to attention to the aesthetic object and discrimination of aesthetic qualities. There will be cases where someone is simply not paying attention through lack of interest, or distraction, and cases where someone may be paying attention but may be doing so in a superficial or careless way. It is also possible that one is paying keen attention, but that attention is not directed appropriately. For example, I might miss the atmosphere of a forest if I always have an eye focused on the forest floor, anticipating the next sighting of a mushroom.

(2) Differences in experience cover a wide range of reasons behind disagreement, including cultural differences in appreciative context, differences in background knowledge and experience of the aesthetic object, and more or less practice of aesthetic criticism (which results in weaker and stronger abilities to discern aesthetic qualities). Wide cultural differences may account for divergence in the types of qualities that are picked out as having positive value, as for example between a North American and a Japanese aesthetic perspective. There may also be variations on a different cultural level. To someone accustomed to the lush vegetation of forested landscapes, the Scottish Highlands may appear denuded and barren. Such critical blind spots occur because one person does not have the cultural background or experience of a particular natural object or environment.

Lack of experience of an aesthetic object often results in a failure to locate aesthetic qualities. This is quite common in cases of 'unscenic nature'. Someone accustomed to grand views may be unable to find aesthetic value in something that is at first glance either unfamiliar or not at all striking. Bogs present a good contrast here, yet with the help of someone who has had some experience exploring and enjoying bogs, one may begin to see their individual aesthetic qualities – the soft, milky texture of bog cotton contrasting with rich, peaty colours. Lack of experience is linked to more or less practice in aesthetic criticism. Inevitably some individuals have more or less experience in aesthetic criticism, or the appreciation of art and natural beauty. Through appreciation we develop the perceptual, imaginative and emotional sensitivity needed to discern aesthetic qualities, to make comparative aesthetic judge-ments and to feel confident enough in our judgements to enter into discus-sions, or even arguments, about them. We develop a vocabulary of aesthetic concepts and learn to make comparisons and deeper and richer aesthetic descriptions. Some individuals will have more practice in the appreciation of natural beauty, others have more practice in art appreciation, others will have both and still others will lack practice in both areas. Depending on where one's experience lies, one is more likely to discern aesthetic qualities.

(3) Prejudice and bias are often pointed to as common reasons for disagreement. Every appreciator comes to an aesthetic object with particular prejudices. Some prejudices may be shared, but many will be too individual to provide a defensible ground of explanation. For example, many of us hate the winter cold, but for some people this hatred may be so vile that it prevents them from seeing the exquisite lacing of ice on trees after an ice storm. Other biases may arise through bad experiences: bee stings, dog bites, or getting caught in stormy weather on a mountaintop may all lead to aversions that make it difficult if not impossible to appreciate bees, dogs or mountaintops. When such prejudices become known, it will be easier to understand why a disagreement has occurred.

(4) The reasons above indicate that there will be different ways we experience the same aesthetic object, and many of them will be equally legitimate experiences (assuming appropriate attention and lack of bias or prejudice). Differences in background knowledge and culture ground varying but still relevant and reasonable aesthetic judgements. A common case of this is someone who has more experience of a place compared to someone who appreciates the same place for the first time. My familiarity with my summer lakeside cottage means that I have wandered through every part of the nearby forest, swam and rowed in the lake and so on. I will be able to describe the various qualities of the local soundscape and smellscape. When I acquaint my visitor to this new aesthetic environment, I expect her to experience many of the same aesthetic qualities, and I hope to help her to come to see those that she does not. She may bring a fresh perspective and discover new qualities that I have never noticed as a result of her particular background and experience. For instance, her more sensitive nose detects a complexity of smells beyond the damp-pine scent that I hardly even notice anymore.

It is also true that experiences and judgements of the same aesthetic object will change over time as we gain more experience through practising dis-cernment of aesthetic qualities, and perhaps have learned something new that enables us to spot an aesthetic quality. This is not to say, however, that one's first appreciation will always be less legitimate. Often our first contact with the aesthetic object will have the most impact, and even if lacking in depth, may gain from a heightened kind of awareness and attention to the object.

This type of experience is sometimes all that we have to go by, since many aesthetic experiences of nature are unrepeatable.

The types of cases discussed in the fourth category show how significant the particularity of an individual can be for grasping the full range of aesthetic qualities in environments. The particularities of individual appreciators are certainly something to contend with when they result in disagreements, but particularities also form the basis of different aesthetic perspectives. These perspectives enable an appreciative community to capture the depth and breadth of aesthetic value, rather than limiting the discovery of that value to a single standard. Finn Arler takes a positive perspective to variety and disagreement:

> Differences and disagreements should not worry us. On the contrary: they broaden the horizon and force us to qualify our own thoughts and experiences. There are things to learn from farmers as well as from landscape painters or any other group of people who have developed a refined sense for qualities through experience and reflection. Disagreement is no reason for treating the different positions as mere expressions of non-rational private preferences to be processed in some sort of utilitarian calculus. Dialogue is a much more interesting alternative, even though formal and impartial procedures like voting may sometimes be the only way to reach decisions.[51]

This is not, of course, to say that all aesthetic descriptions and evaluations will be equally valid. There is a distinct advantage to being open to a range of experiences and to being as inclusive as possible in our discussions and disputes about our aesthetic judgements. It should be possible in most cases to agree on a set of reasonable legitimate descriptions and attributions of value based on different appreciative experiences of the same aesthetic object.

Working Towards Convergence in Aesthetic Judgements

The aim of the seven critical activities is to give justification for one's aesthetic judgements, but, as we have seen, the aesthetic discussion that emerges also involves a form of aesthetic persuasion, where the aim is to secure agreement. I have argued that this method ought to make convergence possible in our judgements. Why should we think that this is possible?

Given differences in background and sensitivity, we can expect that there will be different sensibility groups. For example, one sensibility group might be composed of farmers who experience the hills and dales of their farmlands with their framework. Another sensibility group might comprise tourists visiting those same hills and dales. Within these groups there may be sub-groups, too. I cannot here give empirical predictions about how agreement would actually take place, for my aim is rather to give theoretical grounds for believing that their judgements can have an objective foundation.

Above, I rejected the ideas of a true critic and a standard of taste. What alternative is there for reaching agreement, or for knowing which judgements are sound and which ones are just plain eccentric, if this is not achieved by comparing our judgements to a Humean standard?

Now that we have an understanding of the reasons behind disagreement, the way forward is to discover those reasons in specific cases, and to correct the problem where possible. Poor judges will not be individuals lacking in expert knowledge, but they will be appreciators who suffer from bias, fail to attend properly or to make an effort, and who may not have the background – cultural or experiential – even to begin to appreciate the environment in question. My extensive discussion of disinterestedness in Chapter 5 provides an effective strategy for directing interest appropriately and more impartially, that is, by directing attention to aesthetic qualities as opposed to appreciating the world merely through the narrow scope of one's personal preferences. When disinterestedness is absent, sometimes a fresh perspective from else-where will enable us to attend to the object in virtue of its qualities, or to bring attention back to the object if it has strayed. Removal of all bias is, of course, impossible, and not desirable either, but the task is to pinpoint biases that are limiting, inappropriate or eccentric.

We might still ask, how do we know who is the best judge? Part of the answer is negative in the sense that it will be someone who is not biased or attending inappropriately. Positively, there may be several 'best' judges, according to the demands of the particular aesthetic object, the degree of sensitivity one brings to the object and experience. All that may be needed is appropriate attention and a willing and open perspective, where one brings one's own experience into the situation but at the same time allows the object to speak for itself, as it were. An imaginative approach is also an advantage, as it allows one to go beyond hackneyed or shallow impressions. This has been the spirit of the integrated approach for which I have argued, an approach that acknowledges the centrality of the aesthetic object and also the contribution of the appreciator. Although the demands of good judgement are not unattain-able for many people, some judgements will clearly have more authority than others.

But as I have urged, judges do not belong to a narrow elite of individuals. This is also not true of Kant's or Sibley's approach. Kant's community of taste depends upon the conditions of judgements of taste, such as disinter-estedness and the existence of common mental powers (imagination and understanding), otherwise one would have no grounds for demanding agreement. This community is no select group, as Soper maintains in her defence of Kant against charges of elitism, 'Each judger in these matters is to be regarded, and to regard himself or herself, as exemplary of humanity at large.'[52]

We still have to contend with the problem of differences in background and culture. Even with many biases removed, we should still expect there to be variations in judgements. Here again, it will be mostly a matter of uncovering those differences, and therefore at least having an explanation for the disagreements that occur. Recognising such differences will enable one to identify appreciative groups within which there is convergence, and convergence across groups. In many cases it will be advantageous to have had some experience of the landscape at hand, or landscapes like it, so that one has some familiarity with the aesthetic situation.

It is worth underlining the fact that aesthetic judgements are not too distanced from judgements where we expect few differences (and disagreements) to be present. It is not far-fetched to assume commonality in our 'underlying cognitive-sensory-affective make-up',[53] as Kant has shown us with his *sensus communis*. For example, as I have pointed out, many philosophers have relied on the analogy between aesthetic judgements and colour judgements – if we can assume commonality in colour judgements, then we can assume at least some degree of this also in our aesthetic judgements. This is also where the support of supervenience has a place, since it assumes objectivity in the ascription of non-aesthetic qualities. A robust, relativised supervenience is required in order to account for the range of aesthetic sensibilities (and sensibility groups) that exist. This type of supervenience thesis lacks the definitive objective force of strong aesthetic realism, but such realism is difficult to defend, and does not reflect the complexity of communities of aesthetic judges. The robust view, however, retains stability of some kind in the non-aesthetic–aesthetic dependency relation and the explanations that can be given in respect of it.

Finally, I have put a great deal of emphasis on the communicability of aesthetic judgements. If one accepts that these judgements are not private and unshareable, but rather the kind of judgements that we discuss and argue about, then we are halfway to understanding the importance of communicability for establishing objectivity and agreement. We have also found that aesthetic judgements are susceptible to a perceptual proof, so we establish further grounds for their objectivity through the critical methods described by Sibley. In the next section I expand on the idea of aesthetic communicability to show why I think it is absolutely inseparable from the concept of an aesthetic judgement. Through this discussion I hope to convince the reader further of the objectivity of aesthetic judgements, but, more importantly, to show how aesthetic communication is the foundation of an environmental aesthetic education.

AESTHETIC COMMUNICATION

Sibley's activity of perceptual proof is a kind of aesthetic communication, and it gives a concrete basis and some content to Kant's idea of the 'common sense'. That Sibley thinks there will be some agreement and objectivity in judgements is a result of the successes of such communication. It also shows that aesthetic judgements are essentially about shared experience of the world. Here, I shall expand on my discussion of Kant's idea of the *sensus communis* as the basis of an aesthetic community, for his theory reveals how deeply public our aesthetic judgements are.

Taste as a 'Public Sense'

We have seen that the judgement of taste for Kant is based in the 'common sense', constituted by the harmonious activity of the imagination and the understanding. The capacity to discern aesthetic qualities is common, then, among 'normal' perceivers. The communicability of aesthetic judgements – that they must be communicable to be possible in the first place – says something significant about aesthetic judgements. Kant emphasises that taste is first and foremost a public sense.

He shows this through an interesting contrast that he sets up between the *sensus communis*, understood more generally, and the ordinary meaning of having common sense in an intellectual sense:

> We must here take the *sensus communis* to mean the idea of a sense
> shared [by all of us], i.e., a power to judge that in reflecting takes
> account (a priori), in our thought, of everyone else's way of
> presenting [something], in order *as it were* to compare our own
> judgment with human reason in general and thus escape the illusion
> that arises from the ease of mistaking subjective and private
> conditions for objective ones, an illusion that would have a
> prejudicial influence on the judgment.[54]

The *sensus communis* operates according to three principles: '(1) to think for oneself; (2) to think from the standpoint of everyone else; and (3) to think always consistently. The first is the maxim of an *unprejudiced*, the second of a *broadened*, the third of a *consistent* way of thinking.'[55] These principles indicate that our shared experience depends upon thinking for oneself in a clear, consistent and unprejudiced way, but also being able to think as others do, to put oneself not in the shoes of another but to be able to assume a standpoint beyond one's individual perspective or judgement. Kant gives us a better idea, too, of what he means by communicability more generally. Taste is dependent on this more general idea of the *sensus communis*, and this shows how much Kant views aesthetic engagement as a participatory activity involving 'intimate communication'.[56] Communicability and shared experience are presupposed at a very deep level by aesthetic judgements.

Indeed, this is the project of the first part of the *Critique of Judgment*: to show that a judgement issuing from feeling rather than concepts is communicable, that is, it has import beyond a personal preference. Kant's point is not limited to an attempt to establish the (subjective) universal validity of such judgements. He also wants to show that something assumed to be private – feeling – is actually communicable. Judgements made within the aesthetic sphere become a way of communicating feeling. In so doing, Kant pinpoints a distinctive way that we share our affective experiences with others, and he marks out a special area of human communication.

Aesthetic Conversation

Kant lays the groundwork for the idea of 'aesthetic conversation', which is taken up later by Sibley, and more recently by Ted Cohen. Cohen uses the expression broadly to describe our actual conversations about aesthetic experiences, and also to map out the special features of aesthetic discourse. For examples, he has been particularly interested in studying the phenomena of telling jokes and speaking metaphorically:

> When metaphors go across and jokes work, communities of
> appreciation are realized, but these are essentially unscripted
> communities, because there is no penalty for failing to join them. I
> have been understanding these communities, principally, as what I
> have been calling intimate communities of feeling.[57]

Arto Haapala has also argued for the social relevance of metaphorical language. The power of metaphor lies in its poetic rather than literal character. Not only are metaphors based in a shared understanding of the world: 'Those who get the point and are within the community feel a kind of immediate, spontaneous togetherness.'[58] Although jokes belong to the realm of culture and the arts, the use of metaphor and the use of aesthetic concepts are central in our aesthetic appreciation of nature. The points made by Cohen and Haapala here apply across the range of aesthetic objects and our conversations about them.

The real significance of aesthetic conversation is why agreement matters so much to us. In relation to understanding the nature of aesthetic argument, Cohen explains how aesthetic experience marks out a distinct territory of communication where there is strength to our assertions, and where we do seek agreement, but without forcing our views on others. This kind of communication seeks and encourages shared feeling:

> We want agreement with our [aesthetic] descriptions because we want a shared world, and we need a shared world as an emblem of our shared humanity. I think we seek that in slight remarks, including those that make use of little words like 'graceful' and 'thick', and their slightness is a fit index of the desperate wonder of the task.[59]

Aesthetic judgements entail a motivation to share them, and we seek agreement rather than disagreement. As Peter Railton comments: 'Shared judgment yields a gratifying confirmation and bond, as well as useful evidence that our taste and enjoyment are no fluke.'[60] Such motivation suggests not only that aesthetic judgements may be objective, but that we *want* them to have objective import.

AESTHETIC CRITICISM AND ENVIRONMENTAL AESTHETIC EDUCATION

Aesthetic Criticism

The idea of aesthetic communication of our judgements forms the basis of the enterprise of aesthetic criticism of the environment. This enterprise involves judgements of both positive and negative aesthetic value of individual natural objects and environments, as well as comparative judgements. Because I do not follow positive aesthetics, I believe that some natural and modified environments or objects will be judged to have more value than others. One waterfall is more dramatic than another, one individual of a species more delightfully complex than another individual of a different species.[61]

A promising strategy for making comparative judgements has been recommended by Godlovitch, where rankings are decided according to relative standards. We have families of value, for example, the categorical league of major versus minor waterfalls. Rankings are context-sensitive and depend upon adjusting our expectations to the league in question. Godlovitch puts it frankly: 'Just as there are rotten violinists, so there must be pathetic creeks; just as there is pulp fiction, so there must be junk species; just as there are forgettable meals, so there must be inconsequential forests.'[62] Hepburn also recognises that some parts of nature may be 'irremediably inexpressive, unredeemably characterless, and aesthetically null'.[63] Although some of us may be inclined to find all things in nature beautiful in their own particular way – this waterfall is intimate and elegant in its setting, if not grand – this is not much help when it comes to the concrete aims of conservation decision-making. As much as one may want to resist rankings, they are necessary for determining how to proceed with conservation priorities.

Some of our most heated debates will arise in the context of comparative judgements. It is often the case that people with experience of a particular place, however plain the place appears to the outsider, will insist that is has as much value as a landscape that is obviously magnificent. Indeed, it is the grand landscapes, 'scenic gems', that are protected above all else through landscape designations such as 'Areas of Outstanding Natural Beauty' or 'National Scenic Areas'. One's own sense of place is very often the source of the attribution of aesthetic and other values to a particular landscape, and it is the sway of this type of attachment that is quite strong.[64] This is one of the most common reasons for conflict and disagreement in environmental conservation, at least in relation to the range of values that relate to sense of place (which includes aesthetic value). I cannot give a formula for how to successfully settle these disputes, but I have provided some methods for making reasonable judgements, giving explanations of them, persuading others and helping them to discover aesthetic value and ways to identify factors in disagreements. Also, as I show in the next chapter, although the consensus is to rank scenic gems above other landscapes, we ought to move towards a broader understanding of aesthetic value than is usually reached through the landscape or scenery model of aesthetic appreciation.

Aesthetic criticism and aesthetic education go hand in hand. Important outcomes of critical discourse will be increased in the discovery of aesthetic value in addition to the benefits of communication. As we develop our aesthetic sensibilities, we develop more effective and accurate means of aesthetic criticism. Our evaluations are based on richer aesthetic descriptions, and we may have a better understanding of our own personal experiences, where we're coming from compared to others, and this enables us to know how relevant or irrelevant our own experience will be in discussions about aesthetic values in planning and decision-making. I quote Berleant at length, for he provides an excellent list of the benefits of general environmental criticism, of which aesthetic criticism forms a part:

> It can bring much-needed attention to the aesthetic dimension of environment, so that it assumes an equal place with other, more commonly recognized environmental values – economic, conservation, historical, moral. It can develop an aesthetic appreciation of environment that is as sophisticated as that of any art. And it can promote efforts to design and otherwise shape environment in ways that recognize the importance of its aesthetic

value. As environmental criticism builds a literature of its own, it will gain an authority and influence that match the pervasive importance of its subject matter. Recognizing aesthetic value in environment and appraising it with sensitivity and intelligence constitute a major stage in the difficult process of humanizing our civilization.[65]

Aesthetic Education

The public, communicative characteristic of aesthetic judgements is central to an idea of aesthetic education that is achieved through developing aesthetic sensitivities through aesthetic engagement with environments and all that involves: engagement of the senses, imagination, emotion, cognitive capacities and physical activity as part of this engagement; the practice of making judgements; discovering aesthetic qualities by having others help us to find them, and thus deepening aesthetic understanding through other people's judgements. Although, following Kant and Sibley, I do not believe that an *aim* of appreciation is effective communication or aesthetic education, we can see how the activity of appreciation, especially that of an integrated approach, grounds an environmental aesthetic education.

Any aesthetic education, whether of nature or art, must take place in the setting of first-hand experience. While reproductions of art and representations of nature (e.g. photographs) are sometimes the only alternative available, this is not the point. Rather, we do not develop aesthetic sensitivity from reading a guidebook to a landscape, whether a scientific one or even a tourist guide. Poetic descriptions, like representations of nature, may help, but it is actual engagement with aesthetic qualities, and engagement with other appreciators, that provides the basis of environmental aesthetic education.

Therefore, the most effective environmental education will not be a matter of instruction through environmental interpretation. This method of environmental education involves the use of displays, pamphlets, information boards and other means of conveying environmental knowledge concerning scientific, historical, or other facts about the environment or its objects. While this type of education may supply helpful background knowledge, it has been shown to be ineffective due to a failure to engage interest. More effective methods enable engaged self-learning by evoking interest through exploration and discovery, challenging the individual to be active rather than merely receptive. This may be achieved by enabling the appreciator to relate her or his own experience to the environment, and through alternative types of information such as stories and poems instead of facts.[66]

Douglas Porteous advocates an interesting form of environmental education through 'geoautobiography'. Here, we reintroduce ourselves to places we have had relationships with in the past. Through reflection on our past experience of a place, and recapturing it in words or other means, we develop an awareness of our own aesthetic preferences and are able to articulate them more easily because of the familiar framework: 'self-exploration liberates the environmental imagination, understanding results from doing, and self-knowledge improves future receptiveness to environmental experience and points out both personal blocks and personal biases'.[67] By a Sibleyan sort of extension, we can see how autobiography might be incorporated to good effect in aesthetic criticism. One's own deep experience of a place enables self-exploration, and that would be an important first step to developing capacities for aesthetic appreciation which then become used as an effective means to help others to discover aesthetic value in the places one knows so well.

Developing environmental sensitivity on a general level (to include the aesthetic) is also discussed by geographers through the methods of 'environmental sensitivity training' and 'learning how to see'.[68] The former is a way of developing a sensory awareness of place mainly in the urban context through non-cognitive methods via the senses, imagination and feeling. 'Learning to see' is a way of developing landscape appreciation and, again, involves developing a keen sensitivity to one's surroundings, although in this case it is primarily a visual education, and is therefore limited (this also sets it apart from Sibley's broader idea of helping someone to discern aesthetic qualities).

The discussion above suggests that the most successful methods of aesthetic education will involve the development of aesthetic sensitivity and awareness in the broadest sense through multi-sensuous awareness, imagination and our affective capacities. This not only fits nicely with the methods of aesthetic criticism already set out, but it also reflects the integrated approach for which I have argued, with an emphasis on Hepburn's recommendation that we ought to overcome superficial perspectives by working towards more imaginative and deeper engagement with the natural world.

Imagination in Aesthetic Education

I would like to close this chapter by pointing to the role of imagination in aesthetic education. My discussion of imagination in Chapter 6 showed that this capacity is not reducible to the self-indulgent private world of fantasy. On the contrary, imagination is connected to beliefs, and although its aim is not truth, its force may bring about a kind of disclosure that is shareable. One might say that a community of imagination is like a community of feeling, where we assume some common basis for our aesthetic experiences, despite differences in background experience and sensitivities.

We have seen that aesthetic communication indicates the deep sense in which aesthetic sensibility is public. The Sibleyan model of aesthetic justification reflects a public act of judgement where active perception rather than passive reception is called upon. We fashion our explanation and support through various methods, and in this respect critical activity is performative and creative. Aesthetic appreciation of nature might be described as performative in a fairly rich sense. In relation to art, Philip Alperson writes:

> There is . . . an important sense in which viewing, hearing, reading, judging, scanning, surveying, discussing, criticizing, and all other activities involved in attending to, understanding, and evaluating works of art are themselves performances, not only in the sense that they are performed actions, but also insofar as they contribute to bringing a work to completion or at least to a fuller realization in some sense.[69]

We can extend this idea to the environment as well, since his remarks reflect the appreciative activities discussed in other chapters here: exploratory perception, creative imagination, interpretation, and the justification of our judgements. In the context of dynamic environments, our aesthetic perception participates with that change, responding to what organic processes throw up from one moment to the next. Nature is expressive and it performs in some sense too. It is in relation to its performance that we react and act, improvising in appreciation and interacting with nature through it. Imagination makes new connections between natural qualities and ourselves. It moves us beyond perceptual qualities to make metaphorical and other types of creative relations, expanding our experience and enriching it with meaning. Such imaginative performances depend upon making an imaginative effort, which requires the exercise and practice of our imaginative abilities.

What is imagination's distinctive contribution here to aesthetic education? Again, we return to Kant and his view of imagination's powers to free, 'quicken', animate and expand the mind. The harmonious free play of aesthetic imagination, the stretching of imagination by the sublime, and the heightened mode of imagination in its engagement with 'aesthetic ideas', all point to the essential life force of imagination. Without putting forward a theory of aesthetic education, Kant intimates the centrality of aesthetic imagination to cultivating our aesthetic capacities and thus furthering our feeling of life.[70] Imagination reaches the mind beyond the ordinary and the habitual, and reaches towards poetic and novel engagement with the world. It opens up new horizons of experience. In relation to aesthetic ideas, Anthony Savile explains the Kantian connection between imagination and education:

> The beautiful object, Kant insists, is an expression of an Aesthetic Idea. It is one that strengthens the mind by giving us a new way to

think about the topic which it handles, a new power of thought in dealing (*reflexively* rather than *determinately*) with that theme and its cognates, beneficial for us in the conduct of our lives and in our search for self-understanding. Kant is careful to say that this is as much true of the beauty of nature as of that of art. The psychic strength which we gain is dispositional, of course; through our acquaintance with the beautiful object, we learn to think and feel in new ways about a multitude of things, not just about the particular one that embodies the quickening aesthetic idea.[71]

In order to bring out the active, life-enhancing quality of aesthetic experience, Hepburn also highlights the role of these qualities of the Kantian imagination.[72]

The free play of imagination influenced Friedrich Schiller's theory of aesthetic education, and ideals of Romantic thought. However, I do not want to overemphasise the humanist strand of aesthetic education that emerges from Kant and these other views. While life-enhancement and the cultivation of the mind may lead to greater civility, and perhaps even to a moral attitude towards nature,[73] I want to emphasise how greater perceptual and imaginative awareness lead to an expansion of our capacities to discover aesthetic value in nature. The greater value we find there – value beyond pretty parks and scenic views – the more likely we are to adopt an attitude of respect for nature. Deeper aesthetic sensitivity by no means guarantees respect, but it provides a good starting point. Also, by enriching our aesthetic capacities, we are in a better position in the practical context to make sound aesthetic descriptions and judgements, to provide support for them, and, generally, to be able to locate and define aesthetic value in relation to other environmental values.

NOTES

1. For discussion of the debate between realists and anti-realists, see Alan Goldman, *Aesthetic Value* (Boulder: Westview Press, 1995). For some versions of realism, see Eddy Zemach, *Real Beauty* (University Park, PA: Penn State Press, 1996); Marcia Eaton, 'The Intrinsic, Non-supervenient Nature of Aesthetic Properties, *Journal of Aesthetics and Art Criticism*, 52, 1994.
2. See, for example, Jerrold Levinson, 'Aesthetic Supervenience' in, *Music, Art and Metaphysics* (Ithaca: Cornell University Press, 1990), pp. 134–58; and 'Aesthetic Properties, Evaluative Force and Differences of Sensibility', in Emily Brady and Jerrold Levinson (eds), *Aesthetic Concepts: Essays After Sibley* (Oxford: Oxford University Press, 2001), pp. 61–80.
3. See Levinson's discussion of this in 'Aesthetic Properties, Evaluative Force and Differences of Sensibility'.
4. See, for example, Alan Goldman, 'Realism about Aesthetic Properties', *Journal of Aesthetics and Art Criticism*, 51:1, 1993, pp. 31–7. John Bender, 'Supervenience and

the Justification of Aesthetic Judgments', *Journal of Aesthetics and Art Criticism*, 46:1, 1987, pp. 31–40 and 'Realism, Supervenience, and Irresolvable Aesthetic Disputes', *Journal of Aesthetics and Art Criticism*, 54, 1996.

5. David Hume, 'Of the Standard of Taste', in Eugene Miller (ed.), *Essays Moral, and Political, and Literary* (Indianapolis: Liberty Classics, [1757] 1985).

6. James Shelley, 'Empiricism', in Berys Gaut and Dominic McIver Lopes (eds), *The Routledge Companion to Aesthetics* (London and New York: Routledge, 2001), pp. 45–6.

7. A more recent but slightly different version of an ideal judges standard is put forward by Goldman, 1995.

8. Stan Godlovitch has suggested that nature critics include conservation biologists, restoration ecologists, parks and wildlife managers, and environmental policy planners. Stan Godlovitch, 'Evaluating Nature Aesthetically', in *Journal of Aesthetics and Art Criticism: Special Issue on Environmental Aesthetics*, 56:2, 1998, p. 113. Presumably, we might find aesthetic nature critics among them. Yrjö Sepänmaa refers to such critics as the most appropriate environmental critics, and he argues that, as experts, they will be the best critics. Yrjö Sepänmaa, *The Beauty of Environment: A General Model of Environmental Aesthetics* (Helsinki: Suomalainen Tiedeakatemia, 1986), p. 88.

9. Oswald Hanfling, 'Aesthetic Qualities', in Hanfling (ed.), *Philosophical Aesthetics* (Milton Keynes and Oxford: Open University and Blackwell, 1992), p. 51.

10. Immanuel Kant, *Critique of Judgment*, trans. Werner Pluhar (Indianapolis: Hackett, [1790] 1987), §31, p. 144, Ak. 281.

11. Anthony Savile describes Kant's way of putting the matter thus: 'Matters of taste do not lend themselves to dispute then, but we can at least *argue* about them . . . Kant uses the term ('*streiten*' in German . . .) in an idiosyncratic way. For him, an *argument* is a difference of opinion that does not have a right and wrong answer to it, only it is not one that can be settled by appeal to determinate rules for the application of the concepts involved, and which might fix what intuitable data will close the issue . . . even though determinate proof cannot be supplied to settle a contentious issue, that need not of itself preclude one party to the debate from speaking truly, and another falsely' (Savile's emphasis). Anthony Savile, *Kantian Aesthetics Pursued* (Edinburgh: Edinburgh University Press, 1993), pp. 43–4.

12. Kant, 1987, §8, p. 59, Ak. 215–16.

13. Ibid. §34.

14. Ibid. §31, p. 144, Ak. 281.

15. Ibid. §32, p. 145, Ak. 282.

16. These claims are made at various points in the *Critique of Aesthetic Judgment*, but see also footnote 15 to §38, p. 155.

17. See Kant §20–2, §40.

18. My point is based on Allison's interpretation of Kant's Deduction, as opposed to, for example, Guyer's contention that Kant's argument fails. See Henry Allison, *Kant's Theory of Taste* (Cambridge: Cambridge University Press, 2001), ch. 8.

19. For Carlson's discussion of Walton, see ch. 5, and for his discussion of the 'Human Chauvinistic Aesthetic', see ch. 7, p. 116, in *Aesthetics and the Environment: The Appreciation of Nature, Art and Architecture* (London and New York: Routledge, 2000).

20. John McDowell, 'Aesthetic Value, Objectivity, and the Fabric of the World', in Eva Schaper (ed.), *Pleasure, Preference and Value* (Cambridge: Cambridge University Press, 1983, p. 13.

21. Carlson, 2000, p. 72. According to Carlson, supporters of this view include John Ruskin, John Muir, William Morris, John Constable, George Marsh, Holmes Rolston, Aarne Kinnunen and Robert Elliot.
22. Janna Thompson, 'Aesthetics and the Value of Nature', *Environmental Ethics*, 17, 1995, pp. 291–305.
23. Ibid. p. 293.
24. Ibid. pp. 297–8.
25. Ibid. p. 298.
26. Ibid. p. 300.
27. See Frank Sibley: 'Aesthetic Concepts' (*Philosophical Review*, 68, 1959), revised version reprinted in Frank Sibley, *Approach to Aesthetics: Collected Papers on Philosophical Aesthetics* ed. John Benson, Betty Redfern and Jeremy Roxbee Cox (Oxford: Oxford University Press, 2001), pp. 20–3; and Sibley, 'About Taste', *British Journal of Aesthetics*, 6, 1966, p. 68.
28. Sibley shares with Hume the view that taste is essentially social in character, but I find Sibley's view more egalitarian on the whole.
29. For discussion of this point, see John Benson, 'Sibley After Sibley', in Brady and Levinson, pp. 226–7; and Emily Brady, 'Introduction: Sibley's Vision', in Brady and Levinson, pp. 18–19.
30. Colin Lyas, 'The Evaluation of Art', in Hanfling, *Philosophical Aesthetics*, pp. 355–6.
31. See Sibley, 'Aesthetic Concepts'.
32. John Benson, 'Sibley After Sibley', pp. 224–6.
33. Sibley's discussion is an argument against the kind of view presented by Monroe C. Beardsley, 'On the Generality of Critical Reasons', *Journal of Philosophy*, 59, 1962, pp. 477–80.
34. See Brady, p. 12; and Frank Sibley, 'Philosophy and the Arts', Inaugural Lecture, 23 February 1966, *Inaugural Lectures 1965–1967* (Lancaster: University of Lancaster, 1967), pp. 18–19; reprinted in Benson, Redfern and Roxbee Cox.
35. Hanfling, 'Aesthetic Qualities', pp. 66–7.
36. Frank Sibley, 'Objectivity and Aesthetics', *Proceedings of the Aristotelian Society, Supplementary Volume*, 42 (1968), p. 36; 'Colours', *Proceedings of the Aristotelian Society* (1967–8), pp. 145–66 (both reprinted in Benson, Redfern and Roxbee Cox); Brady, p. 12; and Lyas, pp. 370–7.
37. Sibley discusses these methods in 'Aesthetic Concepts' and 'Aesthetic and Non-aesthetic'. For ideas of aesthetic criticism along similar lines, see Stuart Hampshire, 'Logic and Appreciation' and Arnold Isenberg, 'Critical Communication', in William Elton (ed.), *Aesthetics and Language* (Oxford: Basil Blackwell, 1970). Sibley himself mentions two other articles, John Holloway, 'What are the Distinctive Features of Arguments Used in Criticism of the Arts?', *Proceedings of the Aristotelian Society*, Supplementary vol. 23, 1949, pp. 173–4; and Robert Hoffman, 'Aesthetic Argument', *Philosophical Quarterly*, 11, 1961, pp. 309–12.
38. Sibley, 'Aesthetic and Non-Aesthetic', in Benson, Redfern and Roxbee Cox, p. 37.
39. Ibid.
40. Ibid. p. 38.
41. Ibid. p. 40.
42. Sibley, 'Aesthetic Concepts'. See also Lyas, p. 366.
43. Sibley, 'Aesthetic Concepts', p. 18.
44. Ibid.

45. Ibid.
46. Ibid. p. 19.
47. Ibid.
48. Ibid.
49. There have been psychological and scientific studies that indicate widespread cross-cultural agreement concerning preferences for both artworks and landscapes. For landscapes see Jay Appleton, *The Experience of Landscape* (London: Wiley, 1975); and J. Douglas Porteous, *Environmental Aesthetics: Ideas, Politics and Planning* (London and New York: Routledge, 1996), pp. 24–7.
50. These reasons are based loosely on discussion of the problem of disagreement in Sibley, 'Objectivity and Aesthetics.' See also John Benson's discussion of an unpublished paper by Sibley in, 'Sibley After Sibley', in Brady and Levinson, p. 226.
51. Finn Arler, 'Aspects of Landscape or Nature Quality', *Landscape Ecology*, 15, 2000, p. 295.
52. Kate Soper, *What is Nature?* (Oxford: Blackwell, 1995), p. 233.
53. See Peter Railton's discussion in 'Aesthetic Value, Moral Value, and the Ambitions of Naturalism', in Jerrold Levinson (ed.), *Aesthetics and Ethics: Essays at the Intersection* (Cambridge: Cambridge University Press, 1998), pp. 59–105, esp. pp. 67–74.
54. Kant, 1987, §40, p. 160, Ak. 293. In James Meredith's translation of the *Critique of Judgment*, he translates 'a sense shared' (in the Pluhar translation) as 'public sense'.
55. Ibid. §40, p. 160, Ak. 294. Rudolf Makkreel gives a very interesting discussion of these remarks by Kant in *Imagination and Interpretation in Kant: The Hermeneutical Import of the Critique of Judgment* (Chicago and London: University of Chicago Press, 1990), ch. 8.
56. Kant, §60, p. 231, Ak. 355, and see Kemal, pp. 161–2.
57. Ted Cohen, 'Sibley and the Wonder of Aesthetic Language', in Brady and Levinson, p. 33. See also, Ted Cohen, 'Metaphor and the Cultivation of Intimacy', *Critical Inquiry*, 5, 1978; and *Jokes* (Chicago: University of Chicago Press, 1999).
58. Arto Haapala, 'Metaphors for Living – Living Metaphors', *Danish Yearbook of Philosophy*, 31, 1996, p. 99.
59. Cohen, 2001, p. 34. Cf. Goldman, 1995, pp. 15–16.
60. Railton, p. 71; see also p. 91.
61. Some degree of comparative evaluation appears to be possible on the positive aesthetics model, but only among comparisons of wild nature, and there can be no attributions of negative aesthetic value. See Sepänmaa, 1986, pp. 107–9.
62. Stan Godlovitch, 'Evaluating Nature Aesthetically', *Journal of Aesthetics and Art Criticism: Special Issue: Environmental Aesthetics*, 56:2, 1998, p. 121.
63. R.W. Hepburn, 'Nature in the Light of Art', in *Wonder and Other Essays* (Edinburgh: Edinburgh University Press, 1984), p. 47.
64. Cf. Porteous, p. 252.
65. Arnold Berleant, *The Aesthetics of Environment* (Philadelphia: Temple University Press, 1992), p. 144.
66. See Porteous' discussion of environmental education, pp. 241–8.
67. Ibid. p. 245.
68. Ibid. pp. 245–51.
69. Philip Alperson, 'Performance', in Michael Kelly (ed.), *Encyclopedia of Aesthetics*, vol. 4 (New York and Oxford: Oxford University Press, 1998), p. 466.
70. Kant, §1, p. 44, Ak. 204; Makkreel, ch. 5.
71. Savile, pp. 95–6.

72. Ronald W. Hepburn, *The Reach of the Aesthetic: Collected Essays on Art and Nature* (Aldershot and Burlington: Ashgate, 2001), pp. 66–7.
73. Interestingly, Kant claims that the lover of nature has a greater tendency for moral feeling than the lover of art. See §42, p. 165, Ak. 298.

CHAPTER 8

Aesthetics, Ethics and Environmental Conservation

A esthetic experience is among the most common and accessible ways we come to value nature. Whether walking the dog through a park, jogging through a forest, walking up a mountain, working a field or studying the ecosystem of a canal, in all of these activities we may appreciate the aesthetic qualities of our surroundings for their own sake. The dog-walker pauses to take a deep breath of the fresh country air; the jogger enjoys the bright song of a robin in spring; the farmer appreciates the early morning light across the field; the ecologist marvels at the dance of pond skaters; and the hill-walker reaches out to feel the contrasting texture of moss and rock along the path.

These experiences matter to us, and they also matter to nature because positive aesthetic valuing of the environment may encourage us to care for it. What is the place of the varieties of aesthetic valuing in our endeavours to protect and manage natural environments? The aim of this chapter is to assess the role of aesthetics in normative contexts. In the first part of the chapter, I examine the treatment of aesthetic value in conservation strategy (mainly from a British perspective) and I argue against the narrow approach to it that is often adopted. I put forward a richer conception of aesthetics through the integrated aesthetic and the concept of 'aesthetic character'. In the second part, I consider the sometimes conflicting, sometimes harmonious relationship between aesthetic and ethical values. The chapter concludes with a brief exploration of the question of whether or not aesthetics provides a foundation for environmental ethics.[1]

AESTHETIC VALUE IN ENVIRONMENTAL CONSERVATION

On the one hand, aesthetics is absolutely central to valuing environments. It might even be said that it forms the basis of all other environmental values, such as valuing biodiversity or respecting the life of a species. On the other hand, aesthetic value is not taken very seriously in environmental conservation generally speaking. It is ignored in favour of other values, such as ecological value, or, more generally, scientific value. Environmental values that are believed to be more objective get more attention. In planning cases, for example, ecological value is frequently cited as a key reason for preventing the destruction of a place, often because a rare species' habitat will be destroyed. When there is the opportunity to table it, this sort of reason carries more weight than aesthetic value in one of its many guises as scenic, landscape, visual, recreational or amenity value.

This is not at all an objection to the importance of ecological value or its priority in many cases. Indeed, without its recognition many beautiful places would have been destroyed. Rather, I want to point out that aesthetic value, although apparently a significant factor in our valuing of environments, nonetheless gets short shrift when it comes to actual environmental practice. The fault lies not with turning to scientific value as such, but with favouring it at the expense of aesthetic value. The reasons behind this prejudice are two-fold. Aesthetic value is conceived as too subjective and idiosyncratic to serve as the basis of a strong argument against, say, the plan to build a new airport runway through a natural area. As we have seen, this commonsense view of aesthetics is not supported by critical reflection. Also, aesthetics appears to be given less attention because it is simply considered less important. It is lightweight, less 'serious' than the scientific or the ethical, and associated with, in some sense, luxury, or what we do in our leisure time. There appears to be a major inconsistency between people's actual experiences and enjoyment of nature and the inclusion of this experience, in terms of aesthetic value, in planning and decision-making.

The Scenery Model

When aesthetic value is given a formal place in conservation strategy and decision-making, there is a tendency to value scenic and formal qualities over other kinds of aesthetic features. Landscape conservation strategy in Britain is directed to a great extent by scenic criteria: 'The enjoyment of scenery is one means whereby people most readily come to value the natural heritage. The main experience of people enjoying scenery is a visual one.'[2] This is confirmed in practice by a 1998 survey of Visitors to National Parks carried out by the Countryside Agency of England and Wales, 'The scenery in the Parks is the main source of visitor enjoyment, followed by fresh, clean air, peace and quiet and lack of crowds.'[3] The scenic approach appears to be widespread in North America too, in forestry management, recreation planning, highway construction and landscape architecture.[4]

The main landscape designations in Britain are based on scenic quality and amenity value. The aesthetic is understood mainly in terms of the scenic, while amenity value refers to the use of areas of natural beauty for enjoyment and recreation. In England and Wales there are two landscape-oriented designations, National Parks and 'Areas of Outstanding Natural Beauty' (AONB). The main landscape designation in Scotland is the National Scenic Area (NSA).

There are eleven national parks in England and Wales, which were originally selected according to scenic beauty, recreational value and their accessibility from urban centres.[5] More recently, there has been a move towards a more holistic management strategy, and the aim now is to conserve and enhance, 'natural beauty, wildlife and cultural heritage and to provide opportunities for the understanding and enjoyment of the special qualities of the Park for the public'.[6] National Parks are described as:

> The most beautiful, spectacular and dramatic expanses of country in
> England and Wales . . . The essence of each of these areas is in the
> striking quality and remoteness of much of their scenery, the
> harmony between human activity and nature that they display and
> the opportunities they offer for suitable forms of recreation.[7]

The Lake District is the most well-known National Park, and it is recognised for the diversity of its landscapes (mountains, lakes, dales, pastoral villages) and its cultural heritage in the Romantic movement.

England and Wales have forty-one AONBs (thirty-seven in England covering about 15 per cent of the land), which are described as expanses of countryside that are usually less dramatic and less 'wild' than national park landscapes. They are not, however, perceived as less beautiful, as they are often referred to as the 'jewels' of the English landscape. Nidderdale AONB, for example, is described in this way:

> Nidderdale is located on the eastern flanks of the Yorkshire Pennines
> stretching from the high moorland of Great Whernside south and
> east towards the edge of the Vale of York. The area is crossed by
> deep pastoral, often wooded dales of the Washburn, Laver, Burn and
> the long majestic dale of the Nidd itself. Reservoirs add a further
> dimension to the beauty of the dale. Rich, rolling and wooded
> pastoral scenery, with stone settlements like Lofthouse and Kirkby
> Malzeard, contrast with bleak heather moorland which is broken by
> craggy gritstone outcrops, including the curious shapes of Brimham
> Rocks . . . The landscape is dominated by its millstone grit geology
> giving it a typically dark, sometimes sombre appearance which is

reflected in the stone of buildings and walls, in the heather moorland and in the characteristic grasslands that occur on this type of formation. Glaciation and the differential resistance to weathering of the sand, shale and gritstones produces some of the most dramatic features such as cut off crags on valley sides and wide U-shaped valleys. This is in contrast with the pastoral landscapes of the dales and upland fringes running down to the dale.[8]

AONBs range from more natural to more cultural landscapes, and the way they have been shaped and managed by humans is recognised within their designations. They differ from National Parks in that they generally lack facilities for outdoor recreation, so their designation is based more explicitly on scenic value.[9]

The forty NSAs in Scotland are defined as areas of special protection which represent 'the best of Scotland's scenery'. Glen Coe, part of the Ben Nevis and Glen Coe NSA, was given the following description upon its original designation:

Lying between the 6-mile-long notched ridge of Aonach Eagach and the truncated spurs of Bidean nam Bian, the highest mountain in Argyll (1141m), the glen is an ice worn valley mantled with screes and debris from the mountains. The place called The Study offers impressive vistas of the Three Sisters. Here the River Coe flows westwards over foaming cascades and through clear pools to the calm waters of Loch Achtriochtan. The peaty flats of the lower glen are in sharp contrast to the towering precipices and waterfalls around them.[10]

National Parks are only just now being introduced in Scotland, but, once in place, they will supersede NSA designations in cases where national-park areas overlap or contain NSAs.

The selection process of these prized landscapes and the descriptions given of them are strongly visual in their orientation, and clearly favour the grandly scenic over the unscenic. Visual and formal qualities are expressed through objective descriptions of landform. Less emotive words dominate but expressive and more generally 'sense of place' qualities are sometimes conveyed, as in 'quiet rustic charm', 'intimate, green and silver landscape'.[11] The Glen Coe summary above illustrates this too, although 'foaming cascades' and 'calm waters' lie in the grey area between non-aesthetic and aesthetic qualities.

What is the explanation for the prevalence of the scenic in landscape designations? Generally, one factor is certainly human ocularcentrism, that is, the predominance of the visual sense in our experience of the world and our subsequent preoccupation with it at the expense of other senses and other modes of knowing the world.[12] It is therefore not surprising that a visual bias occurs in landscape tastes as well as in the assessment of aesthetic value in landscape designations. Natural beauty is not equivalent to scenic beauty, but scenic qualities play a central role, at least because vision is our dominant sense.

This scenic bias rests on another key factor, the prevalence of the scenery cult in landscape tastes (which no doubt owes something to the dominance of our visual sense). In Chapter 2, I discussed the landscape or scenery model of aesthetic appreciation as a modern expression of the eighteenth-century theory of the picturesque. This approach to aesthetic appreciation treats landscapes as picture postcards or paintings, and eschews multi-dimensional aesthetic appreciation for a two-dimensional approach, where environments become scenes laid out before us.

Appreciation based narrowly on the scenic results in a superficial grasp of aesthetic qualities. Natural environments place different demands on appreciators than scenes. Unlike the primarily static nature of artworks, especially pictures, natural environments change through growth, decay and the effects of weather and geological change. The scenery model also creates distance between humans and nature, where we act only as observers rather than as part of the environment. Understanding the ontology of natural environments as *environments* rather than scenes is a fundamental view held by just about every philosopher writing in environmental aesthetics.[13]

Another problem is that the scenic orientation is closely related to the attempt to categorise aesthetic value as objective and publicly observable, as if an understanding of aesthetic value in terms of what we can see – the look or appearance of things – demystifies its subjective components. This move is obvious in most landscape-assessment models used by planners. Indeed, such models are often referred to as 'visual assessments'. There are a great variety of landscape-assessment models around, ranging from those that attempt to quantify and measure landscape qualities to more qualitative methods that attempt to incorporate subjective factors.[14] This objectivising strategy is also evident in the highly descriptive nature of most landscape designations and assessments, where the use of more subjectively oriented language is sparse.[15] The approach of conservation agencies is clear: to defend these designations and protect natural areas, an objective basis is required, otherwise developers and others will challenge the status of the designations.[16]

It would be a mistake, however, to assume that conservation strategists and planners themselves necessarily have a narrow understanding of aesthetic value or that there is *no* attempt to capture aesthetic qualities beyond the visual. Many conservationists have a broad understanding of aesthetics that includes aesthetic qualities related to multi-sensuous appreciation, feeling and

emotion, imagination and sense of place.[17] Some recent conservation literature reflects this move towards opening out aesthetic value when it explains
that enjoyment of landscapes primarily involves sense of place, the key
elements of which are described as aesthetic and affective.[18]

The signs are that a broader concept of aesthetics and aesthetic value may
eventually have a larger place in landscape-conservation strategy. Although I
am critical of the scenic approach to aesthetic value, I recognise its place in
appreciation and conservation, for it presents a significant and common
perspective on landscape value. It cannot be denied that the visual impact
of a place is among the first and most fundamental ways we come to appreciate
environments. Also, I sympathise with what conservationists are up against; I
recognise that however narrow their aesthetic basis, these designations are
needed to protect some of the most natural areas in Britain and North
America. Without seeking objectivity, it is difficult to be taken seriously, and
even if conservationists understand that aesthetic appreciation of landscapes is
not merely skin-deep, it is not easy to communicate this clearly and
effectively. Still, a deeper questioning is needed of approaches that reduce
aesthetic value to formal or scenic qualities. Reductive models may be
overturned by encouraging critical reflection on aesthetic appreciation as
the foundation of aesthetic values. The integrated aesthetic is offered here as a
useful way to reconsider what aesthetic appreciation of nature involves
because it shows how more subjective components can be included as part
of valuing while at the same time securing objectivity sufficient for the
justification of attributions of aesthetic value.

Philosophical aesthetics potentially has a practical application in conservation. Just as moral philosophy has enabled a better understanding of our
attitudes towards the environment, through philosophical aesthetics we can
set out a clearer, more accurate understanding of aesthetic value as irreducible
to scenic value or to a type of subjective value. Furthermore, a critical
understanding of environmental aesthetics helps to correct the common view
that aesthetics has only to do with values such as prettiness, beauty or
attractiveness, an assumption often implicit in the scenic model.[19] There are
many categories of aesthetic value, including the ugly, shocking and comic.
We should learn to embrace these values as well to be true to the breadth of
possibilities in aesthetic appreciation and the types of objects and environments we value: bogs and beetles, as well as waterfalls and butterflies.

Subjectivity and Preferences

I mentioned above the common assumption among environmental conservationists and decision-makers that aesthetic appreciation is a subjective matter
which involves personal preferences rather than rational judgement and

debate. The individual experiences that fall into this dimension of human experience are considered personal and individual to a high degree, although some consensus among preferences is recognised. In so far as this view is taken on board, conservationists believe that they face the problem of how to incorporate this subjectivity into planning and decision-making. Consider these lines from a conservation publication: 'Scenery is a difficult subject to debate because "beauty is in the eye of the beholder". What we enjoy is strongly influenced by our individual preferences and taste, and these cannot be measured in any scientific way.'[20]

Landscape-assessment models have some role in the process of most landscape designations. Although not all models are strongly quantitative, the emphasis on measurement is certainly there. In a critical discussion of attempts to quantify aesthetic qualities, Marcia Eaton describes what she calls the 'fallacy of confusing objectivity with quantifiability'. The problem is that objectivity in landscape assessment is assumed to be possible only through quantitative methods. From a philosophical perspective this sounds very odd. Eaton pins down the problem: 'Objectivity is not a matter of reducing things to numeric formulas; it is a matter of grounding one's claims in evidence in such a way that interpersonal agreement or disagreement is meaningful.'[21]

Another implication of the use of more positivist oriented assessment models is their implicit exclusion of non-expert and 'local' input in the selection process. Public consultation is given more of a role in conservation planning and policy now than in earlier years and some approaches to landscape assessment involve public-preference research.[22] However, the views of non-experts are taken less seriously and so have little impact in planning and policy.[23] Their views are perceived as personal opinion and are contrasted with the scientific or economic evidence offered by experts who are uncritically assumed to be wholly objective in their approach. This is unfortunate given that inhabitants (where relevant) and frequent visitors often possess a solid, reliable grasp of the aesthetic value of a place based on experience that has developed in the context of a dynamic environment and in some cases over many years. I do not want to suggest that local knowledge ought to replace expert knowledge, or that it ought to be uncritically integrated into the process. A serious voice ought to be given to local and non-expert aesthetic judgements alongside the voices of experts. A group of this kind engaged in discussion and debate would give a broader and fairer account of the values of a particular environment.

In relation to the practice of aesthetic judgement, the position I put forward in Chapter 7 located intersubjective agreement and found ways to locate and work out sources of disagreement. I rejected the belief that aesthetic judgements express personal preferences and argued that perceptual rather than deductive or inductive proof supports our judgements. As a feature of the integrated aesthetic, my account of aesthetic judgement brought together the particularity of individual aesthetic appreciation with a distinctive kind of objectivity of justification. In light of this, I would argue that the assumption that aesthetic valuing is a subjective matter is based on an unreflective understanding of aesthetics. Rather than support preference-based approaches, an instance of aesthetic appreciation or valuing is better understood as supporting a judgement for which reasonable justification can be given. Accordingly, the consensus that is recognised by landscape conservationists is not based in collecting together preferences, as is assumed in practice, and it should be possible to find agreement among aesthetic judgements. Applied in practice, the integrated aesthetic could provide a richer understanding of aesthetic appreciation and a way around the problem of preferences. It might also support a greater voice for local people in planning contexts because it aims to be an environmental aesthetic that is inclusive of and gives warrant to individual aesthetic experiences. I do not suggest this model naively, or assume that it would be welcomed by those committed to quantitative analyses of environmental values. I offer it as a critical, philosophical perspective for consideration.

Landscape Character Assessments

I now turn to another type of landscape assessment that has become quite important more recently. In the last several years the Countryside Agency for England and Scottish Natural Heritage joined together in a project to instigate a process of *national landscape character assessments* (LCA). Working with landscape architects, surveyors, local councils and the public, they devised a national process for assessing and designating the regional character of various parts of Britain. There are 159 separate, distinctive, character areas in England and Wales. In Scotland, fifty-six landscape character types have been grouped into 350 character areas.[24]

The aim of the assessments is to provide a basis and context to guide management and planning of regional areas and what appear to be more cultural rather than natural landscapes (although, within some of the areas mapped, there are large natural expanses). The AONB, NSA and national-park designations are aimed at grand landscapes, 'scenic gems', while the character assessments are not based explicitly on scenic quality. Instead, they represent a broader conception of landscape because they attempt to 'provide a structured approach to identifying character and distinctiveness as well as value'.[25] Character is defined as 'A distinct, recognisable and consistent pattern of elements in the landscape that makes one landscape different from another; rather than better or worse.'[26] The methodology of LCAs states that they are designed to map landscape character through descriptions of landscape features, elements and characteristics, rather than to evaluate landscape quality.[27]

The practical aim of LCAs is to provide a description of local distinctiveness for the purpose of managing change in these landscapes. Change on a grand scale that does not conform to local character would be prevented, so such designations allow for some protection and guidance in respect to development proposals. Accordingly, the process of assessment is very clearly laid out, and every attempt is made to ensure that the landscape descriptions are 'relatively value-free'. The assessment process proceeds in several stages: defining the scope of the assessment; a desk study to examine natural and cultural factors to determine general landscape character types; a field survey to examine 'aesthetic and perceptual aspects', 'perceived character' and 'condition sensitivity trends'; and classification and description, where the specific mappings of the types and actual landscape areas are made and key characteristics are identified.[28]

Although a role for both subjectivity and objectivity is pointed to as one of the key principles of the approach, subjectivity is construed not as the input of individual appreciators, as one might expect, but rather as the inevitable degree of subjectivity to which the assessors are prone in their judgements. This relatively small degree of subjectivity is explained as preferable because the alternative is to adopt an assessment model which favours quantitative methods in order to avoid subjectivity altogether.[29]

LCAs provide a welcome alternative to scenic designations. They are based on a more holistic idea of landscape, as they include geological features, natural and cultural history and, to some extent, a sense of place: 'To recognise the difference in countryside character is to understand how the many influences upon it combine to give different areas a unique "sense of place".'[30]

Another advantage of the landscape assessments is their whole-hearted inclusion of cultural landscapes, mainly rural ones, since urban areas are not given assessments. Human settlements and human history are very much part of the character of these places, and the designations include discussion of 'Historical and Cultural Influences' as well as 'Buildings and Settlements'. The role of culture is included as shaping landscape character in the past and present, an aspect that is recognised but given less attention in the scenic designations which are intended to capture generally larger expanses of more natural land. This means that the conservation of character areas is focused on the integration of culture and nature that makes the landscape distinctive and valuable rather than on the conservation or management of nature alone.

It is interesting to note how natural landscapes gain precedence in the various designations used. The mainly natural, grand landscapes, those closer on the scale to wilderness, appear to get the designations of AONB, NSA or are included within a National Park, while the others, more cultural land-scapes, are given character assessments. In this respect, character assessments also take account of what are considered to be less scenic landscapes. Ideally, a landscape character description ought to be able to provide guidance on how to manage less traditionally attractive landscapes (although, as I point out below, it is not clear how they incorporate aesthetic judgements).

Despite the strengths of the landscape character approach, they are still aimed almost exclusively at identifying descriptive, objective qualities. The character assessments are explicitly designed to depend more on geology and other landform-related characteristics rather than scenic value because land-form is viewed as significant to defining a landscape's character. Douglas Porteous is critical of the process: 'Government-sponsored research designed to produce maps of "landscape character" rely on remote sensing and professional field survey, and deliberately eschew aesthetic value judgments.'[31] In order to give the strongest foundation possible for their management and protection, the new assessments appear to be seeking a more objective basis than the scenic approach, which is perceived as preference-based.

The problems in this type of approach can be described in terms of a conflict. LCAs aim to capture an area's character, and they attempt to do this as objectively as possible. A significant factor in identifying character is stated as what gives a particular area its distinctiveness for individuals or a com-munity. This factor is expressed through the idea of sense of place in LCA literature. Identification of aesthetic and 'perceptual qualities' is also men-tioned as part of the process, but aesthetic qualities are essentially equated with visual qualities, and perceptual qualities are construed in terms of non-expert perceptions of character, which are assumed to be subjective. If included at all, aesthetic qualities are mentioned through the visual aspects of character or, it seems, as an element within the more overall experience of sense of place. Clear guidance is given for assessors about how to compose relatively value-free assessments that incorporate the subjective or more personal aspects of experiencing character through descriptive language.[32] So, on the one hand, the assessments acknowledge subjectivity, but, on the other hand, they try to express it as objectively as possible. Rather than give adequate and satisfactory explanations of sense of place or how aesthetic qualities are to be conceived of beyond visual qualities, these components of character are simply objectified, and therefore, I believe, misunderstood. Because sense of place and aesthetic qualities are relational by nature, the conflict arises in the attempt to square the human, relational factor with an approach that strives to be value-free.

An example of a specific character description helps to illustrate the problem. The key characteristics of the Morecambe Bay Limestones are described as:

- Wide expanses of shifting intertidal sandflats and saltmarsh, gravelly or muddy beaches, backed by low limestone cliffs.
- Low undulating farmland of pastures divided by drystone walls, with infrequent individual windswept trees but also areas of scrub and broadleaved woodland.
- Conspicuous limestone hills, with cliffs and scree slopes, rising above the low-lying pastures and wetlands.
- A richness of semi-natural habitats, including limestone pavements, scrub, semi-natural coppice woodland, herb-rich grasslands, peaty fenlands and mosslands.
- Inland, scrub woodland including juniper and unimproved grasslands on gently undulating hills, divided by shallow valleys with hedgerows and damson orchards.
- Stately homes set in parkland landscapes with well maintained gardens.[33]

The full description is too lengthy to quote but it is possible to see from the above how descriptively oriented the assessments are. Mainly visual qualities are mentioned, which is also shown by these lines later in the full description: 'The shifting patterns of textures, colour and the play of light across its surface has the effect of constantly changing the visual character of a large part of Morecambe Bay.'[34] There is some reference to expressive qualities, as in, 'a landscape that is intimate and small in scale', which is also the case in some other LCAs.

In moving away from the scenic, character assessments find it difficult to articulate aesthetic qualities, which would appear to confirm the tendency to equate 'aesthetic' with 'scenic' or 'visual'. They refrain from discussion of perceived subjectivity because of the worry that it would weaken their objective foundation; it is as if the concept of landscape character is reduced to an understanding of physical characteristics alone. However, this worry is, as I have argued, based on a false assumption that aesthetic qualities and more general sense-of-place qualities cannot be given anything other than a subjective basis. To be fair, to some extent there is a connection made between physical characteristics and sense of place, but sense of place involves an individual's (or community's) relationship to a place. This aspect of landscape character is given too little attention in the assessments, and it is quite odd that an attempt to define character and distinctiveness would rest so little on a more informed understanding of sense of place and our aesthetic relationship to the land.

LANDSCAPE CHARACTER AND THE INTEGRATED AESTHETIC

Although the landscape designations conceive of landscape more broadly than the scenic approach, I have found them to be overly objective and inadequate in their account of aesthetic value. Overall, a richer understanding and explanation of aesthetic qualities and value is needed. In this section, I develop an alternative account for capturing the aesthetic dimension of landscape character. My position is based on the integrated aesthetic, so while it also relies on descriptive qualities (as non-aesthetic qualities), it is more inclusive of the particularity of aesthetic experience. The aesthetic character of landscapes conceives of the appreciation that underlies character descriptions as contextual and relational, with a robust integration of sub-jective and objective components of experience.

The term 'character' is used in several contexts, perhaps most often when describing people: someone has a strong or weak character, a noble or robust character, and so on. Descriptions include the personality, moral qualities, and physical traits of individuals. Together, these traits provide an overall description of a person, and such descriptions are used in comparing one person to another. The aesthetic character of a thing involves a description of its aesthetic qualities. Sibley makes a number of helpful remarks for under-standing this idea, based on the relationship he sets out between aesthetic and non-aesthetic qualities.

In Chapters 1 and 7, I discussed how aesthetic qualities depend upon non-aesthetic qualities according to Sibley's aesthetic theory. The sombre quality of a mountainscape might emerge from the significant presence of rock, lack of vegetation, or just from the grey colour of the rock. We can simply see non-aesthetic properties in things, but the discrimination of aesthetic qualities usually takes careful attention. In the paper, 'Aesthetic and Nonaesthetic', Sibley holds that 'the particular aesthetic character of something may be said to result from the totality of its relevant non-aesthetic characteristics'.[35] Later, he refines the notion to say that 'the aesthetic character of a work is the quality or assemblage of qualities in virtue of which it may be aesthetically praised or condemned – its grace, serenity'.[36] Sibley seems to be saying that aesthetic character is constituted by descriptions based in aesthetic qualities as well as the non-aesthetic properties they depend upon. By way of a definition, we might say that aesthetic character is a kind of second-order aesthetic quality or property, standing in relation to first-order aesthetic qualities, much as first-order qualities stand to non-aesthetic properties. Aesthetic character is therefore an emergent quality from constituent aesthetic qualities, the overall quality that gives a landscape, artwork, or person a distinctive look or feel.[37]

We should keep in mind that it is likely to be a set of qualities that make up a particular aesthetic character, and that that character is not reducible to one quality. We may get strongly contrasting properties that make up that character, again not reducible to one or the other, as in the delicate strength of a new, spring flower. Often, too, the way we express aesthetic character is not in terms of one quality or property term that sums it up. This might sometimes be possible, but more often we may just list a number of aesthetic qualities, all of which give the thing its character. This expresses the sense in which that character can be understood, as Sibley put it, in terms of a totality of qualities. Finally, we may be unable to put into words the feel of a place, but we nonetheless are certain it *has* a distinctive feel because we can experience it.

The aesthetic–non-aesthetic relationship has particular implications for aesthetic character. First, as we saw in Chapter 7, the relationship is not rule-governed, so we cannot infer from any set of non-aesthetic qualities a particular aesthetic description. Aesthetic character is by nature indeterminate, and a landscape must be experienced first hand to grasp its character. Second, there is an intimate, interactive relationship between the qualities, which means that aesthetic character is sensitive to changes in non- aesthetic properties. The decline of a bird species could alter the character of a place through the absence of a particular birdsong. The introduction of a wind development with its huge, white, whirring wind turbines into a desolate moor would be likely to transform the landscape's dramatically remote character with its windswept and romantic atmosphere into a (still) windswept expanse that now takes on a cultural character through a technological presence. In the context of conservation strategy and planning, the ability to pin down changes in character through the dependency relationship between aesthetic and non-aesthetic qualities enables one to grasp how and why change occurs.

Identifying Aesthetic Character

I have given an account of the grounds of aesthetic character, but how do we go about identifying a particular character? It is not a bottom-up process, but a top-down one. That is, we usually begin by identifying the overall aesthetic impact of a place, a first impression perhaps, and then trace the particular aesthetic and non-aesthetic qualities that give it that character. It might be helpful to consider some general ways of grasping differences between landscapes in order to think about how non-aesthetic qualities structure aesthetic character.

The aesthetic character of landscapes will vary according to at least the following factors: human modification and management of environments; the dynamic forces of nature; and the appreciative situation of the subject. In

Chapter 3, we considered a broad range of environments from the relatively wild to the built environment exemplified by urban centres. Within this range there are a variety of landscape types distinguished by their topographical features. In Britain, for example, one finds: uplands, lowland grasslands and heaths, woodlands and hedgerows, freshwater wetlands, coastlands and islands (and adjacent marine environments), and towns and suburbs. Aesthetic character may be structured according to a variety of particular qualities common to these different sorts of places and any cultural features they have. An urban place is unlikely to be tranquil, except in the very early hours of the morning, and even then it will be a very different sort of tranquillity than would be found in a wilderness area. However, we cannot predict in any determined way aesthetic character based on landscape type, again, first-hand experience is a prerequisite.

Aesthetic character is both defined and changeable according to the dynamic forces of nature and culture, through growth and decay, geological change over centuries, erosion, the day-to-day effects of weather, the effects of human modification and development of natural areas and so on. A useful way to incorporate sensitivity to change into our understanding of aesthetic character would be to conceive of environments as having aesthetic narratives. This idea suggests the dimension of aesthetic qualities as they change over time, and how shifts in qualities affect how aesthetic character unfolds. Much more static aesthetic objects, such as literature or film, also have narratives, as they unfold over time through different sequences of events and images. But in both cases, nature and art, character descriptions are possible. A novel, with its movement from one event or character's thoughts to the next, can still be felt on the whole to be deeply poignant. Even though there are important differences between literary works and natural environments, they also have aesthetic qualities that relate to the more overall quality of aesthetic character. Later, I return to the idea of narrative in environments in my discussion of decisions about how to maintain aesthetic character.

The appreciative situation of the subject is central to attributing a particular aesthetic character to a place, and it is at this point that my account strongly diverges from the LCA approach discussed above. The integrated aesthetic as set out in earlier chapters defines my approach here, so I shall highlight its contribution in the present context. The aesthetic character of a place begins with the perceptual qualities we find there. Visual qualities, sounds, tactile qualities, olfactory and gustatory qualities, all may enable us to identify the aesthetic feel of a place. Besides multi-sensuous engagement, thought, emotion and imagination may come into play to grasp a set of aesthetic qualities upon which aesthetic character rests. The expressive qualities of a landscape are especially relevant. Landscapes very often have distinctive expressive qualities, and sometimes it is this feature alone that defines character. My discussion of Howarth, Carroll and others as well as my own account of expressive qualities in Chapter 6 show how this more subjective dimension of landscape appreciation can be given a non-idiosyncratic role in identifying aesthetic character.

Imagination in relation to aesthetic character enables us to make links and associations to other things, thereby making more vivid aesthetic qualities that define a place's character. Imagining a cleared forest before and after it was cut down serves to emphasise the empty, stark aesthetic character of the place. We can run through the changes over time that led to the clearing of the land, a narrative put together by ourselves through imagination to accompany our present perception. Imagination also works together with our actual memories to expand and deepen our grasp of expressive and perceptual qualities. As a distinct power related to imagination, memory emerges here as a key factor in the relationship between an individual and the land. It creates a less speculative narrative than imagination if we have lived in a place many years before and returned to it, or even if we have heard stories of the place from people who have lived there. Local knowledge is deeply connected to memory, and here such knowledge would contribute an intimate understanding of the evolution of a landscape's aesthetic character.

In line with arguments in earlier chapters concerning the place of knowledge in the integrated aesthetic, grasping aesthetic character in a landscape's present state does not require scientific knowledge. Whatever background knowledge and beliefs particular individuals bring to the experience will have a role in shaping their conception of a landscape's character, and additional knowledge beyond aesthetic experience may enrich their description. When it comes to the practical considerations of conservation decision-making, more specialist knowledge supplements our aesthetic descriptions in order to reach a holistic understanding of the overall character, that is, one which includes natural and cultural history. My aim here has been to sketch out how the integrated aesthetic contributes to discerning the aesthetic dimension of landscape character, and in this respect specialist knowledge is not a necessary condition.

The integrated aesthetic can be used also to support a more informed role for objectivity in the understanding of aesthetics in landscape character. Assuming so-called normal capacities, we ought to recognise the different backgrounds of perceivers coming to the same landscape, more or less knowledge and experience of the place, more or less aesthetic sensitivity, particular biases and preferences, one's mood at the time and so on. We may also need to account for cultural influences that shape the perception of landscape character, such as particular landscape tastes and fads in landscape design. In identifying aesthetic character, idiosyncratic elements in the subject's approach need to be acknowledged and pointed to as reasons for diversity and divergence in character descriptions. The arguments given in Chapter 7 for the justification of aesthetic judgements provide support for aesthetic objectivity with regard to aesthetic character ascriptions.

AESTHETIC CHARACTER AND AESTHETIC INTEGRITY: THE CASE OF THE HARRIS SUPERQUARRY

I now turn to the role of aesthetic character in environmental conservation. The problem that concerns me here is how we ought to manage and maintain the aesthetic character of environments in the face of changes caused by human activity. I argue that we ought to be sensitive to the dynamic aspects of aesthetic character and how the character of individual environments unfolds over time. To give guidance about how to manage potential changes to aesthetic character, I develop the concept of 'aesthetic integrity' as a kind of aesthetic principle for strategy and planning.

The Case of the Harris Superquarry

To provide a framework for my discussion, I introduce a case study, the proposal to build a superquarry on the isle of Harris in the Outer Hebridean islands off the west coast of Scotland. In 1991 Redland Aggregates proposed to extract white anorthosite from Roineabhal mountain near Rodel, which lies near Lingerbay (near the coast on the east side of South Harris). If allowed to go ahead, the project would be huge, lasting over sixty years, and leaving behind 'a crater 370 metres above sea level and 180 metres below it, one kilometre broad and 2 kilometres long'.[38] Computer-simulated aerial photographs show how the superquarry would look in this remote coastal landscape if allowed to go ahead.[39] The change from 'before' to 'after' as shown in the photographs is shocking; there is a great white gouge out of the landscape, as if someone had literally wounded the island. A number of conservation organisations and the local community cited several reasons for rejecting the proposal, and aesthetic concerns were high on the list. The aesthetic character of the place would be destroyed altogether as a result of the sheer scale and pace of change to the environment. Those in favour of the proposal cite economic gain and the creation of jobs in an area that has suffered from depopulation.

The aesthetic character of this part of Harris is the result of minimal human activity. The proposed site is part of the South Lewis, Harris and North Uist National Scenic Area and has been described as:

> wild 'knock' and 'lochan' terrain of brown heather moorland, bare ridges and boggy pools, which spreads inland from a much-indented

coastline where green strips of many small crofting townships fringe sheltered rocky coves.[40]

Viewed from nearby or from the coastline of neighbouring islands, the area has a dominant, rocky coastline, with small mountains behind it, all set beside the brilliant deep blue-green of the sea. Besides the sea, the colours range from greys and browns to the bright green and sea-blue. When the sun shines and it is still, the atmosphere of the place borders on a quiet beauty, but one that is quite the opposite of pastoral beauty. This is a tough environment and its aesthetic qualities are not delicate or fine, but solid, imposing and powerful. The frequent heavy weather on these islands gives them a windswept but uplifting and exhilarating feeling, due to the strong winds and the sea crashing on the coast to the immediate south and east of the mountains. All of these features give the place a dominant character of magnificent sublimity. In addition to the sounds and movement of the sea, the small township of Lingerbay creates some activity in an otherwise quiet locale. Fishing is an important activity in the immediate area, and the wool industry (Harris Tweed) and tourism are other important sources of income for the island.

The superquarry would create great changes to both the look and feel of the place. The look would be altered from magnificently sublime and harmonious in colours and forms, to a stark contrast produced by a great white hole in the shoreline. From the point of view of someone situated near the site, the move from the darkish moor to the edge of a white hole would be abrupt and dislocating in its strangeness. Visual assessment surveys of the island from various offshore points show how it would appear if quarrying began: 'a superquarry on Roineabhal would affect enjoyment not only of the Harris NSA, but of the five other NSAs from which it would be visible – for the astounding clarity of the Hebridean air produces the conditions which allow such distant views'.[41] Interestingly, quarrying has been attempted and abandoned on the site in the past. The white rock of these old attempts is still visible after thirty years, which suggests the difficulties in revegetation and attempts at restoration.[42]

The sublime tranquillity would be interrupted by the jarring noise, dust and ground vibrations from diggers and blasting. These sounds and other effects would disrupt natural sounds from the sea and birdlife. The comings and goings of ships and other work associated with the quarry would create much more activity than at present. The dark night sky, free of light pollution now, would be lit up by lights from work at the quarry and the proposed harbour that would be built. This area is already quite remote and is good reason for leaving it that way.

Reasons for rejecting the quarry and conserving the Lingerbay area range from ecological to aesthetic. I want to pin down the basis of the aesthetic reasons through a discussion of aesthetic character and aesthetic integrity. How might we understand how Harris' aesthetic character would be changed if the quarrying were allowed to proceed?

Aesthetic Character and Conservation

In determining whether such changes are aesthetically desirable or not, should we (1) attempt to restore particular aesthetic features which are no longer apparent in the landscape, and thus restore aesthetic character; or (2) preserve the features as they are, that is, minimise change to aesthetic character; or (3) simply allow for or even welcome changes to that character, as might occur through natural processes or human development?[43] Although my focus here is aesthetic value, I recognise that conservation decisions involve a broad range of concerns, such as ecological and economic values, values that will be, in many cases, more important than aesthetic ones.

My approach to aesthetic character emphasises the need, where possible, to locate a predominant aesthetic character of a place but at the same time I have pointed to the importance of recognising and being open to changes in aesthetic character, a recognition of the narrative of aesthetic character. How might we square this sort of approach with the aims of conservation? I take conservation to be 'about preserving the future as a realisation of the potential of the past . . . [it] is about negotiating the transition from the past to future in such a way as to secure the transfer of maximum significance'.[44] Taking this together with my view of aesthetic character, I suggest a moderate historicist approach to conservation. To explicate this, I turn first to two contrasting views in respect of the role of history in interpreting art, and in art conservation. These are, on the one hand, 'traditionalism', and, on the other, 'historicism'.[45]

Traditionalism holds that artworks remain the same throughout history, and that the only history relevant to their interpretation is the history prior to and at the time of their production. Correct interpretation of an artwork is achieved by viewing it through its original conditions, that is, by reference to the artist's intention and the way the audience of the time would have viewed the work. The assumption here is that the aesthetic character of a work is fixed by its original qualities. If there are changes in its non-aesthetic qualities, such as faded colour, then the rationale of restoration is to restore the artwork to its original condition.

Historicism recognises the historical character of art, which means that the aesthetic character of artworks is historically determined, that is, by events and conditions that affect the work before and after its production. Thus, historical events after the artwork was produced can contribute to its aesthetic character, as well as changes in our perception of it. Understanding and evaluating a work is based on a narrative, rather than a single point in time. Only minimal conservation to prevent deterioration is called for according to this view; changes such as faded colour or the sound of modern instruments are incorporated into the interpretation of a piece.

There are a number of reasons why the traditionalist approach is problematic in the context of art, and these are discussed in debates about interpretation and the idea of 'authentic performance' in music.[46] In the context of landscapes, where change is on a larger scale relative to artworks, the traditionalist model is even more difficult to apply. When the aim of conservation is to preserve or to restore the original features of a landscape, this often involves an attempt to restore an environment to its most 'authentic' state, a state that has eliminated traces of human culture. There are a couple of problems that arise from this sort of aim.

First, which natural state do we choose, pre- or post-glacial, one hundred years ago or five hundred years ago, assuming there was no human activity in these periods? Which of these is the original or authentic state of the landscape? Is it a forested landscape or an early agricultural one? Such a choice will make a significant difference to the aesthetic character of a place, especially if it means reforesting an area. A further disadvantage is that the attempt to return to the natural or authentic manipulates nature, seeks to re-create it and can turn it into a museum piece. This act in itself undermines the aim to free the place of human activity.

In response to this problem, one suggestion might be to return the environment to what its present natural state would have been had there been no human activity. But here too that natural state is difficult to fix, given the contingencies inherent in natural processes. The way in which that environment would evolve might be estimable, but not in precise enough terms to satisfy the demands of restoration.

Second, we might question the coherence of eliminating traces of human culture given that a great number of environments have been affected or even largely formed through human activity. Human activity in a landscape has a significant effect on aesthetic character. Signs of human culture – from the ruins of old cottages to agriculture and farm buildings – usually make a landscape feel less wild, less remote, less 'other'. This is not necessarily a bad thing, but simply an important difference. Aiming to eradicate the cultural aspect from every environment disrespects the narrative of a place and fails to capture the historicity of the place. It may not be desirable in every case to respect every stage of that narrative, especially in cases where there is some human tragedy or environmental catastrophe that a community would rather forget. My point is more about honesty. If we want to be true to the past, then that requires recognition of the human culture that may have been part of shaping that place's character.

Conservation ranges from very minimal management to the dramatic changes of restoration projects. By taking a historicist position, I am not arguing against restoration policy as such, but urging a flexible rather than rigid approach. The changes to landscapes called for by many restoration projects necessarily alter the aesthetic character of a place, and it is this that I am concerned about: extremes. Also, an extreme historicist position might argue against conservation altogether, and encourage us to just leave things alone to take their natural course, to let that narrative unfold in whatever way it will. But this is another extreme I want to avoid. To address some of these issues, in the next section I incorporate the concept of 'diachronic integrity' into an aesthetic context.

Aesthetic Integrity

In 'The Land Ethic' Leopold introduces the concept of integrity as a principle of conservation when he says, 'A thing is right when it tends to preserve the integrity, stability, and beauty of the biotic community. It is wrong when it tends otherwise.'[47] Integrity means the intactness of a thing as sound and unimpaired. As an ecological concept, integrity has been used to describe an ecosystem that is undisturbed by human action, unimpaired, balanced, and stable.[48] As a moral concept, it suggests a solid and unwavering character or an honest and consistent approach to following moral principles. As an aesthetic concept, it implies unity, wholeness and harmony.

Maintaining integrity suggests being 'true to' to something, that is, true to the sort of thing it is, its particular qualities and character, its origins and genesis. A synchronic approach to integrity would give us a position similar to the traditionalists, and we know that this will not do. An alternative, 'diachronic integrity', has been put forward by Alan Holland and John O'Neill. Diachronic integrity defines integrity as being faithful to what has gone before but not in terms of preserving or returning to some natural state, free from human interference, and frozen in time.[49] Use of this concept as a principle of conservation (among others) means that we need to consider environments within a temporal or diachronic context, and with that information then determine the most 'appropriate trajectory' or direction for the narrative to take. When there are multiple narratives to consider, we will need to adjudicate between them to find an appropriate course. Following the lead of diachronic integrity suggests aiming for 'some kind of intactness, and a certain kind of "wholeness" or "continuity" in the notion of an appropriate trajectory'.[50] Being true to the past, where that is construed in terms of a temporal dynamic, rather than an ahistorical state.

Brought into an aesthetic context, diachronic integrity forms the basis of the principle of 'aesthetic integrity'. This principle provides a guide for deciding how to protect the aesthetic character of a landscape. It treats aesthetic features as parts of an integrated whole which constitute the aesthetic character of an environment. It requires that we be true to that character, which means maintaining its soundness while being faithful to its narrative. Finally, it assumes that it is inappropriate to ignore the role that culture has had in shaping the aesthetic character of an environment. Aesthetic integrity as a principle of conservation does not provide a set of criteria, and it will not be a matter of 'measuring' anything. Rather than these approaches, I suggest application of the principle on a case-by-case basis. If this is too wishy-washy for some readers, then we might adopt two loose guidelines that arise from the principle: (1) sensitivity to the diachronic approach: aesthetic integrity requires that we be true to the aesthetic narrative of an environment. This requires us to take on board the history of the environment in question and decide how best to conserve its predominant aesthetic character in relation to past and present changes, and possible changes in the future (as far as these may be within our grasp). (2) Aiming for integrity by avoiding sharp breaks in the narrative through change on a grand scale that creates incongruity and strangeness.

To illustrate how the principle of aesthetic integrity might work in practice, I return to the Harris superquarry. I described the proposed site of the superquarry as a remote, tranquil, windswept rocky coastline, with minimal human activity. Its predominant aesthetic character could be described as magnificently sublime. If the quarry went ahead, the place would be dramatically altered by the introduction of noise, quarry traffic and the transformation of Roineabhal mountain into a white scar on the landscape.

One could attempt to argue that these changes might have positive aesthetic results. The aesthetic character would not be destroyed in the change from mountain to quarry, but merely transformed. There is still aesthetic value to be found there. For example, one might become accustomed to the change, and learn to appreciate the glistening white of the newly quarried hillside, as set against the brilliant blue-green sea. However, the changes proposed in this sort of case constitute too sharp a break from the narrative that has come before, at least because it undermines the predominant character associated with this coastal landscape. Aesthetic integrity would be seriously undermined, even if the new quarry created an aesthetic impact of another distinct kind.

I noted above that adherence to the principle of aesthetic integrity involves following a couple of loose guidelines. Aiming for sensitivity to the narrative of aesthetic character in this case leads to an aesthetic reason against the proposed superquarry. Now, I would like to pick out particular aspects of that context, which are themselves features of an environment's narrative. Familiarity and strangeness, congruity and incongruity, all have to do with a sense of place, a feeling for a place which is based in, although not exclusively, aesthetic character. Familiarity and congruity have positive connotations, strangeness and incongruity have negative connotations, but, in the aesthetic context, I do not want to attach value to them. Familiarity can result in failing to take notice of aesthetic qualities, and congruity can result in ugliness through dullness or orderliness. Incongruity and strangeness will not necessarily undermine integrity; strangeness or a feeling of otherness is the basis of the sublime, and both strangeness and incongruity result in surprises and contrasts that startle in an exciting way. But the positive ways that these features shape aesthetic character and sense of place depend very much on the particular setting and the way in which changes are introduced.

It should be clear by now how likely it is that the white gouge created by the superquarry would create incongruity. A strange, new form would appear, disjointed from the natural undulations of the rocky shore; its scale would be 'inhuman and alien'.[51] The sort of strangeness introduced through the superquarry would not be welcome or of any particular aesthetic interest. It would be a highly technological operation set amidst a non–industrial and relatively wild environment.

Incongruity and strangeness can threaten aesthetic integrity, but what about familiarity and congruity? Here again it is perhaps a case of not too much and not too little familiarity.[52] This sits between two extremes: at one extreme lies the choice of immobilising the dynamism of aesthetic change in the interest of preserving familiarity at all costs; at the opposite extreme lies the choice of overturning familiarity altogether, and in that way dislocating one's sense of place. In the case of congruity it is much the same. Too much congruity leads to tidiness and a taste for perfect beauty, while too little, under some conditions, leads to disfiguring contrasts.

If increased activity and a larger community evolved in this part of Harris, it might not be a problem if it followed the narrative of the place. *Small*-scale quarrying might also be an appropriate way to continue the narrative, assuming that the effects did not create a great impact on the aesthetic character of the island. Aesthetic integrity must be located flexibly and in such a way as to allow character to evolve through change, but in the superquarry case, the changes to the environment would occur on a too huge a scale and at too great a pace to constitute an appropriate trajectory.[53]

In applying the principle of aesthetic integrity I have emphasised a rich notion of aesthetic value which supports more diverse aesthetic categories than the narrow category of the 'scenic'. Although in the Harris case adherence to aesthetic integrity would result in maintaining the scenic character of the island, following the principle will not always be a matter of striving for the most aesthetically pleasing trajectory for any particular landscape's narrative. Rather than a move towards an aestheticisation of the environment, I would argue that we ought to be sensitive to individual character, situation and context, even if that character is relatively unscenic. After all, this seems to be the advantage, in the first place, of adopting a character-oriented approach.

AESTHETICS, ETHICS AND CONSERVATION

The Harris superquarry case illustrates a conflict between economic values on the one hand and aesthetic, ecological, cultural and other values on the other hand. If planning approval is given, jobs and revenue may be created but at the expense of damage to the environment, aesthetic qualities and cultural heritage of South Harris. There appears to be no resolution to these conflicting values. Economic gain is pitted against the need to protect, mainly, the ecological and aesthetic value of the island. In this case, aesthetic and ethical values are in harmony in so far as they belong together on one side of the conflict. But there are other cases where the two values conflict, and where it is impossible to uphold both values. A better understanding of the relationship between these two types of environmental values will further clarify how aesthetic value is situated in relation to more normative environmental concerns.

Conflict between Aesthetic and Ethical Value

> If I am witnessing a spectacularly-coloured sunset from my kitchen window and am taking great pleasure in its beauty, how shall I respond when a friend drops in and informs me that the reason for all the colour is the proliferation of sulphur dioxide in the air? Suppose that the friend also tells me that the sulphur, the result of a factory operating up river, is a pollutant, one with grave consequences for the creatures in the marsh downstream.[54]

In this passage, Cheryl Foster aptly illustrates how aesthetic pleasure conflicts with a moral attitude towards the environment. How are we to assess this type of situation? Are ethical constraints on aesthetic appreciation justifiable or are our aesthetic judgements somehow exempt?

The conflict between aesthetic and ethical values has many different expressions and ways of resolving itself, depending on the position one adopts. My main concern is with situations where some aesthetic aim or consideration conflicts with our moral obligations to nature. I focus on this dimension of the conflict because my aim is to clarify further our understanding of aesthetic value in relation to other environmental values, and to show how it is both distinguished from and related to ethical value. My aim is to set out some critical distinctions and clarifications to untangle the many strands of this difficult problem, rather than to resolve the conflicts in the cases I discuss.[55]

Cases of direct harm arising from human actions with primarily aesthetic aims are common. Many gardening and agricultural practices which produce flowers and other plants in perfect and aesthetically appealing condition use fertilisers that may damage and disrupt ecosystems. Other common examples of conflict arise when one's specific aim is to create aesthetic value in a place through planning and design, but where those plans cause harm to the environment in one way or another. Keekok Lee discusses another variation of a case that might be construed as a kind of direct harm, the National Trust's project to preserve the natural beauty and cultural value of Yew Tree Tarn in the Lake District. Rather than allow the lake to drain through natural geological processes, the Trust has restored the lake and arrested those processes for the sake of (mainly) aesthetic value.[56]

There are also interesting cases of indirect harm, where harm is caused indirectly by humans through some natural object or process. The problem of non-native plant and animal species has created serious debate in environmental conservation. In Britain, a particular variety of rhododendron has been introduced which causes real harm to native ecology. *Rhododendron ponticum* was brought to Britain from Portugal and Spain in 1763, and became a popular garden plant in large estates. The bright, colourful flowers of this common bush have strong aesthetic appeal, and it is valued highly for this reason, even attracting special bus tours in late spring when the bush blooms. *Rhododendron ponticum* is toxic to mammals, and in addition to the dense shade it creates, its roots release poison into the soil, which kills most plant and insect life. In Wales' Snowdonia National Park eradicating this species is a conservation aim in order to protect native ecology, and also, undoubtedly, in an attempt to keep the park wild rather than to support its less genuinely natural species. The tourists want the rhododendrons to stay and are horrified to learn that they are destroyed.[57] The debate over non-native species is complex, and it raises a host of issues I cannot address here. I cite it because it is a common case of conflict between aesthetic, cultural and other values on the one hand, and ecological and moral value on the other. In this particular case, if conservation managers allow the rhododendrons to flourish, they are not fulfilling their obligation to protect the ecology of the park.

There are two aspects of these types of cases that I shall address. First, I ask what the status is of our aesthetic judgements in cases of conflict. Are there moral constraints on the aesthetic value we ascribe to the polluted sunset, the rampant rhododendrons and the attractive tarn? In reply to this I examine the debate between 'moralism' and 'autonomism' in philosophical aesthetics.

Second, if there are no moral constraints on aesthetic valuing, how might we then define the problem of insensitive aesthetic actions? To untangle this problem I make use of Godlovitch's concept of an 'aesthetic offence'.

Moralism and Autonomism

Conflict between aesthetic and ethical value in philosophy has primarily been studied in the context of art. The problem is examined through a debate between two positions, moralism and autonomism (or aestheticism). Moralists, such as Plato, argue for the instrumental value of art as a means to moral education, and claim that moral defects in a work of art count as aesthetic defects. Autonomists, including Kant, argue that artistic value is non-instrumental; its value lies in a distinct, autonomous domain untouched by moral considerations. Art is therefore appreciated for its own sake, so that 'moral defects' never decrease aesthetic value.[58] There are more radical and more moderate varieties of these positions, but I shall limit my discussion to the more moderate ones since they have evolved as more defensible and critically astute compared to their radical counterparts.

The conflict discussed above would be clear to most people, and that the conflict exists in the first place would seem to show that aesthetics and morality are distinct domains, different values that often conflict *because* they have different bases. But this is really the crux of the matter, for some philosophers would argue that the two types of value are not as easily separated as they might first appear.

'Moderate moralism' is a view more recently held by some Anglo-American philosophers.[59] Noël Carroll, for example, holds that, 'some works of art may be evaluated morally . . . and that sometimes the moral defects and/or merits of a work may figure in the aesthetic evaluation of the work'.[60] To support this claim, the reason commonly given is that a moral stance, that is, a concern for humans and what they do, is part of the appreciative stance we take to many aesthetic encounters. In the arts this is most common with narrative artworks such as novels. It is argued that very often our aesthetic and moral interests are so intertwined that they become inseparable. Sometimes moral concerns, such as their role in the portrayal of a character and their actions, are central to the aesthetic effect of the work, as Carroll asserts, 'moral presuppositions play a structural role in the design of many artworks'.[61] While it is sometimes thought that moral considerations detract from aesthetic attention and take us outside the realm of aesthetic appreciation, moderate moralists insist that moral interest increases our engagement and focus by drawing us further into the narrative or content of the work.

This view sounds reasonable, and relative to more radical versions of moralism it is. Its strongest claim is that we cannot disentangle moral and aesthetic interests. In our approach to art, we are emotionally affected by characters, and we care about how their lives turn out, even if they are only part of a fictional world. We are dismayed when injustice prevails, because we disapprove of injustice in the real world. These emotional responses are just what the author expects; they are an integral part of the imaginative response expected to fictional narratives and in that respect they may be seen as inseparable from the aesthetic impact.

According to the moralist, the upshot is that some of our aesthetic judgements are necessarily bound up with moral judgements. An important consequence of this for aesthetic evaluation is that in most cases a moral defect will count as an aesthetic defect. This needs clarification. Narrative art often has moral content; it shows itself in the way characters are developed and ways they act in relation to others in the fictional world they inhabit. Bad things happen in these fictional worlds, and these may be a crucial part of the plots and something we find interesting and enlightening. A moral defect occurs when the moral content is suspect. For example, a novel which clearly takes a sympathetic attitude towards violence against women will be rejected regardless of any aesthetic merit because this sort of moral defect creates an aesthetic defect. It is in this sense that aesthetic and moral value become inseparable for the moralist.

I return to Foster's polluted sunset to consider these issues in the environmental context. She puts forward what appears to be a moralist position in relation to the aesthetic appreciation of nature:

> an attitude that expresses continued enjoyment in an explicitly acknowledged destructive situation indicates a lack of harmony between the perception of beauty and the greater value of life itself. This disjunction between pleasure and the context of pleasure is at bottom irrational: to appreciate genuinely destructive situations is to approve them, and continued (or universalized) approval of this sort would lead, given what we now know through environmental science, to the destruction of life itself. Life provides the context and conditions for aesthetic pleasure.[62]

Should one find the deeply coloured, striking sunset less beautiful upon discovering that much of the colour is due to environmental harm caused by humans?[63] On Foster's account, we cannot find the polluted sunset beautiful because to do so would be to condone life-denying qualities. She wants to show why there are moral constraints on our aesthetic judgement if we know its existence is somehow harmful:

To continue to admire it would be to lend aesthetic approval to an
unnecessary process which has life-denying consequences . . .
Individual aesthetic judgments are rooted in the perceptual features
and patterns of the object's surface, but the practice of aesthetics,
both productive and appreciative, takes place within a wider context
of life-enhancing ethical considerations. That is, the manner and
material of human presence in the natural environment, whether
aesthetic, practical or whimsical, is subject to ethical appraisal.[64]

Foster supports a moralist position in so far as she does not want to separate
aesthetic and moral value. A moral defect counts as an aesthetic defect in her
view, and it is not difficult to see her point. How could we continue to feel
delight in the presence of something that is harming the environment? Yet
something seems to be wrong in her reasoning, and in the reasoning of
moralists more generally. Why is it that aesthetic value takes responsibility, as
it were, in these situations? Morally, we do feel compelled to suppress our
enjoyment, we feel disappointed, betrayed and concerned about environmental
damage, but these are moral reasons not aesthetic reasons. After all, nothing
has changed in the aesthetic qualities of the sunset: the colours remain brilliant.
What *has* changed is that we have come to know that the cause of the beauty is
harmful, however, that is a moral issue and not an aesthetic one. It makes no
sense to say that we feel aesthetically compelled to suppress our pleasure.

What is actually happening in the sunset case is that aesthetic value remains
high, but on *moral* grounds we may decide to turn away from the scene before
us. By turning away we end the aesthetic experience altogether without
changing our aesthetic judgement.[65] Some spectators may continue to enjoy
the scene, but with an added feeling of poignancy. Their aesthetic delight is
accompanied by the conflicting moral feeling of sympathy in the face of
pollution's harm. Still others will feel no conflict at all. From Foster's
perspective, we experience a shift in perception such that we no longer find
the sunset beautiful, and so our aesthetic judgement shifts.

These points need further explanation. Moralists cannot argue that aesthetic disvalue follows from moral disvalue until they have shown how a moral
flaw constitutes an aesthetic flaw. Once again, the two values have different
bases. Aesthetic value is primarily concerned with perceptual qualities and the
emotional and imaginative responses connected to them, as well as the
meanings that come through appreciating these qualities. In this respect
aesthetic evaluation is generally restricted to perceptual, emotional and
imaginative experiential states rather than significantly cognitive ones. Moral
value is primarily concerned with making choices about how one ought to act,
and how one ought to treat humans and the rest of nature. This is not to say
that moral considerations are not part of our aesthetic experiences, nor that

aesthetic considerations are not part of moral deliberation. But aesthetic and moral value are nevertheless distinct and require judgement on their own terms. I may wish to support the eradication of a non-native species on moral grounds, but it would not be inconsistent for me to continue to find that species aesthetically appealing.

The view that I am sketching out is referred to as 'moderate autonomism'. It is a version of autonomism because it argues that aesthetic value lies within the autonomous domain of the aesthetic. Moderate autonomism is more easily defended compared to more radical varieties because although it argues for a clear separation of aesthetic value and moral value, it accepts that moral consideration sometimes come into play in aesthetic appreciation. A recent version which I support is put forward in the context of art by James C. Anderson and Jeffrey T. Dean:

> moral criticism of a work can *surround* [my emphasis] aspects of the moral subject matter of a work, i.e. the moral content of a work can contribute to or detract from aesthetic aspects of a work. What distinguishes our view . . . is our claim that it is never the moral component of the criticism *as such* that diminishes or strengthens the value of an artwork *qua* artwork. In short, both sorts of criticism are appropriate to works of art but the categories of moral and aesthetic criticism always remain conceptually distinct.[66]

Even moderate autonomism may be hard to accept because it might still seem that in our aesthetic experiences it is unclear how the aesthetic and the moral can be teased apart. This may be because, experientially, the two concerns do feel as one in many cases. However, conceptually speaking it is not so difficult to maintain the separation.

Moderate autonomism addresses the feeling that moral considerations ought to have some bearing on aesthetic appreciation but preserves the view that aesthetic judgements are distinct from moral ones. This clarifies how we ought to treat our aesthetic judgements and evaluations in cases of conflict with moral values. However, we are still left with the problem of how to capture the negative effects of actions with an aesthetic aim or the negative effects of existing aesthetic value (as in the rhododendron case). If these negative effects cannot be captured in terms of moral defects or as constrained by our moral obligations, then how are they to be explained?

Aesthetic Offences

In his discussion of 'aesthetic offences' against nature Godlovitch sets out one useful difference between aesthetic and moral offences that helps to support the moderate autonomist's case.[67] Aesthetic offences may be characterised as acts of 'tastelessness': they arise 'in the form of an objectionable intervention; when nature has been uninvitedly sullied or soiled by gratuitous human intrusions which bespeak interference, carelessness or indifference.' His examples include: 'littering a beach, defacement of cliffs by climbers, tearing up paths by mountain bikes, stripping hills for ski runs, river-damming, raw sewage disposal, decimation of species, etc'.[68] The perpetrators of these offences are human beings rather than nature. Godlovitch sides with the view that only humans can be moral agents in the fullest sense, and because of this only they can cause harm. This means that nature cannot offend against itself. We cannot blame nature for the apparent ugliness caused by natural disasters. In the course of constructing their fabulous homes, beavers make a mess, but although nature can be a victim of an aesthetic offence it is otherwise innocent. As Godlovitch puts it, 'Nature is literally a party offended by certain human acts but a party without its own aesthetic view.'[69] I have to set aside the thorny question of whether he is right about this; can nature be an aesthetic, let alone moral, agent in any sense?[70] I am more interested in how an aesthetic offence shows a lack of aesthetic sensitivity, regardless of who or what actually experiences the offence.

What Godlovitch is getting at here is the manner or style of an action, which can be an aesthetic matter. It may take a certain kind of taste to fashion one's actions – be they delicate, careful, subtle, awkward, clumsy, bold, heavy-handed or graceless. These are aesthetic concepts, and they describe the way we do things. There are other ways of doing things, but they are more obviously in the moral domain of concepts, for example, to act considerately or thoughtlessly. Doing something in an aesthetically pleasing or unappealing way does not necessarily make the action better or worse. To do something with grace does not mean the action will be moral – one can kill with grace but the act is still wrong. This way of construing aesthetic offences shows that the moral and aesthetic dimensions of a single act can be distinguished.

In the arts, this manner or style is all important. I am not asserting a strong form/content distinction here, but rather I want to point out how, say, a character is constructed or a plot structured is essential to fashioning the content or moral story in a narrative.[71] The moral story and its representation support each other and work together for the effect they produce. But this does not entail that the two are indistinguishable, or that the failure of one must result in the failure of the other: each *can* stand on its own.

Turning to aesthetic offences against nature, style matters. Wind-energy developments in the form of onshore or offshore collections of wind turbines (often referred to as 'windfarms') present an interesting and currently controversial case of an aesthetic offence. Wind turbines are valued by governments and NGOs alike as a promising new energy source that is clean, efficient and renewable. Although they are often built in 'brownfield' sites or settings already inhabited by technology, many existing turbines are sited in natural, often remote, upland areas where windpower is more easily generated. There is considerable local and national support for wind energy in Britain, but there have also been challenges to proposals by local people, conservation organisations and national conservation agencies. Several proposals have been rejected at planning inquiries, and the controversy continues as new proposals are tabled for turbines to be cited close to or within areas with conservation designations, including National Parks, AONBs and sites of Special Scientific Interest.

When wind turbines are built in upland areas, and in some coastal sites, they can have a strong negative visual impact. The turbines, usually white, are up to 35 metres high with 25–45-metre blade diameters. In some cases there are small to medium groupings, but in others, such as a recent proposal for the Isle of Lewis in Scotland, there may be as many as 300 turbines. Among other problems, critics argue that the turbines destroy scenic beauty and create noise pollution through the sound generated, thus destroying tranquillity. Residents living near to wind farms have complained of the shadows created by the turbines.[72]

Proponents of wind energy argue that wind energy is an excellent source of energy which does not harm the environment because it is clean, non-polluting and relatively unobtrusive compared to nuclear energy.[73] In relation to aesthetic objections, it is argued that many people find the turbines attractive, even 'elegant', and they create a distinct aesthetic impact of another, more cultural, even artistic, kind. Guides have even been produced for tourists to tour wind-farm sites. It is also claimed that they are not noisy at all, although they do introduce new sounds into the landscape where they are situated.

Wind farms present a possible case of an aesthetic offence because although the turbines have been considered by some people to be attractive as design objects, locating them in upland and remote environments has been viewed by others as aesthetically insensitive. Although offshore wind-farm developments have been suggested to address this problem, without sensitivity to the site and its context, an aesthetic offence may still occur.[74]

Many of Godlovitch's examples cover cases where actions are described as tasteless and so count as aesthetic offences, yet they may not have any explicit *aesthetic* aim, for example, wind farms are energy resources even though aesthetic considerations enter into their planning and design. Aesthetic offences also apply to actions with more explicitly aesthetic aims, as in landscape architectural design and some gardening practices. Also, despite the fact that some environmental artworks set out to celebrate or draw attention to nature's forms, they may commit an aesthetic offence, or what

Donald Crawford and Allen Carlson call an 'aesthetic affront' to nature.[75] Earthworks that involve moving tons of earth or rock are disruptive, as they 'forcibly assert their artefactuality over and against nature' and work aesthetically against rather than harmoniously with the aesthetic and ecological features of their sites.[76] New aesthetic qualities are created, but these qualities may create disintegrity in the landscape.

Godlovitch's concept of an aesthetic offence (or indeed the idea of an aesthetic affront) can be usefully applied to explain the negative effects of all kinds of actions with aesthetic and non-aesthetic aims alike. Tastelessness, insensitivity, incongruity and other ways we perform our actions can be described in terms of poor style. Working on improving the style or manner of our actions may help to prevent aesthetic and other types of disvalue. The principle of aesthetic integrity has an application here too for giving guidance on how to avoid committing aesthetic offences.

I have argued that we ought to adopt moderate autonomism's approach to understanding the nature of the relationship between moral and aesthetic value. The conflicts arising between these values in decisions about conservation practices are often serious and may appear unresolvable. Philosophical reflection on this conflict enables us to identify where the real problems lie and who or what actually creates them. With regard to aesthetic value, we need a clear grasp of where it fits into the environmental picture, and how to handle it in relation to other values. I should underline that in my discussion above I do not prioritise aesthetic value over moral value; there may be strong moral reasons to override aesthetic value. My point is that we ought to be careful to distinguish the two types of value.

AESTHETICS AND RESPECT FOR NATURE

Ethical and aesthetic values are distinct from each other but they are not unrelated. As Eaton points out: 'one feels the pull both in the direction of separating aesthetic and moral value as well as connecting them'.[77] At this stage one might ask exactly how to characterise the relationship between them, especially in connection to our attitudes towards the environment. In this section, I explore places of difference and overlap to show how intimate aesthetic and ethical values can sometimes be, and the relevance of this relationship to an attitude of respect for nature.

The Relationship between Aesthetics and Ethics

Ethical practice is importantly concerned with assessing others' actions in relation to one's own beliefs and values, as well as assessing various situations through one's best understanding and choosing the best course for right action. In this sense, ethical concerns are clearly more cognitive and goal-oriented than aesthetic ones. But some commonly held views about the differences between aesthetic and ethics overstate the case. Moral practice is taken to be other-directed and generally more serious in its endeavours. It is often held to be concerned with abstract rules and universal principles. By contrast, aesthetic practice is viewed as reactive, more self-directed (even hedonistic) and concerned with the less serious side of our lives, unrelated to our practical endeavours. It is associated with the subjective and particular, rather than the general.[78]

Artistic activity is creative and active, and we have also seen that the appreciative side of aesthetic experience is active, engaged and even performative. Disinterested appreciation shows how aesthetic attention is other-directed and non-practical but it does not function to cut off appreciators from the concrete aspects of their individual lives. Although moral responsibilities are indeed serious, we are capable of committing aesthetic offences where our aesthetic choices are more serious than choosing the wrong outfit. Conceptions of ethics are brought closer to aesthetics through more concrete interpretations which recognise the particularity of moral agents and the importance of imagination and emotion to moral choice. Moral thinking and justification refer to general principles but they may also involve practices similar to those of art criticism (not unlike Sibley's seven critical activities), such as 'pointing out details we have missed, giving a new kind of emphasis, showing us patterns and relationships that put things in a new light'.[79]

The close relationship between aesthetics and ethics is also conveyed through language which appears to cross over the two domains. 'Sensitivity', 'integrity', 'harmony', 'coherence', 'congruity', 'attentiveness', 'appropriateness', among other terms, highlight an axiological space not easily distinguished into the aesthetic or the ethical in human practice. For example, 'harmony' and 'integrity' have structural connotations, and imply a certain intactness or lack of conflict in formal qualities which we associate with aesthetic appreciation. 'Sensitivity' and 'attentiveness' suggest a careful kind of perception that is a feature of both moral decision-making and attitudes and the appreciation of aesthetic qualities. 'Appropriateness' applies to aesthetic appreciation in terms of attention that is suited to or fits with the object at hand, but it also can be interpreted as having a normative connotation, especially when it is connected to human action. In expressions like 'aesthetic integrity' and 'aesthetic offence', 'aesthetic' serves to clarify the use of the second term in relation to an aesthetic concern, aim or result in relation to one's actions. Our use of such language shows how open these two spaces of value are to each other, and how a kind of cross-fertilisation occurs between them.

Is Aesthetics the Mother of Ethics?[80]

This cross-fertilisation may be expressed in terms of our aesthetic practices supporting and informing our moral practices and our moral practices supporting and informing our aesthetic practices. Most philosophical positions which consider this problem argue that aesthetic skills contribute to developing moral sensitivity, but some have even proposed that ethics is essentially dependent upon aesthetics. I shall explore the first view because it makes a weaker claim that is easier to defend, and it is also compatible with some of my views in relation to the integrated aesthetic and aesthetic education in earlier chapters.

In asking whether or not aesthetics is the mother of ethics, Eaton suggests that, 'In order to understand morality and thus become a mature moral person, one's action must have both appropriate style and content, and this requires aesthetic skills.'[81] And later, 'Aesthetics can become as important as ethics not because making an ethical decision is like choosing wallpaper, but because it is like choosing one story over another.'[82] Eaton's remarks present two strands of thought about how aesthetic skills, such as perceptual sensitivity, imaginative freedom, creativity, emotional expression and so on, help us in our moral lives; first, to make individual moral decisions, and, second, in the overall formation of moral character.

The analogy between moral thinking and art criticism points to the value of perceptual sensitivity for developing moral sensibility. The perceptual skills developed through aesthetic appreciation, for example, the ability to locate and attend to the detail and pattern of formal and other aesthetic qualities, putting together and interpreting the elements of a painting or narrative, enable an awareness of particulars useful, even essential, to increased awareness of the particularities, details and structure of moral situations.

In earlier chapters I pointed to the centrality of a free imagination in Kant's theory of aesthetic judgement, that is, how our aesthetic encounters are unrestrained by conceptual thought and how, through disinterested delight in beauty, we enjoy the free play of imagination with the perceptual qualities of the aesthetic object and revel in the immediate impact of this sort of experience. For Kant, beauty becomes a symbol of morality, that is, the activity of aesthetic experience of beauty gives us the opportunity to experience the kind of freedom we discover in the autonomous act of moral choice.[83] The disinterested, non–utilitarian character of aesthetic experience supports the free, non-goal-oriented activity of the mental powers (a feature that also enables Kant to make an analogy between moral and aesthetic experience). Experience of beauty and its accompanying freedom prepares us in some sense for the freedom characteristic of morality.[84] The experience of the sublime is also significant, for through it we recognise our moral independence and define ourselves in relation to the natural world.[85] Friedrich Schiller took these ideas a practical step further by maintaining that the development of aesthetic skills is a prerequisite to social harmony.[86] For both Kant and Schiller, these skills are developed in the purest way through aesthetic experience, hence the importance of the autonomy of the aesthetic for unhindered practice (but for these thinkers aesthetics is not a means to becoming moral).

Imagination is not the exclusive domain of aesthetics. It is an epistemological tool used in some of our most basic experiences, and according to Kant its activity is a condition of experience itself. But imagination is at its most free in aesthetic experience, and it is exercised most often there, where we are less constrained by practical concerns. Emotion too is hardly exclusive to aesthetics, but we take our emotions for a test drive without obligation in our responses to the fictional worlds of novels, films and other narrative arts. Indeed, according to Aristotle, this is the point of tragic drama, for it offers the opportunity to respond emotionally, even cathartically, to stories and to educate oneself about the appropriateness of those responses. Through aesthetic experience we enjoy imaginative freedom and hone the emotional sensitivity required for making sound moral decisions. Imagination enables us to empathise, envisage alternative scenarios and invent creative solutions to dilemmas. Practised emotion prepares us for sympathy and our own emotional hardships in relation to the decisions we make.

Hume supports this view, if a little prudishly, when he says that: 'a cultivated taste for the polite arts . . . rather improves our sensibility for all the tender and agreeable passions; at the same time that it renders the mind incapable of the rougher and more boisterous emotions'.[87] Hume went further and identified taste as the common sentiment which enables us to locate 'beauty and deformity, vice and virtue'.[88] Hume's remark could be seen as undermining autonomism, but I don't think so. What he shows is that moral and aesthetic capacities may derive from common sources such as taste and delicacy of feeling. This must in some way reveal why we feel a sense of loss – moral and aesthetic – when we feel revulsion at the sight of a mountain severely 'wounded' by a superquarry. The source of the feeling may in fact be common (I am speculating here), and the skills of one may aid the other, but the character of the types of experiences and the bases of each type of value are still distinguishable.

The second strand of thought about how aesthetics supports ethics concerns stories, that is, how we might use aesthetic skills to construct the most ethical real life narratives. R. M. Hare suggests how this might work with the story of moral character. In deciding what kind of person one ought to be, 'it is as if a man were regarding his own life and character as a work of art, and asking how it should best be completed'.[89] Skills of art and aesthetic criticism come to mind here. We judge the style of one's actions as coarse or delicate and borrow terms from the language of criticism such as integrity, harmony, congruity, incongruity, coherence and incoherence to describe moral character and action. Similarly, we may judge the integrity of another person's life narrative or indeed any narratives we encounter. The principle of aesthetic integrity illustrates this in so far as finding integrity in a conservation narrative depends upon locating congruity, critically assessing breaks in the story, and sensitivity to the landscape's past and future existence.

In relation to stories, we may also draw upon the stories we like and approve of in fiction to form our own moral character. We might emulate the qualities of a favourite fictional heroine, or widen our understanding of common dilemmas through different ways fictional characters have solved them, without losing touch with our own real encounters in our own real world. Literary experience does not teach us morals, but it can deepen our understanding of the way people can be, the sorts of choices people make and how people live with those choices. We are unlikely to grasp all of that without imaginatively engaging with the characters and their fictional lives. These views discussed here are recognised by a number of philosophers who want to give a broader picture of our moral lives than one limited to our capacity for reason.[90] Although as natural beings our lives are shaped by nature in ways we cannot choose, we may also turn to nature's 'narratives', the complex relations within ecosystems, for example, to inform our choices about the best way to live. Some forms of ecological lifestyles illustrate this interesting analogy between aesthetic narratives in literature and the natural world.

Aesthetics as a Foundation for Environmental Ethics

We have found that the aesthetic and moral domains are not poles apart, for our ability to exercise aesthetic sensitivity and our ability to make right choices both draw on our capacities of perceptual sensitivity, imagination and feeling. If aesthetics supports ethics in some of the ways described above, what are the implications for our attitude towards the environment?

In his *Land Ethic*, Leopold recognises the strong connection between beauty, truth, and goodness in our approach to the natural world. In fact, we could interpret his ideas as recognising the distinction between aesthetic offences and immoral actions towards nature when he says that in developing an ethical attitude to the environment we need to, 'Examine each question in terms of what is ethically and esthetically right'.[91] To understand what is 'esthetically right' Leopold instructs us to develop our aesthetic sensibility towards nature. Several environmental philosophers have suggested (but not very carefully worked through) the idea that an aesthetically sensitive relationship to nature can engender a benevolent attitude towards it.[92] This attractive idea takes its lead from the strong feeling that people who find beauty in nature are not inclined to harm it. Most writers who have considered the problem recognise that there is no necessary connection between positive aesthetic valuing and a moral attitude towards nature, but nevertheless there is promise in such a proposal. This promise is perhaps most clearly shown by the strong feelings of attachment people develop to particular places and their desire to protect them from change and development.

We have seen that there is a strong consensus among philosophers about how aesthetic practice generally supports and informs moral practice but it would be too hasty, even foolish, to put more faith than this in a developed aesthetic sensibility. The trouble is that the same people who are aesthetically sensitive appreciators of the environment do in fact harm it. For comparison, consider Eaton's example of Nazis who were great lovers of music and art.[93]

A developed aesthetic sensibility is not in itself sufficient to support an environmental ethic. An environmental ethics based in a caring aesthetic is open to some of the same objections raised against theories of ethics of care in moral philosophy. For example, what motivates us to develop a moral attitude towards strangers, and how might one extend circles of care outwards beyond intimate relations? It may be more difficult to engender care for environments that one has not grown to appreciate aesthetically for one reason or another. Many environments first appear strange, even inhospitable, to people un-familiar with them. Familiarity, sensitivity, knowledge and other means by which we develop relations to environments may still be insufficient for a caring attitude. An environmental aesthetic education, as sketched out in Chapter 7, may help here through a kind of appreciative companionship where we share how and why we value aesthetic qualities in a variety of environments, some of which may be strange to our companion. But even if aesthetic engagement and shared experience help to encourage a sympathetic attitude towards nature, moral constraints, such as justice, are probably needed.

This point connects to another worry, that aesthetic sensibility is some-times overrated. Leopold seems to use 'esthetically right' to mean an ethical approach sharpened through aesthetic sensibility. But it is interesting to consider his expression a little differently, as something like the opposite of an aesthetic offence. I'm trying to get at what it is to be aesthetically responsible, as it were. We have some idea of what this would mean on aesthetic grounds from our discussion of aesthetic integrity and aesthetic offences, but how might moral considerations help to inform our aesthetic appreciation? This brings us to the other side of the cross-fertilisation, that is, how ethical practice supports aesthetic practice.

The idea of living one's life as a work of art is attractive, but Hepburn warns us against romanticising such a view: 'Morally speaking, we may not construct ourselves quite as we choose, but only within bounds set by the irreducibly non-aesthetic principles of morality, principles not fashioned but found.'[94] This should give us pause to recognise that an aesthetic stance, like a moral stance, can suffer from undesirable extremes. Aesthetic hedonism would be aesthetic enjoyment out of fancy and a lust of the eyes which devalues the aesthetic object by making it one's own and trivialising it. Aestheticism, another, related extreme, prioritises aesthetic over other values through a shallow and insensitive perception of the world.

In the context of conservation, hedonism comes into play when aesthetic enjoyment turns into a kind of sensuous self-interest, and where one becomes incapable of appreciation that is other-directed. Here, the moral awareness developed through forms of moral practice – struggling through moral dilemmas, learning how to respect others – can help to pull the aesthetic back to a disinterested stance focused on the object. Aestheticism in relation to the environment might be characterised through overly narrow conceptions of aesthetic value, or cases of ignoring engagement with other environmental values in favour of the aesthetic (attempts to beautify regardless of environmental harm come to mind). Aestheticism's superficial and reductive aesthetic approach is corrected by developing a richer, deeper and more diverse valuing of nature. This may be informed by the way in which our imagination and emotions, for example, are developed in different contexts through the complexities of moral situations, and also the fact that we may simply become aware that there are good reasons to consider other values in addition to aesthetic value.

In conclusion, our aesthetic and ethical attitudes towards the environment may be described as two distinct types of relations to the natural environment, but they support each other in valuable ways. The integrated aesthetic as characterised by disinterestedness shows how aesthetic experience turns outwards rather than inwards and gives scope for valuing nature without self-interest or an overly humanising gaze. A consequence of this is the possibility of more intimate engagement with environments, where we deepen and broaden appreciation while maintaining a degree of distance that refrains from a kind of aesthetic appropriation. Appreciation in these terms recognises how sensuous, imaginative, emotional and cognitive engagement engenders self-understanding in relation to birdsongs, mosses, rocks, mountains, skies, trees, rivers and the great variety of other natural phenomena. At the same time it is characterised by aesthetic attention sympathetically directed to qualities that are independent of ourselves in so far as we relate them to phenomena with existences sometimes continuous and sometimes distinct from our own. In this way, the integrated aesthetic can support a relationship between humans and nature based in a kind of 'aesthetic respect' for nature.

NOTES

1. My approach in this chapter, as in others, is principally philosophical. In the area of aesthetic value and landscape, there are a variety of interesting perspectives from geography, landscape research and empirical studies, for example, see Jay Appleton, *The Experience of Landscape* (London: Wiley, 1975) and *The Symbolism of Habitat* (Seattle: Washington University Press, 1990); Stephen Bourassa, *The Aesthetics of Landscape* (London: Belhaven, 1991); Barry Sadler and Allen Carlson (eds), *Environmental Aesthetics: Essays in Interpretation* (Victoria: University of Victoria, 1982); Jack L. Nasar (ed.), *Environmental Aesthetics: Theory, Research and Applications* (Cambridge: Cambridge University Press, 1988); J. Douglas Porteous, *Environmental Aesthetics: Ideas, Politics and Planning* (London and New York: Routledge, 1996); Yi-Fu Tuan, *Topophilia: A Study of Environmental Perception, Attitudes and Value* (Englewood Cliffs, NJ: Prentice Hall, 1974).
2. Scottish Natural Heritage, *National Scenic Areas: Scottish Natural Heritage's Advice to Government*, 1999, p. 9.
3. Countryside Agency, *Visitors to National Parks*, Research Notes Issue CCRN1, 1998, p. 2 (this publication is based on a longer document of the same title, published in 1996).
4. Yuriko Saito, 'Appreciating Nature on its Own Terms', *Environmental Ethics*, 20, 1998, p. 137; and 'Scenic National Landscapes: Common Themes in Japan and the United States', *Essays in Philosophy*, 3:1, 2002 (web journal: www.humboldt.edu/~essays/saito.html); Allen Carlson, *Aesthetics and the Environment: The Appreciation of Nature, Art and Architecture* (London and New York: Routledge, 2000), ch. 3.
5. For an interesting discussion of the national-park designation process and the dominance of the taste for moorlands in their selection, see Marion Shoard, 'The Lure of the Moors', in John R. Gold and Jacquelin Burgess (eds), *Valued Environments* (London: George Allen & Unwin, 1982), pp. 55–73.
6. Council for National Parks, *National Parks*, www.cnp.org.uk/national_parks.htm.
7. Countryside Council for Wales and Countryside Commission, *The National Park Authority: Purposes, Powers and Administration: A Guide for Members of National Park Authorities* (Countryside Commission for Wales, 1993), p. 6.
8. Countryside Agency, 'Areas of Outstanding Natural Beauty', www.countryside.gov.uk/aonb/22_nidd.htm.
9. Countryside Agency, 'Areas of Outstanding Natural Beauty', www.countryside.gov.uk/aonb/.
10. Countryside Commission for Scotland, *Scotland's Scenic Heritage*, 1978, p. 51.
11. Emily Brady and Mary Grant, 'Aesthetic Value in UK Environmental Conservation', Lancaster University, 2001. The research was based on discourse analysis of UK conservation agencies' publications and interviews with planners and strategists in conservation. These particular examples of expressive qualities are from AONBs. See www.countryside.gov.uk/what/aonb/.
12. For a discussion of our visual bias and a richer understanding of our relationship to the world, see, for example, Martin Jay, *Downcast Eyes* (Berkeley: University of California Press, 1993); and David Abrams, *The Spell of the Sensuous* (New York: Vintage, 1996).
13. Allen Carlson, Arnold Berleant, T. J. Diffey, Ronald Hepburn, Yuriko Saito, among others, have discussed the drawbacks of the 'landscape model' of aesthetic appreciation

of nature. See, for example, Yuriko Saito, 'The Aesthetics of Unscenic Nature,' *Journal of Aesthetics and Art Criticism: Special Issue on Environmental Aesthetics*, 56:2, 1998, pp. 101–11; Arnold Berleant, *The Aesthetics of Environment* (Philadelphia: Temple University Press, 1992); Carlson, 2000, chs. 3–4.

14. See Porteous' discussion of various landscape-assessment models in *Environmental Aesthetics: Ideas, Politics and Planning*, esp. pp. 193–204; Marcia Muelder Eaton, *Aesthetics and the Good Life* (London and Toronto: Associated University Presses, 1989), pp. 77–93; and Carlson, 2000, ch. 3. Landscape-assessment models are developed by landscape architects, planners, geographers and others. Within the field of geography, there are strongly positivist models but also the more reflective, subjective-oriented models put forward by human geographers. Yi-Fu Tuan's work is a good representation of the latter.

15. Brady and Grant, 2001.

16. Interestingly, during the Scottish isle of Harris Superquarry public inquiry, Redlands Aggregates argued that Harris' National Scenic Area designation was indefensible because it was grounded in subjective judgements. See 'Landscape', *The Case Against the Harris Superquarry*, www.foe-scotland.org.uk/nation/superquarry1.html. The original Countryside Commission for Scotland report explaining the rationale behind the selection of NSAs in Scotland states quite explicitly that because they found existing, objective landscape-assessment methods unsatisfactory for the selection of NSAs, they used an alternative selection process which was systematic but openly subjective. From a philosophical perspective, one could argue that the selection process had an intersubjectively rational basis, as it depended upon the identification of descriptive and scenic qualities in landscapes by assessors with relevant experience and sensitivity. See *Scotland's Scenic Heritage*, pp. 4–7. The recent review of NSAs in Scotland may be a way to give these designations a more defensible foundation in the planning context.

17. Brady and Grant, 2001.

18. See, for example: Scottish Natural Heritage, 'An Overview', in *Natural Heritage Futures*, www.snh.org.uk/strategy/NHFutures/nhf-OV.htm, 2002; Scottish Natural Heritage's review of NSAs in *National Scenic Areas: A Consultation Document: Summary Document* (Scottish Natural Heritage, 1999); *National Scenic Areas: Scottish Natural Heritage's Advice to Government* (Scottish Natural Heritage, 1999); Brady and Grant, 2001.

19. Some environmental thinkers and strategists dislike the term 'aesthetic' for a number of different reasons. Landscape assessors and planners often equate it with a subjective perspective, while others associate it with up-market tastes. 'Aesthetic appreciation' is suggestive of teaching people to like what the elite think they should like (Brady and Grant, 2001). Still others, including some environmental philosophers, associate it with pleasure and a hedonistic, anthropocentric valuing of nature (see, for example, Keekok Lee, 'Beauty for Ever?', *Environmental Values*, 4, 1995, pp. 213–25). These commonsense connotations can be corrected through a critical understanding of the concept.

20. Scottish Natural Heritage, *National Scenic Areas: A Consultation Document (Summary Document)*, 1999, p. 3. Discussion elsewhere in their publications points to the subjectivity and role of preferences in determining landscape tastes and aesthetic valuing. See Scottish Natural Heritage, *National Scenic Areas: Scottish Natural Heritage's Advice to Government*, 1999, p. 9.

21. Eaton, 1989, pp. 80–1.

22. Recent initiatives to encourage participation and involvement of local people include 'Village Design Statements', 'Planning for Real' and 'Parish Maps'. 'New emphasis on stakeholder participation' is highlighted as important in the development of the new landscape character assessments, and it will be interesting to see how seriously this input is taken. (The Countryside Agency and Scottish Natural Heritage, *Landscape Character Assessment: Guidance for England and Scotland*, 2002, p. 15.)

23. Porteous, pp. 204, 208; Brady and Grant, 2001.

24. LCAs in England fall under the Countryside Agency's 'Countryside Character Initiative', while in Scotland they fall under the strategic framework of Scottish Natural Heritage's 'Natural Heritage Futures'.

25. *Landscape Character Assessment: Guidance for England and Scotland*, p. 3.

26. Ibid. p. 8.

27. Ibid. p. 2.

28. Ibid. p. 13.

29. Ibid. p. 10.

30. Countryside Agency, *Countryside Character Initiative*, www.countryside.gov.uk/cci/character_history.htm.

31. Porteous, p. 208. This point is supported by landscape-character-assessment methods described in *Landscape Character Assessment*, 2002.

32. The guidance states, for example, 'Care must be used in selecting descriptive words. Subjective value judgements should be avoided', *Landscape Character Assessment*, 2002, pp. 43–4; 50.

33. Countryside Commission, *Countryside Character: The Character of England's Natural and Man-made Landscape, Volume 2: North West* (Cheltenham: Countryside Commission, 1998), p. 69 (reprinted on Countryside Agency website: www.countryside.gov.uk/cci/northwest/020.htm).

34. Ibid.

35. Frank Sibley, 'Aesthetic and Nonaesthetic', *Philosophical Review*, 74, 1965, p. 138; and 'Aesthetic Concepts', *Philosophical Review*, 68:4, 1959, pp. 421–50; both reprinted in Frank Sibley, *Approach to Aesthetics: Collected Papers on Philosophical Aesthetics*, ed. John Benson, Betty Redfern and Jeremy Roxbee Cox (Oxford: Oxford University Press, 2001).

36. Frank Sibley, 'Originality and Value', *British Journal of Aesthetics*, 25, 1985, p. 172.

37. I thank Peter Lamarque for helping me to formulate this.

38. Link Quarry Group, 'Introduction', in *The Case Against the Harris Superquarry*, www.foe-scotland.org.uk/nation/superquarry1.html. This document was prepared by groups arguing against the proposal, and includes information about the possible impact of the superquarry on wildlife and the local community. A public inquiry to debate the proposal was held in 1994, and its findings were forwarded to the Environment Minister for Scotland, who refused planning permission for the quarry in November 2000. Redland Aggregates, now Lafarge Redland, has subsequently launched an appeal against the decision. See also: Harry Barton, 'The Isle of Harris Superquarry: Concepts of the Environment and Sustainability', *Environmental Values*, 5, 1996, pp. 97–121; and in the same issue, the guest editorial by Alison Johnson and Andrew Johnson.

39. To view this image, see *The Case Against the Harris Superquarry* website, and Barton, p. 97.

40. 'Landscape', in *The Case Against the Harris Superquarry*. The NSA designation description can be found in *Scotland's Scenic Heritage*, p. 55. The isle of Harris will

also be given a landscape character assessment but there is no description available as yet from Scottish Natural Heritage.

41. 'Landscape', *The Case Against the Harris Superquarry*.

42. Ibid.

43. My focus in the discussion that follows is with conservation more generally rather than the specific problem of ecological restoration.

44. See Alan Holland and Kate Rawles, *The Ethics of Conservation*. Report presented to The Countryside Council for Wales, 1994; also in *The Thingmount Working Paper Series on the Philosophy of Conservation*, TWP 96–01 (Centre for Philosophy, Lancaster University, 1996).

45. For discussion of these topics, see, for example, Anthony Savile, *The Test of Time* (Oxford: Clarendon Press, 1982) and 'The Rationale of Restoration', *Journal of Aesthetics and Art Criticism*, 51:3, 1993, pp. 464–74; Jerrold Levinson, 'Art Works and the Future', in Thomas Anderberg, Tore Nilstun and Ingmar Persson (eds), *Aesthetic Distinction* (Lund: Lund University Press, 1988); and 'Defining Art Historically', *Journal of Aesthetics and Art Criticism*, 47:1, 1989, pp. 19–33. For different views associated with historicism, see Graham McFee, 'The Historicity of Art', *Journal of Aesthetics and Art Criticism*, 38:3, 1980, pp. 302–24 and Arthur Danto, *The Transfiguration of the Commonplace* (Cambridge, MA, and London: Harvard University Press, 1981).

46. One traditionalist view argues for the concept of 'authentic performance', where a piece of music is appropriately performed only if the original conditions of the piece are reproduced as much as possible. There are some interesting parallels between arguments in this debate and arguments concerning environmental conservation that I discuss here. See Stephen Davies, 'Authenticity in Musical Performance', and James O. Young, 'The Concept of Authentic Performance', both in Alex Neill and Aaron Ridley (eds), *Arguing About Art: Contemporary Philosophical Debates* (New York: McGraw Hill, 1995), pp. 62–84.

47. Aldo Leopold, *A Sand Country Almanac* (New York: Oxford University Press, [1949] 1968), pp. 224–5.

48. See James Karr and Ellen Chu, 'Ecological Integrity: Reclaiming Lost Connections', in Laura Westra and John Lemmons (eds), *Perspectives on Ecological Integrity* (Dordrecht: Kluwer, 1995), pp. 40–1. Most approaches to ecological integrity tend to follow a synchronic model of integrity, and one that seeks conservation of the original condition of the ecosystem. This is in sharp contrast to a diachronic approach to the concept.

49. Alan Holland and John O'Neill, 'The Integrity of Nature Over Time: Some Problems', TWP 96–08, *The Thingmount Working Paper Series on the Philosophy of Conservation* (Centre for Philosophy, Lancaster University, 1996).

50. Ibid. pp. 4–5.

51. 'Landscape', *The Case Against the Harris Superquarry*.

52. Holland and O'Neill also use the concept of a mean to understand integrity, see p. 4.

53. Implicit in these reasons for rejecting the superquarry is the *nature* of the proposed changes: a human development on a grand scale which would have a great impact on existing features of a place, a place that is at present remote from *this* type of human activity. The nature of the change is a key factor in considering the appropriate trajectory of a landscape's narrative, which is illustrated by another type of case, where a sharp break is caused by natural rather than human causes. In the case of natural causes, different considerations will arise and affect decisions about what will

constitute an appropriate trajectory. (I thank John O'Neill for drawing my attention to this point.)

54. Cheryl Foster, 'Aesthetic Disillusionment: Environment, Ethics, Art', *Environmental Values*, 1, 1992, p. 212.

55. The context of beauty and harm discussed in the following includes only human causes of harm. I do not address environmental damage caused by natural catastrophes, and I set aside two questions: whether or not nature is capable of causing harm and whether or not the harm caused by humans is aesthetically justifiable.

56. Keekok Lee, 'Beauty For Ever?', *Environmental Values*, 4, 1995, pp. 213–25. Lee argues against the restoration project on the grounds that natural value is more important than aesthetic value in this case. Cheryl Foster provides an interesting discussion of cases of aesthetic value in relation to restoration in 'Restoring Nature in American Culture: An Environmental Aesthetic Perspective', in Paul H. Gobster and R. Bruce Hull (eds), *Restoring Nature: Perspectives from the Humanities and Social Sciences* (Washington: Island Press, 2000).

57. Trevor Lawson, Kate Rawles and Rob Gritten, 'Alien Invasion', *BBC Wildlife Magazine*, 16:9, 1998, pp. 38–40.

58. Writers commonly referred to as moralists include Plato and Leo Tolstoy; autonomists include Kant, Clive Bell and Oscar Wilde. For a fuller discussion of this debate, see Noël Carroll, 'Morality and Aesthetics', in Michael Kelly (ed.), *Encyclopedia of Aesthetics*, vol. 3 (New York and Oxford: Oxford University Press, 1998), pp. 278–82.

59. See for example, Noël Carroll, 'Moderate Moralism', *British Journal of Aesthetics*, 36:3, 1996, pp. 223–38; Berys Gaut, 'The Ethical Criticism of Art', in Jerrold Levinson (ed.), *Aesthetics and Ethics: Essays at the Intersection* (Cambridge: Cambridge University Press, 1998).

60. Carroll, 1996, p. 236.

61. Ibid. p. 233.

62. Foster, 1992, p. 211.

63. Ibid. p. 212.

64. Ibid. pp. 212–13.

65. There may also be situations in which our capacity to perceive aesthetic qualities is 'blocked' by very strong moral objections to the pollution. Marcia Eaton describes this phenomenon where 'one's morality "anaesthetizes" one to the relevant [aesthetic] features'. Marcia Muelder Eaton, 'Morality and Aesthetics: Contemporary Aesthetics and Ethics', in Kelly, 1998, p. 284. This would not be a case where a moral defect counts as an aesthetic defect, but rather aesthetic appreciation cannot get off the ground due to a particular person's moral standpoint. Aesthetic attention becomes impossible because of a distraction caused by moral feeling.

66. James C. Anderson and Jeffrey T. Dean in 'Moderate Autonomism', *British Journal of Aesthetics*, 38:2, 1998, p. 152.

67. Stan Godlovitch, 'Offending Against Nature', *Environmental Values*, 7, 1998, pp. 130–50. Aesthetic offences are classed as a sub-class of a general class of offences which includes breaches of etiquette, legal wrongs, pettiness and others. He does not call the general class an overarching class of moral offences. See Godlovitch, p. 132.

68. Ibid. pp. 134–5.

69. Ibid. p. 136.

70. I will also have to set aside the issue of who actually experiences the offence. It is of course an offence against nature, but who actually *feels* offended is another matter. We

know that some species can suffer, and it may be the case that some species can feel an emotion not unlike the human feeling of being offended, but it is on the whole the potential appreciators of the environment who experience the feeling of being offended. Godlovitch attempts to deal with this issue by making a useful distinction between internal and external natural aesthetic offences. See Godlovitch, p. 135.

71. See also David Hume's remarks on tragedy where he emphasises that the representational aspects of tragic drama are crucial to producing the desired effect. See Hume, 'Of Tragedy', reprinted in Alex Neill and Aaron Ridley (eds), *Arguing About Art: Contemporary Philosophical Debates* (New York: McGraw-Hill, 1995), pp. 198–204.

72. For the case against wind energy see the Country Guardians' website at www.countryguardians.net. For a discussion of both sides of the debate see David Elliott, *Energy, Society and Environment: Technology for a Sustainable Future* (London and New York: Routledge, 1997), pp. 154–76.

73. For the case in favour of wind energy, see The British Wind Energy Association website at www.bwea.com.

74. Wind farms also present a case of a conflict between aesthetic and ethics. Many of the same people who object to siting wind turbines in natural areas also support wind energy. One of the reasons for this is that in principle this alternative type of energy is desirable, so it is the actual proposals for siting the turbines that create the conflict. Furthermore, opposing wind energy results in being branded as anti-environmental. A conflict emerges because, on the one hand, there is the problem of the negative aesthetic value created by siting turbines in beautiful and often remote natural areas. On the other hand, wind energy is 'good' for the environment, that is, it supports an ethical attitude towards the environment in so far as it produces energy that is renewable and so less harmful.

75. Allen Carlson, 'Is Environmental Art an Aesthetic Affront to Nature?', *The Canadian Journal of Philosophy*, 16:4, 1986. pp. 635–50, and reprinted in Carlson, 2000; Donald Crawford, 'Nature and Art: Some Dialectical Relationships', *Journal of Aesthetics and Art Criticism*, 42, 1983, pp. 49–58.

76. Crawford, pp. 56–7; and Emily Brady, 'Rooted Art?: Environmental Art and Our Attachment to Nature', in *IO: Internet Journal of Applied Aesthetics*, vol. 1, Spring 1998, http:/www.lpt.fi/io/io98/brady.html.

77. Eaton, 1998, p. 283. Eaton has written extensively on the relationship between aesthetic and ethics. Her ideas are collected together in her two books: *Aesthetics and the Good Life* (London and Toronto: Associated University Presses, 1989) and *Merit, Aesthetic and Ethical* (Oxford: Oxford University Press, 2001).

78. For a critical discussion of some of these differences see Eaton, 1989; and Ronald W. Hepburn, *The Reach of the Aesthetic: Collected Essays on Art and Nature* (Aldershot and Burlington: Ashgate, 2001), chs 3 and 4.

79. Marcia Cavell, 'Taste and Moral Sense', in David E. W. Fenner (ed.), *Ethics and the Arts: An Anthology* (New York and London: Garland, 1995), p. 295. Eaton also points to Cavell's analogy, see Eaton, 'Aesthetics: The Mother of Ethics?' *Journal of Aesthetics and Art Criticism*, 55:4, 1997, p. 362.

80. Eaton uses this expression for the title of her article 'Aesthetics: The Mother of Ethics?' She attributes the wording to Joseph Brodsky, who contends that aesthetics is the mother of ethics ('Uncommon Visage', *Poets and Writers Magazine*, March–April, 1988, p. 17).

81. Eaton, 1997, p. 361.

82. Ibid. p. 362.
83. Immanuel Kant, *Critique of Judgment*, trans. Werner Pluhar (Indianapolis: Hackett, 1987), §59.
84. Paul Guyer, *Kant and the Experience of Freedom* (Cambridge: Cambridge University Press, 1996), p. 96.
85. Kant, 1987, §23–9.
86. Friedrich Schiller, *On the Aesthetic Education of Man* (Oxford: Clarendon Press, [1795] 1967); Arnold Berleant has developed these ideas further to understand a social aesthetic. See his article, 'On Getting Along Beautifully: Ideas for a Social Aesthetics', in Pauline von Bonsdorff and Arto Haapala (eds), *Aesthetics in the Human Environment* (Lahti, Finland: International Institute of Applied Aesthetics Series, vol. 6, 1999), pp. 12–29.
87. Quoted in Guyer, p. 126.
88. David Hume, *Enquiry Concerning the Principles of Morals*, ed. J. B. Schneewind (Indianapolis: Hackett, [1751] 1983), p. 88.
89. R. M. Hare, *Freedom and Reason* (Oxford: Oxford University Press, 1965), p. 150; cited by Eaton, 1997, p. 362. Several other philosophers have explored this idea, for example see Colin McGinn, *Ethics, Evil and Fiction* (Oxford: Clarendon Press, 1997).
90. Martha Nussbaum is well known for this approach, see *The Fragility of Goodness: Luck and Ethics in Greek Tragedy and Philosophy* (Cambridge: Cambridge University Press, 1986); *Love's Knowledge: Essays on Philosophy and Literature* (Oxford: Oxford University Press, 1990); *Poetic Justice: The Literary Imagination and Public Life* (Boston: Beacon Press, 1996).
91. Leopold, p. 262.
92. Holmes Rolston, III, presents the most recent exploration of the problem in 'From Beauty to Duty: Aesthetics of Nature and Environmental Ethics', in Arnold Berleant (ed.), *Environment and the Arts: Perspectives on Environmental Aesthetics* (Aldershot and Burlington: Ashgate, 2002), pp. 127–42. See also: Eugene Hargrove, *Foundations of Environmental Ethics* (Englewood Cliffs: Prentice-Hall, 1989), ch. 6; John Passmore, *Man's Responsibility for Nature* (London: Duckworth, 1980), p. 189; Robert Elliot, *Faking Nature* (New York: Routledge, 1997), ch. 2. Mark Sagoff takes the view that loving care for nature can be developed through aesthetic experience. See 'Has Nature a Good of its Own?', *Hastings Center Report*, 21, 1991, pp. 32–40.
93. Eaton, 1998, p. 283.
94. Hepburn, 2001, p. 58.

Bibliography

Abrams, David, *The Spell of the Sensuous* (New York: Vintage, 1996).

Ackerman, Diane, *A Natural History of the Senses* (New York: Vintage, 1990).

Allison, Henry, *Kant's Theory of Taste: A Reading of the Critique of Aesthetic Judgment* (Cambridge: Cambridge University Press, 2001).

Alperson, Philip, 'Performance', in Michael Kelly (ed.), *Encyclopedia of Aesthetics*, vol. 4 (New York and Oxford: Oxford University Press, 1998).

Anderson, James C. and Jeffrey T. Dean, 'Moderate Autonomism', *British Journal of Aesthetics*, 38:1, 1998.

Appleton, Jay, *The Experience of Landscape* (London: Wiley, 1975).

Aquinas, Thomas, *Summa Theologiae* (London: Blackfriars, 1964–76).

Arler, Finn, 'Aspects of Landscape or Nature Quality', *Landscape Ecology*, 15, 2000.

Arntzen, Sven ,'Cultural Landscape and Approaches to Nature – Ecophilosophical Perspectives', in Lehari, Laanemets and Sarapik (eds), *Place and Location II* (Tallinn: Estland, 2001).

Attfield, Robin, *The Ethics of Environmental Concern*, 2nd edn (Athens, GA, and London: University of Georgia Press, 1991).

Barton, Harry, 'The Isle of Harris Superquarry: Concepts of the Environment and Sustainability', *Environmental Values*, 5, 1996.

Battersby, Christine, *Gender and Genius: Towards a Feminist Aesthetics* (London: Women's Press, 1989).

——, 'Situating the Aesthetic: A Feminist Defence', in Andrew Benjamin and Peter Osborne (eds), *Thinking Art: Beyond Traditional Aesthetics* (London: ICA, 1991).

Beardsley, Monroe, 'On the Generality of Critical Reasons', *Journal of Philosophy*, 59, 1962.

——, *Aesthetics from Classical Greece to the Present* (Tuscaloosa and London: The University of Alabama Press, 1966).

——, *The Aesthetic Point of View*, ed. Michael Wreen and Donald Callen (Ithaca: Cornell University Press, 1982).

Bell, Clive, *Art* (London: Chatto and Windus, 1931).

Bender, John, 'Supervenience and the Justification of Aesthetic Judgments', *Journal of Aesthetics and Art Criticism*, 46:1, 1987.

——, 'Realism, Supervenience, and Irresolvable Aesthetic Disputes', *Journal of Aesthetics and Art Criticism*, 54, 1996.

Benson, John, 'Sibley After Sibley', in Emily Brady and Jerrold Levinson (eds), *Aesthetic Concepts: Essays After Sibley* (Oxford: Oxford University Press, 2001).

Berleant, Arnold, *The Aesthetics of Environment* (Philadelphia: Temple University Press, 1992).

——, 'The Aesthetics of Art and Nature', in Salim Kemal and Ivan Gaskell, (eds), *Landscape, Natural Beauty and the Arts* (Cambridge: Cambridge University Press, 1993).

——, 'Beyond Disinterestedness', *British Journal of Aesthetics*, 34:3, 1994.

——, *Living in the Landscape: Toward an Aesthetics of Environment* (Lawrence: University Press of Kansas, 1997).

——, 'On Getting Along Beautifully: Ideas for a Social Aesthetics', in Pauline von Bonsdorff and Arto Haapala (eds), *Aesthetics in the Human Environment* (Lahti, Finland: International Institute of Applied Aesthetics Series, vol. 6, 1999).

—— (ed.), *Environment and the Arts: Perspectives on Environmental Aesthetics* (Aldershot and Burlington: Ashgate, 2002).

Berleant, Arnold and Allen Carlson (eds), *Journal of Aesthetics and Art Criticism: Special Issue: Environmental Aesthetics*, 56:2, Spring 1998.

Bonsdorff, Pauline von, *The Human Habitat: Aesthetic and Axiological Perspectives* (Jyväskylä: Gummerus, 1998).

Bonsdorff, Pauline von and Arto Haapala (eds), *Aesthetics in the Human Environment* (Lahti, Finland: International Institute of Applied Aesthetics Series, vol. 6, 1999).

Bourdieu, Pierre, *Distinction: A Social Critique of the Judgement of Taste* (London and New York: Routledge and Kegan Paul, 1984).

Brady, Emily, 'Imagination and the Aesthetic Appreciation of Nature', *Journal of Aesthetics and Art Criticism: Special Issue: Environmental Aesthetics*, 56:2, 1998.

——, 'Don't Eat the Daisies: Disinterestedness and the Situated Aesthetic', *Environmental Values*, 7:1, 1998.

——, 'The City in Aesthetic Imagination', in Arto Haapala (ed.), *The City as Cultural Metaphor: Studies in Urban Aesthetics* (Lahti: International Institute of Applied Aesthetics, 1998).

——, 'Rooted Art?: Environmental Art and Our Attachment to Nature', *IO: Internet Journal of Applied Aesthetics*, vol: 1, 1998, http:/www.lpt.fi/io/io98/brady.html.

——, 'Aesthetics of the Natural Environment', in Vernon Pratt with Jane Howarth and Emily Brady, *Environment and Philosophy* (New York and London: Routledge, 2000).

——, 'Introduction: Sibley's Vision', in Emily Brady and Jerrold Levinson (eds), *Aesthetic Concepts: Essays After Sibley* (Oxford: Oxford University Press, 2001).

——, 'Interpreting Environments', *Essays in Philosophy* 3:1, 2002 (www.humboldt.edu/~essays/).

——, 'Sniffing and Savoring: The Aesthetics of Smells and Tastes', in Andrew Light and Jonathan M. Smith (eds), *The Aesthetics of Everyday Life* (New York: Seven Bridges Press, 2002).

——, 'Aesthetic Character and Aesthetic Integrity in Environmental Conservation', *Environmental Ethics*, 24:2, 2002.

——, 'Aesthetics, Ethics and the Natural Environment', in Arnold Berleant (ed.), *Environment and the Arts: Perspectives on Environmental Aesthetics* (Aldershot and Burlington: Ashgate, 2002).

Brady, Emily and Mary Grant, 'Aesthetic Value in UK Environmental Conservation', Lancaster University, 2001.

Brady, Emily and Jerrold Levinson (eds), *Aesthetic Concepts: Essays After Sibley* (Oxford: Oxford University Press, 2001).

Brady, Joe, 'Aurora Borealis: The Northern Lights', virtual.finland.fi/finfo/english/aurora_borealis.html.

British Wind Energy Association website, www.bwea.com.

Brook, Isis, Without Waste or Destruction: The Aesthetics of Coppicing', *Thingmount Working Paper Series on the Philosophy of Conservation* (Centre for Philosophy, Lancaster University, 1999).

——, 'Can "Spirit of Place" be a Guide to Ethical Building?', in Warwick Fox (ed.), *Ethics and the Built Environment* (London and New York: Routledge, 2000).'

Brook, Isis and Emily Brady, 'Topiary: Ethics and Aesthetics', *Ethics and the Environment: Special Issue: Art, Nature and Social Critique*, forthcoming, 2003.

Budd, Malcolm, 'The Aesthetic Appreciation of Nature', *British Journal of Aesthetics*, 36:3, 1996.

——, 'Delight in the Natural World: Kant on the Aesthetic Appreciation of Nature. Part I: Natural Beauty', *British Journal of Aesthetics*, 38:1, 1998.

——, 'Delight in the Natural World: Kant on the Aesthetic Appreciation of Nature. Part II: Natural Beauty and Morality', *British Journal of Aesthetics*, 38:2, 1998.

——, 'Delight in the Natural World: Kant on the Aesthetic Appreciation of Nature. Part III: The Sublime in Nature', *British Journal of Aesthetics*, 38:3, 1998.

——, 'The Aesthetics of Nature', *Proceedings of the Aristotelian Society*, 2000.

Bullough, Edward, '"Psychical Distance", as a Factor in Art and an Aesthetic Principle', *British Journal of Psychology*, V, 1912.

Burke, Edmund, *A Philosophical Inquiry into the Origin of our Ideas of the Sublime and Beautiful*, ed. J. T. Boulton (London: Basil Blackwell, [1757] 1958).

Callicott, J. Baird and Michael P. Nelson (eds), *The Great New Wilderness Debate* (Athens, GA: University of Georgia Press, 1998).

Carlson, Allen, 'Environmental Ethics and the Dilemma of Aesthetic Education', *Journal of Aesthetic Education*, 10, 1976; reprinted in *Aesthetics and the Environment*.

——, 'Saito on the Correct Aesthetic Appreciation of Nature', *Journal of Aesthetic Education*, 20:2, 1986.

——, 'Is Environmental Art an Aesthetic Affront to Nature?', *The Canadian Journal of Philosophy*, 16:4, 1986; reprinted in *Aesthetics and the Environment*.

——, 'Environmental Aesthetics', in David Cooper (ed.), *A Companion to Aesthetics* (Oxford and Cambridge, MA: Blackwell, 1992).

——, 'Aesthetics and Engagement', *British Journal of Aesthetics*, 33:3, 1993.

——, 'Appreciating Art and Appreciating Nature', in Salim Kemal and Ivan Gaskell (eds), *Landscape, Natural Beauty and the Arts* (Cambridge: Cambridge University Press, 1993); reprinted in *Aesthetics and the Environment*.

——, 'Nature, Aesthetic Appreciation, and Knowledge', *Journal of Aesthetics and Art Criticism*, 53:4, 1995.

——, *Aesthetics and the Natural Environment: The Appreciation of Nature, Art and Architecture* (London and New York: Routledge, 2000).

——, 'Nature Appreciation and the Question of Aesthetic Relevance', in Arnold Berleant (ed.), *Environment and the Arts: Perspectives on Environmental Aesthetics* (Aldershot and Burlington: Ashgate, 2002).

Carroll, Noël, 'Clive Bell's Aesthetic Hypothesis', in George Dickie, Richard Sclafani and Ronald Roblin (eds), *Aesthetics: A Critical Anthology*, 2nd edn (New York: St Martin's Press, 1989).

——, 'Being Moved By Nature: Between Religion and Natural History', in Salim Kemal and Ivan Gaskell (eds), *Landscape, Natural Beauty and the Arts* (Cambridge: Cambridge University Press, 1993).

——, 'Moderate Moralism', *British Journal of Aesthetics*, 36:3, 1996.

——, 'Morality and Aesthetics', in Michael Kelly (ed.), *Encyclopedia of Aesthetics*, vol. 3 (New York and Oxford: Oxford University Press, 1998).

——, *Philosophy of Art: A Contemporary Introduction* (Routledge: London and New York, 1999).

——, *Beyond Aesthetics: Philosophical Essays* (Cambridge: Cambridge University Press, 2001).

Cavell, Marcia, 'Taste and Moral Sense', in David E. W. Fenner (ed.), *Ethics and the Arts: An Anthology* (New York and London: Garland, 1995).

Cohen Ted, 'Metaphor and the Cultivation of Intimacy', *Critical Inquiry*, 5, 1978.

——, *Jokes* (Chicago: University of Chicago Press, 1999).

——, 'Sibley and the Wonder of Aesthetic Language', in Emily Brady and Jerrold Levinson (eds), *Aesthetic Concepts: Essays After Sibley* (Oxford: Oxford University Press, 2001).

Coleridge, Samuel Taylor, *Biographia Literaria*, vol. I [1817] in James Engell and W. Jackson Bate (eds), *The Collected Works of Samuel Taylor Coleridge*, vol. 7 (Princeton: Princeton University Press, 1983).

Collingwood, R. G., *Outlines of a Philosophy of Art* [1925], reprinted in his *Essays in the Philosophy of Art*, ed. Alan Donagan (Bloomington, IN: Indiana University Press, 1964).

——, *The Idea of History* (Oxford: Clarendon Press, 1946).

Cooper, Anthony Ashley (Shaftesbury), *Characteristics of Men, Manners, Opinions, Times, etc.*, ed. J. M. Robertson (London, 1900).

Cooper, David (ed.), *A Companion to Aesthetics* (Oxford and Cambridge, MA: Blackwell, 1992).

Corn, Wanda, *The Art of Andrew Wyeth* (Greenwich: New York Graphic Society, 1973).

Council for National Parks, *National Parks*, www.cnp.org.uk/national_parks.htm.

Country Guardians' website, www.countryguardians.net.

Countryside Agency, *Visitors to National Parks*, Research Notes Issue CCRN1, 1998, p. 2 (this publication is based on a longer document of the same title, published in 1996).

——, 'Areas of Outstanding Natural Beauty', www.countryside.gov.uk/aonb/.

——, Countryside Character Initiative, www.countryside.gov.uk/cci/character_history.htm.

——, 'Areas of Outstanding Natural Beauty', www.countryside.gov.uk/aonb/22_nidd.htm.

Countryside Agency and Scottish Natural Heritage, *Landscape Character Assessment: Guidance for England and Scotland*, 2002.

Countryside Commission, *Countryside Character: The character of England's Natural and Man-made Landscape, Volume 2: North West* (Cheltenham: Countryside Commission, 1998).

Countryside Commission for Scotland, *Scotland's Scenic Heritage*, 1978.

Countryside Council for Wales and Countryside Commission, *The National Park Authority: Purposes, Powers and Administration: A Guide for Members of National Park Authorities* (Countryside Council for Wales, 1993).

Crawford, Donald, 'Nature and Art: Some Dialectical Relationships', *Journal of Aesthetics and Art Criticism*, 42, 1983.

——, 'Comparing Natural and Artistic Beauty', in Salim Kemal and Ivan Gaskell (eds), *Landscape, Natural Beauty and the Arts* (Cambridge: Cambridge University Press, 1993).

——, 'Allen Carlson's Aesthetics of Nature', paper read to American Society of Aesthetics Annual Meeting, Reno, October, 2000.

Crowther, Paul, *Critical Aesthetics and Postmodernism* (Oxford: Clarendon Press, 1993).

——, 'The Significance of Kant's Pure Aesthetic Judgement', *British Journal of Aesthetics*, 36:2, 1996.

Currie, Gregory, *Image and Mind: Film, Philosophy and Cognitive Science* (Cambridge: Cambridge University Press, 1995).

——, 'Imagination and Make-believe', in Berys Gaut and Dominic McIver Lopes (eds), *The Routledge Companion to Aesthetics* (London and New York: Routledge, 2001).

Danto, Arthur, *The Transfiguration of the Commonplace* (Cambridge, MA, and London: Harvard University Press, 1981).

Davies, Stephen, *Musical Meaning and Expression* (Ithaca and London: Cornell University Press, 1994).

——, 'Authenticity in Musical Performance', in Alex Neill and Aaron Ridley (eds), *Arguing About Art: Contemporary Philosophical Debates* (New York: McGraw Hill, 1995).

DeBellis, Mark, 'Music' in Berys Gaut and Dominic McIver Lopes (eds), *Routledge Companion to Aesthetics* (London and New York: Routledge, 2000).

Dewey, John, *Art as Experience* (New York: Perigee, [1934] 1980).

Dickie, George, 'The Myth of the Aesthetic Attitude', *American Philosophical Quarterly*, 1:3, 1964.

Diffey, T. J., 'Natural Beauty without Metaphysics', in Salim Kemal and Ivan Gaskell, *Landscape, Natural Beauty and the Arts* (Cambridge: Cambridge University Press, 1993).

——, 'William Wordsworth', in Michael Kelly (ed.), *Encyclopedia of Aesthetics*, vol. 4 (New York and Oxford: Oxford University Press, 1998).

——, 'Art or Nature?', in Emily Brady and Jerrold Levinson (eds), *Aesthetic Concepts: Essays After Sibley* (Oxford: Oxford University Press, 2001).

Eaton, Marcia Muelder, *Aesthetics and the Good Life* (London and Toronto: Associated University Presses, 1989).

——, 'The Intrinsic, Non-Supervenient Nature of Aesthetic Properties', *Journal of Aesthetics and Art Criticism*, 52, 1994.

——, 'Aesthetics: The Mother of Ethics?', *Journal of Aesthetics and Art Criticism*, 55:4, 1997.

——, 'The Role of Aesthetics in Designing Sustainable Landscapes', in Yrjö Sepänmaa (ed.), *Real World Design: The Foundations and Practice of Environmental Aesthetics*, *Proceedings of the XIIIth International Congress of Aesthetics*, vol. II (Lahti: University of Helsinki – Lahti Research and Training Centre, 1997).

——, 'The Beauty that Requires Health', in Joan Nassauer (ed.), *Placing Nature: Culture and Landscape Ecology* (Washington: Island Press, 1997).

——, 'Fact and Fiction in the Aesthetic Appreciation of Nature', *Journal of Aesthetics and Art Criticism*, 56:2, 1998.

——, 'Morality and Aesthetics: Contemporary Aesthetics and Ethics', in Michael Kelly (ed.), *Encyclopedia of Aesthetics*, vol. 3, (New York and Oxford: Oxford University Press, 1998).

——, *Merit, Aesthetic and Ethical* (Oxford and New York: Oxford University Press, 2001).

Eco, Umberto, *Art and Beauty in the Middle Ages*, trans. Hugh Bredin (New Haven and London: Yale University Press, 1986).

——, *The Aesthetics of Thomas Aquinas*, trans. Hugh Bredin (Cambridge, MA: Harvard University Press, 1988).

Elliot, Robert, *Faking Nature* (London and New York: Routledge, 1997).

Elliott, David, *Energy, Society and Environment: Technology for a Sustainable Future* (London and New York: Routledge, 1997).

Elliott, R. K., 'Imagination in the Experience of Art', *Royal Institute of Philosophy Lectures, vol. six, 1971–1972: Philosophy and the Arts* (New York: St Martin's Press, 1974).

——, 'Imagination: A Kind of Magical Faculty', in Paul Crowther (ed.), *Collected Essays of R. K. Elliott* (Aldershot and Burlington: Ashgate, forthcoming).

Feagin, Susan, *Reading with Feeling* (Ithaca: Cornell University Press, 1996).

Fenner, David E. W., *The Aesthetic Attitude* (Atlantic Highlands: Humanities Press, 1996).

Fisher, John Andrew, 'What the Hills Are Alive With: In Defense of the Sounds of Nature', *Journal of Aesthetics and Art Criticism: Special Issue: Environmental Aesthetics*, 56:2, 1998.

——, 'The Value of Natural Sounds', *Journal of Aesthetic Education: Symposium on Natural Aesthetics*, 33:3, 1999.

Foster, Cheryl, 'Aesthetic Disillusionment: Environment, Ethics, Art', *Environmental Values*, 1, 1992.

——, 'Schopenhauer's Subtext on Natural Beauty', *British Journal of Aesthetics*, 32:1, 1992.

——, 'The Narrative and the Ambient in Environmental Aesthetics', *Journal of Aesthetics and Art Criticism, Special Issue: Environmental Aesthetics*, 56:2, 1998.

——, 'Texture: Old Material, Fresh Novelty', in Pauline von Bonsdorff and Arto Haapala (eds), *Aesthetics in the Human Environment*, (Lahti, Finland: International Institute of Applied Aesthetics Series vol. 6, 1999).

——, 'Restoring Nature in American Culture: An Environmental Aesthetic Perspective', in Paul H. Gobster and R. Bruce Hull (eds), *Restoring Nature: Perspectives from the Humanities and Social Sciences* (Washington: Island Press, 2000).

Fudge, Robert, 'Imagination and the Science-Based Aesthetic Appreciation of Unscenic Nature', *Journal of Aesthetics and Art Criticism*, 59:3, 2001.

Gaut, Berys, 'The Ethical Criticism of Art', in Jerrold Levinson (ed.), *Aesthetics and Ethics: Essays at the Intersection* (Cambridge: Cambridge University Press, 1998).

Gaut, Berys and Dominic McIver Lopes (eds), *The Routledge Companion to Aesthetics* (London and New York: Routledge, 2001).

Gilpin, William, *Three Essays*, 2nd edn (London: R. Blamire, 1794).

Godlovitch, Stan, 'Icebreakers: Environmentalism and Natural Aesthetics', *Journal of Applied Philosophy*, 11:1, 1994.

——, 'Carlson on Appreciation', *Journal of Aesthetics and Art Criticism*, 55, 1997.

——, 'Evaluating Nature Aesthetically', *Journal of Aesthetics and Art Criticism: Special Issue on Environmental Aesthetics*, 56:2, 1998.

——, 'Offending Against Nature', *Environmental Values*, 7, 1998.

——, 'Valuing Nature and the Autonomy of Natural Aesthetics', *British Journal of Aesthetics*, 38:2, 1998.

Gold, John R. and Jacquelin Burgess (eds), *Valued Environments* (London: George Allen & Unwin, 1982).

Goldman, Alan, 'Properties, Aesthetic', in David Cooper (ed.), *A Companion to Aesthetics* (Oxford and Cambridge, MA: Blackwell, 1992).

——, 'Realism about Aesthetic Properties', *Journal of Aesthetics and Art Criticism*, 51:1, 1993.

——, *Aesthetic Value* (Boulder: Westview Press, 1995).

——, 'The Aesthetic', in Berys Gaut and Dominic McIver Lopes (eds), *The Routledge Companion to Aesthetics* (London and New York: Routledge, 2001).

Guyer, Paul, *Kant and the Claims of Taste* (Cambridge, MA, and London: Harvard University Press, 1979).

——, *Kant and the Experience of Freedom: Essays on Aesthetics and Morality* (Cambridge: Cambridge University Press, 1996).

Haapala, Arto, 'Metaphors for Living – Living Metaphors', *Danish Yearbook of Philosophy*, 31, 1996.

Haldane, John, 'Admiring the High Mountains', *Environmental Values*, 3:3, 1994.

Hampshire, Stuart, 'Logic and Appreciation', in William Elton (ed.), *Aesthetics and Language* (Oxford: Basil Blackwell, 1970).

Hanfling, Oswald (ed.), *Philosophical Aesthetics* (Oxford and Milton Keynes: Blackwell and The Open University, 1992).

——, 'Aesthetic Qualities', in Hanfling (ed.), *Philosophical Aesthetics* (Oxford and Milton Keynes: Blackwell and the Open University, 1992).

——, 'Five Kinds of Distance', *British Journal of Aesthetics*, 40:1, 2000.

Hare, R. M., *Freedom and Reason* (Oxford: Oxford University Press, 1965).

Hargrove, Eugene C., *Foundations of Environmental Ethics* (Englewood Cliffs: Prentice-Hall, 1989).

Hegel, G. F. W., *Aesthetics: Lectures on Fine Art*, trans. T. M. Knox (Oxford: Clarendon Press, 1975).

Hepburn, Ronald W., 'Contemporary Aesthetics and the Neglect of Natural Beauty', in *Wonder and Other Essays* (Edinburgh: Edinburgh University Press, 1984). First published in Bernard Williams and Alan Montefiore (eds), *British Analytical Philosophy* (London: Routledge and Kegan Paul, 1966).

——, 'Nature in the Light of Art', in *Wonder and Other Essays* (Edinburgh: Edinburgh University Press, 1984).

——, *Wonder and Other Essays* (Edinburgh: Edinburgh University Press, 1984).

——, 'Trivial and Serious in Aesthetic Appreciation of Nature', in Salim Kemal and Ivan Gaskell (eds), *Landscape, Natural Beauty and the Arts* (Cambridge: Cambridge University Press, 1993), and reprinted in *The Reach of the Aesthetic: Essays on Art and Nature* (Aldershot and Burlington: Ashgate, 2001).

——, 'Landscape and Metaphysical Imagination', *Environmental Values*, 5, 1996.

——, 'Nature Humanised: Nature Respected', *Environmental Values*, 7, 1998.

——, *The Reach of the Aesthetic: Essays on Art and Nature* (Aldershot and Burlington: Ashgate, 2001).

Herman, Barbara, *The Practice of Moral Judgment* (Cambridge, MA, and London: Harvard University Press, 1993).

Hermeren, Goran, *The Nature of Aesthetic Qualities* (Lund: Lund University Press, 1988).

Heyd, Thomas, 'Aesthetic Appreciation and the Many Stories About Nature,' *British Journal of Aesthetics*, 41, 2001.

Holland, Alan and John O'Neill in 'The Integrity of Nature Over Time: Some Problems', TWP 96–08, *The Thingmount Working Paper Series on the Philosophy of Conservation* (Centre for Philosophy, Lancaster University, 1996).

Holland, Alan and Kate Rawles, *The Ethics of Conservation*. Report presented to The Countryside Council for Wales, 1994; reprinted in *The Thingmount Working Paper Series on the Philosophy of Conservation*, TWP 96–01 (Centre for Philosophy, Lancaster University, 1996).

Howarth, Jane, 'Nature's Moods', *British Journal of Aesthetics*, 35:2, 1995.

Hume, David, *Enquiry Concerning the Principles of Morals*, ed. J. B. Schneewind (ed.) (Indianapolis: Hackett, [1751] 1983).

——, 'Of the Standard of Taste', in *Essays Moral, and Political, and Literary* ed. Eugene Miller (Indianapolis: Liberty Classics, [1757] 1985).

——, 'Of Tragedy', reprinted in Alex Neill and Aaron Ridley (eds), *Arguing About Art: Contemporary Philosophical Debates* (New York: McGraw-Hill, 1995).

Isenberg, Arnold, 'Critical Communication', in William Elton (ed.), *Aesthetics and Language* (Oxford: Basil Blackwell, 1970).

Jay, Martin, *Downcast Eyes* (Berkeley: University of California Press, 1993).

Johnson, Alison and Andrew Johnson, 'Editorial' *Environmental Values*, 5, 1996.

Kant, Immanuel, *Observations on the Feeling of the Beautiful and the Sublime*, trans. John T. Goldthwait (Berkeley and Los Angeles: University of California Press, [1764] 1960).

——, *Critique of Pure Reason*, trans. Norman Kemp Smith (London: Macmillan, [1781; 1787] 1929).

——, *Critique of Practical Reason*, trans. Lewis White Beck (Indianapolis: Bobbs-Merrill, [1787] 1956).

——, *Critique of Judgment*, trans. Werner Pluhar (Indianapolis: Hackett, [1790] 1987).

——, *Metaphysics of Morals*, (1797) in *Ethical Philosophy*, trans. James Ellington (Indianapolis: Hackett, 1983).

——, *Anthropology from A Pragmatic Point of View*, trans. Mary J. Gregor (The Hague: Nijhoff, [1798] 1974).

Karr, James and Ellen Chu, 'Ecological Integrity: Reclaiming Lost Connections', in Laura Westra and John Lemmons (eds), *Perspectives on Ecological Integrity* (Dordrecht: Kluwer, 1995).

Kearney, Richard, *The Poetics of Imagining* (Edinburgh: Edinburgh University Press, 1998).

——, *The Wake of Imagination* (London: Hutchinson, 1988).

Kelly, Michael (ed.), *Encyclopedia of Aesthetics*, vols 1–4 (New York and Oxford: Oxford University Press, 1998).

Kemal, Salim, *Kant's Aesthetic Theory*, 2nd edn (New York: St Martin's Press, 1997).

Kemal, Salim and Ivan Gaskell (eds), *Landscape, Natural Beauty and the Arts* (Cambridge: Cambridge University Press, 1993).

Kemp, Gary, 'The Aesthetic Attitude', *British Journal of Aesthetics*, 39:4, 1999.

Kieran, Matthew, 'In Defence of Critical Pluralism', *British Journal of Aesthetics*, 36:3, 1996.

Kivy, Peter, *Sound Sentiment* (Philadelphia: Temple University Press, 1989).

Knight, Richard Payne, *An Analytical Inquiry into the Principles of Taste* (London, 1805).

Koerner, Joseph, *Caspar David Friedrich and the Subject of Landscape* (London: Reaktion Books, 1990).

Korsmeyer, Carolyn, *Making Sense of Taste: Food and Philosophy* (Ithaca: Cornell University Press, 1999).

Lamarque, Peter, 'In and Out of Imaginary Worlds', in John Skorupski and Dudley Knowles (eds), *Virtue and Taste, Philosophical Quarterly Supplementary Series*, vol. 2 (Oxford: Blackwell, 1993).

Langewiesche, William, *Inside the Sky: A Meditation on Flight* (New York: Vintage Books, 1998).

Lawson, Trevor, Kate Rawles and Rob Gritten, 'Alien Invasion', *BBC Wildlife Magazine*, 16:9, 1998.

Lee, Keekok, 'Beauty for Ever?', *Environmental Values*, 4, 1995.

——, *The Natural and the Artefactual: The Implications of Deep Science and Deep Technology for Environmental Philosophy* (Lanham: Lexington Books, 1999).

Leopold, Aldo, *Sand County Almanac* (New York, Oxford University Press, [1949] 1968).

Levinson, Jerrold, 'Properties and Related Entities', *Philosophy and Phenomenological Research*, 39, 1978.

——, 'Particularisation of Attributes', *Australasian Journal of Philosophy*, 58:2, 1980.

——, 'Art Works and the Future', in Thomas Anderberg, Tore Nilstun and Ingmar Persson (eds), *Aesthetic Distinction* (Lund: Lund University Press, 1988).

——, 'Defining Art Historically', *Journal of Aesthetics and Art Criticism*, 47:1, 1989.

——, 'Aesthetic Supervenience', in *Music, Art, and Metaphysics* (Ithaca: Cornell University Press, 1990).

——, 'Pleasure, Aesthetic', in David Cooper (ed.), *A Companion to Aesthetics* (Oxford and Cambridge, MA: Blackwell, 1992).

——, *The Pleasures of Aesthetics: Philosophical Essays* (Ithaca: Cornell University Press, 1996).

——, 'Aesthetic Properties, Evaluative Force and Differences of Sensibility', in Emily Brady and Jerrold Levinson (eds), *Aesthetic Concepts: Essays After Sibley* (Oxford: Oxford University Press, 2001).

Link Quarry Group, *The Case Against the Harris Superquarry*, www.foe-scotland.org.uk/nation/superquarry1.html.

Lyas, Colin, 'The Evaluation of Art', in Oswald Hanfling (ed.), *Philosophical Aesthetics* (Oxford and Milton Keynes: Blackwell and The Open University, 1992).

Mabey, Richard, *Flora Britannica* (London Sinclair Stevenson, 1996).

McDowell, John, 'Aesthetic Value, Objectivity, and the Fabric of the World', in Eva Schaper (ed.), *Pleasure, Preference and Value* (Cambridge: Cambridge University Press, 1983).

McFee, Graham, 'The Historicity of Art', *Journal of Aesthetics and Art Criticism*, 38:3, 1980.

Makkreel, Rudolf, *Imagination and Interpretation in Kant: The Hermeneutical Import of the Critique of Judgment* (Chicago and London: University of Chicago Press, 1990).

Mannison, Don, 'A Prolegomenon to a Human Chauvinistic Aesthetic', in D. Mannison, M. Robbie and R. Routley (eds), *Environmental Philosophy* (Canberra: Australian National University, 1980).

Matthews, Patricia, 'Scientific Knowledge and the Aesthetic Appreciation of Nature', *Journal of Aesthetics and Art Criticism*, 60:1, 2002.

Moore, Ronald, 'Appreciating Natural Beauty', *Journal of Aesthetic Education: Symposium on Natural Aesthetics*, 33:3, 1999.

Moran, Richard, 'The Expression of Feeling in Imagination', *The Philosophical Review*, 103:1, 1994.

Moriarty, Paul Veatch and Mark Woods, 'Hunting ‡ Predation', *Environmental Ethics*, 19:4, 1997.

Murdoch, Iris, *The Sovereignty of the Good* (London: Routledge, [1970] 1991).

Nagel, Ernst, *The Structure of Science: Problems in the Logic of Scientific Explanation* (Indianapolis and Cambridge: Hackett, 1979).

Nasar, Jack L. (ed.), *Environmental Aesthetics: Theory, Research and Applications* (Cambridge: Cambridge University Press, 1988).

Nash, Roderick, *Wilderness and the American Mind*, rev. edn (New Haven and London: Yale University Press, 1967).

Nicolson, Marjorie Hope, *Mountain Gloom and Mountain Glory: The Development of the Aesthetics of the Infinite* (New York: Norton, 1959).

Nietzsche, Friedrich, *On the Genealogy of Morals*, trans. Walter Kaufmann (New York: Vintage Books, 1969).

Novitz, David, *Knowledge, Fiction and Imagination* (Philadelphia: Temple University Press, 1987).

——, *The Boundaries of Art* (Philadelphia: Temple University Press, 1992).

Nussbaum, Martha, *The Fragility of Goodness: Luck and Ethics in Greek Tragedy and Philosophy* (Cambridge: Cambridge University Press, 1986).

——, *Love's Knowledge: Essays on Philosophy and Literature* (Oxford: Oxford University Press, 1990).

O'Neill, John, 'The Varieties of Intrinsic Value', *The Monist*, 75, 1992.

O'Neill, Onora, *Constructions of Reason* (Cambridge: Cambridge University Press, 1989).

Passmore, John, *Man's Responsibility to Nature* (London: Duckworth, 1980).

Plumwood, Val, *Feminism and the Mastery of Nature* (London: Routledge, 1993).

Poe, Edgar Allen, 'A Descent into the Maelström', in *The Complete Tales and Poems of Edgar Allen Poe* (New York: Modern Library, 1938).

Porteous, J. Douglas, *Environmental Aesthetics: Ideas, Politics and Planning* (London and New York: Routledge, 1996).

Railton, Peter, 'Aesthetic Value, Moral Value, and the Ambitions of Naturalism', in Jerrold Levinson (ed.), *Aesthetics and Ethics: Essays at the Intersection* (Cambridge: Cambridge University Press, 1998).

Rolston, III, Holmes, *Environmental Ethics: Duties to and Values in the Natural World* (Philadelphia: Temple University Press, 1988).

——, 'Does Aesthetic Appreciation of Landscapes Need to Be Science-based?', *British Journal of Aesthetics*, 35:4, 1995.

——, 'Nature for Real: Is Nature a Social Construct?', in T. D. J. Chappell (ed.), *The Philosophy of Environment* (Edinburgh: Edinburgh University Press, 1997).

——, 'Aesthetic Experience in Forests', *Journal of Aesthetics and Art Criticism: Special Issue: Environmental Aesthetics*, 56:2, 1998.

——, 'From Beauty to Duty: Aesthetics of Nature and Environmental Ethics', in Arnold Berleant (ed.), *Environment and the Arts: Perspectives on Environmental Aesthetics* (Aldershot and Burlington: Ashgate, 2002).

Ross, Stephanie, *What Gardens Mean* (Chicago and London: Chicago University Press, 1998).

Ruskin, John, *Modern Painters*, edited and abridged by David Barrie (London: Pilkington Press, [1873] 1987).

——, *Stones of Venice*, ed. J. Morris (London: Faber and Faber, [1851, 1853] 1981).

Sadler, Barry and Allen Carlson (eds), *Environmental Aesthetics: Essays in Interpretation* (Victoria: University of Victoria, 1982).

Sagoff, Mark, 'Has Nature a Good of its Own?', *Hastings Center Report*, 21, 1991.

Saito, Yuriko, 'Is There a Correct Aesthetic Appreciation of Nature?', *Journal of Aesthetic Education*, 18:4, 1984.

——, 'The Japanese Appreciation of Nature', *British Journal of Aesthetics*, 25:3, 1985.

——, 'The Japanese Aesthetics of Imperfection and Insufficiency', *Journal of Aesthetics and Art Criticism*, 55:4, 1997.

——, 'The Aesthetics of Unscenic Nature', *Journal of Aesthetics and Art Criticism: Special Issue: Environmental Aesthetics*, 56:2, 1998.

——, 'Appreciating Nature on Its Own Terms', *Environmental Ethics*, 20, 1998.

——, 'Environmental Directions for Aesthetics and the Arts', in Arnold Berleant (ed.), *Environment and the Arts: Perspectives on Environmental Aesthetics* (Aldershot and Burlington: Ashgate, 2002).

——, 'Scenic National Landscapes: Common Themes in Japan and the United States', *Essays in Philosophy*, 3:1, 2002 (wwww.humboldt.edu/~essays/saito.html).

Santayana, George, *The Sense of Beauty: Being the Outline of Aesthetic Theory* (New York: Dover, [1896] 1955).

Savile, Anthony, *The Test of Time* (Oxford: Clarendon Press, 1982).

——, 'The Rationale of Restoration', *Journal of Aesthetics and Art Criticism* 51:3, 1993.

——, *Kantian Aesthetics Pursued* (Edinburgh: Edinburgh University Press, 1993).

——, *Aesthetic Reconstructions* (Oxford: Basil Blackwell, 1988).

Schaper, Eva, *Studies in Kant's Aesthetics* (Edinburgh: Edinburgh University Press, 1979).

Schiller, Friedrich, *On the Aesthetic Education of Man* (Oxford: Clarendon Press, [1795] 1967).

Schopenhauer, Arthur, *The World as Will and Representation*, vols. I and II, trans. E. F. J. Payne (New York: Dover, [1818] 1966).

Scottish Natural Heritage, *National Scenic Areas: A Consultation Document: Summary Document* (Scottish Natural Heritage, 1999).

——, *National Scenic Areas: Scottish Natural Heritage's Advice to Government* (Scottish Natural Heritage, 1999).

——, 'An Overview', in *Natural Heritage Futures*, www.snh.org.uk/strategy/NHFutures/nhf-OV.htm, 2002.

——, www.biodiversitystories.co.uk.

Scruton, Roger, *Art and Imagination* (London: Methuen, 1974).

——, *The Aesthetics of Architecture* (London: Methuen, 1979).

——, 'Imagination', in David Cooper (ed.), *A Companion to Aesthetics* (Oxford: Blackwell, 1992).

——, *Modern Philosophy* (London: Sinclair Stevenson, 1994).

Sepänmaa, Yrjö, *The Beauty of Environment: A General Model for Environmental Aesthetics* (1st edn: Helsinki: Suomalainen Tiedeakatemia, 1986; 2nd edn: Denton: Environmental Ethics Books, 1992).

—— (ed.), *Real World Design: The Foundations and Practice of Environmental Aesthetics*, *Proceedings of the XIIIth International Congress of Aesthetics*, vol. II (Lahti: University of Helsinki, Lahti Research and Training Centre, 1997).

Shelley, James, 'Empiricism' in Berys Gaut and Dominic McIver Lopes (eds), *The Routledge Companion to Aesthetics* (London and New York: Routledge, 2001).

Shoard, Marion, 'The Lure of the Moors' in John R. Gold and Jacquelin Burgess (eds), *Valued Environments* (London: George Allen & Unwin, 1982).

Shusterman, Richard, *Pragmatist Aesthetics: Living Beauty, Rethinking Art* (Oxford: Blackwell, 1992).

——, 'Pragmatism', in Berys Gaut and Dominic McIver Lopes (eds), *The Routledge Companion to Aesthetics* (London and New York: Routledge, 2001).

Sibley, Frank, 'About Taste', *British Journal of Aesthetics*, 6, 1966.

——, 'Aesthetic Concepts', *Philosophical Review*, 68:4, 1959; revised version reprinted in *Approach to Aesthetics: Collected Papers on Philosophical Aesthetics*.

——, 'Aesthetic and Nonaesthetic', *Philosophical Review*, 74, 1965; reprinted in *Approach to Aesthetics: Collected Papers on Philosophical Aesthetics*.

——, 'Philosophy and the Arts', Inaugural Lecture, 23 February 1966, *Inaugural Lectures 1965–1967* (Lancaster: University of Lancaster, 1967); reprinted in *Approach to Aesthetics: Collected Papers on Philosophical Aesthetics*.

——, 'Colours', *Proceedings of the Aristotelian Society* (1967–8); reprinted in *Approach to Aesthetics: Collected Papers on Philosophical Aesthetics*.

——, 'Objectivity and Aesthetics', *Proceedings of the Aristotelian Society, Supplementary Volume*, 42 (1968); reprinted in *Approach to Aesthetics: Collected Papers on Philosophical Aesthetics*.

——, 'Originality and Value', *British Journal of Aesthetics*, 25 (1985); reprinted in *Approach to Aesthetics: Collected Papers on Philosophical Aesthetics*.

——, 'Some Notes on Ugliness', in John Benson, Betty Redfern and Jeremy Roxbee Cox (eds), *Approach to Aesthetics: Collected Papers on Philosophical Aesthetics* (Oxford: Oxford University Press, 2001).

——, 'Tastes, Smells, and Aesthetics', in John Benson, Betty Redfern and Jeremy Roxbee Cox (eds), *Approach to Aesthetics: Collected Papers on Philosophical Aesthetics* (Oxford: Oxford University Press, 2001).

——, *Approach to Aesthetics: Collected Papers on Philosophical Aesthetics*, ed. John Benson, Betty Redfern and Jeremy Roxbee Cox (Oxford: Oxford University Press, 2001).

Soper, Kate, *What is Nature?* (Oxford: Blackwell, 1995).

Spackman, John, 'Expression Theory of Art', in Michael Kelly (ed.), *Encyclopedia of Aesthetics*, vol. 2 (New York and Oxford: Oxford University Press, 1998).

Stecker, Robert, 'The Correct and the Appropriate in the Aesthetic Appreciation of Nature', *British Journal of Aesthetics*, 37:4, 1997.

——, 'Interpretation' in Berys Gaut and Dominic McIver Lopes (eds), *The Routledge Companion to Aesthetics* (London and New York: Routledge, 2001).

Stock, Kathleen, *The Nature and Value of Imaginative Responses to the Fiction Film*, Ph.D. dissertation, 2002.

Stolnitz, Jerome, *Aesthetics and Philosophy of Art Criticism* (Boston: Houghton Mifflin, 1960).

——, 'On the Origins of "Aesthetic Disinterestedness"', *Journal of Aesthetics and Art Criticism*, 20, 1961.

Strawson, Peter, 'Imagination and Perception', in *Freedom and Resentment* (London: Methuen, 1974).

Thomas, Keith, *Man and the Natural World* (New York: Pantheon, 1983).

Thompson, Janna, 'Aesthetics and the Value of Nature', *Environmental Ethics*, 17, 1995.

Thoreau, Henry David, 'Solitude' in 'Walden: or, Life in the Woods', in *Walden and Civil Disobedience* (New York: New American Library, [1854] 1963).

——, 'Walking' (1862), in *The Natural History Essays*, reprinted in Susan J. Armstrong and Richard G. Botzler (eds), *Environmental Ethics: Divergence and Convergence* (New York: McGraw-Hill, 1993).

Townsend, Dabney, 'The Picturesque', *Journal of Aesthetics and Art Criticism*, 55:4, 1997.

Tuan, Yi-Fu, *Topophilia: A Study of Environmental Perception, Attitudes and Value* (Englewood Cliffs, NJ: Prentice-Hall, 1974).

——, 'Desert and Ice: Ambivalent Aesthetics', in Salim Kemal and Ivan Gaskell (eds), *Landscape, Natural Beauty and the Arts* (Cambridge: Cambridge University Press, 1993).

Urmson, J. O., 'What Makes a Situation Aesthetic?', *Proceedings of the Aristotelian Society*, Supplementary Volume, XXXI, 1957.

Uvedale, Price, *On the Picturesque*, ed. T. D. Lauder (Edinburgh: Caldwell, Lloyd and Co., 1842).

Walton, Kendall, 'Categories of Art', *Philosophical Review*, 79, 1970.

——, *Mimesis as Make-Believe* (Cambridge: Harvard University Press, 1990).

Warnock, Mary, *Imagination* (London: Faber and Faber, 1976).

White, Alan, *The Language of Imagination* (Oxford: Blackwell, 1990).

Wilson, Alexander, *The Culture of Nature* (Blackwell: Oxford, 1992).

Young, James O., 'The Concept of Authentic Performance', in Alex Neill and Aaron Ridley (eds), *Arguing About Art: Contemporary Philosophical Debates* (New York: McGraw Hill, 1995).

Zangwill, Nick, 'Formal Natural Beauty', *Proceedings of the Aristotelian Society*, New Series, vol. CI, 2001.

Zemach, Eddy, *Real Beauty* (University Park, PA: Penn State Press, 1996).

Ziff, Paul, 'Anything Viewed', in Esa Saarinen Risto Hilpinen, Ilkka Niiniluoto and Merrill Provence Hintikka (eds), *Essays in Honour of Jaakko Hintikka* (Dordrecht: Reidel, 1979).

Index